THE GNOSTIC RELIGION

Hans Jonas was born and educated in Germany. He left in 1933, when Hitler came into power, and in 1940 joined the British Army in the Middle East. Since the war he has taught at Hebrew University in Jerusalem and Carleton University in Ottawa. He is now Alvin Johnson Professor of Philosophy on the Graduate Faculty of Political and Social Science at the New School for Social Research in New York. Professor Jonas is also the author of, among other books, *The Phenomenon of Life* (1966).

THE GNOSTIC RELIGION

The Message of the Alien God and the
Beginnings of Christianity

by Hans Jonas

Second edition, revised

Beacon Press   Boston

First published in 1958 by Beacon Press

Copyright © 1958 by Hans Jonas

Enlarged edition first published as a Beacon Paperback in 1963

Copyright © 1963 by Hans Jonas

Beacon Press books are published under the auspices
of the Unitarian Universalist Association

Printed in the United States of America

International Standard Book Number: 0–8070–5799–1

Fourth printing, March 1972

Contents

Part II. Gnostic Systems of Thought

Acknowledgments

The publishers thank the following for giving permission to quote or translate from the works mentioned:

Clarendon Press: *The Republic of Plato,* trans. F.M. Cornford; W. Kohlhammer: *A Manichaean Psalm-book,* ed. and trans. C.R.C. Allberry, and *Kephalaia,* ed. and trans. H. J. Polotsky and A. Böhlig; Oxford University Press: *The Dialogues of Plato,* trans. B. Jowett, and *The Student's Oxford Aristotle,* ed. W. D. Ross; Rascher & Cie., and the C. G. Jung-Institut: *Evangelium Veritatis,* ed. and trans. M. Malinine, H. C. Puech, G. Quispel; Routledge & Kegan Paul, Ltd.: *Plato's Cosmology,* F. M. Cornford; University Press, Cambridge: *Origen: Contra Celsum,* trans. H. Chadwick; Akademie-Verlag, Berlin: *Die gnostischen Schriften des koptischen Papyrus Berolinensis 8502,* ed. and trans. W. Till.

Special acknowledgment is made to the generosity shown by W. Kohlhammer, Stuttgart, and by Rascher & Cie., Zürich, in permitting extensive quotation from the *Manichaean Psalm-book* and the *Evangelium Veritatis* respectively, either of them *editio princeps* of most important new texts in the field.

With respect to the Second Edition, acknowledgments are due to the following for permitting substantial use of articles by the author, previously published by them:

Akademie-Verlag, Berlin: *Studia Patristica* VI ("Evangelium Veritatis and the Valentinian Speculation"); *Gnomon,* Heidelberg ("Evangelium Veritatis . . ."); *Social Research,* New York ("Gnosticism and Modern Nihilism"); University of Chicago Press: *The Journal of Religion* ("The Secret Books of the Egyptian Gnostics"); Vandenhoeck & Ruprecht, Göttingen: *Kerygma und Dogma* ("Gnosis und moderner Nihilismus").

C.H. *Corpus Hermeticum*

G *Ginza. Der Schatz oder das Grosse Buch der Mandäer,* by M. Lidzbarski (tr.), Göttingen, 1925

GT "Gospel of Truth": *Evangelium Veritatis,* by M. Malinine, H. C. Puech, G. Quispel (ed. and tr.), Zürich, 1956

J *Das Johannesbuch der Mandäer,* by M. Lidzbarski (ed. and tr.), Giessen, 1915

For Lore Jonas

Preface

Out of the mist of the beginning of our era there looms a pageant of mythical figures whose vast, superhuman contours might people the walls and ceiling of another Sistine Chapel. Their countenances and gestures, the roles in which they are cast, the drama which they enact, would yield images different from the biblical ones on which the imagination of the beholder was reared, yet strangely familiar to him and disturbingly moving. The stage would be the same, the theme as transcending: the creation of the world, the destiny of man, fall and redemption, the first and the last things. But how much more numerous would be the cast, how much more bizarre the symbolism, how much more extravagant the emotions! Almost all the action would be in the heights, in the divine or angelic or daimonic realm, a drama of pre-cosmic persons in the supranatural world, of which the drama of man in the natural world is but a distant echo. And yet that transcendental drama before all time, depicted in the actions and passions of manlike figures, would be of intense human appeal: divinity tempted, unrest stirring among the blessed Aeons, God's erring Wisdom, the Sophia, falling prey to her folly, wandering in the void and darkness of her own making, endlessly searching, lamenting, suffering, repenting, laboring her passion into matter, her yearning into soul; a blind and arrogant Creator believing himself the Most High and lording it over the creation, the product, like himself, of fault and ignorance; the Soul, trapped and lost in the labyrinth of the world, seeking to escape and frightened back by the gatekeepers of the cosmic prison, the terrible archons; a Savior from the Light beyond venturing into the nether world, illumining the darkness, opening a path, healing the divine breach: a tale of light and darkness, of knowledge and ignorance, of serenity and passion, of conceit and pity, on the scale not of man but of eternal beings that are not exempt from suffering and error.

The tale has found no Michelangelo to retell it, no Dante and no Milton. The sterner discipline of biblical creed weathered the storm of those days, and both Old and New Testament were left to inform the mind and imagination of Western man. Those teachings which, in the feverish hour of transition, challenged, tempted, tried to twist the new faith are forgotten, their written record buried in the tomes of their refuters or in the sands of ancient lands. Our art and literature and much else would be different, had the gnostic message prevailed.

Where the painter and the poet are silent, the scholar must, from its fragments, reconstruct the vanished world and with his feebler means bring its form to life. He can do so better now than ever before, as the sands have begun to yield up some of the buried trust. This resuscitation is of more than antiquarian interest: with all its strangeness, its violence to reason, its immoderateness of judgment, that world of feeling, vision, and thought had its profundity, and without its voice, its insights, and even its errors, the evidence of humanity is incomplete. Rejected as it was, it represents one of the possibilities then offered at the crossroads of creeds. Its glow throws light upon the beginnings of Christianity, the birth pangs of our world; and the heirs of a decision made long ago will better understand their heritage by knowing what once competed with it for the soul of man.

The investigation of Gnosticism is almost as old as Gnosticism itself. Chiefly by its own choosing—being the aggressor—it was an embattled cause from the beginning and thus came under the scrutiny of those whose cause it threatened to subvert. The investigation, carried on in the heat of conflict, was that of a prosecutor. Attorneys for the prosecution were the Fathers of the early Church, stating its case against the heresies in lengthy works (we have no record of the defense, if there was any); and they inquired into the spiritual ancestry of Gnosticism as part of their undertaking to expose its error. Their writings, therefore, provide not only our main —until recently, our sole—source of knowledge of gnostic teaching itself, but also the earliest theory about its nature and origin. To them, their finding that Gnosticism, or what in it distorted the Christian truth, hailed from Hellenic philosophy, amounted to an indictment: to us, it must still count as a hypothesis, among alternative ones, relevant for the historical diagnosis of the phenomenon, and must be considered on its merits.

The last of the major heresiologists to deal extensively with the

gnostic sects, Epiphanius of Salamis, wrote in the fourth century
A.D. From then on, with the danger past and the polemical interest
no longer alive, oblivion settled down on the whole subject, until
the historical interest of the nineteenth century returned to it in the
spirit of dispassionate inquiry. By reason of subject matter it still
fell into the domain of the theologian, like everything connected
with the beginnings of Christianity. But the Protestant theologians
(mostly German) who engaged in the new investigation approached their task as historians who are no longer party to the
conflict, though intellectual trends of their own time might sway
their sympathies and judgments.

It was then that diverse schools of thought about the historical
nature of Gnosticism began to spring up. Naturally enough, the
Hellenic, and more particularly "Platonic," thesis of the Church
Fathers was revived, and not merely on their authority, for suggestive aspects of the literary evidence, including gnostic use of philosophical terms, as well as the general probabilities of the age,
almost inevitably at first point in that direction. Indeed there hardly
seemed to be a choice of alternatives as long as only Judaeo-
Christian and Greek thought were reckoned with as the forces
which could exert influence in that period. But somehow the division of the quantity that is Gnosticism by these known factors leaves
too large a remainder, and from the early nineteenth century the
"Hellenic" school was confronted by an "oriental" one which argued
that Gnosticism derived from an older "oriental philosophy."
Though this position reflected a correct instinct, it suffered from the
weakness that it operated with an ill-defined and really unknown
magnitude—that oriental philosophy the nature and previous existence of which were inferred from the facts of Gnosticism itself
rather than independently established. The position gained firmer
ground, however, once the mythological rather than the philosophical character of what was felt to be oriental in Gnosticism was
recognized and the search for the mysterious philosophy abandoned.
It is generally true to say that to this day the "Greek" and
"oriental" emphases shift back and forth according to whether the
philosophical or the mythological, the rational or the irrational facet
of the phenomenon is seen as decisive. The culmination of the
Greek and rational thesis may be found at the end of the century

in Adolf von Harnack's famous formula that Gnosticism is "the acute Hellenization of Christianity."

Meanwhile, however, the scientific scene changed with the classical scholar and the orientalist entering the field where before the theologian had been alone. The investigation of Gnosticism became part of the comprehensive study of the whole age of later Antiquity in which a variety of disciplines joined hands. Here it was the younger science of the orientalists which could add most to what theology and classical philology had to offer. The vague concept of generally "oriental" thought gave way to a concrete knowledge of the several national traditions mingling in the culture of the time; and the concept of Hellenism itself was modified by the inclusion of these distinct heterogeneous influences in its hitherto predominantly Greek picture. As to Gnosticism in particular, the acquaintance with such massively mythological material as the Coptic and Mandaean texts dealt a blow to the "Greek-philosophical" position from which it never fully recovered, though in the nature of the case it can never be entirely abandoned either. Diagnosis became largely a matter of genealogy, and for this the field was thrown wide open: one by one, or in varying combinations, the different oriental filiations suggested by the rainbow colors of the material—Babylonian, Egyptian, Iranian—were elaborated to determine the principal "whence" and "what" of Gnosis, with the overall result that its picture became more and more syncretistic. The latest turn in the quest for one dominant line of descent is to derive Gnosticism from Judaism: a needful correction of a previous neglect, but in the end probably no more adequate to the total and integral phenomenon than other partial and partially true explanations. Indeed, so far as traceable pedigrees of elements go, all investigations of detail over the last half century have proved divergent rather than convergent, and leave us with a portrait of Gnosticism in which the salient feature seems to be the absence of a unifying character. But these same investigations have also gradually enlarged the range of the phenomenon beyond the group of Christian heresies originally comprised by the name, and in this greater breadth, as well as in the greater complexity, Gnosticism became increasingly revealing of the whole civilization in which it arose, and whose all-pervading feature was syncretism.

Both the wealth of historical detail and the atomization of the subject into motifs from separate traditions are well reflected in Wilhelm Bousset's work of 1907, *Hauptprobleme der Gnosis* (Principal Problems of Gnosticism), which typified a whole school and for long dominated the field. The present work is not entirely of that lineage. When, many years ago, under the guidance of Rudolf Bultmann, I first approached the study of Gnosticism, the field was rich with the solid fruit of philology and the bewildering harvest of the genetic method. To these I neither presumed nor intended to add. My aim, somewhat different from that of the preceding and still continuing research, but complementary to it, was a philosophic one: to understand the spirit speaking through these voices and in its light to restore an intelligible unity to the baffling multiplicity of its expressions. That there was such a gnostic spirit, and therefore an essence of Gnosticism as a whole, was the impression which struck me at my initial encounter with the evidence, and it deepened with increasing intimacy. To explore and interpret that essence became a matter, not only of historical interest, as it substantially adds to our understanding of a crucial period of Western mankind, but also of intrinsic philosophical interest, as it brings us face to face with one of the more radical answers of man to his predicament and with the insights which only that radical position could bring forth, and thereby adds to our human understanding in general.

The results of these prolonged studies are published in German under the title *Gnosis und spätantiker Geist,* of which the first volume appeared in 1934, the second—because of the circumstances of the times—only in 1954, and the third and concluding one is still to come. The present volume, while retaining the point of view of the larger work and restating many of its arguments, is different in scope, in organization, and in literary intention. For one thing, it keeps to the area which is by general consent termed gnostic and refrains from striking out into the wider and more controversial ground where the other work, by an extension of meaning, attempts to uncover the presence of a metamorphized "gnostic principle" in manifestations quite different from the primary ones (as in the systems of Origen and Plotinus). This restriction in scope is due not to a change of view but merely to the kind of book this is intended to be. Then, much of the more difficult philosophical elaboration, with its too technical language—the cause for much complaint in the German volumes—has been excluded from this treatment, which strives to reach the general educated reader as well as the scholar. Methodological discussions and scholarly controversy have been ruled out for the same reason (excepting occasional footnotes). On the other hand, in some respects the present volume goes beyond the earlier presentation: certain texts are more fully interpreted, as in the extensive commentaries to the "Hymn of the Pearl" and the *Poimandres*; and it has been possible to include new material of recent discovery. Inevitably, although this is a new book and not a translation, it does duplicate, with some rephrasing, certain parts of the German work.

All sources are rendered in English. Translations from the Greek and Latin are my own, unless stated otherwise. Mandaean texts are given in my English version of Lidzbarski's German translation, and a similar procedure has been adopted with Coptic, Syriac, Persian, and other texts: where there exists a translation in only one modern language, other than English (usually German or French, as with much of the Coptic material), I have translated this into English; where several translations exist (as with much of the Eastern-Manichaean material and the "Hymn of the Pearl"), I arrived, by their synopsis and the exercise of my judgment, at some composite version as the one that seemed best to me.

I make grateful acknowledgment to my German publishers, Vandenhoeck and Ruprecht in Göttingen, who, in so fine a point as the relation of this to the earlier treatment of the same subject, left me entirely free to use my judgment and sense of fitness. My other acknowledgment is to Miss Jay Macpherson of Victoria College, Toronto, scholar and poet, who with great patience and unfailing linguistic tact, by comment, approval and disapproval throughout the writing of this book, helped me in the English formulation of my thought without thrusting on me a style not my own.

H. J.

New Rochelle, N. Y.
November 1957

Preface to the Second Edition

This second edition of *The Gnostic Religion* has been enlarged by two substantial additions: a new chapter (12), dealing with the great find at Nag Hamadi in Egypt, of whose contents too little was known at the time of the first writing of this book to permit more than a few references and quotations; and, for an epilogue to the historical subject as a whole, an essay relating Gnosticism to more recent and even to contemporary forms of spiritual life: "Gnosticism, Nihilism, and Existentialism." The text of the first edition of *The Gnostic Religion* has been retained in its entirety, unchanged except for a few minor corrections.

The new epilogue, as printed here, is the revised version of an article first published in 1952.* Since parts of that article were later incorporated in the body of this book, its present reproduction as an epilogue—to avoid major duplications—omits from its text two passages which the reader at those points is asked to look up in the main body of the book: they do remain integral to the argument of the essay considered as an entity by itself. That argument, venturing into a confrontation of ancient Gnosticism with things highly modern, transcends the strict terms of the historical study to which this book is otherwise committed. But the understanding of ancient Gnosticism itself is advanced by discussing, however speculatively, its relationships to contemporary religious and spiritual phenomena; and even the understanding of the latter may profit from such an undertaking.

H. J.

New Rochelle, N.Y.
July 1962

* "Gnosticism and Modern Nihilism," *Social Research* 19 (1952), pp. 430-452. An expanded German version, "Gnosis und moderner Nihilismus," appeared in *Kerygma und Dogma* 6 (1960), pp. 155-171.

Note on the Occasion
of the Third Printing (1970)

Great changes have taken place in the field of Gnosticism since this book was first published. Only the barest beginnings of information on the famous Nag Hammadi documents were then in the public domain. Of the about fifty-three or more tractates, only the Gospel of Truth had been published and could just be inserted with a few quotations into my text. It was evident from the first, and has become ever more so, that the stunning chance discovery of 1946 marks a turning point in our knowledge of things Gnostic. Never before has a single archaeological find so radically altered the state of documentation for a whole field. From great scarcity we were overnight catapulted into great wealth with regard to original sources uncontaminated by secondary tradition. Yet circumstances conspired to make the opening up of this treasure to international scholarship frustratingly slow. Such progress as had been made by 1962 was taken account of in this second edition (Chapter 12); it still represented a minor fraction of the total corpus. Things have moved forward since. Work has at last been pooled, and teams of scholars are busy on all thirteen codices.* At this moment it looks as if the main body of the new evidence will be in our hands within the next few years. It is the Coptologists' day. Everybody else is holding his breath and, if wise, his hand. A summing up of the new knowledge and its import for the gnostic image as a whole will be a prime necessity some day, but must wait. On the other hand, the student has a right to find in a 1970 reprinting some guidance for making his own way to the evidence at its present intermediate stage. I have tried to serve this purpose by bringing the Supplementary Bibliography up to the beginning of 1970 and paying special attention to the Nag Hammadi complex. In this, I received valuable help from Professors James M. Robinson and David M. Scholer. An Addendum to Chapter 12 provides a key for converting its references to individual tractates into the system of numeration that has meanwhile become standard.

*UNESCO, by arrangement with the United Arab Republic, plans to publish photographic plates. For the English-speaking world, The Coptic Gnostic Library Project of the Institute for Antiquity and Christianity at the Claremont University Center serves, under the directorship of James M. Robinson, as a coordinating center for research and publication. It is preparing an English edition to appear at Brill in Leiden.

THE GNOSTIC RELIGION

Chapter 1. *Introduction: East and West in Hellenism*

Any portrayal of the Hellenistic era must begin with Alexander the Great. His conquest of the East (334-323 B.C.) marks a turning point in the history of the ancient world. Out of the conditions it created grew a cultural unity larger than any that had existed before, a unity which was to last for almost a thousand years until destroyed in its turn by the conquests of Islam. The new historical fact made possible, and indeed intended, by Alexander was the union of West and East. "West" means here the Greek world centered around the Aegaean; "East," the area of the old oriental civilizations, stretching from Egypt to the borders of India. Although Alexander's political creation fell apart with his death, the merging of cultures proceeded undisturbed through the succeeding centuries, both as regional processes of fusion within the several kingdoms of the Diadochi and as the rise of an essentially supra-national, Hellenistic, culture common to them all. When finally Rome dissolved the separate political entities in the area and transformed them into provinces of the Empire, she simply gave form to that homogeneity which in fact had long prevailed irrespective of dynastic boundaries.

In the larger geographical framework of the Roman Empire, the terms "East" and "West" assume new meanings, "East" being the Greek and "West" the Latin half of the Roman world. The Greek half, however, comprised the whole Hellenistic world, in which Greece proper had become a minor part; that is, it comprised all that part of Alexander's heritage which had not slipped back into "barbarian" control. Thus in the enlarged perspective of the Empire the East is constituted by a synthesis of what we first distinguished as the Hellenic West and the Asiatic East. In the permanent division of Rome from the time of Theodosius into an Eastern and a Western Empire, the cultural situation finds final political expression: under Byzantium the unified eastern half of the world came at last to form that Greek empire which Alexander

3

had envisioned and which Hellenism had made possible, although the Persian renascence beyond the Euphrates had diminished its geographical scope. The parallel division of Christendom into a Latin and a Greek Church reflects and perpetuates the same cultural situation in the realm of religious dogma.

It is this spatio-cultural unity, created by Alexander and existing in turn as the kingdoms of the Diadochi, as the eastern provinces of Rome, as the Byzantine Empire, and concurrently as the Greek Church, a unity bound together in the Hellenistic-oriental synthesis, which provides the setting for those spiritual movements with which this book is concerned. In this introductory chapter we have to fill in their background by saying something more about Hellenism in general and by clarifying on the one hand some aspects of its two components, namely, Hellas and Asia, and on the other the manner of their meeting, marriage, and common issue.

(a) THE PART OF THE WEST

What were the historical conditions and circumstances of the development we have indicated? The union which Alexander's conquest initiated was prepared for on both sides. East and West had each progressed previously to the maximum degree of unification in its own realm, most obviously so in political terms: the East had been unified under Persian rule, the Greek world under the Macedonian hegemony. Thus the conquest of the Persian monarchy by the Macedonian was an event involving the whole "West" and the whole "East."

No less had cultural developments prepared each side, though in a very different manner, for the roles they were destined to play in the new combination. Cultures can best mix when the thought of each has become sufficiently emancipated from particular local, social, and national conditions to assume some degree of general validity and thereby become transmissible and exchangeable. It is then no longer bound to such specific historical facts as the Athenian polis or the oriental caste society but has passed into the freer form of abstract principles that can claim to apply to all mankind, that can be learned, be supported by argument, and compete with others in the sphere of rational discussion.

Greek Culture on the Eve of Alexander's Conquests

When Alexander appeared, Hellas had, both in point of fact and in its own consciousness, reached this stage of cosmopolitan maturity, and this was the positive precondition of his success, which was matched by a negative one on the oriental side. For more than a century the whole evolution of Greek culture had been leading in this direction. The ideals of a Pindar could hardly have been grafted onto the court of a Nebuchadnezzar or an Artaxerxes and the bureaucracies of their realms. Since Herodotus, "the father of history" (fifth century B.C.), Greek curiosity had interested itself in the customs and opinions of the "barbarians"; but the Hellenic way was conceived for and suited to Hellenes alone, and of them only those who were freeborn and full citizens. Moral and political ideals, and even the idea of knowledge, were bound up with very definite social conditions and did not claim to apply to men in general—indeed, the concept of "man in general" had for practical purposes not yet come into its own. However, philosophical reflection and the development of urban civilization in the century preceding Alexander led gradually to its emergence and explicit formulation. The sophistic enlightenment of the fifth century had set the individual over against the state and its norms and in conceiving the opposition of nature and law had divested the latter, as resting on convention alone, of its ancient sanctity: moral and political norms are relative. Against their skeptical challenge, the Socratic-Platonic answer appealed, not indeed to tradition, but to conceptual knowledge of the intelligible, i.e., to rational theory; and rationalism carries in itself the germ of universalism. The Cynics preached a revaluation of existing norms of conduct, self-sufficiency of the private individual, indifference to the traditional values of society, such as patriotism, and freedom from all prejudice. The internal decline of the old city-states together with the loss of their external independence weakened the particularistic aspect of their culture while it strengthened the consciousness of what in it was of general spiritual validity.

In short, at the time of Alexander the Hellenic idea of culture had evolved to a point where it was possible to say that one was a Hellene not by birth but by education, so that one born a barbarian could become a true Hellene. The enthroning of reason as the highest part in man had led to the discovery of man as such, and at the same time to the conception of the Hellenic way as a general humanistic culture. The last step on this road was taken when the Stoics later advanced the proposition that freedom, that highest good of Hellenic ethics, is a purely inner quality not dependent on external conditions, so that true freedom may well be found in a slave if only he is wise. So much does all that is Greek become a matter of mental attitude and quality that participation in it is open to every rational subject, i.e., to every man. Prevailing theory placed man no longer primarily in the context of the polis, as did Plato and still Aristotle, but in that of the cosmos, which we sometimes find called "the true and great polis for all." To be a good citizen of the cosmos, a *cosmopolites,* is the moral end of man; and his title to this citizenship is his possession of *logos,* or reason, and nothing else— that is, the principle that distinguishes him as man and puts him into immediate relationship to the same principle governing the universe. The full growth of this cosmopolitan ideology was reached under the Roman Empire; but in all essential features the universalistic stage of Greek thought was present by Alexander's time. This turn of the collective mind inspired his venture and was itself powerfully reinforced by his success.

Cosmopolitanism and the New Greek Colonization

Such was the inner breadth of the spirit which Alexander carried into the outward expanses of the world. From now on, Hellas was everywhere that urban life with its institutions and organization flourished after the Greek pattern. Into this life the native populations could enter with equal rights by way of cultural and linguistic assimilation. This marks an important difference from the older Greek colonization of the Mediterranean coastline, which established purely Greek colonies on the fringes of the great "barbarian" hinterland and envisaged no amalgamation of colonists and natives. The colonization following in the footsteps of Alexander intended from the outset, and indeed as part of his own political program, a symbiosis of an entirely new kind, one which though most obviously a Hellenization of the East required for its success a certain reciprocity. In the new geopolitical area the Greek element no longer clung to geographic continuity with the mother country, and generally with what had hitherto been the Greek world, but spread far into the continental expanses of the Hellenistic Empire. Unlike the earlier colonies, the cities thus founded were not daughter cities of individual metropoles but were fed from the reservoir of the cosmopolitan Greek nation. Their main relations were not to one another and to the distant mother city but each acted as a center of crystallization in its own environment, that is, in relation to its indigenous neighbors. Above all, these cities were no longer sovereign states but parts of centrally administered kingdoms. This changed the relation of the inhabitants to the political whole. The classical city-state engaged the citizen in its concerns, and these he could identify with his own, as through the laws of his city he governed himself. The large Hellenistic monarchies neither called for nor permitted such close personal identification; and just as they made no moral demands on their subjects, so the individual detached himself in regard to them and as a *private* person (a status hardly admitted in the Hellenic world before) found satisfaction of his social needs in voluntarily organized associations based on community of ideas, religion, and occupation.

The nuclei of the newly founded cities were as a rule constituted by Greek nationals; but from the outset the inclusion of compact native populations was part of the plan and of the charter by which each city came into being. In many cases such groups of natives were thus transformed into city populations for the first time, and into the populations of cities organized and self-administering in the Greek manner. How thoroughly Alexander himself understood his policy of fusion in racial terms as well is shown by the famous marriage celebration at Susa when in compliance with his wishes ten thousand of his Macedonian officers and men took Persian wives.

The Hellenization of the East

The assimilating power of such an entity as the Hellenistic city must have been overwhelming. Participating in its institutions and ways of life, the non-Hellenic citizens underwent rapid Hellenization, shown most plainly in their adoption of the Greek language: and this in spite of the fact that probably from the beginning the non-Hellenes outnumbered the born Greeks or Macedonians. The tremendous subsequent growth of some of these cities, like Alexandria or Antioch, can be explained only by the continual influx of native oriental populations, which yet did not change the Hellenistic character of the communities. Finally, in the Seleucid kingdom, in Syria and Asia Minor, even originally oriental cities transformed themselves through the adoption of Hellenic corporative constitutions and the introduction of gymnasia and other typical institutions into cities of the Greek type and received from the central government the charter granting the rights and duties of such cities. This was a kind of refounding, evidence of the progress of Hellenization and at the same time a factor adding momentum to it. Besides the cities, the Greek-speaking administration of the monarchies was of course also a Hellenizing agent.

The invitation suggested in the formula that one is a Hellene not by birth but by education was eagerly taken up by the more responsive among the sons of the conquered East. Already in the generation after Aristotle we find them active in the very sanctuaries of Greek wisdom. Zeno, son of Mnaseas (i.e., Manasseh), founder of the Stoic school, was of Phoenician-Cypriote origin: he learned Greek as an adopted language, and throughout his long teaching career at Athens his accent always remained noticeable. From then until the end of antiquity the Hellenistic East produced a continual stream of men, often of Semitic origin, who under Greek names and in the Greek language and spirit contributed to the dominant civilization. The old centers of the Aegaean area remained in existence, but the center of gravity of Greek culture, now the universal culture, had shifted to the new regions. The Hellenistic cities of the Near East were its fertile seedbeds: among them Alexandria in Egypt was pre-eminent. With names generally Hellenized, we can mostly no longer determine whether an author from Apameia or Byblos in Syria, or from Gadara in Trans-Jordan, is of Greek or Semitic race; but in these melting-pots of Hellenism the question finally becomes irrelevant—a third entity had come into being.

In the newly founded Greek cities the result of the fusion was Greek from the outset. In other places the process was gradual, and continued into the period of late antiquity: people became converted to Hellenism as one might change one's party or creed, and this was still going on at a time when movements of renascence of national languages and literatures were already under way. The earliest, indeed anachronistic, example of such a situation is provided by the familiar events of the Maccabaean period in Palestine in the second century B.C. Even as late as the third century A.D., after five hundred years of Hellenistic civilization, we observe a native of the ancient city of Tyre, Malchus son of Malchus, becoming a prominent Greek philosophic writer and at the instance of his Hellenic friends changing (or suffering them to change) his Semitic name first to the Greek *Basileus*,[1] then to *Porphyrius*,[2] thereby symbolically declaring his adherence to the Hellenic cause together with his Phoenician extraction. The interesting point in this case is that at the same time the counter-movement was gathering momentum in his native country—the creation of a Syrian vernacular literature associated with the names of Bardesanes, Mani, and Ephraem. This movement and its parallels everywhere were part of the rise of the new popular religions against which Hellenism was forced to defend itself.

Later Hellenism: The Change from Secular to Religious Culture

With the situation just indicated the concept of Hellenism underwent a significant change. In late antiquity the unchallenged universalism of the first Hellenistic centuries was succeeded by an age of new differentiation, based primarily on spiritual issues and only secondarily also of a national, regional, and linguistic character. The common secular culture was increasingly affected by a mental polarization in religious terms, leading finally to a breaking up of the former unity into exclusive camps. Under these new circumstances, "Hellenic," used as a watchword *within* a world already thoroughly Hellenized, distinguishes an embattled cause from its Christian or gnostic opponents, who yet, in language and literary form, are themselves no less part of the Greek milieu. On this common ground Hellenism became almost equivalent to conservatism and crystallized into a definable doctrine in which the whole

---

[1] "King"—the literal translation of Malchus.

[2] "The purple-clad"—an allusion to his original name as well as to the major industry of his native city, purple-dyeing.

tradition of pagan antiquity, religious as well as philosophical, was for the last time systematized. Its adherents as well as its opponents lived everywhere, so that the battlefield extended over the whole civilized world. But the rising tide of religion had engulfed "Greek" thought itself and transformed its own character: Hellenistic secular culture changed into a pronouncedly religious pagan culture, both in self-defense against Christianity and from an inner necessity. This means that in the age of the rising world-religion, Hellenism itself became a denominational creed. This is how Plotinus and still more Julian the Apostate conceived their Hellenic, i.e., pagan, cause, which in Neoplatonism founded a kind of church with its own dogma and apologetic. Doomed Hellenism had come to be a particular cause on its own native ground. In this hour of its twilight the concept of Hellenism was at the same time broadened and narrowed. It was broadened in so far as, in the final entrench-ment, even purely oriental creations like the religions of Mithras or of Attis were counted in with the Hellenistic tradition that was to be defended; it was narrowed in that the whole cause became a party cause, and more and more that of a minority party. Yet, as we have said, the whole struggle was enacted within a Greek frame-work, that is, within the frame of the one universal Hellenic culture and language. So much is this the case that the victor and heir in this struggle, the Christian Church of the East, was to be pre-dominantly a Greek church: the work of Alexander the Great tri-umphed even in this defeat of the classical spirit.

The Four Stages of Greek Culture

We can accordingly distinguish four historical phases of Greek culture: (1) before Alexander, the classical phase as a national culture; (2) after Alexander, Hellenism as a cosmopolitan secular culture; (3) later Hellenism as a pagan religious culture; and (4) Byzantinism as a Greek Christian culture. The transition from the first to the second phase is for the most part to be explained as an autonomous Greek development. In the second phase (300 B.C.—first century B.C.) the Greek spirit was represented by the great rival schools of philosophy, the Academy, the Epicureans, and above all the Stoics, while at the same time the Greek-oriental synthesis was progressing. The transition from this to the third phase, the turning to religion of ancient civilization as a whole and of the Greek mind with it, was the work of profoundly un-Greek forces which, originating in the East, entered history as new factors. Between the rule of Hellenistic secular culture and the final defensive position of a late Hellenism turned religious lie three centuries of revolutionary spiritual movements which effected this transformation, among which the gnostic movement occupies a prominent place. With these we have to deal later.

(b) THE PART OF THE EAST

So far we have considered the role of the Greek side in the combination of West and East, and in doing so started from the internal preconditions that enabled Hellenic culture to become a world civilization following upon Alexander's conquests. These preconditions had of course to be matched by preconditions on the oriental side which explain the role of the East in the combination —its apparent or real passivity, docility, and readiness for assimilation. Military and political subjection alone is not sufficient to explain the course of events, as the comparison with other conquests of areas of high culture shows throughout history, where often enough the victor culturally succumbs to the vanquished. We may even raise the question whether in a deeper sense, or at least partially, something of the kind did not also happen in the case of Hellenism; but what is certainly manifest at first is the unequivocal ascendancy of the Greek side, and this determined at least the form of all future cultural expression. What, then, was the condition of the oriental world on the eve of Alexander's conquest to explain its succumbing to the expansion of Greek culture? And in what shape did native oriental forces survive and express themselves under the new conditions of Hellenism? For naturally this great East with its ancient and proud civilizations was not simply so much dead matter for the Greek form. Both questions, that concerning the antecedent conditions and that concerning the manner of survival, are incomparably harder to answer for the oriental side than the parallel ones were for the Greek side. The reasons for this are as follows.

In the first place, for the time before Alexander, in contrast with the wealth of Greek sources we are faced with an utter paucity of oriental ones, except for the Jewish literature. Yet this negative fact, if we may take it as a sign of literary sterility, is itself a historical testimony which confirms what we can infer from Greek sources about the contemporary state of the Eastern nations.

Moreover, this vast East, unified in the Persian Empire by sheer force, was far from being a cultural unity like the Greek world. Hellas was the same everywhere; the East, different from region to region. Thus an answer to the question regarding cultural preconditions would have to fall into as many parts as there were cultural entities involved. This fact also complicates the problem of Hellenism itself as regards its oriental component. Indeed, Gustav Droysen, the originator of the term "Hellenism" for the post-Alexandrian Greek-oriental synthesis, has himself qualified the term by stating that in effect as many different kinds of Hellenism evolved as there were different national individualities concerned. In many cases, however, these local factors are little known to us in their original form. Nevertheless, the overall homogeneity of the ensuing Hellenistic development suggests some overall similarity of conditions. In fact, if we except Egypt, we can discern in the pre-Hellenistic Orient certain universalistic tendencies, beginnings of a spiritual syncretism, which may be taken as a counterpart to the cosmopolitan turn of the Greek mind. Of this we shall have more to say.

Finally, in the period after Alexander the supremacy of pan-Hellenic civilization meant precisely that the East itself, if it aspired to literary expression at all, had to express itself in the Greek language and manner. Consequently the recognition of such instances of self-expression as voices of the East within the totality of Hellenistic literature is for us frequently a matter of subtle and not unequivocally demonstrable distinction: that is to say, the situation created by Hellenism is itself an ambiguous one. With the interesting methodological problem this presents we shall have to deal later.

These are some of the difficulties encountered in any attempt to clarify the picture of the Eastern half of the dual fact which we call Hellenism. We can nonetheless obtain a general though partly conjectural idea, and we shall briefly indicate as much of it as is necessary for our purpose. First a few words about the state of the Eastern world on the eve of the Greek conquest that accounts for its lethargy at first and the slowness of its reawakening afterwards.

The East on the Eve of Alexander's Conquests

Political Apathy and Cultural Stagnation. Politically, this state was determined by the sequence of despotic empires that had swept over the East in the preceding centuries. Their methods of conquest and rule had broken the political backbone of the local populations and accustomed them passively to accept each new master in the change of empires. The destinies of the central power were undisputed fate for the subject peoples, who were simply thrown in with the spoils. At a much later time, Daniel's vision of the four kingdoms still reflects this passive relation of the oriental peoples to the succession of political powers. So it came about that three battles which broke the military might of the Persian monarchy delivered to the victor an enormous empire of innumerable peoples which had become estranged from the idea of self-determination and did not even feel the urge to take a hand in the decision. The only serious local resistance of a popular nature was encountered by Alexander in Tyre and Gaza, which had to be reduced in long-drawn-out sieges. This exception was no accident: the Phoenician city—and Gaza's case was probably similar—was in spite of its vassal relation to the Great King a sovereign polity, and its citizens fought for their own cause in the long-standing Phoenician-Greek rivalry for sea power.

The political apathy was matched by a cultural stagnation, arising in part from different causes. In the old centers of oriental civilization, on the Euphrates and on the Nile, which prior to the Persian epoch were also the centers of political power, after several thousand years of existence all intellectual movement had come to a standstill, and only the inertia of formidable traditions was left. We cannot go here into explanations which would lead us far from our path; we simply note the fact, which especially in the case of Egypt is very obvious indeed. We may, however, remark that the immobility that our dynamic predilections are inclined to derogate as petrifaction could also be regarded as a mark of the perfection which a system of life has attained—this consideration may well apply in the case of Egypt.

In addition, the Assyrian and Babylonian practice of expatriating and transplanting whole conquered peoples, or more accurately their socially and culturally leading strata, had destroyed the forces of cultural growth in many of the regions outside the old centers. This fate had in many cases overtaken peoples of a more youthful cultural age who were still to unfold their potentialities. For the imperial manageability thus gained, the central power paid with the drying up of the potential sources of its own regeneration. Here we have doubtless one of the reasons for the torpor of the old centers we mentioned before: by breaking the national and regional vital forces throughout the kingdom, they had as it were surrounded themselves with a desert, and under these conditions the isolated summit of power was denied the benefit of whatever rejuvenating influences might have come from below. This may in part explain the state of paralysis in which the East seems to have been sunk prior to Alexander and from which it was delivered by the revivifying influence of the Hellenic spirit.

Beginnings of Religious Syncretism. Yet this same state of affairs contained also some positive conditions for the role which the East was to play in the Hellenistic age. It is not just that the prevailing passivity, the absence of consciously resisting forces, facilitated assimilation. The very weakening of the strictly local aspects of indigenous cultures meant the removal of so many obstacles to a merging in a wider synthesis and thus made possible the entry of these elements into the common stock. In particular, the uprooting and transplantation of whole populations had two significant effects. On the one hand, it favored the disengagement of cultural contents from their native soil, their abstraction into the transmissible form of teachings, and their consequently becoming available as elements in a cosmopolitan interchange of ideas—just as Hellenism could use them. On the other hand, it favored already a pre-Hellenistic syncretism, a merging of gods and cults of different and sometimes widely distant origins, which again anticipates an important feature of the ensuing Hellenistic development. Biblical history offers examples of both these processes.

The earliest description of the genesis of an intentional religious syncretism is found in the narrative in II Kings 17:24-41 concerning the new inhabitants settled by the Assyrian king in evacuated Samaria, that well-known story of the origin of the Samaritan sect which closes with the words:

So these nations feared the Lord, and served their graven images, both their children and their children's children: as did their fathers, so do they unto this day.

On a world-wide scale religious syncretism was later to become a decisive characteristic of Hellenism: we see here its inception in the East itself.

Beginnings of Theological Abstraction in Jewish, Babylonian, and Persian Religion. Even more important is the other development we mentioned, the transformation of the substance of local cultures into ideologies. To take another classic example from the Bible, the Babylonian exile forced the Jews to develop that aspect of their religion whose validity transcended the particular Palestinian conditions and to oppose the creed thus extracted in its purity to the other religious principles of the world into which they had been cast. This meant a confrontation of ideas with ideas. We find the position fully realized in Second Isaiah, who enunciated the pure principle of monotheism as a world cause, freed from the specifically Palestinian limitations of the cult of Jahweh. Thus the very uprooting brought to fulfillment a process which had started, it is true, with the older prophets.

The uniqueness of the Jewish case notwithstanding, certain parallels to these developments can be discerned elsewhere in the political disintegration of the East or can be inferred from the later course of events. Thus, after the overthrow of Babylon by the Persians the Old-Babylonian religion ceased to be a state cult attached to the political center and bound up with its functions of rule. As one of the institutions of the monarchy it had enjoyed a defined official status, and this connection with a local system of secular power had supported and at the same time limited its role. Both support and restriction fell away with the loss of statehood. The release of the religion from a political function was an uprooting comparable to the territorial uprooting of Israel. The fate of subjection and political impotence in the Persian Empire forced the Babylonian religion to stand henceforth on its spiritual content alone. No longer connected with the institutions of a local power-system and enjoying the prestige of its authority, it was thrown back upon its inherent *theological* qualities, which had to be formulated as such if they were to hold their own against other religious systems which had similarly been set afloat and were now competing for the minds of men. Political uprooting thus led to a liberation of spiritual substance. As a subject for speculation, the generalized principle acquired a life of its own and unfolded its abstract implications. We may discern here the working of a historical law which helps us to understand many mental developments of later antiquity. In the case of the Babylonian religion, the success of this movement toward abstraction is apparent in its later form as it emerged into the full light of Hellenism. In a one-sided development of its original astral features, the older cult was transformed into an abstract doctrine, the reasoned system of *astrology,* which simply by the appeal of its thought-content, presented in Greek form, became a powerful force in the Hellenistic world of ideas.

In a comparable manner, to take a final example, the Old Persian religion of Mazdaism detached itself from its native Iranian soil. Carried over all the countries from Syria to India by the numerically small ruling nation, it had in the midst of the religious plurality of the Persian Empire already found itself in something like a cosmopolitan situation. Through the fall of the Empire it lost with the support also the odium of a foreign rule and henceforth shared in the countries outside Persia proper with other creeds the burdens and advantages of diaspora. Here again, out of the less-defined national tradition there was extracted an unequivocal metaphysical principle which evolved into a system of general intellectual significance: the system of theological dualism. This dualistic doctrine in its generalized content was to be one of the great forces in the Hellenistic syncretism of ideas. In Persia itself the national reaction which led in succession to the founding of the Parthian and neo-Persian kingdoms was prepared for and accompanied by a religious restoration which in its turn was forced to systematize and dogmatize the content of the old folk-religion, a process in some ways analogous to the contemporary creation of the Talmud. Thus in the homeland and in the diaspora alike, the changing conditions produced a similar result: the transformation of traditional religion into a theological system whose characteristics approach those of a rational doctrine.

We may suppose comparable processes to have taken place throughout the East, processes by which originally national and local beliefs were fitted to become elements of an international exchange of ideas. The general direction of these processes was toward dogmatization, in the sense that a principle was abstracted from the body of tradition and unfolded into a coherent doctrine. Greek influence, furnishing both incentive and logical tools, everywhere brought this process to maturity; but as we have just tried to show, the East itself had on the eve of Hellenism already initiated it in significant instances. The three we have mentioned were chosen with particular intent: Jewish monotheism, Babylonian astrology, and Iranian dualism were probably the three main spiritual forces that the East contributed to the configuration of Hellenism, and they increasingly influenced its later course.

So much for what we called "preconditions." We may just pause to note the fact that the first cosmopolitan civilization known to history, for so we may regard the Hellenistic, was made possible by catastrophes overtaking the original units of regional culture. Without the fall of states and nations, this process of abstraction and interchange might never have occurred on such a scale. This is true, though less obviously, even for the Greek side, where the political decline of the polis, this most intensive of particularistic formations, provided a comparable negative precondition. Only in the case of Egypt, which we omitted in our survey, were conditions entirely different. In the main, however, it was from Asia, whether Semitic or Iranian, that the forces issued that were actively operative in the Hellenistic synthesis together with the Greek heritage: thus we can confine our sketch to the Asiatic conditions.

The East Under Hellenism

Having dealt with the preconditions, we must briefly consider the destiny of the East under the new dispensation of Hellenism. The first thing we note is that the East became silent for several centuries and was all but invisible in the overpowering light of the Hellenic day. With regard to what followed from the first century A.D. onward, we may call this opening stage the period of latency of the oriental mind and derive from this observation a division of the Hellenistic age into two distinct periods: the period of manifest Greek dominance and oriental submersion, and the period of reaction of a renascent East, which in its turn advanced victoriously in a kind of spiritual counterattack into the West and reshaped the universal culture. We are speaking of course in terms of intellectual and not of political events. In this sense, Hellenization of the East prevails in the first period, orientalization of the West in the second, the latter process coming to an end by about 300 A.D. The result of both is a synthesis which carried over into the Middle Ages.

The Submersion of the East. About the first period we can be brief. It was the age of the Seleucid and Ptolemaic kingdoms, particularly characterized by the efflorescence of Alexandria. Hellenism triumphed throughout the East and constituted the general culture whose canons of thought and expression were adopted by everyone who wished to participate in the intellectual life of the age. Only the Greek voice was heard: all public literary utterance was in its idiom. In view of what we said about the entering of orientals into the stream of Greek intellectual life, the muteness of the East cannot be construed as a lack of intellectual vitality on the part of its individuals: it consists rather in its not speaking for itself, in its own name. Anyone who had something to say had no choice but to say it in Greek, not only in terms of language but also in terms of concept, ideas, and literary form, that is, as ostensibly part of the Greek tradition.

To be sure, the Hellenistic civilization, wide open and hospitable, had room for creations of the oriental mind once they had assumed the Greek form. Thus the formal unity of this culture covered in fact a plurality, yet always as it were under the official Greek stamp. For the East, this situation engendered a kind of mimicry which had far-reaching consequences for its whole future. The Greek mind on its part could not remain unaffected: it was the recognition of the difference in what was called "Greek" before and after Alexander that prompted Droysen to introduce the term "Hellenistic" in distinction to the classical "Hellenic." "Hellenistic" was intended to denote not just the enlargement of the polis culture to a cosmopolitan culture and the transformations inherent in this process alone but also the change of character following from the reception of oriental influences into this enlarged whole.

However, the anonymity of the Eastern contributions makes these influences in the first period hard to identify. Men like Zeno, whom we mentioned before, wished to be nothing but Hellenes, and their assimilation was as complete as any such can be. Philosophy generally ran on very much in the tracks laid down by the native Greek schools; but toward the end of the period, about two centuries after Zeno, it too began to show significant signs of change in its hitherto autonomous development. The signs are at first by no means unambiguous. The continuing controversy about Posei-donius of Apameia (about 135-50 B.C.) well illustrates the difficulty of any confident attribution of influences and in general the uncertainty as to what in this period is genuinely Greek and what tinged with orientalism. Is the fervent astral piety that pervades his philosophy an expression of the Eastern mind or not? Both sides can be argued, and probably will continue to be, though there can be no doubt that, whether or not he was Greek by birth, to his own mind his thought was truly Greek. In this case, so in the general picture: we cannot demand a greater certainty than the complex nature of the situation admits. Faced with the peculiar anonymity, we might even say pseudonymity, that cloaks the oriental element, we must be content with the general impression that oriental influences in the broadest sense were at work throughout this period in the domain of Greek thought.

A clearer case is presented by the growing literature on "the wisdom of the barbarians" that made its appearance in Greek letters: in the long run it did not remain a matter of merely antiquarian interest but gradually assumed a propagandist character. The initiative of Greek authors in this field was taken up in the old centers of the East, Babylon and Egypt, by native priests, who turned to composing accounts of their national histories and cultures in the Greek language. The very ancient could always count on a respectful curiosity on the part of the Greek public, but as this was increasingly accompanied by a receptivity toward the spiritual contents themselves, the antiquarians were encouraged imperceptibly to turn into teachers and preachers.

The most important form, however, in which the East contributed at this time to the Hellenistic culture was in the field not of literature but of cult: the religious *syncretism* which was to become the most decisive fact in the later phase begins to take shape in this first period of the Hellenistic era. The meaning of the term "syncretism" may be extended, and usually is, to cover secular phenomena as well; and in this case the whole Hellenistic civilization may be called syncretistic, in that it increasingly became a mixed culture. Strictly speaking, however, syncretism denotes a religious phenomenon which the ancient term "theocrasy," i.e., mixing of gods, expresses more adequately. This is a central phenomenon of the period and one to which we, otherwise familiar with the intermingling of ideas and cultural values, have no exact parallel in our contemporary experience. It was the ever-growing range and depth of just this process that eventually led over from the first to the second, the religious-oriental, period of Hellenism. The theocrasy expressed itself in myth as well as in cult, and one of its most important logical tools was allegory, of which philosophy had already been making use in its relation to religion and myth. Of all the phenomena noted in this survey of the first period of Hellenism, it is in this religious one that the East is most active and most itself. The growing prestige of Eastern gods and cults within the Western world heralded the role which the East was to play in the second period, when the leadership passed into its hands. It was a religious role, whereas the Greek contribution to the Hellenistic whole was that of a secular culture.

In sum, we may state of the first half of Hellenism, which lasts roughly until the time of Christ, that it is in the main characterized by this Greek secular culture. For the East, it is a time of preparation for its re-emergence, comparable to a period of incubation. We can only guess from its subsequent eruption at the profound transformations that must have occurred there at this time under the Hellenistic surface. With the one great exception of the Maccabaean revolt, there is hardly any sign of oriental self-assertion within the Hellenistic orbit in the whole period from Alexander to Caesar. Beyond the borders, the founding of the Parthian kingdom and the revival of Mazdaism parallel the Jewish case. These events do little to disturb the general picture of Hellas as the assimilating and the East as the assimilated part during this period.

Greek Conceptualization of Eastern Thought. Nevertheless, this period of latency was of profound significance in the life history of the East itself. The Greek monopoly of all forms of intellectual expression had for the oriental spirit simultaneously the aspects of suppression and of liberation: suppression because this monopoly deprived it of its native medium and forced a dissimulation upon the expression of its own contents; liberation because the Greek conceptual form offered to the oriental mind an entirely new possibility of bringing to light the meaning of its own heritage. We have seen that the lifting of generally communicable spiritual principles out of the mass of popular tradition was under way on the eve of Hellenism; but it was with the logical means provided by the Greek spirit that this process came to fruition. For Greece had invented the *logos,* the abstract concept, the method of theoretical exposition, the reasoned system—one of the greatest discoveries in the history of the human mind. This formal instrument, applicable to any content whatsoever, Hellenism made available to the East, whose self-expression could now benefit from it. The effect, delayed in its manifestation, was immeasurable. Oriental thought had been non-conceptual, conveyed in images and symbols, rather disguising its ultimate objects in myths and rites than expounding them logically. In the rigidity of its ancient symbols it lay bound; from this imprisonment it was liberated by the vivifying breath of Greek thought, which gave new momentum and at the same time adequate tools to whatever tendencies of abstraction had been at work before. At bottom, oriental thought remained mythological, as became clear when it presented itself anew to the world; but it had learned in the meantime to bring its ideas into the form of *theories* and to employ rational concepts, instead of sensuous imagery alone, in expounding them. In this way, the definite formulation of the systems of dualism, astrological fatalism, and transcendent monotheism came about with the help of Greek conceptualization. With the status of metaphysical doctrines they gained general currency, and their message could address itself to all. Thus the Greek spirit delivered Eastern thought from the bondage of its own symbolism and enabled it in the reflection of the *logos* to discover itself. And it was with the arms acquired from the Greek arsenal that the East, when its time came, launched its counteroffensive.

The Eastern "Underground." Inevitably the blessings of a development of this kind are not unmixed, and the dangers inherent in it for the genuine substance of oriental thought are obvious. For one thing, every generalization or rationalization is paid for with the loss of specificity. In particular, the Greek ascendancy naturally tempted oriental thinkers to profit from the prestige of everything Greek by expressing their cause not directly but in the disguise of analogues gleaned from the Greek tradition of thought. Thus, for instance, astrological fatalism and magic could be clothed in the garments of the Stoic cosmology with its doctrines of sympathy and cosmic law, religious dualism in the garment of Platonism. To the mentality of assimilation this was certainly a rise in the world; but the mimicry thus initiated reacted upon the further growth of the Eastern mind and presents peculiar problems of interpretation to the historian. The phenomenon which Oswald Spengler called, with a term borrowed from mineralogy, "pseudomorphosis" will engage our attention as we go on (see below, Ch. 2, *d*).

There was another, perhaps still profounder, effect which Greek ascendancy had upon the inner life of the East, an effect which was to become manifest only much later: the division of the oriental spirit into a surface and a sub-surface stream, a public and a secret tradition. For the force of the Greek exemplar had not only a stimulating but also a repressive effect. Its selective standards acted like a filter: what was capable of Hellenization was passed and gained a place in the light, that is, became part of the articulate upper stratum of the cosmopolitan culture; the remainder, the radically different and unassimilable, was excluded and went underground. This "other" could not feel itself represented by the conventional creations of the literary world, could not in the general message recognize its own. To oppose its message to the dominant one it had to find its own language; and to find it became a process of long toil. In the nature of things it was the most genuine and original tendencies of the spirit of the East, those of the future rather than of the past, that were subjected to this condition of subterranean existence. Thus the spiritual monopoly of Greece caused the growth of an invisible East whose secret life formed an antagonistic under-current beneath the surface of the public Hellenistic civilization. Processes of profound transformation, far-reaching new departures, must have been under way in this period of submergence. We do not know them, of course; and our whole description, conjectural as it is, would be without foundation were it not for the sudden eruption of a new East which we witness at the turn of the era and from whose force and scale we can draw inferences as to its incuba-tion.

The Re-emergence of the East

What we do witness at the period roughly coinciding with the beginnings of Christianity is an explosion of the East. Like long-pent-up waters its forces broke through the Hellenistic crust and flooded the ancient world, flowing into the established Greek forms and filling them with their content, besides creating their own new beds. The metamorphosis of Hellenism into a religious oriental culture was set on foot. The time of the breakthrough was probably determined by the coinciding of two complementary conditions, the maturing of the subterranean growth in the East, which enabled it to emerge into the light of day, and the readiness of the West for a religious renewal, even its deeply felt need of it, which was grounded in the whole spiritual state of that world and disposed it to respond eagerly to the message of the East. This complemen-tary relation of activity and receptivity is not unlike the converse one which obtained three centuries earlier when Greece advanced into the East.

The Novelty of Revived Eastern Thought. Now it is important to recognize that in these events we are dealing, not with a reaction of the *old* East, but with a novel phenomenon which at that crucial hour entered the stage of history. The "Old East" was dead. The new awakening did not mean a classicist resuscitation of its time-honored heritage. Not even the more recent conceptualizations of earlier oriental thought were the real substance of the movement. Traditional dualism, traditional astrological fatalism, traditional monotheism were all drawn into it, yet with such a peculiarly new twist to them that in the present setting they subserved the repre-sentation of a novel spiritual principle; and the same is true of the use of Greek philosophical terms. It is necessary to emphasize this fact from the outset because of the strong suggestion to the contrary created by the outer appearances, which have long misled historians into regarding the fabric of thought they were confronted with, except for its Christian part, as simply made up of the remnants of older traditions. They all do in fact appear in the new stream: symbols of old oriental thought, indeed its whole mythological heritage; ideas and figures from Biblical lore; doctrinal and terminological elements from Greek philosophy, particularly Platonism. It is in the nature of the syncretistic situation that all these different elements were available and could be combined at will. But syncretism itself provides only the outer aspect and not the essence of the phenomenon. The outer aspect is confusing by its compositeness, and even more so by the associations of the old names. However, though these associations are by no means irrelevant, we can discern a new spiritual center around which the elements of tradition now crystallize, the unity behind their multiplicity; and this rather than the syncretistic means of expression is the true entity with which we are confronted. If we acknowledge this center as an autonomous force, then we must say that it makes use of those elements rather than that it is constituted by their confluence; and the whole which thus originated will in spite of its manifestly synthetic character have to be understood not as the product of an uncommitted eclecticism but as an original and determinate system of ideas.

Yet this system has to be elicited as such from the mass of disparate materials, which yield it only under proper questioning, that is, to an interpretation already guided by an anticipatory knowledge of the underlying unity. A certain circularity in the proof thus obtained cannot be denied, nor can the subjective element involved in the intuitive anticipation of the goal toward which the interpretation is to move. Such, however, is the nature and risk of historical interpretation, which has to take its cues from an initial impression of the material and is vindicated only by the result, its intrinsic convincingness or plausibility, and above all by the progressively confirmatory experience of things falling into their place when brought into contact with the hypothetical pattern.

Major Manifestations of the Oriental Wave in the Hellenistic World. We have now to give a brief enumeration of the phenomena in which the oriental wave manifests itself in the Hellenistic world from about the beginning of the Christian era onward. They are in the main as follows: the spread of Hellenistic Judaism, and especially the rise of Alexandrian Jewish philosophy; the spread of Babylonian astrology and of magic, coinciding with a general growth of fatalism in the Western world; the spread of diverse Eastern mystery-cults over the Hellenistic-Roman world, and their evolution into spiritual mystery-religions; the rise of Christianity; the efflorescence of the gnostic movements with their great system-formations inside and outside the Christian framework; and the transcendental philosophies of late antiquity, beginning with Neo-pythagoreanism and culminating in the Neoplatonic school.

All these phenomena, different as they are, are in a broad sense interrelated. Their teachings have important points in common and even in their divergences share in a common climate of thought: the literature of each can supplement our understanding of the others. More obvious than kinship of spiritual substance is the recurrence of typical patterns of expression, specific images and formulas, through-out the literature of the whole group. In Philo of Alexandria we encounter, besides the Platonic and Stoic elements with which the Jewish core is overlaid, also the language of the mystery-cults and the incipient terminology of a new mysticism. The mystery-religions on their part have strong relations to the astral complex of ideas. Neoplatonism is wide open to all pagan, and especially East-ern, religious lore having a pretense to antiquity and a halo of spirituality. Christianity, even in its "orthodox" utterances, had from the outset (certainly as early as St. Paul) syncretistic aspects, far exceeded however in this respect by its heretical offshoots: the gnostic systems compounded everything—oriental mythologies, as-trological doctrines, Iranian theology, elements of Jewish tradition, whether Biblical, rabbinical, or occult, Christian salvation-eschatol-ogy, Platonic terms and concepts. Syncretism attained in this period its greatest efficacy. It was no longer confined to specific cults and the concern of their priests but pervaded the whole thought of the age and showed itself in all provinces of literary expression. Thus, none of the phenomena we have enumerated can be considered apart from the rest.

Yet the syncretism, the intermingling of given ideas and

images, i.e., of the coined currencies of the several traditions, is of course a formal fact only which leaves open the question of the mental content whose external appearance it thus determines. Is there a one in the many, and what is it? we ask in the face of such a compound phenomenon. What is the organizing force in the syncretistic matter? We said before by way of preliminary assertion that in spite of its "synthetic" exterior the new spirit was not a directionless eclecticism. What then was the directing principle, and what the direction?

The Underlying Unity: Representativeness of Gnostic Thought. In order to reach an answer to this question, one has to fix one's attention upon certain characteristic mental attitudes which are more or less distinctly exhibited throughout the whole group, irrespective of otherwise greatly differing content and intellectual level. If in these common features we find at work a spiritual principle which was not present in the given elements of the mixture, we may identify this as the true agent of it. Now such a novel principle can in fact be discerned, though in many shadings of determinateness, throughout the literature we mentioned. It appears everywhere in the movements coming from the East, and most conspicuously in that group of spiritual movements which are comprised under the name "gnostic." We can therefore take the latter as the most radical and uncompromising representatives of a new spirit, and may consequently call the *general principle,* which in less unequivocal representations extends beyond the area of gnostic literature proper, by way of analogy the "gnostic principle." Whatever the usefulness of such an extension of the meaning of the name, it is certain that the study of this particular group not only is highly interesting in itself but also can furnish, if not *the* key to the whole epoch, at least a vital contribution toward its understanding. I personally am strongly inclined to regard the whole series of phenomena in which the oriental wave manifests itself as different refractions of, and reactions to, this hypothetical gnostic principle, and I have elsewhere argued my reasons for this view.[3] However far such a view may be granted, it carries in its own meaning the qualification that what can be thus identified as a common denomi-

[3] H. Jonas, *Gnosis und spätantiker Geist,* I and II, 1, *passim;* see especially the introduction to vol. I, and Ch. 4 of vol. II, 1.

nator can wear many masks and admits of many degrees of dilu-
tion and of compromise with conflicting principles. It may thus in
many cases itself be only one of the elements in a complex set of
intellectual motives, only partially effective and imperfectly realized
in the resulting whole. But it is a novel factor wherever it makes
itself felt, and its most unadulterated revelation is to be found in
the gnostic literature properly so called. To this we now turn, re-
serving for later (Part III) the attempt to place its message within
the wider setting of contemporary culture.

PART I

Gnostic Literature—Main Tenets,
Symbolic Language

Chapter 2. *The Meaning of Gnosis and the Extent of the Gnostic Movement*

(*a*) SPIRITUAL CLIMATE OF THE ERA

At the beginning of the Christian era and progressively throughout the two following centuries, the eastern Mediterranean world was in profound spiritual ferment. The genesis of Christianity itself and the response to its message are evidence of this ferment, but they do not stand alone. With regard to the environment in which Christianity originated, the recently discovered Dead Sea Scrolls have added powerful support to the view, reasonably certain before, that Palestine was seething with eschatological (i.e., salvational) movements and that the emergence of the Christian sect was anything but an isolated incident. In the thought of the manifold *gnostic* sects which soon began to spring up everywhere in the wake of the Christian expansion, the spiritual crisis of the age found its boldest expression and, as it were, its extremist representation. The abstruseness of their speculations, in part intentionally provocative, does not diminish but rather enhances their symbolic representativeness for the thought of an agitated period. Before narrowing down our investigation to the particular phenomenon of Gnosticism, we must briefly indicate the main features that characterize this contemporary thought as a whole.

First, all the phenomena which we noted in connection with the "oriental wave" are of a decidedly *religious* nature; and this, as we have repeatedly stated, is the prominent characteristic of the second phase of Hellenistic culture in general. Second, all these currents have in some way to do with *salvation*: the general religion of the period is a religion of salvation. Third, all of them exhibit an exceedingly *transcendent* (i.e., transmundane) conception of God and in connection with it an equally transcendent and other-worldly idea of the goal of salvation. Finally, they maintain a radical *dualism* of realms of being—God and the world, spirit and matter, soul and body, light and darkness, good and evil, life and death—and

31

consequently an extreme polarization of existence affecting not only man but reality as a whole: the general religion of the period is a *dualistic transcendent religion of salvation.*

(*b*) THE NAME "GNOSTICISM"

Turning to Gnosticism in particular, we ask what the name means, where the movement originated, and what literary evidence it left. The *name* "Gnosticism," which has come to serve as a collective heading for a manifoldness of sectarian doctrines appearing within and around Christianity during its critical first centuries, is derived from *gnosis,* the Greek word for "knowledge." The emphasis on *knowledge* as the means for the attainment of salvation, or even as the form of salvation itself, and the claim to the possession of this knowledge in one's own articulate doctrine, are common features of the numerous sects in which the gnostic movement historically expressed itself. Actually there were only a few groups whose members expressly called themselves Gnostics, "the Knowing ones"; but already Irenaeus, in the title of his work, used the name "gnosis" (with the addition "falsely so called") to cover all those sects that shared with them that emphasis and certain other characteristics. In this sense we can speak of gnostic schools, sects, and cults, of gnostic writings and teachings, of gnostic myths and speculations, even of gnostic religion in general.

In following the example of the ancient authors who first extended the name beyond the self-styling of a few groups, we are not obliged to stop where their knowledge or polemical interest did and may treat the term as a class-concept, to be applied wherever the defining properties are present. Thus the extent of the gnostic area can be taken as narrower or broader, depending on the criterion employed. The Church Fathers considered Gnosticism as essentially a Christian heresy and confined their reports and refutations to systems which either had sprouted already from the soil of Christianity (e.g., the Valentinian system), or had somehow added and adapted the figure of Christ to their otherwise heterogeneous teaching (e.g., that of the Phrygian Naassenes), or else through a common Jewish background were close enough to be felt as competing with and distorting the Christian message (e.g., that of

Simon Magus). Modern research has progressively broadened this traditional range by arguing the existence of a *pre-Christian Jewish* and a *Hellenistic pagan* Gnosticism, and by making known the *Mandaean* sources, the most striking example of Eastern Gnosticism outside the Hellenistic orbit, and other new material. Finally, if we take as a criterion not so much the special motif of "knowledge" as the dualistic-anticosmic spirit in general, the religion of *Mani* too must be classified as gnostic.

(c) THE ORIGIN OF GNOSTICISM

Asking next the question where or from what historical tradition Gnosticism originated, we are confronted with an old crux of historical speculation: the most conflicting theories have been advanced in the course of time and are still in the field today. The early Church Fathers, and independently of them Plotinus, emphasized the influence upon a Christian thinking not yet firmly consolidated of *Plato* and of misunderstood Hellenic philosophy in general. Modern scholars have advanced in turn Hellenic, Babylonian, Egyptian, and Iranian origins and every possible combination of these with one another and with Jewish and Christian elements. Since in the material of its representation Gnosticism actually is a product of syncretism, each of these theories can be supported from the sources and none of them is satisfactory alone; but neither is the combination of all of them, which would make Gnosticism out to be a mere mosaic of these elements and so miss its autonomous essence. On the whole, however, the oriental thesis has an edge over the Hellenic one, once the meaning of the term "knowledge" is freed from the misleading associations suggested by the tradition of classical philosophy. The recent Coptic discoveries in Upper Egypt (see below, sec. *e*) are said to underline the share of a heterodox occultist Judaism, though judgment must be reserved pending the translation of the vast body of material.[1] Some connection of Gnosticism with the beginnings of the *Cabbala* has in any case to be assumed, whatever the order of cause and effect. The violently anti-Jewish bias of the more prominent gnostic systems is by itself not incompatible with Jewish heretical origin at some distance. Inde-

[1] See Chapt. 12.

pendently, however, of who the first Gnostics were and what the main religious traditions drawn into the movement and suffering arbitrary reinterpretation at its hands, the movement itself transcended ethnic and denominational boundaries, and its spiritual principle was new. The Jewish strain in Gnosticism is as little the orthodox Jewish as the Babylonian is the orthodox Babylonian, the Iranian the orthodox Iranian, and so on. Regarding the case made out for a preponderance of Hellenic influence, much depends on how the crucial concept of "knowledge" is to be understood in this context.

(d) THE NATURE OF GNOSTIC "KNOWLEDGE"

"Knowledge" is by itself a purely formal term and does not specify *what* is to be known; neither does it specify the psychological manner and subjective significance of possessing knowledge or the ways in which it is acquired. As for *what* the knowledge is about, the associations of the term most familiar to the classically trained reader point to *rational* objects, and accordingly to natural reason as the organ for acquiring and possessing knowledge. In the gnostic context, however, "knowledge" has an emphatically religious or supranatural meaning and refers to objects which we nowadays should call those of faith rather than of reason. Now although the relation between faith and *knowledge* (*pistis* and *gnosis*) became a major issue in the Church between the gnostic heretics and the orthodox, this was not the modern issue between faith and *reason* with which we are familiar; for the "knowledge" of the Gnostics with which simple Christian faith was contrasted whether in praise or blame was not of the rational kind. *Gnosis* meant pre-eminently knowledge *of God,* and from what we have said about the radical transcendence of the deity it follows that "knowledge of God" is the knowledge of something naturally unknowable and therefore itself not a natural condition. Its objects include everything that belongs to the divine realm of being, namely, the order and history of the upper worlds, and what is to issue from it, namely, the salvation of man. With objects of this kind, knowledge as a mental act is vastly different from the rational cognition of philosophy. On the one hand it is closely bound up with revelationary experience, so that *reception* of the truth either through sacred and secret lore or through inner illumination re-places rational argument and theory (though this extra-rational basis may then provide scope for independent speculation); on the other hand, being concerned with the secrets of salvation, "knowledge" is not just theoretical information about certain things but is itself, as a modification of the human condition, charged with perform-ing a function in the bringing about of salvation. Thus gnostic "knowledge" has an eminently practical aspect. The ultimate "ob-ject" of gnosis is God: its event in the soul transforms the knower himself by making him a partaker in the divine existence (which means more than assimilating him to the divine essence). Thus in the more radical systems like the Valentinian the "knowledge" is not only an instrument of salvation but itself the very form in which the goal of salvation, i.e., ultimate perfection, is possessed. In these cases knowledge and the attainment of the known by the soul are claimed to coincide—the claim of all true mysticism. It is, to be sure, also the claim of Greek *theoria,* but in a different sense. There, the object of knowledge is the universal, and the cognitive relation is "optical," i.e., an analogue of the visual relation to objec-tive form that remains unaffected by the relation. Gnostic "knowl-edge" is about the particular (for the transcendent deity is still a particular), and the relation of knowing is mutual, i.e., a being known at the same time, and involving active self-divulgence on the part of the "known." There, the mind is "informed" with the forms it beholds and while it beholds (thinks) them: here, the subject is "transformed" (from "soul" to "spirit") by the union with a reality that in truth is itself the supreme subject in the situation and strictly speaking never an object at all.

These few preliminary remarks are sufficient to delimitate the gnostic type of "knowledge" from the idea of rational theory in terms of which Greek philosophy had developed the concept. Yet the suggestions of the term "knowledge" as such, reinforced by the fact that Gnosticism produced real thinkers who unfolded the con-tents of the secret "knowledge" in elaborate doctrinal systems and used abstract concepts, often with philosophical antecedents, in their exposition, have favored a strong tendency among theologians and historians to explain Gnosticism by the impact of the Greek ideal of knowledge on the new religious forces which came to the fore at that time, and more especially on the infancy of Christian thought. The genuine theoretical aspirations revealed in the higher type of gnostic speculation, bearing out as it seemed the testimony of the early Church Fathers, led Adolf von Harnack to his famous formulation that Gnosticism was "the acute Hellenization of Christianity," while the slower and more measured evolution of orthodox theology was to be regarded as its "chronic Hellenization." The medical analogy was not meant to designate Hellenization as such as a disease; but the "acute" stage which provoked the reaction of the healthy forces in the organism of the Church was understood as the hasty and therefore disruptive anticipation of the same process that in its more cautious and less spectacular form led to the incorporation of those aspects of the Greek heritage from which Christian thought could truly benefit. Perspicacious as this diagnosis is, as a definition of Gnosticism it falls short in both the terms that make up the formula, "Hellenization" and "Christianity." It treats Gnosticism as a solely Christian phenomenon, whereas subsequent research has established its wider range; and it gives way to the Hellenic appearance of gnostic conceptualization and of the concept of *gnosis* itself, which in fact only thinly disguises a heterogeneous spiritual substance. It is the genuineness, i.e., the underivative nature, of this substance that defeats all attempts at derivation that concern more than the outer shell of expression. About the idea of "knowledge," the great watchword of the movement, it must be emphasized that its objectification in articulate systems of thought concerning God and the universe was an autonomous achievement of this substance, not its subjection to a borrowed scheme of theory. The combination of the practical, salvational concept of knowledge with its theoretical satisfaction in quasi-rational systems of thought —the rationalization of the supranatural—was typical of the higher forms of Gnosticism and gave rise to a kind of speculation previously unknown but never afterwards to disappear from religious thought.

Yet Harnack's half-truth reflects a fact which is almost as integral to the destiny of the new oriental wisdom as its original substance: the fact called by Spengler "pseudomorphosis" to which we have alluded before. If a different crystalline substance happens to fill the hollow left in a geological layer by crystals that have dis-

integrated, it is forced by the mold to take on a crystal form not its
own and without chemical analysis will mislead the observer into
taking it for a crystal of the original kind. Such a formation is
called in mineralogy a "pseudomorphosis." With the inspired intuition that distinguished him, amateur as he was in the field,
Spengler discerned a similar situation in the period under view and
argued that the recognition of it must govern the understanding of
all its utterances. According to him, disintegrating Greek thought is
the older crystal of the simile, Eastern thought the new substance
forced into its mold. Leaving aside the wider historical vista within
which Spengler places his observation, it is a brilliant contribution
to the diagnosis of a historical situation and if used with discrimina-
tion can greatly help our understanding.

(e) SURVEY OF SOURCES

What are the sources, that is, the literature, from which we have
to reconstruct the image of this forgotten creed? The following
survey aims at representativeness rather than completeness. We
have to divide the sources into original and secondary ones, of
which until fairly recently almost none but the latter were known.
We shall take this group first.

Secondary or Indirect Sources

1. The struggle against Gnosticism as a danger to the true faith
occupied a large space in early Christian literature, and the writings
devoted to its refutation are by their discussion, by the summaries
they give of gnostic teachings, and frequently also by extensive verbatim quotation from gnostic writings the most important secondary source of our knowledge. We may add that until the nineteenth
century they were (apart from Plotinus' treatise) the only source,
as the victory of the Church naturally led to the disappearance of
the gnostic originals. Of this group we name the great polemical
works of the Fathers Irenaeus, Hippolytus, Origen, and Epiphanius
in Greek and Tertullian in Latin. Another Father, Clement of
Alexandria, left among his writings an extremely valuable collection
of Greek *Excerpts* from the writings of Theodotus, a member of the
Valentinian school of Gnosticism, representing its Eastern ("Ana-

tolian") branch. Of its Italic branch Epiphanius has preserved an entire literary document, Ptolemaeus' *Letter to Flora*. In the case of such complete, or almost complete, renderings of the subject of the attack (among which may be counted also Hippolytus' reports on the Naassenes and on the book *Baruch*), our distinction between secondary and primary sources of course becomes blurred. It is in the nature of the case that all the originals preserved through this medium, whether whole or in part (the latter is the rule), were Greek. Taken together, these patristic sources give information about a large number of sects, all of them at least nominally Christian, though in some cases the Christian veneer is rather thin. A unique contribution from the pagan camp concerning this group is the treatise of Plotinus, the Neoplatonic philosopher, *Against the Gnostics, or against those who say that the Creator of the World is evil and that the World is bad* (*Enn.* II. 9). It is directed against the teachings of one particular Christian gnostic sect which cannot be definitely identified with any individual one named in the patristic catalogues but clearly falls into one of their major groupings.

2. After the third century the anti-heretical writers had to concern themselves with the refutation of *Manichaeism*. They did not consider this new religion as part of the gnostic heresy, which in its narrower sense had by then been disposed of; but by the broader criteria of the history of religion it belongs to the same circle of ideas. Of the very extensive Christian literature we need name only the *Acta Archelai,* the works of Titus of Bostra (Greek), of St. Augustine (Latin), and of Theodore bar Konai (Syriac). Here too a philosophically trained pagan author, Alexander of Lycopolis (in Egypt), writing one generation after Mani, supplements the Christian chorus.

3. In a qualified way, some of the *mystery-religions* of late antiquity also belong to the gnostic circle, insofar as they allegorized their ritual and their original cult-myths in a spirit similar to the gnostic one: we may mention the mysteries of Isis, Mithras, and Attis. The sources in this case consist of reports by contemporary Greek and Latin, mostly pagan, writers.

4. A certain amount of veiled information is scattered in *rabbinical* literature, though on the whole, unlike the Christian prac-

tice, silence was there considered the more effective way of dealing with heresy.

5. Finally, the branch of *Islamic* literature that deals with the variety of religions, late as it is, contains valuable accounts, especially of the Manichaean religion but also of some more obscure gnostic sects whose writings had survived into the Islamic period.

In language these secondary sources are Greek, Latin, Hebrew, Syriac, and Arabic.

Primary or Direct Sources

These for the most part have come to light only since the nineteenth century and are constantly being added to through fortunate archaeological finds. The following enumeration is independent of order of origin and discovery.

1. Of inestimable value for the knowledge of Gnosticism outside the Christian orbit are the sacred books of the *Mandaeans,* a sect which survives in a few remnants in the region of the lower Euphrates (the modern Iraq), no less violently anti-Christian than anti-Jewish, but including among its prophets John the Baptist in opposition to and at the expense of Christ. This is the only instance of the continued existence of a gnostic religion to the present day. The name is derived from the Aramaic *manda,* "knowledge," so that "Mandaeans" means literally "Gnostics." Their scriptures, written in an Aramaic dialect closely related to that of the Talmud, make up the largest corpus—with the possible exception of the next group—of original gnostic writings in our possession. It includes mythological and doctrinal treatises, ritual and moral teaching, liturgy, and collections of hymns and psalms, these last containing some profoundly moving religious poetry.

2. A constantly growing group of sources is constituted by the Christian *Coptic-gnostic* writings, mostly of the Valentinian school or the larger family of which this school is the outstanding member. Coptic was the Egyptian vernacular of the later Hellenistic period, descended from the ancient Egyptian with an admixture of Greek. The promotion of this popular language to use as a literary medium reflects the rise of a mass-religion as against the Greek secular culture of the Hellenistically educated. Until recently, the bulk of

the Coptic-gnostic writings in our possession, such as the *Pistis Sophia* and the *Books of Jeû*, represented a rather low and degenerate level of gnostic thought, belonging to the declining stage of the Sophia speculation. But lately (about 1945) a sensational find at Nag-Hammadi (Chenoboskion) in Upper Egypt has brought to light a whole library of a gnostic community, containing in Coptic translation from the Greek hitherto unknown writings of what may be termed the "classical" phase of gnostic literature: among them one of the major books of the Valentinians, the *Gospel of Truth*—if not by Valentinus himself, certainly dating back to the founding generation of the school—of which the mere existence and title had been known from Irenaeus. With the exception of this one part of one codex, just published in full (1956), and some excerpts from other parts, the remainder of the extensive new material (thirteen codices, some fragmentary, some almost intact, totaling about 1000 papyrus pages and presenting about forty-eight writings) has not yet been made known. On the other hand, one codex of the older Coptic discoveries, after sixty years in the Berlin Museum, has recently (1955) for the first time been published in its gnostic parts, of which the most important is the *Apocryphon of John,* a main work of the Barbelo-Gnostics already used by Irenaeus in his account of this second-century system. (This and another writing of this collection, the somewhat later *Wisdom of Jesus Christ,* are also found in the unedited part of the Nag-Hammadi library—the *Apocryphon* in no less than three versions, evidence of the esteem it enjoyed.)

3. Also in the Coptic language is the library of *Manichaean* papyri discovered in Egypt in 1930, the editing of which is still in progress. Dating back to the fourth century A.D., the very badly preserved codices, estimated at about 3500 pages, have so far yielded one of Mani's own books, known before by title and, like all his writings, believed irretrievably lost: the *Kephalaia,* i.e., "Chapters"; a (the?) *Psalm-Book* of the early Manichaean community; also part of a collection of *Homilies* (sermons) from the first generation after Mani. Barring the Dead Sea Scrolls, this find is easily the greatest event for the history of religion which archaeology has provided within this generation. Like the Mandaean corpus, the Coptic Manichaean corpus contains doctrinal as well as poetic ma-

terial. In this case the translation is presumably from the Syriac, though the interposition of a Greek translation cannot be ruled out.

4. Another group of original, though later, sources for the Manichaean religion, this time in its Eastern form, is the so-called Turfan fragments in Persian and Turkish, found in explorations at the oasis of Turfan in Chinese Turkestan at the beginning of this century; to which must be added two Chinese texts also found in Turkestan, a hymn scroll and a treatise quoted by the name of its discoverer and editor Pelliot. These documents—also not yet edited in full—are evidence of the flowering of a gnostic religion so far away as central Asia.

5. Longest known to Western scholars has been the corpus of Greek writings attributed to *Hermes Trismegistus* and often quoted as *Poimandres,* which strictly speaking is the name of the first treatise only. The extant corpus, first published in the sixteenth century, is the remnant of an Egyptian Hellenistic literature of revelation, called "Hermetic" because of the syncretistic identification of the Egyptian god Thoth with the Greek Hermes. A number of references and quotations in late classical writers, both pagan and Christian, add to the sources for Hermetic thought. This literature, not as a whole but in certain portions, reflects gnostic spirit. The same goes for the closely related *alchemistic* literature and some of the Greek and Coptic *magical papyri,* which show an admixture of gnostic ideas. The Hermetic *Poimandres* treatise itself, in spite of some signs of Jewish influence, is to be regarded as a prime document of independent pagan Gnosticism.

6. There is, finally, gnostic material in some of the New Testament *Apocrypha,* like the Acts of Thomas and the Odes of Solomon—in both these cases in the shape of poems which are among the finest expressions of gnostic sentiment and belief.

In terms of language, these original sources are Greek, Coptic, Aramaic, Persian, Turkish, and Chinese. (The term "original" does not here exclude ancient translations, like the Turkish and Chinese and most of the Coptic documents.)

This survey gives some idea of the wide geographical and linguistic range of gnostic sources and the great variety of gnostic groups. Accordingly we can speak of *the* gnostic doctrine only as an abstraction. The leading Gnostics displayed pronounced intellectual individualism, and the mythological imagination of the whole movement was incessantly fertile. Non-conformism was almost a principle of the gnostic mind and was closely connected with the doctrine of the sovereign "spirit" as a source of direct knowledge and illumination. Already Irenaeus (*Adv. Haer.* I. 18. 1) observed that "Every day every one of them invents something new." The great system builders like Ptolemaeus, Basilides, Mani erected ingenious and elaborate speculative structures which are original creations of individual minds yet at the same time variations and developments of certain main themes shared by all: these together form what we may call the simpler "basic myth." On a less intellectual level, the same basic content is conveyed in fables, exhortations, practical instructions (moral and magical), hymns, and prayers. In order to help the reader to see the unity of the whole field before entering into the detailed treatment, we shall outline this "basic myth" that can be abstracted from the confusing variety of the actual material.

(f) ABSTRACT OF MAIN GNOSTIC TENETS

Theology

The cardinal feature of gnostic thought is the radical dualism that governs the relation of God and world, and correspondingly that of man and world. The deity is absolutely transmundane, its nature alien to that of the universe, which it neither created nor governs and to which it is the complete antithesis: to the divine realm of light, self-contained and remote, the cosmos is opposed as the realm of darkness. The world is the work of lowly powers which though they may mediately be descended from Him do not know the true God and obstruct the knowledge of Him in the cosmos over which they rule. The genesis of these lower powers, the Archons (rulers), and in general that of all the orders of being outside God, including the world itself, is a main theme of gnostic speculation, of which we shall give examples later. The transcendent God Himself is hidden from all creatures and is unknowable by natural concepts. Knowledge of Him requires supranatural revelation and illumination and even then can hardly be expressed otherwise than in negative terms.

Cosmology

The universe, the domain of the Archons, is like a vast prison whose innermost dungeon is the earth, the scene of man's life. Around and above it the cosmic spheres are ranged like concentric enclosing shells. Most frequently there are the seven spheres of the planets surrounded by the eighth, that of the fixed stars. There was, however, a tendency to multiply the structures and make the scheme more and more extensive: Basilides counted no fewer than 365 "heavens." The religious significance of this cosmic architecture lies in the idea that everything which intervenes between here and the beyond serves to separate man from God, not merely by spatial distance but through active demonic force. Thus the vastness and multiplicity of the cosmic system express the degree to which man is removed from God.

The spheres are the seats of the Archons, especially of the "Seven," that is, of the planetary gods borrowed from the Babylonian pantheon. It is significant that these are now often called by Old Testament names for God (Iao, Sabaoth, Adonai, Elohim, El Shaddai), which from being synonyms for the one and supreme God are by this transposition turned into proper names of inferior demonic beings—an example of the pejorative revaluation to which Gnosticism subjected ancient traditions in general and Jewish tradition in particular. The Archons collectively rule over the world, and each individually in his sphere is a warder of the cosmic prison. Their tyrannical world-rule is called *heimarmene,* universal Fate, a concept taken over from astrology but now tinged with the gnostic anti-cosmic spirit. In its physical aspect this rule is the law of nature; in its psychical aspect, which includes for instance the institution and enforcement of the Mosaic Law, it aims at the enslavement of man. As guardian of his sphere, each Archon bars the passage to the souls that seek to ascend after death, in order to prevent their escape from the world and their return to God. The Archons are also the creators of the world, except where this role is reserved for their leader, who then has the name of *demi-*

urge (the world-artificer in Plato's *Timaeus*) and is often painted with the distorted features of the Old Testament God.

Anthropology

Man, the main object of these vast dispositions, is composed of flesh, soul, and spirit. But reduced to ultimate principles, his origin is twofold: mundane and extra-mundane. Not only the body but also the "soul" is a product of the cosmic powers, which shaped the body in the image of the divine Primal (or Archetypal) Man and animated it with their own psychical forces: these are the appetites and passions of natural man, each of which stems from and corresponds to one of the cosmic spheres and all of which together make up the astral soul of man, his "psyche." Through his body and his soul man is a part of the world and subjected to the *heimarmene*. Enclosed in the soul is the spirit, or "pneuma" (called also the "spark"), a portion of the divine substance from beyond which has fallen into the world; and the Archons created man for the express purpose of keeping it captive there. Thus, as in the macrocosm man is enclosed by the seven spheres, so in the human microcosm again the pneuma is enclosed by the seven soul-vestments originating from them. In its unredeemed state the pneuma thus immersed in soul and flesh is unconscious of itself, benumbed, asleep, or intoxicated by the poison of the world: in brief, it is "ignorant." Its awakening and liberation is effected through "knowledge."

Eschatology

The radical nature of the dualism determines that of the doctrine of salvation. As alien as the transcendent God is to "this world" is the pneumatic self in the midst of it. The goal of gnostic striving is the release of the "inner man" from the bonds of the world and his return to his native realm of light. The necessary condition for this is that he *knows* about the transmundane God and about himself, that is, about his divine origin as well as his present situation, and accordingly also about the nature of the world which determines this situation. As a famous Valentinian formula puts it,

What liberates is the knowledge of who we were, what we became; where we were, whereinto we have been thrown; whereto we speed, wherefrom we are redeemed; what birth is, and what rebirth.

(*Exc. Theod.* 78. 2)

This knowledge, however, is withheld from him by his very situation, since "ignorance" is the essence of mundane existence, just as it was the principle of the world's coming into existence. In particular, the transcendent God is unknown in the world and cannot be discovered from it; therefore revelation is needed. The necessity for it is grounded in the nature of the cosmic situation; and its occurrence alters this situation in its decisive respect, that of "ignorance," and is thus itself already a part of salvation. Its bearer is a messenger from the world of light who penetrates the barriers of the spheres, outwits the Archons, awakens the spirit from its earthly slumber, and imparts to it the saving knowledge "from without." The mission of this transcendent savior begins even before the creation of the world (since the fall of the divine element preceded the creation) and runs parallel to its history. The knowledge thus revealed, even though called simply "the knowledge of God," comprises the whole content of the gnostic myth, with everything it has to teach about God, man, and world; that is, it contains the elements of a theoretical system. On the practical side, however, it is more particularly "knowledge of the way," namely, of the soul's way out of the world, comprising the sacramental and magical preparations for its future ascent and the secret names and formulas that force the passage through each sphere. Equipped with this *gnosis,* the soul after death travels upwards, leaving behind at each sphere the psychical "vestment" contributed by it: thus the spirit stripped of all foreign accretions reaches the God beyond the world and becomes reunited with the divine substance. On the scale of the total divine drama, this process is part of the restoration of the deity's own wholeness, which in pre-cosmic times has become impaired by the loss of portions of the divine substance. It is through these alone that the deity became involved in the destiny of the world, and it is to retrieve them that its messenger intervenes in cosmic history. With the completion of this process of gathering in (according to some systems), the cosmos, deprived of its elements of light, will come to an end.

Morality

In this life the *pneumatics,* as the possessors of gnosis called themselves, are set apart from the great mass of mankind. The immediate illumination not only makes the individual sovereign in the sphere of knowledge (hence the limitless variety of gnostic doctrines) but also determines the sphere of action. Generally speaking, the pneumatic morality is determined by hostility toward the world and contempt for all mundane ties. From this principle, however, two contrary conclusions could be drawn, and both found their extreme representatives: the ascetic and the libertine. The former deduces from the possession of gnosis the obligation to avoid further contamination by the world and therefore to reduce contact with it to a minimum; the latter derives from the same possession the privilege of absolute freedom. We shall deal later with the complex theory of gnostic libertinism. In this preliminary account a few remarks must suffice. The law of "Thou shalt" and "Thou shalt not" promulgated by the Creator is just one more form of the "cosmic" tyranny. The sanctions attaching to its transgression can affect only the body and the psyche. As the pneumatic is free from the *heimarmene,* so he is free from the yoke of the moral law. To him all things are permitted, since the pneuma is "saved in its nature" and can be neither sullied by actions nor frightened by the threat of archontic retribution. The pneumatic freedom, however, is a matter of more than mere indifferent permission: through intentional violation of the demiurgical norms the pneumatic thwarts the design of the Archons and paradoxically contributes to the work of salvation. This antinomian libertinism exhibits more forcefully than the ascetic version the *nihilistic* element contained in gnostic acosmism.

Even the reader unfamiliar with the subject will realize from the foregoing abstract that, whatever heights of conceptualization gnostic theory attained to in individual thinkers, there is an indissoluble mythological core to gnostic thought as such. Far remote from the rarefied atmosphere of philosophical reasoning, it moves in the denser medium of imagery and personification. In the following chapters we have to fill in the framework of our generalized account with the substance of gnostic metaphor and myth, and on the other hand present some of the elaborations of this basic content into speculative systems of thought.

Chapter 3. *Gnostic Imagery and Symbolic Language*

At his first encounter with gnostic literature, the reader will be struck by certain recurrent elements of expression which by their intrinsic quality, even outside the wider context, reveal something of the fundamental experience, the mode of feeling, and the vision of reality distinctively characteristic of the gnostic mind. These expressions range from single words with symbolic suggestion to extensive metaphors; and more than for their frequency of occurrence, they are significant for their inherent eloquence, often enhanced by startling novelty. In this chapter we shall consider some of them. The advantage of this line of approach is that it confronts us with a level of utterance more fundamental than the doctrinal differentiation into which gnostic thought branched out in the completed systems.

Especially rich in the kind of original coinage that displays the stamp of the gnostic mind with telling force is the *Mandaean* literature. This wealth of expressiveness is at least in part the obverse of its poorness on the theoretical side; it is also connected with the fact that owing to their geographical and social remoteness from Hellenistic influence the Mandaeans were less exposed than most to the temptation to assimilate the expression of their ideas to Western intellectual and literary conventions. In their writings mythological fantasy abounds, the compactness of its imagery unattenuated by any ambition toward conceptualization, its variety unchecked by care for consistency and system. Although this lack of intellectual discipline often makes tedious the reading of their larger compositions, which are highly repetitious, the unsophisticated colorfulness of mythical vision that permeates them offers ample compensation; and in Mandaean poetry the gnostic soul pours forth its anguish, nostalgia, and relief in an unending stream of powerful symbolism. For the purposes of this chapter, we shall accordingly draw heavily on this source, without thereby wishing

48

to exaggerate the importance of the Mandaeans in the general picture of Gnosticism.

(a) THE "ALIEN"

"In the name of the great first alien Life from the worlds of light, the sublime that stands above all works": this is the standard opening of Mandaean compositions, and "alien" is a constant attribute of the "Life" that by its nature is alien to this world and under certain conditions alien within it. The formula quoted speaks of the "first" Life "that stands above all works," where we have to supply *of creation,* i.e., above the world. The concept of the alien Life is one of the great impressive word-symbols which we encounter in gnostic speech, and it is new in the history of human speech in general. It has equivalents throughout gnostic literature, for example Marcion's concept of the "alien God" or just "the Alien," "the Other," "the Unknown," "the Nameless," "the Hidden"; or the "unknown Father" in many Christian-gnostic writings. Its philosophic counterpart is the "absolute transcendence" of Neoplatonic thought. But even apart from these theological uses where it is one of the predicates of God or of the highest Being, the word "alien" (and its equivalents) has its own symbolic significance as an expression of an elemental human experience, and this underlies the different uses of the word in the more theoretical contexts. Regarding this underlying experience, the combination "the alien life" is particularly instructive.

The alien is that which stems from elsewhere and does not belong here. To those who do belong here it is thus the strange, the unfamiliar and incomprehensible; but their world on its part is just as incomprehensible to the alien that comes to dwell here, and like a foreign land where it is far from home. Then it suffers the lot of the stranger who is lonely, unprotected, uncomprehended, and uncomprehending in a situation full of danger. Anguish and homesickness are a part of the stranger's lot. The stranger who does not know the ways of the foreign land wanders about lost; if he learns its ways too well, he forgets that he is a stranger and gets lost in a different sense by succumbing to the lure of the alien world and becoming estranged from his own origin. Then he has become a "son of the house." This too is part of the alien's fate. In his alienation from himself the distress has gone, but this very fact is the culmination of the stranger's tragedy. The recollection of his own alienness, the recognition of his place of exile for what it is, is the first step back; the awakened homesickness is the beginning of the return. All this belongs to the "suffering" side of alienness. Yet with relation to its origin it is at the same time a mark of excellence, a source of power and of a secret life unknown to the environment and in the last resort impregnable to it, as it is incomprehensible to the creatures of this world. This superiority of the alien which distinguishes it even here, though secretly, is its manifest glory in its own native realm, which is outside this world. In such position the alien is the remote, the inaccessible, and its strangeness means majesty. Thus the alien taken absolutely is the wholly transcendent, the "beyond," and an eminent attribute of God.

Both sides of the idea of the "Alien," the positive and the negative, alienness as superiority and as suffering, as the prerogative of remoteness and as the fate of involvement, alternate as the characteristics of one and the same subject—the "Life." As the "great first Life" it partakes in the positive aspect alone: it is "beyond," "above the world," "in the worlds of light," "in the fruits of splendor, in the courts of light, in the house of perfection," and so forth. In its split-off existence in the world it tragically partakes in the interpenetration of both sides; and the actualization of all the features outlined above, in a dramatic succession that is governed by the theme of salvation, makes up the metaphysical history of the light exiled from Light, of the life exiled from Life and involved in the world—the history of its alienation and recovery, its "way" down and through the nether world and up again. According to the various stages of this history, the term "alien" or its equivalents can enter into manifold combinations: "my alien soul," "my worldsick heart," "the lonely vine," apply to the human condition, while "the alien man" and "the stranger" apply to the messenger from the world of Light—though he may apply to himself the former terms as well, as we shall see when we consider the "redeemed redeemer." Thus by implication the very concept of the "alien" includes in its meaning all the aspects which the "way" explicates in the form of temporally distinct phases. At the same time it most directly expresses the basic experience which first led to this conception of the "way" of existence—the elementary experience of alienness and transcendence. We may therefore regard the figure of the "alien Life" as a primary symbol of Gnosticism.

(b) "BEYOND," "WITHOUT," "THIS WORLD," AND "THE OTHER WORLD"

To this central concept other terms and images are organically related. If the "Life" is originally alien, then its home is "outside" or "beyond" this world. "Beyond" here means beyond everything that is of the cosmos, heaven and its stars included. And "included" literally: the idea of an absolute "without" limits the world to a closed and bounded system, terrifying in its vastness and inclusiveness to those who are lost in it, yet finite within the total scope of being. It is a power-system, a demonic entity charged with personal tendencies and compulsive forces. The limitation by the idea of the "beyond" deprives the "world" of its claim to totality. As long as "world" means "the All," the sum total of reality, there is only "the" world, and further specification would be pointless: if the cosmos ceases to be the All, if it is limited by something radically "other" yet eminently real, then it must be designated as "this" world. All relations of man's terrestrial existence are "in this world," "of this world," which is in contrast to "the other world," the habitation of "Life." Seen from beyond, however, and in the eyes of the inhabitants of the worlds of Light and Life, it is our world which appears as "that world." The demonstrative pronoun has thus become a relevant addition to the term "world"; and the combination is again a fundamental linguistic symbol of Gnosticism, closely related to the primary concept of the "alien."

(c) WORLDS AND AEONS

It is in line with this view of things that "world" comes to be used in the plural. The expression "the worlds" denotes the long chain of such closed power-domains, divisions of the larger cosmic system, through which Life has to pass on its way, all of them equally alien to it. Only by losing its status of totality, by becoming particularized and at the same time demonized, did the concept "world" come to admit of plurality. We might also say that "world" denotes a collective rather than a unity, a demonic family rather than a unique individual. The plurality denotes also the labyrinthine aspect of the world: in the worlds the soul loses its way and wanders about, and wherever it seeks an escape it only passes from one world into another that is no less world. This multiplication of demonic systems to which unredeemed life is banished is a theme of many gnostic teachings. To the "worlds" of the Mandaeans correspond the "aeons" of Hellenistic Gnosticism. Usually there are seven or twelve (corresponding to the number of the planets or the signs of the zodiac), but in some systems the plurality proliferates to dizzying and terrifying dimensions, up to 365 "heavens" or the innumerable "spaces," "mysteries" (here used topologically), and "aeons" of the *Pistis Sophia*. Through all of them, representing so many degrees of separation from the light, "Life" must pass in order to get out.

> You see, O child, through how many bodies [elements?], how many ranks of demons, how many concatenations and revolutions of stars, we have to work our way in order to hasten to the one and only God.
>
> (*C.H.* IV. 8)

It is to be understood even where it is not expressly stated that the role of these intervening forces is inimical and obstructive: with the spatial extent they symbolize at the same time the anti-divine and imprisoning power of this world. "The way that we have to go is long and endless" (G 433);[1] "How wide are the boundaries of these worlds of darkness!" (G 155);

> Having once strayed into the labyrinth of evils,
> The wretched [Soul] finds no way out . . .
> She seeks to escape from the bitter chaos,
> And knows not how she shall get through.
>
> (Naassene Psalm, Hippol. V. 10. 2)

Apart from all personification, the whole of space in which life finds itself has a malevolently spiritual character, and the "demons"

---

[1] Mandaean quotations are based on the German translation by M. Lidzbarski, "G" standing for *Ginza: Der Schatz oder das Grosse Buch der Mandäer,* Göttingen, 1925, "J" for *Das Johannesbuch der Mandäer,* Giessen, 1915. Numbers after the letter indicate pages of these publications.

themselves are as much spatial realms as they are persons. To overcome them is the same thing as to pass through them, and in breaking through their boundaries this passage at the same time breaks their power and achieves the liberation from the magic of their sphere. Thus even in its role as redeemer the Life in Mandaean writings says of itself that it "wandered through the worlds": or as Jesus is made to say in the Naassene Psalm, "All the worlds shall I journey through, all the mysteries unlock."

This is the spatial aspect of the conception. No less demonized is the time dimension of life's cosmic existence, which also is represented as an order of quasi-personal powers (e.g., the "Aeons"). Its quality, like that of the world's space, reflects the basic experience of alienness and exile. Here too we meet the plurality we observed there: whole series of ages stretch between the soul and its goal, and their mere number expresses the hold which the cosmos as a principle has over its captives. Here again, escape is achieved only by passing through them all. Thus the way of salvation leads through the temporal order of the "generations": through chains of unnumbered generations the transcendent Life enters the world, sojourns in it, and endures its seemingly endless duration, and only through this long and laborious way, with memory lost and regained, can it fulfill its destiny. This explains the impressive formula "worlds and generations" which constantly occurs in Mandaean writings: "I wandered through worlds and generations," says the redeemer. To the unredeemed soul (which may be that of the redeemer himself), this time perspective is a source of anguish. The terror of the vastness of cosmic spaces is matched by the terror of the times that have to be endured: "How long have I endured already and been dwelling in the world!" (G 458).

This twofold aspect of the cosmic terror, the spatial and the temporal, is well exhibited in the complex meaning of the gnostically adapted Hellenistic concept of "Aeon." Originally a time-concept purely (duration of life, length of cosmic time, hence eternity), it underwent personification in pre-gnostic Hellenistic religion—possibly an adaptation of the Persian god Zervan—and became an object of worship, even then with some fearsome associations. In Gnosticism it takes a further mythological turn and becomes a class-name for whole categories of either divine, semi-divine, or demonic beings. In the last sense "the Aeons" represent with temporal as well as spatial implications the demonic power of the universe or (as in the *Pistis Sophia*) of the realm of darkness in its enormity. Their extreme personification may sometimes all but obliterate the original time aspect, but in the frequent equating of "aeons" with "worlds" that aspect is kept alive as part of a meaning become rather protean through the drifts of mythical imagination.[2]

The feeling inspired by the time aspect of cosmic exile finds moving expression in words like these:

In that world [of darkness] I dwelt thousands of myriads of years, and nobody knew of me that I was there. . . . Year upon year and generation upon generation I was there, and they did not know about me that I dwelt in their world.

(G 153 f.)[3]

or (from a Turkish Manichaean text):

Now, O our gracious Father, numberless myriads of years have passed since we were separated from thee. Thy beloved shining living countenance we long to behold. . . .

(*Abh. d. Pr. Akad.* 1912, p. 10)

The immeasurable cosmic duration means separation from God, as does the towering scale of cosmic spaces, and the demonic quality of both consists in maintaining this separation.

[2] In the singular, "aeon" can simply mean "the world," and is as "this aeon" in Jewish and Christian thought opposed to "the coming aeon": here the model was probably the Hebrew word *olam* (Aram. *alma*), whose original meaning of "eternity" came to include that of "world." The Mandaean plural *almaya* can mean "worlds" and "beings," the latter in a personal (superhuman) sense. Personification is joined to the New Testament concept of "this aeon" by expressions like "the god [or, "the rulers"] of this aeon."

[3] These are words spoken by the savior; but how close his situation is to that of the life exiled in the world in general, i.e., of those to be saved, is shown by the words with which he is sent forth on his mission: "Go, go, our son and our image. . . . The place to which thou goest—grievous suffering awaits thee in those worlds of darkness. Generation after generation shalt thou remain there, until we forget thee. Thy form will remain there, until we read for thee the mass for the dead" (G 152 f.).

(*d*) THE COSMIC HABITATION AND THE STRANGER'S SOJOURN

For the world as a whole, vast as it appears to its inhabitants, we have thus the visual image of an enclosed cell—what Marcion contemptuously called *haec cellula creatoris*—into which or out of which life may move. "To come from outside" and "to get out" are standard phrases in gnostic literature. Thus the Life or the Light "has come into this world," "has travelled here"; it "departs into the world," it can stand "at the outer rim of the worlds" and thence, "from without," "call into" the world. We shall later deal with the religious significance of these expressions: at present we are concerned with the symbolic topology and with the immediate eloquence of the imagery.

The sojourn "in the world" is called "dwelling," the world itself a "dwelling" or "house," and in contrast to the bright dwellings, the "dark" or the "base" dwelling, "the mortal house." The idea of "dwelling" has two aspects: on the one hand it implies a temporary state, something contingent and therefore revocable—a dwelling can be exchanged for another, it can be abandoned and even allowed to go to ruin; on the other hand, it implies the dependence of life on its surroundings—the place where he dwells makes a decisive difference to the dweller and determines his whole condition. He can therefore only change one dwelling for another one, and the extra-mundane existence is also called "dwelling," this time in the seats of Light and Life, which though infinite have their own order of bounded regions. When Life settles in the world, the temporary belonging thus established may lead to its becoming "a son of the house" and make necessary the reminder, "Thou wert not from here, and thy root was not of the world" (G 379). If the emphasis is on the temporary and transient nature of the worldly sojourn and on the condition of being a stranger, the world is called also the "inn," in which one "lodges"; and "to keep the inn" is a formula for "to be in the world" or "in the body." The creatures of this world are the "fellow-dwellers of the inn," though their relation to it is not that of guests: "Since I was one and kept to myself, I was a stranger to my fellow-dwellers in the inn" ("Hymn of the Pearl" in the *Acta Thomae*).

The same expressions can refer also to the body, which is eminently the "house" of life and the instrument of the world's power over the Life that is enclosed in it. More particularly, "tent" and "garment" denote the body as a passing earthly form encasing the soul; these too, however, can also be applied to the world. A garment is donned and doffed and changed, the earthly garment for that of light.

Cut off from its fountainhead, the Life languishes in the bodily garment:

I am a Mana[4] of the great Life. Who has made me live in the Tibil,[5] who has thrown me into the body-stump?

(G 454)

A Mana am I of the great Life. Who has thrown me into the suffering of the worlds, who has transported me to the evil darkness? So long I endured and dwelt in the world, so long I dwelt among the works of my hands.

(G 457 f.)

Grief and woe I suffer in the body-garment into which they transported and cast me. How often must I put it off, how often put it on, must ever and again settle my strife[6] and not behold the Life in its sh'kina.[7]

(G 461)

From all this arises the question addressed to the great Life: "Why hast thou created this world, why hast thou ordered the tribes [of Life] into it out of thy midst?" (G 437). The answer to such questions differs from system to system: the questions themselves are more basic than any particular doctrine and immediately reflect the underlying human condition.

[4] See Glossary at end of chapter, pp. 97-99.
[5] See Glossary, p. 98.
[6] "Settle my strife": formula for "die."
[7] See Glossary, p. 98.

(e) "LIGHT" AND "DARKNESS," "LIFE" AND "DEATH"

We have to add a few words about the antithesis of light and darkness that is so constant a feature in this account. Its symbolism meets us everywhere in gnostic literature, but for reasons we shall discuss later its most emphatic and doctrinally important use is to be found in what we shall call the *Iranian* strain of Gnosticism, which is also one component of Mandaean thought. Most of the following examples are taken from this area and therefore imply the Iranian version of gnostic dualism. Irrespective of the theoretical context, however, the symbolism reflects a universal gnostic attitude. The first alien Life is the "King of Light," whose world is "a world of splendor and of light without darkness," "a world of mildness without rebellion, a world of righteousness without turbulence, a world of eternal life without decay and death, a world of goodness without evil. . . . A pure world unmixed with ill" (G 10). Opposed to it is the "world of darkness, utterly full of evil, . . . full of devouring fire . . . full of falsehood' and deceit. . . . A world of turbulence without steadfastness, a world of darkness without light . . . a world of death without eternal life, a world in which the good things perish and plans come to naught" (G 14). Mani, who most completely adopted the Iranian version of dualism, commences his doctrine of origins, as reported in the *Fihrist,* an Arabic source, as follows: "Two beings were at the beginning of the world, the one Light, the other Darkness." On this assumption the existing world, "this" world, is a mixture of light and darkness, yet with a preponderance of darkness: its main substance is darkness, its foreign admixture, light. In the given state of things, the duality of darkness and light coincides with that of "this world" and "the other world," since darkness has embodied its whole essence and power in this world, which now therefore is *the* world of darkness.[8] The equation "world (cos-

[8] The king of primal darkness is even in the pre-cosmic stage called "the King of this world" and "of these aeons," although according to the system the "world" stems only from a mingling of the two principles. A Mandaean parallel to Mani's teaching about the origins whose opening sentence we quoted above reads: "Two kings there were, two natures were created: one king of this world and one king of outside the worlds. The king of these aeons put on a sword and a crown

mos) = darkness" is in fact independent of and more basic than the particular theory of origins just exemplified, and as an expression of the given condition admits of widely divergent types of derivation, as we shall see later. The equation as such is symbolically valid for Gnosticism in general. In the Hermetic Corpus we find the exhortation, "Turn ye away from the dark light" (*C.H.* I. 28), where the paradoxical combination drives home the point that even the light so called in this world is in truth darkness. "For the cosmos is the fulness of evil, God the fulness of good" (*C.H.* VI. 4); and as "darkness" and "evil," so is "death" a symbol of the world as such. "He who is born of the mother is brought forth into death and the cosmos: he who is reborn of Christ is transported into life and the Eight [i.e., removed from the power of the Seven]" (*Exc. Theod.* 80. 1). Thus we understand the Hermetic statement quoted in Macrobius (*In somn. Scip.* I. 11) that the soul "through as many deaths as she passes spheres descends to what on earth is called life."

(f) "MIXTURE," "DISPERSAL," THE "ONE," AND THE "MANY"

To return once more to the Iranian conception, the idea of two original and opposite entities leads to the metaphor of "mixture" for the origin and composition of this world. The mixture is, however, an uneven one, and the term essentially denotes the tragedy of the portions of the Light separated from its main body and immersed in the foreign element.

I am I, the son of the mild ones [i.e., the beings of Light]. Mingled am I, and lamentation I see. Lead me out of the embracement of death.
(Turfan fragment M 7)

They brought living water[9] and poured it into the turbid water;[9] they brought shining light and cast it into the dense darkness. They

---

of darkness [etc.]" (J 55). Logically speaking, this is inconsistent; but symbolically it is more genuinely gnostic than Mani's abstraction, since the principle of "darkness" is here from the outset *defined* as that of the "world" from whose gnostic experience it had first been conceived. "World" is determined by darkness, and "darkness" solely by world.

[9] See Glossary, pp. 97 and 99, respectively.

brought the refreshing wind and cast it into the scorching wind. They brought the living fire and cast it into the devouring fire. They brought the soul, the pure Mana, and cast it into the worthless body.

(J 56)

The mixing is here expressed in terms of the five basic elements of the Manichaean scheme, which obviously underlies this Mandaean text.

Thou hast taken the treasure of Life and cast it onto the worthless earth. Thou hast taken the word of Life and cast it into the word of mortality.

(G 362)

As it entered the turbid water, the living water lamented and wept. . . . As he mingled the living water with the turbid, darkness entered the light.

(J 216)

Even the messenger is subject to the fate of mixture:

Then the living fire in him became changed. . . . His splendor was impaired and dulled. . . . See how the splendor of the alien man is diminished!

(G 98 f.)

In Manichaeism the doctrine of mixing, with its counterpart of unmixing, forms the basis of the whole cosmological and soteriological system, as will be shown in a later chapter.

Closely connected with the idea of "mixing" is that of "dispersal." If portions of the Light or the first Life have been separated from it and mixed in with the darkness, then an original unity has been split up and given over to plurality: the splinters are the sparks dispersed throughout the creation. "Who took the song of praise, broke it asunder and cast it hither and thither?" (J 13). The very creation of Eve and the scheme of reproduction initiated by it subserve the indefinite further dispersion of the particles of light which the powers of darkness have succeeded in engulfing and by this means endeavor to retain the more securely. Consequently, salvation involves a process of gathering in, of re-collection of what has been so dispersed, and salvation aims at the restoration of the original unity.

I am thou and thou art I, and where thou art I am, and in all things am I dispersed. And from wherever thou willst thou gatherest me; but in gathering me thou gatherest thyself.[10]

This self-gathering is regarded as proceeding *pari passu* with the progress of "knowledge," and its completion as a condition for the ultimate release from the world:

He who attains to this gnosis and gathers himself from the cosmos . . . is no longer detained here but rises above the Archons;[11]

and by proclaiming this very feat the ascending soul answers the challenge of the celestial gatekeepers:

I have come to know myself and have gathered myself from everywhere. . . .[12]

It is easy to see from these quotations that the concept of unity and unification, like that of plurality, diversity, and dispersal, has an inward as well as metaphysical aspect, i.e., applies to the individual self as it does to universal being. It is a mark of the higher, or more philosophical, forms of Gnosis that these two aspects, complementary from the beginning, come to ever more complete coincidence; and that the increasing realization of the internal aspect purifies the metaphysical one of the cruder mythological meanings it had to begin with. To the Valentinians, whose spiritualized symbolism marks an important step on the road of de-mythologizing, "unification" is the very definition of what the "knowledge of the Father" is to achieve for "each one":

It is by means of Unity that each one shall receive himself back again. Through knowledge he shall purify himself of diversity with a view to Unity, by engulfing (devouring) the Matter within himself like a flame, Darkness by Light and Death by Life.

(GT 25:10-19)

It must be noted that in the Valentinian system the same achievement is ascribed to *gnosis* on the plane of universal being where

[10] From a fragment of the gnostic Gospel of Eve preserved by Epiphanius (*Haer*. 26. 3).
[11] *Ibid.*, 26. 10.
[12] *Ibid.*, 26. 13; the passage is quoted below in full, p. 168.

the "restoring of Unity" and the "engulfing of Matter" mean no less than the actual dissolution of the whole lower world, i.e., sensible nature as such—not by an act of external force but solely by an inner event of mind: "knowledge" on a transcendental scale. We shall see later (Ch. 8) by what speculative principle the Valentinians established this objective and ontological efficacy of what at first sight seems to be a merely private and subjective act; and how their doctrine justified the equating of individual unification with the reuniting of the universe with God.

Both the universal (metaphysical) and the individual (mystical) aspects of the idea of unity and its opposites became abiding themes of succeeding speculation as it moved even farther away from mythology. Origen, whose proximity to gnostic thought is obvious in his system (duly anathematized by the Church), viewed the whole movement of reality in the categories of the loss and recovery of metaphysical Unity.[13] But it was Plotinus who in his speculation drew the full mystical conclusions from the metaphysics of "Unity versus Plurality." Dispersal and gathering, ontological categories of total reality, are at the same time action-patterns of each soul's potential experience, and unification within *is* union with the One. Thus emerges the Neoplatonic scheme of the inner ascent from the Many to the One that is ethical on the first rungs of the ladder, then theoretical, and at the culminating stage mystical.

Endeavor to ascend into thyself, gathering in from the body all thy members which have been dispersed and scattered into multiplicity from that unity which once abounded in the greatness of its power. Bring together and unify the inborn ideas and try to articulate those that are confused and to draw into light those that are obscured.

(Porphyr. *Ad Marcell.* x)

It was probably through the writings of Porphyry that this Neoplatonic conception of unification as a principle of personal life came to Augustine, in whose intensely subjective manner the emphasis at last shifts from the metaphysical aspect entirely to the moral one.

[13] See Jonas, *Gnosis und spätantiker Geist,* II, 1, pp. 175-223.

Since through the iniquity of godlessness we have seceded and dissented and fallen away from the one true and highest God and dissipated ourselves into the many, split up by the many and cleaving to the many: it was necessary that . . . the many should have joined in clamor for the coming of One (Christ) . . . and that we, disencumbered from the many, should come to One . . . and, justified in the justice of One, be made One.

(*Trin.* IV. 11)

By continence we are collected into the One from which we have declined to the many.

(*Confess.* X. 14; cf. *Ord.* I. 3)

The "dispersal" has finally received what we should nowadays call an existentialist meaning: that of the soul's "distraction" by the manifold concerns and lures of the world acting through the senses of the body; that is, it has been turned into a psychological and ethical concept within the scheme of individual salvation.

(g) "FALL," "SINKING," "CAPTURE"

For the manner in which life has got into its present plight there are a number of expressions, most of them describing the process as a passive one, some giving it a more active turn. "The tribe of souls"[14] was transported here from the house of Life" (G 24); "the treasure of Life which was fetched from there" (G 96), or "which was brought here." More drastic is the image of falling: the soul or spirit, a part of the first Life or of the Light, fell into the world or into the body. This is one of the fundamental symbols of Gnosticism: a pre-cosmic fall of part of the divine principle underlies the genesis of the world and of human existence in the majority of gnostic systems. "The Light fell into the darkness" signifies an early phase of the same divine drama of which "the Light shone in the darkness" can be said to signify a later phase. How this fall originated and by what stages it proceeded is the subject of greatly divergent speculations. Except in Manichaeism and related Iranian types, where the whole process is initiated by the powers of darkness, there is a voluntary element in

[14] See Glossary, p. 98.

the downward movement of the divine: a guilty "inclination" of the Soul (as a mythical entity) toward the lower realms, with various motivations such as curiosity, vanity, sensual desire, is the gnostic equivalent of original sin. The fall is a pre-cosmic one, and one of its consequences is the world itself, another the condition and fate of the individual souls in the world.

The Soul once turned toward matter, she became enamored of it, and burning with the desire to experience the pleasures of the body, she no longer wanted to disengage herself from it. Thus the world was born. From that moment the Soul forgot herself. She forgot her original habitation, her true center, her eternal being.[15]

Once separated from the divine realm and engulfed by the alien medium, the movement of the Soul continues in the downward direction in which it started and is described as "sinking": "How long shall I sink within all the worlds?" (J 196). Frequently, however, an element of violence is added to this description of the fall, as in the metaphors relating to captivity, of which we shall see more when we study the Manichaean system. Here some Mandaean examples will suffice. "Who has carried me into captivity away from my place and my abode, from the household of my parents who brought me up?" (G 323). "Why did ye carry me away from my abode into captivity and cast me into the stinking body?" (G 388).[16]

The term "cast" or "thrown" occurring in the last quotation requires some comment. Its use, as we have seen before, is not confined to the metaphor of captivity: it is an image in its own right and of very wide application—life has been cast (thrown) into the world and into the body. We have met the expression associated with the symbolism of the "mixture," where it is used for the origin of the cosmos as well as for that of man: "Ptahil [17] threw the form which the Second [Life] had formed into the world of darkness. He made creations and formed tribes outside the Life" (G 242). This passage refers to the cosmogonic activity of the demiurge: in the anthropogony the image is repeated, and it is there that it has

---

[15] El Châtibî of the Harranites: for continuation of this text, see below, p. 162, note 15.

[16] Prison, ball and chain, bond, and knot are frequent symbols for the body.

[17] See Glossary, p. 98.

its main significance. "Ptahil took a hidden Mana which was given to him from the house of Life, brought it hither and threw it into Adam and Eve" (*ibid.*). This is the constantly recurring expression for the ensouling of man by his unauthorized creator. That this is not an event planned in the scheme of Life but a violence done to it and to the divine order is evident from the remorse which the demiurge feels afterwards. "Who has stultified me, so that I was a fool and cast the soul into the body?" (G 393).[18] Even in the Valentinian formula quoted before (see p. 45), though it belongs to a branch of Gnosticism inclined to categories more of internal motivation than of external force to expound the prehistory of the Soul, we encountered the expression "whereinto we have been thrown." The jarring note which this concrete term introduces into the series of abstract and neutral verbs preceding it in the formula (forms of "to be" and "to become") is certainly intended. The impact of the image has itself a symbolic value in the gnostic account of human existence. It would be of great interest to compare its use in Gnosticism with its use in a very recent philosophical analysis of existence, that of Martin Heidegger.[19] All we wish to say here is that in both cases "to have been thrown" is not merely a description of the past but an attribute qualifying the given existential situation as determined by that past. It is from the gnostic experience of the present situation of life that this dramatic image of its genesis has been projected into the past, and it is part of the mythological expression of this experience. "Who has cast me into the affliction of the worlds, who transported me into the evil darkness?" (G 457) asks the Life; and it implores, "Save us out of the darkness of this world into which we are thrown" (G 254). To the question the Great Life replies, "It is not according to the will of the Great Life that thou hast come there" (G 329): "That house in which thou dwellest, not Life has built it" (G 379): "This world was not created according to the wish of the Life" (G 247). We

---

[18] The remorse of the creator is also encountered in Christian Gnosticism. In the *Book of Baruch* we even see him pleading—unsuccessfully—with the supreme God, "Lord, let me destroy the world which I made, for my spirit [*pneuma*] is fettered into the human beings and I will deliver it thence" (Hippol. V. 26. 17).

[19] For *Geworfenheit* see his *Sein und Zeit*, Halle, 1927, pp. 175 ff. A comparison of gnostic and existentialist views is attempted below in the Epilogue, pp. 320-340.

shall later learn what these negative answers mean in terms of a positive mythology. Gnostic myth is precisely concerned with translating the brute factuality experienced in the gnostic vision of existence, and directly expressed in those queries and their negative answers, into terms of an explanatory scheme which derives the given state from its origins and at the same time holds out the promise of overcoming it.

The Life thus "thrown" into the world expresses its condition and mood there in a group of metaphors which we shall now consider. For the most part these refer in the gnostic sources, not to "man" in the ordinary sense, but to a symbolic-mythological being, a divine figure dwelling in the world in a peculiar and tragic role as victim and savior at once. Since, however, this figure according to the meaning of the system is the prototype of man, whose destiny in its full force he suffers in his own person (frequently his name is Man, though the figure can also be female), we are justified in taking the first-person accounts of his suffering as projections of the experience of those who make him speak thus, even if such statements refer to pre-cosmic events. In the following account we shall accordingly not differentiate, and shall think of man's existence in the world, to whatever phase or personage of the mythical drama the statement may refer.

(h) FORLORNNESS, DREAD, HOMESICKNESS

All the emotional implications which our initial analysis revealed in the concept of the "alien" as such find explicit utterance in gnostic myth and poetry. Mandaean narratives and hymns, the Valentinian fantasies about the adventures of the erring Sophia, the long-drawn-out lamentations of the *Pistis Sophia,* abound with expressions of the frightened and nostalgic state of the soul forlorn in the world. We select a few examples.

Manda d'Hayye[20] spake unto Anosh:[20] Fear not and be not dismayed, and say not, They have left me alone in this world of the evil ones. For soon I will come to thee. . . . [Anosh, left alone in the world, meditates upon the created world, especially upon the planets and their

[20] See Glossary, pp. 98 and 97, respectively.

various gifts and influences: he is overcome with fear and the desolation of loneliness:] The evil ones conspire against me. . . . They say to one another, In our own world the call of Life shall not be heard, it [the world] shall be ours. . . . Day in, day out I seek to escape them, as I stand alone in this world. I lift up mine eyes unto Manda d'Hayye, who said unto me, Soon I come to thee. . . . Daily I lift mine eyes to the way upon which my brothers walk, to the path upon which Manda d'Hayye shall come. . . . Manda d'Hayye came, called to me, and said unto me, Little Enosh, why art thou afraid, why didst thou tremble? . . . Since terror overcame thee in this world, I came to enlighten thee. Be not afraid of the evil powers of this world.

(G 261 ff.)

Looking forward to its liberation, the abandoned Soul speaks:

O how shall I rejoice then, who am now afflicted and afraid in the dwelling of the evil ones! O how shall my heart rejoice outside the works which I have made in this world! How long shall I wander, and how long sink within all the worlds?

(J 196)

The forlornness of the Life from beyond sojourning in the world is movingly expressed:

A vine am I, a lonely one, that stands in the world. I have no sublime planter, no keeper, no mild helper to come and instruct me about every thing.

(G 346)

The feeling of having been forgotten in the foreign land by those of the other world recurs again and again:

The Seven oppressed me and the Twelve became my persecution. The First [Life] has forgotten me, and the Second does not enquire after me.

(J 62)

The question form which so conspicuously abounds in Mandaean literature reflects with peculiar vividness the groping and helplessness of the Life lost in the alien world. Some passages in the following extracts have been quoted before:

I consider in my mind how this has come about. Who has carried me into captivity away from my place and my abode, from the household of my parents who brought me up? Who brought me to the guilty ones, the sons of the vain dwelling? Who brought me to the rebels who make war day after day?

(G 328)

I am a Mana of the great Life. I am a Mana of the mighty Life. Who has made me live in the Tibil, who has thrown me into the body-stump? . . . My eyes, which were opened from the abode of light, now belong to the stump. My heart, which longs for the Life, came here and was made part of the stump. It is the path of the stump, the Seven will not let me go my own path. How I must obey, how endure, how must I quiet my mind! How I must hear of the seven and twelve mysteries, how must I groan! How must my mild Father's Word dwell among the creatures of the dark!

(G 454 f.)

These will suffice as examples from Mandaean literature. We note the tone of lamentation which is a characteristic of the Eastern sources.

We have quoted before (sec. *c*) from the Naassene "Psalm of the Soul." Of all the Greek sources it most dramatically describes the plight of the Soul in the labyrinth of the hostile world. The text is hopelessly corrupted, and any rendering of it can only be tentative: the general content, however, is sufficiently clear. The Soul, a third principle somehow placed between the first two of Spirit and Chaos, has become immersed in the latter. In the unworthy form in which she has been clothed she struggles and toils. A prey of Death, she now has regal power and beholds the light, now is plunged into misery and weeps. Lamented [21] she rejoices, lamenting she is condemned, condemned she dies, forever to be reborn. Thus she wanders about in a labyrinth of evils and finds no way out. It is for her sake that Jesus asks the Father to send him forth with the seals that enable him to pass through the Aeons and to unlock their Mysteries (Hippol. V. 10. 2).

Finally we quote some of the lamentations of the *Pistis Sophia,* chap. 32:

[21] Sc., at bodily death? The three clauses beginning here make up the most doubtful passage in the whole text.

O Light of Lights, in which I have had faith from the beginning, hearken now to my repentance.[22] Deliver me, O Light, for evil thoughts have entered into me. . . . I went, and found myself in the darkness which is in the chaos beneath, and I was powerless to hasten away and to return to my place, for I was afflicted by all the Emanations of the Authades [the Arrogant One]. . . . And I cried for help, but my voice did not carry out of the darkness, and I looked upwards so that the Light in which I had faith might come to my help. . . . And I was in that place, mourning and seeking the Light that I had seen on high. And the watchmen of the gates of the Aeons sought me, and all those who stay within their Mystery mocked me. . . . Now, O Light of Lights, I am afflicted in the darkness of the chaos. . . . Deliver me out of the matter of this darkness, so that I shall not be submerged in it. . . . My strength looked up from the midst of the chaos and from the midst of the darknesses, and I waited for my spouse, that he might come and fight for me, and he came not.

(i) NUMBNESS, SLEEP, INTOXICATION

The emotional categories of the last section may be said to reflect general human experiences which may spring up and find expression anywhere, though rarely in such emphatic forms. Another series of metaphors referring to the human condition in the world is more uniquely gnostic and recurs with great regularity throughout the whole range of gnostic utterance, regardless of linguistic boundaries. While earthly existence is on the one hand, as we just saw, characterized by the feelings of forlornness, dread, nostalgia, it is on the other hand described also as "numbness," "sleep," "drunkenness," and "oblivion": that is to say, it has assumed (if we except drunkenness) all the characteristics which a former time ascribed to the state of the dead in the underworld. Indeed, we shall find that in gnostic thought the world takes the place of the traditional underworld and is itself already the realm of the dead, that is, of those who have to be raised to life again. In some respects this series of metaphors contradicts the previous one: unconsciousness excludes fear. This is not overlooked in the detailed narrative of the myths: it is only the awakening from the state of unconsciousness ("ignorance"), effected from without, that reveals

[22] A guilty fall has taken place.

to man his situation, hitherto hidden from him, and causes an outburst of dread and despair; yet in some way these must have been at work already in the preceding state of ignorance, in that life shows a tendency to hold fast to it and to resist the awakening.

How did the state of unconsciousness come about, and in what concrete terms is it described? The "throw" as such would account for a numbness of the fallen soul; but the alien medium itself, the world as a demonic entity, has an active share in it. In the Manichaean cosmogony as related by Theodore bar Konai we read:

As the Sons of Darkness had devoured them, the five Luminous Gods [the sons of the Primal Man, and the substance of all the souls later dispersed in the world] were deprived of understanding, and through the poison of the Sons of Darkness they became like a man who has been bitten by a mad dog or a serpent.[23]

The unconsciousness is thus a veritable infection by the poison of darkness. We are dealing here, as in the whole group of the metaphors of sleeping, not with a mythological detail, a mere episode in a narrative, but with a fundamental feature of existence in the world to which the whole redemptional enterprise of the extramundane deity is related. The "world" on its part makes elaborate efforts to create and maintain this state in its victims and to counteract the operation of awakening: its power, even its existence, is at stake.

They mixed me drink with their cunning and gave me to taste of their meat. I forgot that I was a king's son, and served their king. I forgot the Pearl for which my parents had sent me. Through the heaviness of their nourishment I sank into deep slumber.
("Hymn of the Pearl" in the *Acta Thomae*)

Of the most constant and widest use is probably the image of "sleep." The Soul slumbers in Matter. Adam, the "head" of the race and at the same time symbol of mankind, lies in deep slumber, of a very different kind from that of the biblical Adam: men in

[23] See also the parallel description in a Turfan fragment: "[Ahriman] captured the fair Soul and fettered it within the impurity. Since he had made it blind and deaf, it was unconscious and confused, so that [at first] it did not know its true origin" (Salemann, *Bull. Acad. Impér. des Sciences St-Petersbourg,* 1912). [See below, p. 341, "Corrections and Additions."]

general are "asleep" in the world. The metaphor expresses man's total abandonment to the world. Certain figures of speech under-line this spiritual and moral aspect. Men are not just asleep but "love" the sleep ("Why will ye love the sleep, and stumble with them that stumble?"—G 181); they have abandoned themselves to sleep as well as to drunkenness (*C.H.* I. 27). Even realizing that sleep is the great danger of existence in the world is not enough to keep one awake, but it prompts the prayer:

According to what thou, great Life, saidst unto me, would that a voice might come daily to me to awaken me, that I may not stumble. If thou callest unto me, the evil worlds will not entrap me and I shall not fall prey to the Aeons.

(G 485)

The metaphor of sleep may equally serve to discount the sensa-tions of "life here" as mere illusions and dreams, though night-marish ones, which we are powerless to control; and there the similes of "sleep" join with those of "erring" and "dread":

What, then, is that which He desires man to think? This: "I am as the shadows and phantoms of the Night." When the light of dawn appears, then this man understands that the Terror which had seized upon him, was nothing. . . . As long as Ignorance inspired them with terror and confusion, and left them unstable, torn and divided, there were many illusions by which they were haunted, and empty fictions, as if they were sunk in sleep and as if they found themselves a prey to troubled dreams. Either they are fleeing somewhere, or are driven in-effectually to pursue others; or they find themselves involved in brawls, giving blows or receiving blows; or they are falling from great heights . . . [etc., etc.]: until the moment when those who are passing through all these things, wake up. Then, those who have been experiencing all these confusions, suddenly see nothing. For they are nothing—namely, phantasmagoria of this kind.

(GT 28:24-29:32)

Since the gnostic message conceives itself as the counter-move to the design of the world, as the call intended to break its spell, the metaphor of sleep, or its equivalents, is a constant component of the typical gnostic appeals to man, which accordingly present themselves as calls of "awakening." We shall therefore meet these metaphors again and again when we deal with the "call."

The metaphors of intoxication require special comment. The "drunkenness" of the world is a phenomenon peculiarly characteristic of the spiritual aspect of what the Gnostics understood by the term "world." It is induced by the "wine of ignorance" (*C.H.* VII. 1), which the world everywhere proffers to man. The metaphor makes it clear that ignorance is not a neutral state, the mere absence of knowledge, but is itself a positive counter-condition to that of knowledge, actively induced and maintained to prevent it. The ignorance of drunkenness is the soul's ignorance of itself, its origin, and its situation in the alien world: it is precisely the awareness of alienness which the intoxication is meant to suppress; man drawn into the whirlpool and made oblivious of his true being is to be made one of the children of this world. This is the avowed purpose of the powers of the world in proffering their wine and holding their "feast." The drunkenness of ignorance is opposed by the "sobriety" of knowledge, a religious formula sometimes intensified to the paradox of "sober drunkenness." [24] Thus in the Odes of Solomon we read:

From the Lord's spring came speaking water in abundance to my lips. I drank and was drunken with the water of everlasting life, yet my drunkenness was not that of ignorance, but I turned away from vanity.

(Ode XI. 6-8)

He who thus possesses knowledge . . . [is like] a person who, having been intoxicated, becomes sober and having come to himself reaffirms that which is essentially his own.

(GT 22:13-20)

The orgiastic feast prepared by the world for the seduction of man, or more generally of the alien Life from beyond, is repeatedly described in extensive scenes in Mandaean writings. The following example occupies many pages in the original and is here greatly

---

[24] Probably a coinage of Philo Judaeus which gained wide currency in mystical literature: cf. Hans Lewy, *Sobria ebrietas* (*Beihefte zur ZNW* 9, Giessen, 1929).

abridged. For the reader unfamiliar with Mandaean mythology we may just explain that Ruha is the demonic mother of the Planets and as the evil spirit of this world the main adversary of the sons of light.[25]

Ruha and the Planets began to forge plans and said, "We will entrap Adam and catch him and detain him with us in the Tibil. When he eats and drinks, we will entrap the world. We will practise embracing in the world and found a community in the world. We will entrap him with horns and flutes, so that he may not break away from us. . . . We will seduce the tribe of life and cut it off with us in the world . . . [G 113 f.]. Arise, let us make a celebration: arise, let us make a drinking-feast. Let us practise the mysteries of love and seduce the whole world! . . . The call of Life we will silence, we will cast strife into the house, which shall not be settled in all eternity. We will kill the Stranger. We will make Adam our adherent and see who then will be his deliverer. . . . We will confound his party, the party that the Stranger has founded, so that he may have no share in the world. The whole house shall be ours alone. . . . What has the Stranger done in the house, that he could found himself a party therein?" They took the living water and poured turbid [water] into it. They took the head of the tribe and practised on him the mystery of love and of lust, through which all the worlds are inflamed. They practised on him seduction, by which all the worlds are seduced. They practised on him the mystery of drunkenness, by which all the worlds are made drunken. . . . The worlds are made drunk by it and turn their faces to the Suf-Sea.[26] (G 120 ff.)

We have only a few remarks to add to this powerful scene. The main weapon of the world in its great seduction is "love." Here we encounter a widespread motif of gnostic thought: the mistrust of sexual love and sensual pleasure in general. It is seen as the eminent form of man's ensnarement by the world: "The

[25] Ruha, literally "spirit." The perversion of this term to denote the highest personification of evil is an interesting episode in the history of religion, all the more paradoxical in view of the fact that the full title of this anti-divine figure is Ruha d'Qudsha, i.e., "the Holy Spirit." But this very paradox indicates the cause: the violent hostility to Christian doctrine, whose Founder according to Mandaean tradition had stolen and falsified the message of his master, John the Baptist. But an ambivalence in the figure of the "Holy Spirit," understood as female, is noticeable also in Christian Gnosticism, as will be seen when we deal with the Sophia speculation.

[26] See Glossary, p. 98.

spiritual man shall recognize himself as immortal, and love as the cause of death" (*C.H.* I. 17); "He who has cherished the body issued from the error of love, he remains in the darkness erring, suffering in his senses the dispensations of death" (*ibid.* 19). More than sexual love is involved in this role of *eros* as the principle of mortality (to Plato it was the principle of the striving for immortality). The lust for the things of this world in general may take on many forms, and by all of them the soul is turned away from its true goal and kept under the spell of its alien abode.

> Love not the world, neither the things that are in the world. If any man love the world, the love of the Father is not in him. For all that is in the world, the lust of the flesh, and the lust of the eyes, and the pride of life, is not of the Father, but is of the world.
>
> (I John 2:15-16)

The three propensities mentioned here, "the lust of the flesh," "the lust of the eyes," and "the pride of life," later serve Augustine as main categories of the general "temptation" of the world (see *Confess.* X. 41 ff.). The "mystery of love" in the Mandaean text is a mythological version of the same idea.

(*j*) THE NOISE OF THE WORLD

The Mandaean scene of the conspiracy of the world prompts an additional observation. The orgiastic feast, intended to draw man into its drunken whirl, has besides intoxication another aspect: its noise is to drown out the "call of Life" and deafen man to the voice of the alien Man.

> They shall not hear the words of the alien Man who has come here. . . . Since we have created Adam, he shall come and obey us and our father Ptahil.
>
> (G 244)

> Come let us make him hear a great upheaval, that he may forget the heavenly voices.
>
> (J 62)

However, as in view of the essential foolishness of the world-powers might be expected, the din has also a very different and ultimately self-defeating effect:

As their noise fell upon Adam's ear, he awoke from his slumber and lifted his eyes to the place of the light. He called his helpers, called the mild faithful Uthras. He spoke to Hibil-Uthra [here instead of Manda d'Hayye], the man who had made him hear his voice: "What has happened in the house, that the sound of the din rises up to heaven?" As Adam spoke thus, a tear gathered itself together in his eye. . . . I came near him, took him by his right hand, and made his heart rest again on its support.

(G 126)

Thus the world's own weapon turns against it: meant to deafen and confuse, it also frightens and causes Adam to look toward the stranger, to strain his ears toward the other voice.

(k) THE "CALL FROM WITHOUT"

"An Uthra calls from without and instructs Adam, the man" (G 387, J 225); "At the gate of the worlds stands Kushta (Truth) and speaks a question into the world" (J 4); "It is the call of Manda d'Hayye. . . . He stands at the outer rim of the worlds and calls to his elect" (G 397). The transmundane penetrates the enclosure of the world and makes itself heard therein as a call. It is the one and identical call of the other-worldly: "One call comes and instructs about all calls" (G 90); it is the "call of Life" or "of the great Life," which is equivalent to the breaking of light into the darkness: "They [the Uthras] shall make heard the call of Life and illumine the mortal house" (G 91). It is directed into the world: "I sent a call out into the world" (G 58); in its din it is discernible as something profoundly different: "He called with heavenly voice into the turmoil of the worlds" (J 58).

The symbol of the call as the form in which the transmundane makes its appearance within the world is so fundamental to Eastern Gnosticism that we may even designate the Mandaean and Manichaean religions as "religions of the call." [27] The reader will remember the close connection which obtains in the New Testament between hearing and faith. We find many examples of it in Mandaean writings: faith is the response to the call from beyond that

[27] "Caller of the Call" is the title of the Manichaean missionary; and as late as in Islam the word for mission is "call," for missionary, "caller."

cannot be seen but must be heard. Manichaean symbolism went so far as to hypostatize "Call" and "Answer" into separate divine figures (see below, p. 82). In the "Hymn of the Pearl," the "letter" which the celestials send to their exiled kinsman in the world turns on arrival into "voice":

Like a messenger was the letter which the King had sealed with his right hand. . . . He flew like an eagle and alighted beside me and became wholly speech. At the sound of his voice I awoke and arose from my slumber . . . and directed my steps that I might come to the light of our home. The letter who had awakened me I found before me on the way, the letter who with his voice had awakened me from sleep. . . .

In the Valentinian elaboration, the call is specifically the calling by "name," i.e., the person's mystic spiritual name, from eternity "inscribed" with God in the "book of the living": [28]

Those whose names He knew in advance, were called at the end, so that he who knows, is he whose name has been spoken by the Father. For he whose name has not been pronounced, is ignorant. Truly, how should a person be able to hear, if his name has not been called? For he who remains ignorant until the end, is a creature of "Oblivion" and will be destroyed with it. If this is not the case, why have these miserable ones received no name, why do they not hear the call?

(GT 21:25-22:2)

Finally, the call can also be the apocalyptic call announcing the end of the world:

A call rang out over the whole world, the splendor departed from every city. Manda d'Hayye revealed himself to all the children of men and redeemed them ·from the darkness into the light.

(G 182)

(l) THE "ALIEN MAN"

The call is uttered by one who has been sent into the world for this purpose and in whose person the transcendent Life once more

---

[28] This idea, like the whole "name"—and "book"—mysticism so conspicuous in the Gospel of Truth, points to certain Jewish speculations as the probable source; but the motif may have been widespread in oriental thought—see, in the Mandaean psalm quoted on p. 80, the line "who calls my name, his name I call."

takes upon itself the stranger's fate: he is the Messenger or Envoy —in relation to the world, the Alien Man. Ruha says to the Planets:

> The man does not belong to us, and his speech is not your speech. He has no connection with you. . . . His speech comes from without.
>
> (G 258)

The name "the alien" indicates the kinds of reception he finds down here: the welcoming exultation of those who feel themselves alien and exiled here ("Adam felt love for the Alien Man whose speech is alien, estranged from the world"—G 244); the shocked surprise of the cosmic powers who do not comprehend what is happening in their midst ("What has the Stranger done in the house, that he could found himself a party therein?"—G 122); finally, the hostile banding together of the sons of the house against the intruder ("We will kill the Stranger. . . . We will confound his party, so that he may have no share in the world. The whole house shall be ours alone"—G 121 f.). The immediate effect of his appearance down here is forcefully described in the Gospel of Truth:

> When the Word appeared, the Word which is in the hearts of those who pronounce It—and It was not only a sound, but It had taken on a body as well—a great confusion reigned among the vessels, for some had been emptied, others filled; some were provided for, others were overthrown; some were sanctified, still others were broken to pieces. All the spaces (?) were shaken and confused, for they had no fixity nor stability. "Error" was agitated, not knowing what it should do. It was afflicted, and lamented and worried because it knew nothing. Since the Gnosis, which is the perdition of "Error" and all its Emanations, approached it, "Error" became empty, there being nothing more in it.
>
> (GT 26:4-27)

Thus, to retrieve its own, Life in one of its unfallen members once more undertakes to descend into the dungeon of the world, "to clothe itself in the affliction of the worlds" and to assume the lot of exile far from the realm of light. This we may call the second descent of the divine, as distinct from the tragic earlier one which led to the situation that now has to be redeemed. Whereas formerly the Life now entangled in the world got into it by way of "fall," "sinking," "being thrown," "being taken captive," its entrance this time is of a very different nature: sent by the Great Life and invested with authority, the Alien Man does not fall but betakes himself into the world.

> One call comes and instructs about all calls. One speech comes and instructs about all speech. One beloved Son comes, who was formed from the womb of splendor. . . . His image is kept safe in its place. He comes with the illumination of life, with the command which his Father imparts. He comes in the garment of living fire and betakes himself into thy [Ruha's] world.
>
> (G 90)

> I am Yokabar-Kushta, who have gone forth from my Father's house and come hither. I have come hither with hidden splendor and with light without end.
>
> (G 318)

The going forth and coming hither have to be taken literally in their spatial meaning: they really lead, in the sense of an actual "way," from outside into the enclosure of the world, and in the passage have to penetrate through all its concentric shells, i.e., the manifold spheres or aeons or worlds, in order to get to the innermost space, where man is imprisoned.

> For his sake send me, Father!
> Holding the seals will I descend,
> through all the Aeons will I take my way,
> all the Mysteries will I unlock,
> the forms of the gods will I make manifest,
> the secrets of the sacred Way,
> known as Knowledge, I will transmit.
>
> (Naassene "Psalm of the Soul")

This passage through the cosmic system is in the nature of a breaking through, thereby already a victory over its powers.

> In the name of him who came, in the name of him who comes, and in the name of him who is to be brought forth. In the name of that Alien Man who forced his way through the worlds, came, split the firmament and revealed himself.
>
> (G 197)

Here we have the reason why the mere call of awakening from outside is not enough: not only must men be awakened and called to return, but if their souls are to escape the world, a real breach must be made in the "iron wall" of the firmament, which bars the way outward as well as inward. Only the real act of the godhead in itself entering the system can make that breach: "He broke their watchtowers and made a breach in their fastness" (J 69). "Having penetrated into terror's empty spaces, He placed Himself at the head of those who were stripped by Oblivion" (Gosp. of Truth, p. 20, 34-38). Thus already by the mere fact of his descent the Messenger prepares the way for the ascending souls. Depending on the degree of spiritualization in different systems, however, the emphasis may shift increasingly from this mythological function to the purely religious one embodied in the call as such and the teaching it has to convey, and thereby also to the individual response to the call as the human contribution to salvation. Such is the function of Jesus in the Valentinian Gospel of Truth:

> Through Him He enlightened those who were in darkness because of "Oblivion." He enlightened them and indicated a path for them; and that path is the Truth which He taught them. It was because of this that "Error" became angry with Him, persecuted Him, oppressed Him, annihilated Him.

> (GT 18:16-24)

Here, incidentally, we have as much as the "Christian" Gnostics in general could make of the passion of Christ and of the reason for it: it is due to the enmity of the powers of the lower creation (the cosmic principle: "Error"—usually personified in the Archons), threatened in their dominion and very existence by his mission; and often enough, the suffering and death they are able to inflict upon him are not real at all.[29]

Now in the last analysis he who comes is identical with him to whom he comes: Life the Savior with the life to be saved. The Alien from without comes to him who is alien in the world, and

---

[29] Not so, it must be added, in the Gospel of Truth: there, indeed, for once the utterances on Christ's suffering betray an emotional fervor and sense of mystery ("Oh! great, sublime Teaching") which suggest for it a religious significance far surpassing what is usual in so-called Christian Gnosticism, including most of the known Valentinian literature itself.

the same descriptive terms can in a striking way alternate between the two. Both in suffering and in triumph, it is often impossible to distinguish which of the two is speaking or to whom a statement refers. The prisoner here is also called "the alien man" (cf. J 67 ff., where the name is applied to the man to be saved), and he regains as it were this quality through the encounter with the Alien sent from without:

> I am an alien man. . . . I beheld the Life and the Life beheld me. My provisions for the journey come from the Alien Man whom the Life willed and planted. I shall come amongst the good whom this Alien Man has loved.
>
> (G 273)

There is a strong suggestion of an active-passive double role of one and the same entity. Ultimately the descending Alien redeems himself, that is, that part of himself (the Soul) once lost to the world, and for its sake he himself must become a stranger in the land of darkness and in the end a "saved savior." "The Life supported the Life, the Life found its own" (*Mandäische Liturgien,* p. 111).

This seeking, finding, and gathering of its own is a long-drawn-out process bound to the spatio-temporal form of cosmic existence. "I wandered through worlds and generations until I came to the gate of Jerusalem" (J 243). This leads to the idea that the savior does not come just once into the world but that from the beginning of time he wanders in different forms through history, himself exiled in the world, and revealing himself ever anew until, with his gathering-in complete, he can be released from his cosmic mission (the doctrine is most completely presented in the Pseudo-Clementine *Homilies*—see quotation from III. 20 on p. 230). Apart from the changing human incarnations, the constant form of his presence is precisely the other-worldly call resounding through the world and representing the alien in its midst; and between his manifestations he walks invisible through time.

> From the place of light have I gone forth,
> from thee, bright habitation.
> I come to feel the hearts,
> to measure and try all minds,
> to see in whose heart I dwell,

in whose mind I repose.
Who thinks of me, of him I think:
who calls my name, his name I call.
Who prays my prayer from down below,
his prayer I pray from the place of light. . . .
I came and found
the truthful and believing hearts.
When I was not dwelling among them,
yet my name was on their lips.
I took them and guided them up to the world of light. . . .

(G 389 f.)

(*m*) THE CONTENT OF THE CALL

What is it that the call has come to communicate to men? Its content is determined by its aim of "awakening," the simple naming of which may sometimes be the whole message itself, and nearly always is the opening part of it. "I am the call of awakening from sleep in the Aeon of the night," begins an excerpt from a scripture of the Peratae in Hippolytus (*Refut.* V. 14. 1). Here the call as such is its own content, since it simply states what its being sounded will effect: the awakening from sleep. This awakening is constantly designated as the essence of his mission either by the messenger himself or by those who send him.

I am a word, a son of words, who have come in the name of Jawar. The great Life called, charged and prepared me, me, Anosh [Man], the great Uthra the son of mighty ones. . . . It sent me forth to watch over this era, to shake out of their sleep and raise up those that slumber. It said to me: "Go, gather thee a following from the Tibil. . . . Elect, and draw the elect out of the world. . . . Instruct the souls, that they may not die and perish, nor be kept back in the dense darkness. . . . When thou comest to the earth Tibil, the evil ones shall not know of thee. . . . Fear not and be not dismayed, and say not, I stand here alone. When fear overcomes thee, we shall all be beside thee. . . ."

(G 295 f.)

They bestowed upon the guardians a sublime call, to shake up and make to rise those that slumber. They were to awaken the souls that had stumbled away from the place of light. They were to awaken them and shake them up, that they might lift their faces to the place of light.

(G 308)

Accordingly, the first effect of the call is always described as "awaking," as in the gnostic versions of the story of Adam (see next section). Often the merely formal exhortation, "Wake from your slumber" (or "from drunkenness," or, less frequently, "from death"), with metaphorical elaboration and in different phrasings, constitutes the sole content of the gnostic call to salvation. However, this formal imperative implicitly includes the whole speculative framework within which the ideas of sleep, drunkenness, and waking assume their specific meanings; and as a rule the call makes this framework explicit as part of its own content, that is, it connects the command to awake with the following doctrinal elements: the *reminder* of the heavenly origin and the transcendent history of man; the *promise* of redemption, to which also belongs the redeemer's account of his own mission and descent to this world; and finally the practical *instruction* as to how to live henceforth in the world, in conformity with the newly won "knowledge" and in preparation for the eventual ascent. Now, these three elements contain in a nutshell the complete gnostic myth, so that the gnostic call of awakening is a kind of abbreviation of gnostic doctrine in general. The gnosis transmitted by the message and compressed in it into a few symbolic terms is the total cosmogonic-soteriological myth within whose narrative the event of this message itself constitutes one phase, in fact the turning point with which the total movement is reversed. This compendious "knowledge" of the theoretical whole has its practical complement in the knowledge of the right "way" to liberation from the captivity of the world. In the numerous literary versions of the call, one or the other of these aspects may preponderate or be expressed exclusively: the reminder of origin, the promise of salvation, the moral instruction.

We shall quote some of these calls of awakening from gnostic literature, beginning with Manichaean examples. The first of such calls in the rigidly constructed Manichaean world-drama occurs before the beginning of our world and is addressed to the Primal Man, who is lying unconscious in the depths after being defeated and swallowed up in the first pre-cosmic contest of light and darkness. The following scene is from the Syriac account of Theodore bar Konai.

Then the Living Spirit called with a loud voice; and the voice of the Living Spirit became like to a sharp sword and laid bare the form of the Primal Man. And he spoke to him:

Peace be unto thee, good one amidst the wicked,
luminous one amidst the darkness,
God who dwells amidst the beasts of wrath
who do not know his[30] honor.

Thereupon Primal Man answered him and spoke:

Come for the peace of him who is dead,
come, oh treasure of serenity and peace!

and he spoke further to him:

How is it with our Fathers,
the Sons of Light in their city?

And the Call said unto him: It is well with them. And Call and Answer joined each other and ascended to the Mother of Life and to the Living Spirit. The Living Spirit put on the Call and the Mother of Life put on the Answer, her beloved son.[31]

Here the call apparently has the form of a simple salutation. As such, however, it includes the *reminder* of the divine origin of the one saluted, that is, the reawakening of the knowledge of himself, lost through the poison of the darkness, and at the same time the *promise* of his salvation: the address "Good one amidst the wicked," etc., represents the reminder, the salutation "Peace be unto thee" the promise. The touching inquiry of the Primal Man about the sons of light in their city must be understood in connection with

[30] Text: their.

[31] To explain the last sentence: the Mother of Life had created the Primal Man, whom the "Answer" now represents as the expression of his awakened true Self. The Living Spirit for his part had sent out the "Call" like a messenger. Both are now put on like garments by those from whom they originated, i.e., they are reunited with their source. As mentioned before, the personification of "Call" and "Answer" is a feature of Manichaean speculation (Jackson renders "Appellant" and "Respondent"). Thus, just as in the passage quoted from Theodore bar Konai, the hymn fragment in M 33 from Turfan relates how the primal Father abandons the "Spirit" (here equivalent to the Primal Man) to the enemies, the Mother of Life intercedes with him for their captive Son, the god Chroshtag ("Call") is sent to him, the freed god as "Answer" ascends, and the Mother welcomes the Son home. (Reitzenstein, *Das iranische Erlösungsmysterium*, p. 8.)

the fact that he had gone forth to his destiny for their protection. Awaking from his stupefaction, he wants to know whether the sacrifice has fulfilled its purpose.

Another version of this scene has come to light in the Turfan fragment M 7:

> Shake off the drunkenness in which thou hast slumbered,
> awake and behold me!
> Good tidings to thee from the world of joy
> from which I am sent for thy sake.

And he answered him who is without suffering:

> I am I, the son of the mild ones.
> Mingled am I and lamentation I see.
> Lead me out of the embracement of death.

[The messenger speaks:]

> Power and prosperity of the Living
> unto thee from thy home!
> Follow me, son of mildness,
> set upon thy head the crown of light.[32]

Detached from the mythological context, we find the call addressed to the soul in general in another Turfan text, the so-called "Abridged Mass of the Dead."

> My soul, O most splendid one, . . . whither hast thou gone? Return again. Awake, soul of splendor, from the slumber of drunkenness into which thou hast fallen . . . , follow me to the place of the exalted earth where thou dwelledst from the beginning. . . .[33]

We pass to the Mandaean literature, where versions of the call of awakening are extremely numerous, addressed either to Adam (not identical with Primal Man) or to the indefinite number of the believers in the world. The symbolism connected with Adam will

---

[32] After the translation of Andreas in Reitzenstein, *Hellenistiche Mysterienreligionen*, 3rd ed., 1927, p. 58; also in his *Das iranische Erlösungsmysterium*, p. 3. Cf. Jackson, p. 257: "From the Light and the Gods am I, and become a stranger to them; come together upon me are the enemies, and by them I am dragged down to the dead" (M 7). Cf. *ibid.*, p. 256, "I have become a stranger (an alien) from the Great Majesty."

[33] *Das Iranische Erlösungsmysterium*, pp. 11 ff.

be dealt with later on; here we shall say merely that the biblical motif of his sleep in the Garden is turned into a symbol of the human condition in the world. A precise parallel to the Manichaean versions is the following passage.

> They created the messenger and sent him to the head of the generations. He called with heavenly voice into the turmoil of the worlds. At the messenger's call Adam, who lay there, awoke . . . and went to meet the messenger: "Come in peace, thou messenger, envoy of the Life, who hast come from the house of the Father. How firmly planted in its place is the dear fair Life! And how sits here my dark· form in lamentation!" Then replied the messenger: ". . . All remembered thee with love and . . . sent me to thee. I have come and will instruct thee, Adam, and release thee out of this world. Hearken and hear and be instructed, and rise up victorious to the place of light."

(J 57)

The instruction mentioned here is frequently included in the call as the explication of the command "Sleep not," and sometimes grows into lengthy moral homilies which monopolize the whole content of the call and by their sheer extent make of the basic situation simply a literary fiction.

> An Uthra calls from without and instructs Adam the man. He speaks unto Adam: "Slumber not nor sleep, and forget not that with which thy Lord hath charged thee. Be not a son of the house, and be not called a sinner in the Tibil. Love not pleasant-smelling garlands and take not pleasure in a fair woman. . . . Love not lust nor deceiving shadows. . . . At thy going out and thy coming in see that thou forget not thy Lord [etc., etc.]. . . . Adam, behold the world, that it is a thing wholly without substance, . . . in which thou must place no trust. The scales stand prepared, and of thousands they choose one. . . . Scented garlands fade, and the beauty of woman becomes as if it had never been. . . . All works pass away, take their end and are as if they had never been." [34]

[34] Identical in G 387 f. and J 225 f. This still keeps comparatively close to the fictitious situation of the call. In G 16-27 we have over twelve pages of exhortations introduced by what is little more than a formula: "Me the pure messenger my Lord called and charged, saying: Go and call a voice to Adam and all his tribes, and instruct them about every thing, about the high King of Light . . . and about the worlds of light, the everlasting ones. Speak with him, that his heart may be enlightened. . . . Teach knowledge to Adam, Eve his wife, and all their

Sometimes the call of awakening is immediately connected with the summons to leave the world: it is at the same time the message of death, and is then followed by the ascent of the soul, as in the following example.

The savior approached, stood at Adam's pillow, and awakened him from his sleep. "Arise, arise, Adam, put off thy stinking body, thy garment of clay, the fetter, the bond . . . for thy time is come, thy measure is full, to depart from this world. . . ."

(G 430)

Sometimes the whole content of the call is concentrated in the one admonition to be watchful of oneself:

I sent a call out into the world: Let every man be watchful of himself. Whosoever is watchful of himself shall be saved from the devouring fire.

(G 58)

The typical formula of awakening has passed also into the New Testament, where it occurs in Eph. 5:14 as an anonymous quotation:

Wherefore he saith, Awake thou that sleepest, and arise from the dead, and Christ shall give thee light.

In conclusion we quote from the *Poimandres* the Hellenistic rendering of the call of awakening, which has become detached from the myth and is used as a stylistic device of religious-ethical exhortation.

---

tribes. Tell them . . . ," and now follows a collection of the most various exhortations, warnings, and commandments, held together by their anti-cosmic attitude: here are a few examples: "[95] Love ye not gold and silver and the possessions of this world. For this world perishes and passes away. . . . [103] With truthfulness and faith and pure speech of the mouth ransom ye the soul from darkness to light, from error to truth, from unbelief to belief in your Lord. He who ransoms a soul is worth to me generations and worlds. [134] When someone passes from the body, weep not nor raise lamentation over him. . . . [135] Go, ye poor, miserable and persecuted, weep for yourselves; for so long as ye are in the world, your sins increase upon you. [155] Mine elect, put no trust in the world in which ye live, for it is not yours. Put your trust in the fair works that ye perform. [163] Exalt not the Seven and the Twelve, the rulers of the world . . . for they lead astray the tribe of souls that was transported hither from the house of life." The collection concludes with the words, "This is the first teaching which Adam the head of the living tribe received." (The bracketed numbers indicate paragraphs in Lidzbarski's edition.)

O ye people, earthborn men, who have abandoned yourselves to drunkenness and sleep and to ignorance of God—become sober! cease from your intoxication, from the enchantment of irrational sleep! . . . Why, O earthborn men, have ye given yourselves over to death, being vested with power to partake in immortality? Change your ways, ye fellow-travellers of error and companions of ignorance; turn ye away from the dark light [i.e., of the cosmos], take part in immortality and forsake corruption.[35]

(C.H. I. 27 f.)

(n) THE RESPONSE TO THE CALL

How does the one called respond to the call and to its content? The first effect of the call is of course the awakening from the deep slumber of the world. Then, however, the reaction of the one awakened to his situation as revealed in the call and to the demands made upon him can be of different kinds, and significant dialogues between the called and the caller may ensue. In the Manichaean cosmogony according to Theodore bar Konai, for instance, Adam's first reaction to the wakening and the information he receives about himself is an outburst of acute terror at his situation:

Jesus the Luminous approached the innocent Adam. He awakened him from the sleep of death, so that he might be delivered from the many demons. And as a man who is just and finds a man possessed by a mighty demon and calms him by his power—so was Adam because that Friend found him sunk in deepest slumber, awakened him, made him stir, shook him awake, drove away from him the seducing Demon and removed the mighty Archon [here female] away from him into bonds. And Adam examined himself and discovered who he was. Jesus showed him the Fathers on high and his own Self [36] cast into all things, to the teeth of panthers and elephants, devoured by them that

[35] Cf. C.H. VII. 1 f.: "Whither are ye carried, O ye drunken men who have drained the unmixed wine [lit. "word"] of ignorance . . . stop and become sober, and look up with the eyes of the heart. . . . Seek the guide who will lead ye by the hand to the gates of knowledge where is the brilliant light that is pure of darkness, where none is drunken but all are sober and turn their hearts to see Him whose will it is to be seen."

[36] Either Jesus' or Adam's, but more probably the first: see below, p. 228 ff., the doctrine of the Jesus patibilis.

devour, consumed by them that consume, eaten by the dogs, mingled and bound in all that is, imprisoned in the stench of darkness. He raised him up and made him eat of the tree of life. Then Adam cried and lamented: terribly he raised his voice like a roaring lion, tore [his dress], smote his breast, and spoke: "Woe, woe unto the shaper of my body, unto those who fettered my soul, and unto the rebels that enslaved me!"

A similar though more muted tone of lamentation met us in the preceding section as first response to the call (in the Turfan fragment M 7 and in the Mandaean passage J 57).

More primitively human is Adam's reaction in the Mandaean text G 430 f., whose beginning we quoted on p. 85. There, as we saw, the call of awakening coincides with the message of death, and the continuation shows the earthbound soul terrified at the prospect of having to depart and clinging desperately to the things of this world:

When Adam heard this, he lamented his fate and wept. [He argues his indispensability in the world:] "Father! If I come with thee, who will be guardian in this wide Tibil? . . . Who will harness the oxen to the plow, and who will guide the seed into the soil? . . . Who will clothe the naked, . . . who settle the strife in the village?" [The messenger of Life:] "Have no regret, Adam, for this place in which thou dwelledst, for this place is desolate. . . . The works shall be wholly abandoned and shall not come together again. . . ." [Then Adam begs that his wife Eve, his sons and his daughters may accompany him on the way. The messenger informs him that in the house of Life there is no body nor kinship. Then he instructs him about the way:] "The way that we have to go is long and endless. . . . Overseers are installed there, and watchmen and toll-collectors sit beside it. . . . The scales stand prepared, and of thousands they choose one soul that is good and enlightened." Thereupon Adam departed from his body [he turns back once more and regrets his body], then he began his journey through the ether. [Even here the dialogue continues; again Adam laments his body, once more he asks for Eve—although he has known that he "would have to depart alone, to settle his strife alone." Finally he is told:] "Calm thyself and be silent, Adam, and the peace of the good enfold thee. Thou goest and risest up to thy place, and thy wife Eve shall rise up after thee. Then all the generations shall come to an end and all creatures perish."

Thus the call to the individual is connected with the general eschatology of the return of all souls.

To the different meanings of the lamentation with which the awakened soul first responds to the call we must add its complaint about, even its accusation of, the Great Life itself, which is called to account for the unnatural condition just revealed to the soul. Thus in the version of the call in G 387 f. (p. 84) we read:

As Adam heard this, he lamented and wept over himself. He spoke to the Uthra of Life: "If you know that this is so, why have you carried me away from my place into captivity and cast me into the stinking body . . . ?" Thereupon he replied unto him: "Be silent, Adam, thou head of the whole tribe. The world which is to be we cannot suppress. Arise, arise, worship the Great [Life] and submit thyself, that the Life may be thy savior. The Life be thy savior, and do thou ascend and behold the place of light."

Ultimately the soul calls the Great Life to account for the existence of the world as such and for its own exile there: that is, it asks the great "Why?" which, far from being appeased by the awakening and the reminder of its origin, is powerfully stirred up by them and becomes a main concern of the gnosis just initiated. This query is even called "the lawsuit concerning the world" which Adam is to present directly to the First Life itself.

"Do thou, Adam, ascend and present thy lawsuit to the Great First Life, thy lawsuit concerning the world in which thou dwellest. Say unto the Great Life: 'Why hast thou created this world, why hast thou ordered the tribes there away out of thy midst, why hast thou cast strife into the Tibil? Why dost thou ask now for me and my whole tribe?'"
(G 437)

The answer to this type of question is the major object of the various gnostic speculations about the beginnings: some of its forms will be dealt with when we come to the treatment of the different systems.

For the most part, however, the response to the call is not of this problematical kind but one of joyous and grateful acceptance. "The Gospel of Truth is joy for those who have received from the Father of Truth the grace of knowing Him" (opening words of the Gospel of Truth).

If a person has the Gnosis, he is a being from on high. If he is called, he hears, replies, and turns towards Him who calls him, in order to reascend to Him. And he knows what he is called. Having the Gnosis, he performs the will of Him who called him. He desires to do that which pleases Him, and he receives repose. [Each?] one's name comes to him. He who thus possesses the Gnosis, knows whence he came and whither he goes.[37]

(GT 22:3-15)

Joy to the man who has rediscovered himself and awakened!

(GT 30:13 f.)

We often meet in this context the sequence of "hearing" and "believing" so familiar from the New Testament:

Adam heard and *believed*. . . . Adam received *Truth*. . . . Adam gazed upwards full of *hope* and ascended. . . .

(J 57)

Here we have the triad faith, knowledge, and hope as response to the hearing of the call. Elsewhere love is mentioned in the same context: "Adam felt *love* for the Alien Man whose speech is alien and estranged from the world" (G 244). "For each one loves Truth, since Truth is the Mouth of the Father; His Tongue is the Holy Ghost . . ." (Gosp. of Truth, p. 26. 33-36). The Christian reader is of course familiar with St. Paul's triad of faith, hope, and charity (I Cor. 13:13), which, not without reason and perhaps with intent, omits knowledge and extols love as the greatest of them all.

Mandaean poetry gives wonderful expression to the gratefully believing acceptance of the message and the ensuing conversion of the heart and renewal of life. Some examples may conclude this account.

From the day when we beheld thee,
from the day when we heard thy word,
our hearts were filled with peace.
We believed in thee, Good One,
we beheld thy light and shall not forget thee.
All our days we shall not forget thee,
not one hour let thee from our hearts.

[37] Cf. the fuller version of this Valentian formula in *Exc. Theod*. 78. 2; see above p. 45.

For our hearts shall not grow blind,
these souls shall not be held back.

(G 60)

From the place of light have I gone forth,
from thee, bright habitation . . .
An Uthra from the house of Life accompanied me.
The Uthra who accompanied me from the house of the Great Life
held a staff of living water in his hand.
The staff which he held in his hand
was full of leaves of excellent kind.
He offered me of its leaves,
and prayers and rituals sprang complete from it.
Again he offered me of them,
and my sick heart found healing
and my alien soul found relief.
A third time he offered me of them,
and he turned upwards the eyes in my head
so that I beheld my Father and knew him.
I beheld my Father and knew him,
and I addressed three requests to him.
I asked him for mildness in which there is no rebellion.
I asked him for a strong heart
to bear both great and small.
I asked him for smooth paths
to ascend and behold the place of light.

(G 377 f.)

From the day when I came to love the Life,
from the day when my heart came to love the Truth,
I no longer have trust in anything in the world.
In father and mother
I have no trust in the world.
In brothers and sisters
I have no trust in the world . . .
In what is made and created
I have no trust in the world.
In the whole world and its works
I have no trust in the world.
After my soul alone I go searching about,
which to me is worth generations and worlds.
I went and found my soul—

what are to me all the worlds? . . .
I went and found Truth
as she stands at the outer rim of the worlds . . .

(G 390 f.)

(o) GNOSTIC ALLEGORY

This account of gnostic imagery and symbolic language would be incomplete without some remarks on the peculiar use of allegory in gnostic writings. Allegory, probably an invention of the philosophers, was widely used in Greek literature as a means of making the tales and figures of mythical lore conform to enlightened thought. By taking the concrete entities and episodes of classical myth as symbolic expressions of abstract ideas, such time-honored elements of tradition and popular belief could be so conceptualized that a general consensus of truth seemed to unite the most advanced intellectual insight with the wisdom of the past. Thus Zeus became equated with the cosmic "reason" of the Stoics, and other Olympic gods with particular manifestations of the universal principle. Arbitrary as the method was, it could claim to elicit the true meaning of the ancient lore and in the conceptual translation to present it stripped of the symbolic cloak. At the same time it bestowed upon contemporary ideas the prestige of venerable antiquity. Thus the tendency was a harmonizing one, and with all boldness of interpretation in the individual cases conservative, essentially respectful of tradition: one homogeneous heritage of knowledge about the highest things was seen to comprehend oldest and newest and to teach the same things under different forms. In consequence, the myth, however freely handled, was never contradicted nor were its own valuations controverted. In the first century A.D., that is, at the time when the gnostic movement was gathering momentum, Philo of Alexandria put allegory, hitherto chiefly an instrument for adapting myth to philosophy, into the service of religion itself in his effort to establish a congruency between his Jewish creed and his Platonizing philosophy. The system of scriptural allegory evolved in his school was bequeathed as a model to the early Fathers of the Church. Here again the purpose is that of integration and synthesis.

Gnostic allegory, though often of this conventional type, is in its most telling instances of a very different nature. Instead of taking over the value-system of the traditional myth, it proves the deeper "knowledge" by reversing the roles of good and evil, sublime and base, blest and accursed, found in the original. It tries, not to demonstrate agreement, but to shock by blatantly subverting the meaning of the most firmly established, and preferably also the most revered, elements of tradition. The rebellious tone of this type of allegory cannot be missed, and it therefore is one of the expressions of the revolutionary position which Gnosticism occupies in late classical culture. Of the three examples we shall discuss, two concern subjects from the Old Testament, which supplied the favorite material for gnostic perversions of meaning, and the third uses a motif from Greek mythology.

Eve and the Serpent

We have met before (pp. 69, 86) with the gnostic interpretation of Adam's sleep in Eden, which implies a very unorthodox conception of the author of this sleep and of the garden in which it takes place. The recently published *Apocryphon of John* spells out this comprehensive revision of the Genesis tale in what purports to be a revelation of the Lord to John the disciple. About the garden:

> The first Archon (Ialdabaoth) brought Adam (created by the Archons) and placed him in paradise which he said to be a "delight" [38] for him: that is, he intended to deceive him. For their (the Archons') delight is bitter and their beauty is lawless. Their delight is deceit and their tree was hostility. Their fruit is poison against which there is no cure, and their promise is death to him. Yet their tree was planted as "tree of life": I shall disclose to you the mystery of their "life"—it is their Counterfeit Spirit,[39] which originated from them so as to turn him away,[40] so that he might not know his perfection.
>
> (55:18-56:17, Till)

About the sleep:

> Not as Moses said "He made him sleep," but he enshrouded his perception with a veil and made him heavy with unperceptiveness—as he said himself through the prophet (Is. 6:10): "I will make heavy

[38] Translation of *Eden*.
[39] A perverting imitation of the genuine, divine Spirit.
[40] From the Light.

the ears of their hearts, that they may not understand and may not see."

(58:16-59:5)

Now in the same oppositional vein is the gnostic view of the *serpent* and its role in inducing Eve to eat of the tree. For more than one reason, not the least of which was the mention of "knowledge," the biblical tale exerted a strong attraction upon the Gnostics. Since it is the serpent that persuades Adam and Eve to taste of the fruit of knowledge and thereby to disobey their Creator, it came in a whole group of systems to represent the "pneumatic" principle from beyond counteracting the designs of the Demiurge, and thus could become. as much a symbol of the powers of redemption as the biblical God had been degraded to a symbol of cosmic oppression. Indeed, more than one gnostic sect derived its name from the cult of the *serpent* ("Ophites" from the Gk. *ophis;* "Naassenes" from the Heb. *nahas*—the group as a whole being termed "ophitic"); and this position of the serpent is based on a bold allegorizing of the biblical text. This is the version found in the ophitic summary of Irenaeus (I. 30. 7): the transmundane Mother, Sophia-Prunikos, trying to counteract the demiurgic activity of her apostatical son Ialdabaoth, sends the serpent to "seduce Adam and Eve into breaking Ialdabaoth's command." The plan succeeds, both eat of the tree "of which God [i.e., the Demiurge] had forbidden them to eat. But when they had eaten, they knew the power from beyond and turned away from their creators." It is the first success of the transcendent principle against the principle of the world, which is vitally interested in preventing knowledge in man as the inner-worldly hostage of Light: the serpent's action marks the beginning of all *gnosis* on earth which thus by its very origin is stamped as opposed to the world and its God, and indeed as a form of rebellion.

The Peratae, sweepingly consistent, did not even shrink from regarding the historical *Jesus* as a particular incarnation of the "general serpent," i.e., the serpent from Paradise understood as a principle (see below). In the barbelo-gnostic (non-ophitic) *Apocryphon of John* this identification, made almost inevitable in the course of its argument, is only narrowly evaded by playing on the difference between the "tree of life" and the "tree of the knowledge of good and evil": of the latter Christ indeed causes man to eat against the Archon's commandment, while the serpent, acting for the other tree and identified with Ialdabaoth, is left in its traditional role of corrupter (this, none too convincingly, in reply to the disciple's startled question, "Christ, was it not the serpent who taught her?"). Thus, with the merging of the figures just avoided, part of the serpent's function has passed over to Christ. The Valentinians, on the other hand, though not involving Jesus in the Paradise action itself, drew an allegorical parallel between him and the *fruit* from the tree: by being affixed to a "wood," [41] he "became a Fruit of the Knowledge of the Father, which did *not,* however, bring perdition upon those who ate it" (Gosp. of Truth, 18. 25 f.). Whether the denial simply contrasts the new to the old event (after the manner of St. Paul) or is meant to rectify the Genesis account itself must in this instance be left undecided. But the latter is clearly the case elsewhere and very much the gnostic fashion (cf. the repeated, blunt "not as Moses said" in the Apocryphon of John).

By Mani's time (third century) the gnostic interpretation of the Paradise story and Jesus' connection with it had become so firmly established that he could simply put Jesus in the place of the serpent with no mention of the latter: "He raised [Adam] up and made him eat of the tree of life" (see above, p. 87). What was once a conscious boldness of allegory had become itself an independent myth that could be used without a reference to (and perhaps even a memory of) the original model. The revolutionary genesis of the motif is probably forgotten at this stage. This goes to show that, unlike the allegory of the Stoics or of syncretistic literature in general, gnostic allegory is itself the source of a new mythology: it is the revolutionary vehicle of its emergence in the face of an entrenched tradition, and since it aims at subverting the latter, the principle of this allegory must be paradox and not congruency.

Cain and the Creator

Also to the ophitic circle belongs the next example, taken from Hippolytus' account of the Peratae (*Refut.* V. 16. 9 f.):

This general Serpent is also the wise Word of Eve. This is the mystery of Eden: this is the river that flows out of Eden. This is also

[41] ξύλον as a translation of Heb. *ēts* = "tree," and its matter, "wood": so that the phrase could also mean "hung on a tree"; cf. Acts 10:40; Deut. 21:22.

the mark that was set on Cain, whose sacrifice the god of this world did not accept whereas he accepted the bloody sacrifice of Abel: for the lord of this world delights in blood. This Serpent is he who appeared in the latter days in human form at the time of Herod. . . .

The elevation of Cain, prototype of the outcast, condemned by God to be "a fugitive and a vagabond" on earth, to a pneumatic symbol and an honored position in the line leading to Christ is of course an intentional challenge to ingrained valuations. This opting for the "other" side, for the traditionally infamous, is a heretical method, and much more serious than a merely sentimental siding with the underdog, let alone mere indulgence in speculative freedom. It is obvious that allegory, normally so respectable a means of harmonizing, is here made to carry the bravado of non-conformity. Perhaps we should speak in such cases, not of allegory at all, but of a form of polemics, that is, not of an exegesis of the original text, but of its tendentious rewriting. Indeed, the Gnostics in such cases hardly *claimed* to bring out the correct meaning of the original, if by "correct" is meant the meaning *intended* by its author—seeing that this author, directly or indirectly, was their great adversary, the benighted creator-god. Their unspoken claim was rather that the blind author had unwittingly embodied something of the truth in his partisan version of things, and that this truth can be brought out by turning the intended meaning upside down.

The figure of Cain, after which a gnostic sect called itself (for the Cainites, see Iren. I. 31. 2), is only the most prominent example of the working of the method. In the construction of a complete series of such countertypes, stretching through the ages, a rebels' view of history as a whole is consciously opposed to the official one. The siding with Cain extends consistently to all the "rejected" among Scriptural figures: the passage quoted above continues with a like elevation of Esau, who "did not receive the blind blessing but became rich outside without accepting anything from the blind one" (*loc. cit.* 9); and Marcion, whose hate of the Old Testament creator-god led him to the most radical conclusions in all respects, taught that Christ descended into hell solely to redeem Cain and Korah, Dathan and Abiram, Esau, and all nations which did not acknowledge the God of the Jews, while Abel, Enoch, Noah, Abraham, and so on, because they served the creator and his law and ignored the true God, were left down below (cf. p. 140, note 11).

Prometheus and Zeus

The third example is added mainly to show that we are dealing here with a general principle of gnostic allegory and not with a particular attitude toward the Old Testament alone. It is true that the blasphemous degrading of the Most High of former religion to a demonic power and the consequent revision of status of his friends and foes found its preferred material in the Jewish tradition: there alone the prestige of the sacred original, the gravity of its claims, the devotion of its believers, gave to the gnostic reversal that flavor of provocation and scandal which was an intended effect of the novel message. With the Olympians literary fancy could play much more freely without outrage to pious feelings. They were taken less seriously, even by their conventional believers, and on the whole the Gnostics ignored them: yet the position of *Zeus* as the highest god of the pantheon was reverend enough to make *his* degradation a grave matter, and so he can occasionally be subjected to the same treatment as we saw accorded the biblical Lord of Creation. The alchemist Zosimos in his treatise *Omega* (paras. 3 f., p. 229, lines 16 ff., Berthelot) divides mankind into those "under" and those "over" the *heimarmene,* and calls the latter "the tribe of the philosophers":[42] these, he says, are "over the heimarmene in that they neither are gladdened by its happiness, for they master their pleasures, nor are cast down by its misfortunes . . . , nor do they even accept the fair gifts it offers." Of the others he says that they "follow in the procession of the heimarmene" and are "in every respect its acolytes." Then he continues with an allegory: for this reason Prometheus advises Epimetheus in Hesiod (*Erga* I. 86 f.) " 'never to accept a gift from Olympian Zeus, but to send it back': thus he teaches his brother through philosophy to refuse the gifts of Zeus, i.e. of the heimarmene." It is the identification of Zeus with the heimarmene that makes of the Hesiod quotation a gnostic

---

[42] "Philosopher" here means what in gnostic terminology is more normally called "pneumatic"; through this use it comes to be a term for the true alchemist, who has the mystical power to transform the base elements into noble ones: hence "the philosophers' stone."

allegory. The identification implies the parallel one of Prometheus, his challenger and victim, with the type of the "spiritual" man whose loyalty is not to the god of this world but to the transcendent one beyond. Thus in a paradoxical way the status of Zeus as the highest principle of the cosmos is taken over from tradition, but with reversed values: because the opponent of Prometheus is this cosmic ruler, the interpreter takes the rebel's side and makes the latter the embodiment of a principle superior to the whole universe. The victim of the older mythology becomes the bearer of the gospel in the new. Here again the allegory consciously shocks the piety of a whole religious culture powerfully entrenched in the Hellenistic environment. It must be noted that to identify the *Jupiter summus exsuperantissimus* of imperial religion with the heimarmene is not really to misjudge him, for the necessity of cosmic destiny was a legitimate aspect of his divine power. The point is that the gnostic revaluation of the cosmos as such (for which "heimarmene" had come to stand as the repulsive symbol) brought down along with it its highest divinity, and it is precisely his cosmic power which now makes Zeus an object of contempt. If we wished to speak mythologically ourselves, we might say that Zeus now suffers the fate to which he condemned his own predecessors and that the revolt of the Titans against his own rule achieves a belated victory.

Appendix to Chapter 3: Glossary of Mandaean Terms

Anosh (or **Enosh**). "Man," one of the Uthras, eternal but temporarily exiled in the world of darkness.

Firmly grounded, steadied. Almost identical with "blessed," predicated mainly of the highest and faultless Uthras.

Kushta. Truth, truthfulness, the true faith; also faithfulness and sincerity in the dealings of the believers with the highest Being and with one another. To "pass Kushta" means to exchange the handclasp of brotherhood. Sometimes personified.

Living water. Flowing water, which is of sublime origin and flows in streams, all of which the Mandaeans called "Jordans" (possibly an indication of the geographical origin of the Mandaean community). This alone can be used ritually, i.e., for the frequent baptisms which are a main feature of the Mandaean cult. For this reason the Mandaeans can only settle close to rivers. The expression "living water" is probably taken over from the Old Testament (see Gen. 26:19, Lev. 14:5, 50). The opposite is stagnant water and the troubled waters of the sea—see under "Turbid water."

Mana.   Spiritual being of pure divinity, also the divine spirit in man: the Great Mana (also Mana of Glory) is the highest godhead. Original meaning probably "vessel," "jar."

Manda.   Knowledge: equivalent of the Greek *gnosis*.

Manda d'Hayye.   "Knowledge of life": the gnosis personified in the central divine savior-figure of Mandaean religion, called forth by the Life in the worlds of light and sent down into the lower world. The combination is used exclusively as a proper name.

Ptahil.   One of the Uthras; as the executor of the cosmogonic designs of a group of Uthras, most directly connected with the fashioning of this world: he is thus the Mandaean Demiurge. The name Ptah-il is that of the Egyptian artisan-god *Ptah* with the semitic *-il* ("god") suffixed to it. That the name for the Demiurge was taken from the Egyptian pantheon is doubtless connected with the symbolic role of Egypt as the representative of the material world (see under "Suf-Sea"; cf. p. 117 f.).

Ruha.   "Spirit," more fully also Ruha d'Qudsha, "Holy Spirit" (!), the chief female demon of the Mandaeans, mother of the seven Planets and thoroughly evil: for explanation see Ch. 3, note 25.

Sh'kina.   "Habitation," viz., of beings of light (e.g., of the Life, of individual Uthras): by the Mandaeans mostly used in the literal sense, with the connotation of glory as the light-aura surrounding these beings like a dwelling; sometimes, however, also in the personified sense which the term had acquired in Jewish speculation (cf. Mani's *sh'kinas,* equivalent to "aeons," the personified powers surrounding the highest godhead).

Suf-Sea.   The Red Sea through which the children of Israel had to pass on the exodus from Egypt: in gnostic as well as in Alexandrian-Jewish speculation this was allegorically referred to the exodus of the soul from the body, or from the world, so that the Red Sea came to be a symbol for the dividing waters between this and the other world. By an easy vowel-transition from *suf* (reed) to *sof* (end) the Suf-Sea could be interpreted as "sea of the end," i.e., of death.

Tibil.   The Old Testament *tēvēl,* "earth," "terra firma," used by the Mandaeans as a name for the terrestrial world, always with the connotation of baseness opposed to the purity of the divine world.

Tribe of souls.   Name for the totality of the believers, i.e., the Mandaeans.

Turbid water. Troubled water, lit. "water of the Abyss [or Chaos]": the original matter of the world of darkness with which the living water mingled.

Uthra. Name for divine beings beneath the Great Mana and the First Life, comparable to the angels and archangels of Jewish and Christian lore. It has ousted the common semitic *mal'ach* for angel used throughout the Old Testament: where the older term occurs in Mandaean writings it denotes genii of sorcery or evil spirits. The literal meaning of Uthra is "wealth," "abundance," denoting these beings as emanations from the divine fullness. They were generated (partly in orders of mediate descent) within the world of light, and in their entirety, with their respective sh'kinas, make up that world. Some of them, however, are fallible (see under "Firmly grounded").

Worlds. *Almaya,* can also mean "beings," sometimes also, in spite of the plural form, simply the singular "world"; mostly not certain which of the different meanings is intended in the given case.

PART II

Gnostic Systems of Thought

After the survey of the semantic *elements,* which emphasized the common ground rather than the doctrinal differentiations of gnostic thought, we turn now to the larger units of theory in which the gnostic view of things was elaborated, that is, to the consciously constructed *systems* of gnostic speculation. From the great number of these we can offer here only a selection representative of the major types, and even there considerations of space oblige us to sacrifice some of their wealth of mythological detail.

Gnostic speculation had its task set for it by the basic tenets of the gnostic view of things. This as we have seen comprised a certain conception of the world, of man's alienness within it, and of the transmundane nature of the godhead. These tenets as it were constituted the vision of reality as given here and now. But that which is, especially if it is of such a disturbing kind, must have had a *history* by which it has come to be as it is and which explains its "unnatural" condition. The task of speculation, then, is to account in a historical narrative for the present state of things, to derive it from first beginnings and thereby to explain its riddle—in other words, to lift the vision of reality into the light of *gnosis.* The manner in which this task is performed is invariably *mythological,* but the resulting myth, apart from its general plan, is in many cases a work of free invention by individual authors, and with all its borrowing from popular tradition not a product of folklore.[1] Its symbolism is highly deliberate, and in the hands of the prominent system-builders becomes an instrument, wielded with great virtuosity, for the communication of sophisticated ideas. The mythological character of these speculations must nevertheless not be underrated. The dramatic nature and the psychological significance of the truths to be conveyed called for this medium, in which personification is the legitimate form of expression. In the following study we shall begin with relatively simple specimens of gnostic theory and progress to more elaborate ones.

[1] To the student of religion it is, by reason of this borrowing, a depository of ancient and in part long-petrified material; but the new context imbues this material with meanings often widely divergent from the original ones.

Chapter 4. *Simon Magus*

The Fathers of the Church regarded Simon Magus as the father of all heresy. He was a contemporary of the apostles and a Samaritan, and Samaria was notoriously unruly in matters of religion and regarded with suspicion by the orthodox. When the apostle Philip came there to preach the gospel, he found the movement of Simon in full swing, with Simon saying of himself, and the people concurring with him, that he was "the Power of God that is called the great" (Acts 8:10). This means that he preached not as an apostle but as himself a messiah. The story of his subsequent conversion, though not necessarily that of his baptism, must be wrong (if indeed the Simon of the Acts and the heresiarch of the Fathers are one and the same person, which has been seriously doubted) as in none of the heresiological accounts of the Simonian teaching from the second and third centuries is there an indication that the position of Jesus was granted by the sect, except for his having been a precursory incarnation of Simon himself. By all accounts—even if we discount the story of the Acts as relating to a different person, and date the gnostic prophet of the same name one or two generations later—Simonianism was from the start and remained strictly a rival message of obviously independent origin; that is to say, Simon was not a dissident Christian, and if the Church Fathers cast him in the role of the arch-heretic, they implicitly admitted that Gnosticism was not an inner-Christian phenomenon. On the other hand, the terms in which Simon is said to have spoken of himself are testified by the pagan writer Celsus to have been current with the pseudo-messiahs still swarming in Phoenicia and Palestine at his time about the middle of the second century. He has heard a number of them himself, and records thus a typical sermon of theirs:[1]

[1] He introduces what he calls "the most perfect type among the men in that region" with these words: "There are many who prophesy at the slightest excuse for some trivial cause both inside and outside temples; and there are some who wander about begging and roaming around cities and military camps; and they pretend to be moved as if giving some oracular utterance. It is an ordinary and common custom for each one to say . . . ," and there follows the speech we quote.

I am God (or a son of God, or a divine Spirit). And I have come. Already the world is being destroyed. And you, O men, are to perish because of your iniquities. But I wish to save you. And you see me returning again with heavenly power. Blessed is he who has worshipped me now! But I will cast everlasting fire upon all the rest, both on cities and on country places. And men who fail to realize the penalties in store for them will in vain repent and groan. But I will preserve for ever those who have been convinced by me.[2]

A singular feature of Simon's terrestrial journey was that he took about with him a woman called Helena whom he said he had found in a brothel in Tyre and who according to him was the latest and lowliest incarnation of the fallen "Thought" of God, redeemed by him and a means of redemption for all who believed in them both. The following exposition will explain the doctrinal meaning of this piece of showmanship; the picturesqueness and effrontery of the exhibition should be savored by itself.[3]

The developed Simonian doctrine, whether it was his own work or that of his school, has been preserved by a number of later writers beginning with Justin Martyr (who himself grew up in the district of Samaria) and including Irenaeus, Hippolytus, Tertullian, and Epiphanius. A source of great value is the writings entitled *Recognitions* and *Homilies,* purporting to be by Clement of Rome and therefore called the "Clementines" or "Pseudo-Clementines." We shall give here a synthesis of all these accounts, only occasionally indicating the particular source.

"There is one Power, divided into upper and lower, begetting itself, increasing itself, seeking itself, finding itself, being its own mother, its own father . . . , its own daughter, its own son . . . , One, root of the All." This One, unfolded, "is he who stands, stood and shall stand: he stands above in the unbegotten Power; he stood

---

[2] Celsus continues: "Having brandished these threats they then go on to add incomprehensible, incoherent and utterly obscure utterances, the meaning of which no intelligent person could discover; for they are meaningless and nonsensical, and give a chance for any fool or sorcerer to take the words in whatever sense he likes." (Origen, *Contra Celsum* VII. 9, tr. Chadwick, pp. 402-3).

[3] Simon is unjustly, and unnecessarily, robbed of an original and provocative trait if one tries with a recent author to explain the whore away as a slander or misunderstanding of the earliest Christian writers (G. Quispel, *Gnosis als Weltreligion,* p. 69).

below in the stream of the waters [i.e., the world of matter], begotten in the image; he shall stand above with the blessed infinite Power when his image shall be perfected" (Hippol. *Refut.* VI. 17. 1-3). How does this self-division into upper and lower come about? In other words, how does the original Being cause for itself the necessity of its later self-restoration? It is characteristic of the following speculation that no original world of darkness or of matter is assumed to oppose the primal being, but that the dualism of existing reality is derived from an inner process within the one divinity itself. This is a distinctive feature of the Syrian and Alexandrian *gnosis* and its major difference from the Iranian type of gnostic speculation, which starts from a dualism of pre-existent principles. The subtlest account ascribed to Simon of the self-division of the divine unity is found comparatively late, in Hippolytus, who copied it from a purportedly Simonian treatise entitled "The Great Exposition"; somewhat simplified, it runs like this:

The one root is unfathomable Silence, pre-existent limitless power, existing in singleness. It bestirs itself and assumes a determinate aspect by turning into Thinking (*Nous,* i.e., Mind), from which comes forth the Thought (*Epinoia*) conceived in the singleness. Mind and Thought are no longer one but two: in his Thought the First "appeared to himself from himself and thereby became a Second." Thus through the act of reflection the indeterminate and only negatively describable power of the Root turns into a positive principle committed to the object of its thinking, even though that object is itself. It is still One in that it contains the Thought in itself, yet already divided and no longer in its original integrity. Now, the whole sequel, here and in other speculations of this type, depends on the fact that the Greek words *epinoia* and *ennoia,* like the more frequent *sophia* (wisdom) of other systems, are feminine, and the same is true of their Hebrew and Aramaic equivalents. The Thought begotten by the original One is in relation to it a female principle; and responding to her capacity to conceive the Mind (Nous) assumes the male role. His name becomes "Father" when his Thought calls him thus, that is, addresses him and appeals to him in his generative function. Thus the original split comes about by the Nous' "educing himself from himself and making manifest to himself his own thought." [4] The manifested Epinoia beholds the Father and hides him as the creative power within herself, and to that extent the original Power is drawn into the Thought, making an androgynous combination: the Power (or Mind) is the upper and the Epinoia the lower element. Though conjoined in a unity, they are at the same time ranged opposite each other, and in their duality make apparent the distance between. The upper principle, the great Power, is in this combination the Mind of the All, governing everything and male: the lower principle, the great Thought, is the one bringing forth everything and female. [5]

From here on—turning now to the more authentic sources—the hypostatized and personified female figure of the Epinoia (or, alternatively, Ennoia), who has absorbed into herself the generative power of the Father, is the subject of the further divine history, which has been set in motion by the first act of reflection. This history is one of *creation* or a series of creations, and the specifically gnostic feature of the process is that it is one of progressive *deterioration* (alienation) in which the Epinoia, the bearer of the creative powers separated from their source, loses control over her own creations and more and more falls victim to their self-assertive forces. It is with the fall, suffering, degradation, and eventual redemption

[4] Nearest to this description of the first step of divine self-multiplication come certain Mandaean ones and, in the Greek area, that in the Apocryphon of John (preserved in Coptic translation). "He 'thought' His own likeness when He saw it in the pure Light-water that surrounded Him. And His Thought [*ennoia*] became efficacious and made herself manifest. Out of the splendor of the Light she stood herself before Him: this is the Power-before-the-All which became manifest; this is the perfect Forethought of the All, the Light that is the image of the Light, the likeness of the Invisible. . . . She is the first Ennoia, His likeness" (Apocr. of John, 27. 1 ff., Till).

[5] Summarized from Hippol. VI. 18. In the original the account is much longer and much more involved, and it goes on to an elaborate physical theory of the universe. The Great Exposition is certainly not by Simon himself, and perhaps Hippolytus was even mistaken in ascribing it to the Simonian sect at all. Actually the only connecting link with the Simonian doctrine as related everywhere else is the female "Thought" of God, who is here, however, not subjected to the degradations of the Helena story. If I have nevertheless included this opening speculation of the Great Exposition in the account of "Simon," it was because this typical example of gnostic half-mythical play with highly abstract concepts had to be presented somewhere, and Hippolytus' ascription, right or wrong, is an excuse for doing it here.

of this female hypostasis of the divine that the older reports on Simon are alone concerned. Apparently with nothing in their source like the conceptual deduction of the Great Exposition they introduce the female entity with the simple statement that she is "the first Thought of His (the divine) mind, the universal mother through whom He in the beginning had it in mind to create angels and archangels." The account goes on: "This Ennoia, springing forth from Him[6] and perceiving her Father's intention, descended to the lower regions and, anticipating Him, generated angels and powers, by whom this world was then made. After she had brought them forth, she was detained by them out of envy because they did not want to be thought someone else's progeny. The Father was totally unknown to them: his Thought, however, was detained by those angels and powers who had emanated from her and was dragged down from the highest heavens into the cosmos. And she suffered all manner of abuse from them, that she might not return upward to her Father, and this went so far that she was even enclosed in human flesh and migrated for centuries as from vessel to vessel into different female bodies. And since all the Powers contended for her possession, strife and warfare raged among the nations wherever she appeared. Thus she was also that Helen about whom the Trojan war was fought, and in this manner Greeks and barbarians beheld a phantasm of the truth. Migrating from body to body, suffering abuse in each, she at last became a whore in a brothel, and this is the 'lost sheep.' "[7] For her sake God descended in the person of Simon; and a main point of the latter's gospel consisted precisely in declaring that the whore from Tyre traveling around with him was the fallen Ennoia of the highest God, i.e., of himself, and that world salvation was bound up with her redemption by him. We must here add to the account quoted from Irenaeus (*et al.*) that every "He" or "His" referring to the divine Father was "I" etc. in Simon's own words; that is, he declared *himself* to be the God of the absolute beginning, "He who

[6] A recollection of the myth describing the birth of Pallas Athena from the head of Zeus.

[7] Iren. I. 23. 2, with some insertions from the parallel accounts in the *Homilies* (II.25), Hippolytus (VI. 19), and Tertullian (*De animo* Ch. 34).

stands," and recounted the begetting of the Ennoia, the creation of the angels through her, and indirectly even the unauthorized creation of the world by them, as his own deeds.

"Therefore [he says] he came, first to raise up her and release her from her bonds, and then to bring salvation to all men through knowledge of him. For since the angels ruled the world evilly, because each of them coveted the mastery, he has come to set things right, and has descended, transforming and assimilating himself to the virtues and powers and angels, so that (eventually) among men he appeared as a man, though he was not one, and was thought to have suffered in Judaea, though he did not suffer." (The relation to Jesus is more specifically defined in Simon's statement that he, himself the highest power, appeared in Judaea as Son, in Samaria as Father and in other nations as Holy Spirit.) The transformation of the savior in his descent through the spheres is a widespread motif in gnostic eschatology, and Simon himself according to Epiphanius describes it thus:

In every heaven I took on a different form, according to the form of the beings in each heaven, that I might remain concealed from the ruling angels and descend to the Ennoia, who is called also Prunikos[8] and Holy Spirit, through whom I created the angels, who then created the world and man.

(*Haer.* XXI. 2. 4)

To continue Irenaeus' account: "The prophets uttered their prophecies inspired by the angels that made the world; wherefore those who placed their hope in himself and his Helena need no longer heed them and might freely do what they liked. For by his grace men were saved, not by righteous deeds. For works are not in their nature good [or bad], but by external dispensation: the angels who made the world decreed them as such, by precepts of this kind to bring men into servitude. Wherefore he promised that the world should be dissolved and that his own should be liberated from the dominion of those who made the world" (Iren. *Adv. Haer.* I. 23. 2-3). Simon's Helena was also called *Selēnē* (Moon), which suggests the mythological derivation of the figure from the ancient

---

[8] "The prurient"—usually in gnostic texts in the connection "Sophia-Prunikos," about whom we shall have to say more when we deal with the Valentinian speculation.

moon-goddess.[9] The number of thirty disciples also mentioned in the *Recognitions* likewise suggests lunar origin. This feature as we shall see has persisted into the pleroma speculation of the Valentinians, where the Sophia and her consort are the last two of thirty Aeons. The basis for the transference of the lunar theme to the symbolism of salvation is the waning and waxing of the moon, which in the old nature mythology was sometimes represented as a rape and recovery. In the gnostic spiritualization, "Moon" is merely the exoteric name of the figure: her true name is Epinoia, Ennoia, Sophia, and Holy Spirit. Her representation as a harlot is intended to show the depth to which the divine principle has sunk by becoming involved in the creation.

The disputations of the Pseudo-Clementines emphasize the anti-Judaistic aspect of Simon's teaching. According to this source he professes "a Power of the immeasurable and ineffable light, whose magnitude is to be held incomprehensible, which Power even the creator of the world does not know, nor the lawgiver Moses, nor your teacher Jesus" (*Rec.* II. 49). In this polemical context he singles out the highest of the angels who created the world and divided it among themselves, and identifies this leader with the God of the Jews: out of the seventy-two nations of the earth the Jewish people fell by lot to him (*loc. cit.* 39).[10] Sometimes, passing over the figure of the Ennoia, he simply states that this demiurge was originally sent out by the good God to create the world but established himself here as an independent deity, that is, gave himself out to be

[9] Some Greek mythological speculation seems to have associated the Homeric Helen with the moon, whether prompted by the similarity of Helēnē and Selēnē, or by her fate (abduction and recovery) interpreted as a nature myth, or by Homer's once comparing her appearance to that of Artemis. One story had it that the egg which Leda found dropped from the moon; and the late Homer commentator Eustathius (twelfth century A.D.) mentions that there are some who say that Helen fell down to earth from the moon, and that she was taken back up when the will of Zeus was accomplished. When and by whom this was said, Eustathius does not state; neither does he say (or imply) that in this form of the myth Helen served as a symbol of the *anima*. It is therefore impermissible to extract from his testimony the conclusion that "already in antiquity Helen was regarded as image of the fallen Soul," as does G. Quispel in explanation of the Simonian doctrine (*Gnosis als Weltreligion*, pp. 64 f.). Even if granted, the point would prove as little against the historicity of Simon's earthly companion as does the earlier myth of a dying and resurrected god against that of Christ.

[10] This idea is also found elsewhere in gnostic literature, e.g., in Basilides.

the Most High and holds captive in his creation the souls which belong to the supreme God (*loc. cit.* 57). The fact that what is elsewhere told of the abduction of the Ennoia is here related of the plurality of the souls shows that the Ennoia is the general Soul which we have met e.g. in the Psalm of the Naassenes: her incarnation in the Tyrian Helena is thus an added trait peculiar to Simon.

Regarding the character of the world-god, Simon—as Marcion did later with particular vehemence—proves his inferiority from his creation, and he determines his nature, in contrast to the "goodness" of the transcendent God, by the quality of "justice" interpreted in the vicious sense as was the fashion of the time. (With this contrast we shall deal at greater length in connection with Marcion.) We have seen already that the antinomianism resulting from this interpretation of the world-god and his law leads straight to libertinism, which we shall find in other gnostic sects as a fully fledged doctrine.

In conclusion, let us hear what Simon says to Peter about the novelty of his teaching: "Thou indeed as one stupefied continually as it were stoppest thine ears that they may not be polluted by blasphemy and takest to flight, finding nothing to reply; and the unthinking people assenting unto thee will yet approve thee as one teaching what is familiar to them: but me they will execrate, as one who professes novel and unheard-of things" (*loc. cit.* 37). This speech rings too true to have been invented by an opponent like the author of the Clementines: disputations of this kind must actually have taken place, if not between Simon and Peter themselves, then between their followers of the first or second generation, and subsequently ascribed to the original protagonists. What then was the thing "novel and unheard-of"? In the last analysis, nothing else than the profession of a transcendent power beyond the creator of the world which at the same time can appear within the world even in the basest forms and if it knows itself can despise him. In brief, the unheard-of is the revolt against the world and its god in the name of an absolute spiritual freedom.

Simon traveled around as a prophet, miracle-worker, and magician, apparently with a great deal of showmanship. The extant sources, of course, being Christian, draw a none too sympathetic picture of his person and doings. According to them he performed also at the imperial court at Rome and met a bad end there while attempting to fly.[11] It is of interest, though in a context far removed from ours, that in Latin surroundings Simon used the cognomen *Faustus* ("the favoured one"): this in connection with his permanent cognomen "the Magician" and the fact that he was accompanied by a Helena whom he claimed to be the reborn Helen of Troy shows clearly that we have here one of the sources of the Faust legend of the early Renaissance. Surely few admirers of Marlowe's and Goethe's plays have an inkling that their hero is the descendant of a gnostic sectary, and that the beautiful Helen called up by his art was once the fallen Thought of God through whose raising mankind was to be saved.[12]

[11] According to at least one source, however, this was an attempted ascension meant as the end and consummation of his terrestrial mission and announced in these words: "Tommorrow I shall leave you impious and wicked ones and shall repair above to God whose power I am, even if become weak. Whereas ye have fallen, behold, I am He-who-stands. And I ascend to the Father and shall tell him: me too, thy Son the Standing, they wished to cause to fall, but I had no dealings with them but returned to myself" (*Actus Vercellensis* 31). Peter then by a prayer really "caused him to fall" from mid-air, thus bringing his career to an end.

[12] Cf. E. M. Butler, *The Myth of the Magus,* Cambridge University Press, 1948; *The Fortunes of Faust,* Cambridge University Press, 1952.

Chapter 5. *The "Hymn of the Pearl"*

In the Simonian doctrine we have introduced a specimen of what we shall call the Syrian-Egyptian gnosis. We follow this with an introductory example of the other main type of gnostic specula-tion, which for reasons to be explained later we shall call the Iranian one. Strictly speaking, the text chosen for a first representation of this type is not a systematic but a poetic composition, which clothes the central part of the Iranian doctrine in the garment of a fable apparently dealing with human actors, and in concentrating upon the eschatological part of the divine drama omits its first, cosmo-gonic part. It is nevertheless in its vividness and subtle naïveté such an immediately captivating document of gnostic feeling and thought alike that no better introduction to the whole type could be provided. The more theoretical, cosmogonic chapter of the doctrine will be supplied later in the account of Mani's teaching. After the calculated brazenness of Simon Magus, the moving tenderness of the following poem will come as a striking contrast.

The so-called "Hymn of the Pearl" is found in the apocryphal Acts of the Apostle Thomas, a gnostic composition preserved with orthodox reworkings that are relatively slight: the text of the Hymn itself is entirely free of these. "Hymn of the Pearl" is a title given to it by modern translators: in the Acts themselves it is headed "Song of the Apostle Judas Thomas in the land of the Indians."[1] In view of the didactic intention and narrative form of the poem, "hymn" is perhaps not exactly appropriate. It is with the rest of the Acts extant in a Syriac and a Greek version, the Syriac being the original one (or an immediate descendant of the original, which was doubtlessly Syriac). In our rendering, based mainly on the Syriac text, we shall disregard the metrical divisions and treat the text as a prose narrative.

[1] Supposed to have been composed when he was imprisoned there.

(a) THE TEXT

When I was a little child and dwelt in the kingdom of my Father's house and delighted in the wealth and splendor of those who raised me, my parents sent me forth from the East, our homeland, with provisions for the journey.[2] From the riches of our treasure-house they tied me a burden: great it was, yet light, so that I might carry it alone. . . .[3] They took off from me the robe of glory which in their love they had made for me, and my purple mantle that was woven to conform exactly to my figure,[4] and made a covenant with me, and wrote it in my heart that I might not forget it: "When thou goest down into Egypt and bringest the One Pearl which lies in the middle of the sea which is encircled by the snorting serpent, thou shalt put on again thy robe of glory and thy mantle over it and with thy brother our next in rank be heir in our kingdom."

I left the East and took my way downwards, accompanied by two royal envoys, since the way was dangerous and hard and I was young for such a journey; I passed over the borders of Maishan, the gathering-place of the merchants of the East, and came into the land of Babel and entered within the walls of Sarbûg. I went down into Egypt, and my companions parted from me. I went straightway to the serpent and settled down close by his inn until he should slumber and sleep so that I might take the Pearl from him. Since I was one and kept to myself, I was a stranger to my fellow-dwellers in the inn. Yet saw I there one of my race, a fair and well-favored youth, the son of kings [lit. "anointed ones"]. He came and

[2] We have met this symbol already in the Mandaean literature (see above p. 79), where differently from here the provision is intended for the return of the souls, but for this purpose also brought down by the alien man in his own journey: it is the transmundane spiritual instruction, the gnosis, which he communicates to the faithful. A similar symbolic meaning has probably to be assumed for the "burden" from the heavenly treasure-house mentioned in the next sentence.

[3] The burden as described in the ommitted lines consists of *five* precious substances, which clearly connects the "Prince" of this tale with the Primal Man of Manichaean speculation: see below, p. 216 f.

[4] For the symbolism of the garment, see above, p. 56.

attached himself to me, and I made him my trusted familiar to whom I imparted my mission. I [he?] warned him [me?] against the Egyptians and the contact with the unclean ones. Yet I clothed myself in their garments, lest they suspect me as one coming from without to take the Pearl and arouse the serpent against me. But through some cause they marked that I was not their countryman, and they ingratiated themselves with me, and mixed me [drink] with their cunning, and gave me to taste of their meat; and I forgot that I was a king's son and served their king. I forgot the Pearl for which my parents had sent me. Through the heaviness of their nourishment I sank into deep slumber.

All this that befell me, my parents marked, and they were grieved for me. It was proclaimed in our kingdom that all should come to our gates. And the kings and grandees of Parthia and all the nobles of the East wove a plan that I must not be left in Egypt. And they wrote a letter to me, and each of the great ones signed it with his name.

From thy father the King of Kings, and from thy mother, mistress of the East, and from thy brother, our next in rank, unto thee, our son in Egypt, greeting. Awake and rise up out of thy sleep, and perceive the words of our letter. Remember that thou art a king's son: behold whom thou hast served in bondage. Be mindful of the Pearl, for whose sake thou hast departed into Egypt. Remember thy robe of glory, recall thy splendid mantle, that thou mayest put them on and deck thyself with them and thy name be read in the book of the heroes and thou become with thy brother, our deputy, heir in our kingdom.

Like a messenger was the letter that the King had sealed with his right hand against the evil ones, the children of Babel and the rebellious demons of Sarbûg. It rose up in the form of an eagle, the king of all winged fowl, and flew until it alighted beside me and became wholly speech. At its voice and sound I awoke and arose from my sleep, took it up, kissed it, broke its seal, and read. Just as was written on my heart were the words of my letter to read. I remembered that I was a son of kings, and that my freeborn soul desired its own kind. I remembered the Pearl for which I had been sent down to Egypt, and I began to enchant the terrible and snorting serpent. I charmed it to sleep by naming over it my Father's name, the name of our next in rank, and that of my mother, the queen of the East. I seized the Pearl, and turned to repair home to my Father. Their filthy and impure garment I put off, and left it behind in their land, and directed my way that I might come to the light of our homeland, the East.

My letter which had awakened me I found before me on my way; and as it had awakened me with its voice, so it guided me with its light that shone before me, and with its voice it encouraged my fear, and with its love it drew me on. I went forth. . . .[5] My robe of glory which I had put off and my mantle which went over it, my parents . . . sent to meet me by their treasurers who were entrusted therewith. Its splendor I had forgotten, having left it as a child in my Father's house. As I now beheld the robe, it seemed to me suddenly to become a mirror-image of myself: myself entire I saw in it, and it entire I saw in myself, that we were two in separateness, and yet again one in the sameness of our forms. . . .[6] And the image of the King of kings was depicted all over it. . . . I saw also quiver all over it the movements of the gnosis. I saw that it was about to speak, and perceived the sound of its songs which it murmured on its way down: "I am that acted in the acts of him for whom I was brought up in my Father's house, and I perceived in myself how my stature grew in accordance with his labors." And with its regal movements it pours itself wholly out to me, and from the hands of its bringers hastens that I may take it; and me too my love urged on to run towards it and to receive it. And I stretched towards it and took it and decked myself with the beauty of its colors. And I cast the royal mantle about my entire self. Clothed therein, I ascended to the gate of salutation and adoration. I bowed my head and adored the splendor of my Father who had sent it to me, whose commands I had fulfilled as he too had done what he promised. . . . He received me joyfully, and I was with him in his kingdom, and

[5] The stages of the return journey correspond to those of the descent.
[6] We pass over an extensive description of the robe.

all his servants praised him with organ voice, that he had promised that I should journey to the court of the King of kings and having brought my Pearl should appear together with him.

(b) COMMENTARY

The immediate charm of this tale is such that it affects the reader prior to all analysis of meaning. The mystery of its message speaks with its own force, which almost seems to dispense with the need for detailed interpretation. Perhaps nowhere else is the basic gnostic experience expressed in terms more moving and more simple. Yet the tale is a symbolic one as a whole and employs symbols as its parts, and both the total symbolism and its component elements have to be explained. We shall begin with the latter.

Serpent, Sea, Egypt

If we take it for granted that the Father's house in the East is the heavenly home and defer the question as to the meaning of the Pearl, we have to explain the symbols of Egypt, the serpent, and the sea. The *serpent* we meet here for the second time in the gnostic world of images (see above, p. 93 f.); but differently from its meaning in the Ophitic sects, where it is a pneumatic symbol, it is here, in the form of the earth-encircling dragon of the original chaos, the ruler or evil principle of this world. The *Pistis Sophia* (Ch. 126, p. 207, Schmidt) says, "The outer darkness is a huge dragon whose tail is in its mouth." The Acts themselves, in a passage outside the Hymn, offer a more detailed characterization of this figure through the mouth of one of its dragon-sons:

I am the offspring of the serpent-nature and a corrupter's son. I am a son of him who . . . sits on the throne and has dominion over the creation beneath the heavens, . . . who encircles the sphere, . . . who is outside (around) the ocean, whose tail lies in his mouth.

(para. 32)

There are many parallels to this other meaning of the serpent in gnostic literature. Origen in his work *Contra Celsum* (VI. 25. 35) describes the so-called "diagram of the Ophites," where the seven circles of the Archons are placed within a larger circle which is called the Leviathan, the great dragon (not identical, of course, with the "serpent" of the system), and also the *psyche* (here "world-soul"). In the Mandaean system this Leviathan is called Ur and is the father of the Seven. The mythological archetype of this figure is the Babylonian Ti'amat, the chaos-monster slain by Marduk in the history of creation. The closest gnostic parallel to our tale is to be found in the Jewish apocryphal Acts of Kyriakos and Julitta (see Reitzenstein, *Das iranische Erlösungsmysterium,* p. 77), where the prayer of Kyriakos relates, also in the first person, how the hero, sent out by his Mother into the foreign land, the "city of darkness," after long wandering and passing through the waters of the abyss meets the dragon, the "king of the worms of the earth, whose tail lies in his mouth. This is the serpent that led astray through passions the angels from on high; this is the serpent that led astray the first Adam and expelled him from Paradise. . . ." [7] There too a mystical letter saves him from the serpent and causes him to fulfill his mission.

Sea or *waters* is a standing gnostic symbol for the world of matter or of darkness into which the divine has sunk. Thus, the Naassenes interpreted Ps. 29: 3 and 10, about God's inhabiting the abyss and His voice ringing out over the waters, as follows: The many waters is the multifarious world of mortal generation into which the god Man has sunk and out of whose depth he cries up to the supreme God, the Primal Man, his unfallen original (Hippol. V. 8. 15). We quoted (p. 104 f.) Simon's division of the One into him who "stands above in the unbegotten Power" and him who "stood below in the stream of the waters, begotten in the image." The Peratae interpreted the Red Sea (Suf-Sea), which has to be passed on the way to or from Egypt, as the "water of corruption," and identified it with Kronos, i.e., "time," and with "becoming" (*ibid*. 16. 5). In the Mandaean *Left Ginza* III we read: "I am a great Mana . . . who dwelt in the sea . . . until wings were formed for me and I raised my wings to the place of light." The apocryphal Fourth Book of Ezra, an apocalypse, has in chap. xiii.

---

[7] In the *Acta Thomae* (para. 32) these and many other acts of seduction are attributed to the *son* of the original serpent, from whose speech we have quoted the description of his progenitor.

an impressive vision of the Man who flies up "from the heart of the sea." The fish symbolism of early Christianity must also be noted in this connection.

Egypt as a symbol for the material world is very common in Gnosticism (and beyond it). The biblical story of Israel's bondage and liberation lent itself admirably to spiritual interpretation of the type the Gnostics liked. But the biblical story is not the only association which qualified Egypt for its allegorical role. From ancient times Egypt had been regarded as the home of the cult of the dead, and therefore the kingdom of Death; this and other features of Egyptian religion, such as its beast-headed gods and the great role of sorcery, inspired the Hebrews and later the Persians with a particular abhorrence and made them see in "Egypt" the embodiment of a demonic principle. The Gnostics then turned this evaluation into their use of Egypt as a symbol for "this world," that is, the world of matter, of ignorance, and of perverse religion: "All ignorant ones [i.e., those lacking gnosis] are 'Egyptians,'" states a Peratic dictum quoted by Hippolytus (V. 16. 5).

We noted before that generally the symbols for world can serve also as symbols for the body and vice versa; this is true also for the three just treated: "sea" and "dragon" occasionally denote the body in Mandaean writings, and regarding "Egypt" the Peratae, to whom it is otherwise "the world," also said that "the body is a little Egypt" (Hippol. V. 16. 5; similarly the Naassenes, *ibid*. 7. 41).

The Impure Garment

That the stranger puts on the garments of the Egyptians belongs to the widespread symbolism of the "garment" which we met before (p. 56). The purpose stated here, that of remaining incognito to the Egyptians, connects that symbolism with a theme found throughout Gnosticism in numerous variations: the savior comes into the world unknown to its rulers, taking on by turns their various forms. We met the doctrine in Simon Magus, connected with the passage through the spheres. In a Mandaean text we read, "I concealed myself from the Seven, I compelled myself and took on bodily form" (G 112). In fact this theme combines two different ideas, that of the ruse by which the Archons are outwitted, and that of the sacrificial necessity for the savior to "clothe himself in the affliction of the worlds" in order to exhaust the powers of the world, i.e., as part of the mechanism of salvation itself. And if we look at our text closely, we realize that the King's Son has actually no choice but to put on the terrestrial garments, seeing that he has left his own in the upper realm. It is obvious also, and in spite of its paradoxicality part of the logic of the process itself, that the familiarity with the "Egyptians" made possible by this change of garments to some extent defeats the purpose of the messenger's protection by making him a partaker in their meat and drink. The Egyptians, though they do not recognize his origin or mission (in that case they would have aroused the dragon against him), perceive his difference from themselves and are anxious to make him one of them. They succeed precisely for the reason that his concealment succeeded: namely, his having a body. Thus the means of concealment from the cosmic powers becomes almost by necessity a cause of self-alienation which imperils the whole mission. This is part of the divine predicament: the necessary condition of the savior's success at the same time introduces the greatest threat of failure.

The Letter

The tribulations of the messenger and his temporary succumbing are described in the metaphors of sleep and intoxication which were dealt with in Chap. 3 (see "Numbness," "Sleep," "Intoxication," p. 68 ff.). His recovery of consciousness through the voice of the letter belongs to the general imagery connected with the "call" (see The "Call from Without," p. 74 f.) The "letter" in particular is the theme of the entire Ode XXIII from the apocryphal Odes of Solomon, of which we render here one stanza.

> His plan of salvation became like unto a letter,
>   his will came down from on high
> and was dispatched like an arrow
>   which is driven mightily from the bow.
> Many hands reached out for the letter
>   to snatch it, to take it and read it;
> but it eluded their fingers.
> They were afraid of it and of the seal upon it,

having no power to break the seal,
  for the force of the seal was stronger than they.
                                                    (5-9)

We may note that the Mandaeans, reversing the direction, called the *soul* departing from the body "a well-sealed letter dispatched out of the world whose secret nobody knew . . . the soul flies and proceeds on its way . . ." (*Mandäische Liturgien,* p. 111). But more naturally the letter is the embodiment of the call going *into* the world and reaching the soul dormant here below, and this in the context of our narrative creates a curious contrapuntal play of meaning. The caller in gnostic symbolism is the messenger, and the called the sleeping soul. Here, however, the called sleeper is himself the messenger, the letter therefore a duplication of his role as he on his part duplicates that of the divine treasure he came to retrieve from the world. If we add to this the duplication of the messenger's figure in his heavenly garment, his mirror-image with which he is reunited at the completion of his mission, we perceive some of the logic of that strain of eschatological symbolism which has been summarized in the expression, "the saved savior."

The Conquering of the Serpent and the Ascent

The manner in which the messenger overcomes the serpent and snatches the treasure from it is barely narrated in our text. It simply states that the serpent is put to sleep, that is, experiences what the messenger has experienced before. What is here briefly attributed to a charm is in other sources explained by the fact that the Light is as much poison to the Darkness as the Darkness is to the Light. Thus in the Manichaean cosmogony the Primal Man, seeing his impending defeat in the encounter with the forces of Darkness, "gave himself and his five sons as food to the five sons of Darkness, as a man who has an enemy mixes a deadly poison in a cake and gives it to him" (according to Theodore bar Konai). By this sacrificial means the furor of the Darkness is actually "appeased." Here the connection of the gnostic savior-motif with the old sun-myth of nature religion is obvious: the theme of the hero's allowing himself to be devoured by the monster and vanquishing it from within is extremely widespread in mythology all over the world. Its transposition from nature religion to the symbolism of salvation we witness in the Christian myth of Christ's harrowing hell, which properly belongs in a dualistic setting and is hardly genuinely Christian. In the Odes of Solomon we read:

> Hell beheld me and became weak: Death spewed me out and many with me: gall and poison was I to him: I descended with him to the uttermost depth of Hell: his feet and head became strengthless. . . .

> (Ode XLII, 11-13)

The Mandaeans most literally preserved the original, non-spiritualized form of the myth. In their main treatise on the descent of the savior into the lower worlds, Hibil, the savior-god, thus describes his adventure:

> Karkûm the great flesh-mountain said unto me: Go, or I shall devour thee. When he spake thus to me, I was in a casing of swords, sabres, lances, knives, and blades, and I said unto him: Devour me. Then . . . he swallowed me half-way: then he spewed me forth. . . . He spewed venom out of his mouth, for his bowels, his liver and his reins were cut to pieces.

> (G 157)

The author of the Hymn was obviously not interested in such crudities.

The ascent starts with the discarding of the impure garments[8] and is guided and spurred on by the letter, which is light and voice at the same time. It has thus the function ascribed to Truth in a parallel passage from the Odes of Solomon:

> I ascended up to the light as if on the chariot of Truth,
> the Truth guided and led me.
> She brought me over gulfs and abysses
> and bore me upward out of gorges and valleys.
> She became to me a harbor of salvation
> and laid me in the arms of life everlasting.

> (Ode XXXVIII, 1-3)

In our narrative, however, the guidance of the letter ceases at what we must call the climax of the ascent, the encounter of the returning

[8] About this we shall hear more in the ascent-doctrine of the *Poimandres*.

son with his garment. This fascinating symbol requires special comment.

The Heavenly Garment; the Image

In the Mandaean Liturgies for the Dead we read the standard formula: "I go to meet my image and my image comes to meet me: it caresses and embraces me as if I were returning from captivity" (e.g., in G 559). The conception is derived from an Avesta[9] doctrine according to which after the death of a believer "his own religious conscience in the form of a fair maiden" appears to his soul and replies to his question as to who she is,

> I am, O youth of good thoughts, good words, good deeds, good conscience, none other than thine own personal conscience. . . . Thou hast loved me . . . in this sublimity, goodness, beauty . . . in which I now appear unto thee.
>
> (*Hādōkht Nask* 2. 9 ff.)

The doctrine was taken over by the Manichaeans: cf. F 100 of the Turfan fragments, where it is said that the soul after death is met by the garment, the crown (and other emblems) and "the virgin like unto the soul of the truthful one." And in the Coptic-Manichaean genealogy of the gods we find among the divine emanations the "figure of light that comes to meet the dying," also called "the angel with the garment of light." In our narrative the garment has become this figure itself and acts like a person. It symbolizes the heavenly or eternal self of the person, his original idea, a kind of double or *alter ego* preserved in the upper world while he labors down below: as a Mandaean text puts it, "his image is kept safe in its place" (G 90). It grows with his deeds and its form is perfected by his toils.[10] Its fullness marks the fulfillment of his task and therefore his release from exile in the world. Thus the encounter with this divided-off aspect of himself, the recognition of it as his own image, and the reunion with it signify the real moment of his salvation. Applied to the messenger or savior as it is here and elsewhere, the conception leads to the interesting

[9] Avesta is the canon of Zoroastrian writings as redacted in the Sassanian period.
[10] Cf. the reverse of this idea in *The Picture of Dorian Gray*.

theological idea of a twin brother or eternal original of the savior remaining in the upper world during his terrestrial mission. Duplications of this kind abound in gnostic speculation with regard to divine figures in general wherever their function requires a departure from the divine realm and involvement in the events of the lower world. For the interpretation of our text, these considerations strongly suggest that the Second ("next in rank") repeatedly mentioned as staying with his parents, and together with whom the King's Son is to be heir in his Father's house, is another such duplication, and in fact the same as the garment: he is actually no longer mentioned where otherwise we should most expect him to be mentioned, namely, after the stranger's triumphant return. In the latter's reunion with his own garment, the figure of the brother seems to have been reabsorbed into a unity.

The Transcendental Self

The double of the savior is as we have seen only a particular theological representation of an idea pertaining to the doctrine of man in general and denoted by the concept of the Self. In this concept we may discern what is perhaps the profoundest contribution of Persian religion to Gnosticism and to the history of religion in general. The Avesta word is *daena,* for which the orientalist Bartholomae lists the following meanings: "1. religion, 2. inner essence, spiritual ego, individuality; often hardly translatable." [11]

In the Manichaean fragments from Turfan, another Persian word is used, *grev,* which can be translated either by "self" or by "ego." It denotes the metaphysical person, the transcendent and true subject of salvation, which is not identical with the empirical soul. In the Chinese Manichaean treatise translated by Pelliot, it is called "the luminous nature," "our original luminous nature," or "inner nature," which recalls St. Paul's "inner man"; Manichaean hymns call it the "living self" or the "luminous self." The Mandaean "Mana" expresses the same idea and makes particularly clear the identity between this inner principle and the highest godhead; for "Mana" is the name for the transmundane Power of Light, the first deity, *and* at the same time that for the transcendent,

[11] See Reitzenstein, *Hellenistische Mysterienreligionen,* 3rd ed., 1927, p. 409.

non-mundane center of the individual ego.[12] The same identity is expressed in the Naassene use of the name "Man" or "Adam" for the highest God and for his sunken counterpart.

In the New Testament, especially in St. Paul, this transcendent principle in the human soul is called the "spirit" (*pneuma*), "the spirit in us," "the inner man," eschatologically also called "the new man." It is remarkable that Paul, writing in Greek and certainly not ignorant of Greek terminological traditions, never uses in this connection the term *"psyche,"* which since the Orphics and Plato had denoted the divine principle in us. On the contrary, he *opposes,* as did the Greek-writing Gnostics after him, "soul" and "spirit," and "psychic man" [13] and "pneumatic man." Obviously the Greek meaning of *psyche,* with all its dignity, did not suffice to express the new conception of a principle transcending all natural and cosmic associations that adhered to the Greek concept. The term *pneuma* serves in Greek Gnosticism generally as the equivalent of the expressions for the spiritual "self," for which Greek, unlike some oriental languages, lacked an indigenous word. In this function we find it also in the so-called Mithras Liturgy with adjectives like "holy" and "immortal," contrasted with the *psyche* or the "human psychical power." The alchemist Zosimos has "our luminous *pneuma,*" "the inner pneumatic man," etc. In some of the Christian Gnostics it is called also the "spark" and the "seed of light."

It is between this hidden principle of the terrestrial person and its heavenly original that the ultimate recognition and reunion takes place. Thus the function of the garment in our narrative as the celestial form of the invisible because temporarily obscured self is one of the symbolic representations of an extremely widespread and, to the Gnostics, essential doctrine. It is no exaggeration to say that the discovery of this transcendent inner principle in man and the supreme concern about its destiny is the very center of gnostic religion.

[12] The Mandaeans, incidentally, sometimes connect the phrase "the hidden Adam" with the term "Mana" when used in relation to man.

[13] The Authorized Version renders *psychikos* by "natural."

The Pearl

This brings us to our last question: What is the meaning of the Pearl? The answer to this question determines also the meaning of the story as a whole. As a mythographic detail, the question is easily answered. In the glossary of gnostic symbolism, "pearl" is one of the standing metaphors for the "soul" in the supranatural sense. It could therefore have been listed simply with the equivalent terms dealt with in the preceding survey. Yet it is more of a secret name than the more direct terms of that enumeration; and it also stands in a category by itself by singling out one particular aspect, or metaphysical condition, of that transcendent principle. Whereas almost all the other expressions can apply equally to divinity unimpaired and to its sunken part, the "pearl" denotes specifically the latter in the fate that has overtaken it. The "pearl" is essentially the "lost" pearl, and has to be retrieved. The fact of the pearl's being enclosed in an animal shell and hidden in the deep may have been among the associations that originally suggested the image. The Naassenes, interpreting in their own way Matt. 7:6, called "understandings and intelligences and men" (i.e., the "living" elements in the physical cosmos) "the pearls of that Formless One cast into the formation [i.e., the body]" (Hippol. *Refut.* V. 8. 32). When the soul is *addressed* as "pearl" (as happens in a Turfan text), it is to remind it of its origin, but also to emphasize its preciousness to the celestial ones who seek for it, and also to contrast its worth to the worthlessness of its present surroundings, its luster to the darkness in which it is immersed. The address is used by the "Spirit" as the opening of his message of salvation. In the text referred to he goes on to call the soul a "king" for whose sake war was waged in heaven and earth and the envoys were sent.

And for thy sake the gods went forth and appeared and destroyed Death and killed Darkness. . . . And I have come, who shall deliver from evil. . . . And I shall open before thee the gate in every heaven . . . and show thee the Father, the King for ever; and lead thee before him in a pure garment.[14]

[14] Reitzenstein, *Das iranische Erlösungsmysterium*, pp. 22 ff.

Now, if this is the message addressed to the Pearl, the reader, who remembers the story from the Acts of Thomas, must be struck by the fact that this is also the message addressed to him who went forth to recover the Pearl: he too is assured that the "gods," the great ones in his Father's kingdom, care about his deliverance, he too is reminded of his kingly origin, and he too is guided upward by the "letter," that is, the Spirit or the Truth; finally he too is led before the Father in pure garments. In other words, the fate of the *messenger* has drawn to itself all the characteristics which would aptly describe the fate of the Pearl, while in the Hymn the Pearl itself remains a mere object, and even as such entirely undescribed. So much is it here merely the symbol for a task on whose execution the messenger's own destiny depends that it is all but forgotten in the story of his return, and its handing over to the King is barely mentioned. Thus, if our poem is sometimes called "The Hymn of the Soul," its content seems to justify this designation in the figure of the Prince alone: whatever it has to tell about the soul's condition and destiny, it tells through *his* experiences. This has led some interpreters to believe that the Pearl stands here simply for the "self" or the "good life" of the envoy which he has to find on his terrestrial journey, this terrestrial journey being a trial to which he is subjected in order that he may prove himself: which means that he himself, and not the Pearl, represents the "soul" in general, and that the journey was really undertaken not for the Pearl's sake but for his own. In this case the Pearl, the object of the quest, would have no independent status apart from the quest: it would be rather an expression for the latter, which may then be designated as "self-integration."

Much as such an interpretation seems to be supported by the symbolism of the heavenly garment which grows with the traveler's deeds, etc., the allegorical meaning of the Pearl itself is too firmly established in gnostic myth[15] to allow of its being dissolved into a

[15] Cf., e.g., the extensive allegory of the "Holy Church" in the Manichaean *Kephalaia* (p. 204), which may be summarized thus: The raindrop falls from above into the sea and forms in the oyster-shell into a pearl; the divers descend into the depths of the sea to bring up this pearl; the divers give it to the merchants, and the merchants give it to the kings. The allegory then equates: the raindrop—with the spoil that was carried off in the beginning, i.e., the living Soul; the oyster-shell— with the flesh of mankind in which the Soul is gathered and laid up as pearl; the

mere moral function; and as undoubtedly as the envoy's experiences can be substituted for those of the Pearl, if this is to represent the soul, just as undoubtedly is the recovery of the Pearl itself the primary concern of the Celestials which prompts the mission of the Son with its otherwise unnecessary dangers to himself. The Pearl is an entity in its own right; it fell into the power of Darkness prior to the sending out of the Prince, and for its sake he is ready to assume the burden of descent and exile, thereby inevitably reproducing some of the features of the "pearl's" own fate.

In fact, the interpreters' puzzle, the interchangeability of the subject and object of the mission, of savior and soul, of Prince and Pearl, is the key to the true meaning of the poem, and to gnostic eschatology in general. We can confidently take the King's Son to be the Savior, a definite divine figure, and not just the personification of the human soul in general. Yet this unique position does not prevent him from undergoing in his own person the full force of human destiny, even to the extent that he the savior himself has to be saved. Indeed, this is an irremissible condition of his saving function. For the parts of divinity lost to the darkness can be reached only down there in the depth in which they are swallowed up; and the power which holds them, that of the world, can be overcome only from within. This means that the savior-god must assimilate himself to the forms of cosmic existence and thereby subject himself to its conditions. The Christian reader must not confuse this necessity with the orthodox interpretation of Christ's passion. Since the gnostic concept of salvation has nothing to do with the remission of sin ("sin" itself having no place in gnostic doctrine, which puts "ignorance" in its place), there is in the savior's descent nothing of vicarious suffering, of atonement as a condition for divine forgiveness, and, with the one exception of Marcion, nothing even of a ransom by which the captive souls

divers—with the apostles; the merchants—with the enlighteners of the heavens (sun and moon as agents of salvation in the Manichaean myth); the kings and nobles—with the Aeons of the Greatness. Cf. Matthew 13:45 f. A Mandaean example should be added: "The treasurers of this world assembled and said 'Who has carried away the pearl which illumined the perishable house? In the house which it left the walls cracked and collapsed'" (G 517): the "house" may be the body but is more probably the world, in which case the "pearl" is the general soul or the sum of all souls (whose removal according to Mani leads to the world's collapse), and this should also be the meaning of the Pearl in our poem.

have to be bought back. Rather, the idea is either that of a technical necessity imposed by the conditions of the mission, namely, the nature of the system, far from the divine realm, into which the messenger has to penetrate and whose laws he cannot cancel for himself, or that of a ruse by which the Archons are to be deceived. In the latter version the suffering or temporary succumbing of the savior may not be real at all but merely apparent and part of the deception.[16] This of course is not the case in our poem, where the stranger's predicament is quite real; yet even here his trials are an outcome of the inevitable dangers of his mission and not part of its very meaning. To put it differently, they *imperil* the success of his mission and are triumphantly overcome, whereas in the Christian account the trials are the very *means and manner* of the fulfillment of the mission. With this cardinal difference in mind, we may still say that there is a sacrificial element in the savior's descent according to our poem, in that he was willing for the Pearl's sake to take upon himself an exile's fate and to duplicate in his person the history of that which he came to redeem: the Soul.

If in addition we are right in discerning in the King's Son certain features of the Primal Man of Manichaean doctrine, he also duplicates the fate of that pre-cosmic divinity in which the present condition of the Soul, i.e., the Pearl, originated. Indeed, as we shall see when we come to the Manichaean cosmogony, all these successive and mutually analogous phases of the world-drama, notwithstanding their cosmic significance, symbolize also the tribulations and triumphs of the human soul. The reference to the Primal Man in particular supplies a final link in the solution of our riddle. It is not for nothing that a pre-cosmic (and mediately cosmogonic) eternal divinity bears the name "Man": the souls dispersed in the world are his "Light-Armor," part of his original substance, which he lost to the Darkness in the primordial fight (the "spoil carried off" in the allegory quoted, note 15), so that he is actually present in every human soul, exiled, captive, stunned; and if the Prince as his later representation comes to recover these lost elements, he in a sense really seeks his own, and his work *is* one of reintegration

---

[16] This is the interpretation put by many Christian Gnostics upon the passion of Christ, the so-called Docetism.

of the divine self—even of his own self, only not in the sense pertaining to an individual person. If, then, there is this metaphysical, though not numerical, identity between the messenger and the Pearl, every hearer of the tale can legitimately, without confounding personal identities, recognize in the adventures of the messenger the story of his own earthbound soul, see his own fate as part *and* analogue of the deity's, yet at the same time also as the latter's object. Thus in the proper perspective the competing interpretations resolve themselves as not really alternative but complementary.

Chapter 6. *The Angels That Made the World. The Gospel of Marcion*

The "Hymn of the Pearl" did not relate how the Pearl got into the power of the Darkness. Simon Magus did so, if rather briefly in the extant renderings, with regard to the divine Ennoia or Sophia, which in his system corresponds to the Pearl of the Hymn. As we have seen, she had been abducted into the creation by her own offspring, the world-creating angels, in their ignorant conceit and lust for godlike power. The divine origin, though at some remove, of these cosmic agencies, and therefore the conception of the whole story as one of divine failure, is an integral point in this type of speculation, indeed its explanatory principle. The same derivation could not well be supplied for the dragon which holds the Pearl in captivity. If, as its Babylonian archetype suggests, it embodies the power of the primordial chaos, then its principle was anti-divine from the beginning, and its character evil or "dark" in a sense different from the delusion and folly of Simon's erring angels. We indicated (p. 105) that on this point the two main types of gnostic speculation divide. Whereas the Iranian speculation had to explain how the original Darkness could engulf elements of Light, the Syrian-Egyptian speculation saw its major task in deriving the dualistic rift itself, and the ensuing predicament of the divine in the system of creation, from the one and undivided source of being; and this it did by way of an extensive genealogy of divine states evolving from one another which described the progressive darkening of the divine Light in mental categories. The really important difference rests, not so much in the pre-existence or otherwise of a realm of Darkness independent of God, but in whether the tragedy of the divine is forced upon it from outside or is motivated from within itself. The latter can be the case even in the face of a pre-existing Darkness or Matter if its role is the passive one of tempting members of the upper realm into material creativity rather than the active one of invading the realm of Light. In this form, adopted by some systems, the Iranian scheme of two opposed original principles could be brought within the scope of the Syrian-Egyptian scheme of divine guilt and error.[1]

It might be argued that for the existing state of things and the concern of salvation based upon it, which was after all the chief concern of gnostic religion, it made no appreciable difference whether one or the other kind of prehistory was adopted, for both led essentially to the same result: whether it is the demiurgical angels "ruling the world evilly," or the demons of primordial Darkness, that hold the souls in captivity, "salvation" means salvation from their power and the savior has to overcome them as his enemies. This is true, and if it were otherwise the two theoretical types could not both be expressions of the gnostic spirit, for which the negative evaluation of the cosmos is fundamental. Yet it is by no means religiously irrelevant whether the world is regarded as the expression of an inferior principle or whether its substance is seen as outright devilish. And it is the Syrian-Egyptian type which, with its subtler and more intriguing deductive task, is not only more ambitious speculatively and more differentiated psychologically than the rigid Iranian type of dualism but also the one of the two which can do full systematic justice to the redemptional claim of *gnosis* so central to gnostic religion: this because its opposite, "ignorance" as a *divine* event, is accorded a metaphysical role in the very origination of the cosmos and in sustaining the dualistic situation as such. We shall have to say more about this aspect when dealing with the Valentinian system. Even at this stage it is obvious that the Syrian-Egyptian scheme allows the greater speculative variety, and that, once the character of this world and of its immediate lords and creators was established, as it was in the general gnostic view almost as a matter of course, the theoretical center of gravity would shift to the elaboration of the *mediate* stages between these cosmocratic deities and the primary godhead from which they had sprung: the tendency would then be to multiply figures and lengthen the genealogy—for the sake of spiritual differentiation no less than for the sake of widening the distance between

[1] A version of this kind is even reported as a variant of the Manichaean doctrine, which by the overwhelming evidence of the sources is the classical representative of the Iranian type, describing the kingdom of Darkness as the first aggressor and the history of the world as the prolonged struggle between the two principles (see Jonas, *Gnosis,* I, p. 301).

the lower world and the unfallen realm of Light. To explain this very noticeable tendency we may also assume simply a growing speculative interest in the upper worlds as such which found its satisfaction only in an increasing manifoldness. At any rate, in the light of what eventually emerged, the genealogy of Simon with its two steps of Ennoia and world-creating angels must appear as a very modest beginning.

(a) THE ANGELS THAT MADE THE WORLD

By far the majority of the Christian gnostic systems listed by the heresiologists belong to the Syrian type, even when incorporating the original Darkness in the Platonizing form of a passive matter. This is not to say that they all indulged in the kind of transcendental genealogy which we indicated. In fact, wherever either "angels" or the "demiurge" are said to be the creators and rulers of the world, even without having their line of descent from the supreme God traced, we deal with a principle not outright evil, but rather inferior and degenerate, as the cause and essence of creation.

Thus *Carpocrates,* without any attempt at deduction (as far as Irenaeus' report goes), simply states that the world was made by angels "that are lower by far than the unbegotten Father": Jesus and all souls which like his remained pure and strong in their memory of the unbegotten Father can despise the creators and pass through them (Iren. I. 25. 1-2). *Menander* taught similarly to Simon that the First Power is unknown to all and the world made by angels, who he "like Simon says are emanated from the Ennoia": he claims by magic to be able to conquer these world-rulers *(loc. cit.* 23. 5). *Saturninus,* passing over the Ennoia, or any such female principle, taught according to Irenaeus simply that "the one unknown Father made the angels, archangels, powers and dominions. The world, however, and everything in it, was made by seven particular angels, and man too is a work of the angels," of whom the Jewish god is one. These angels he describes in turn as feeble artisans and as rebellious. Christ came to destroy the god of the Jews. As a particular trait,[2] Saturninus acknowledges besides these angels also the devil, who "is an angel who is an

[2] Shared with Marcion and the Valentinians.

enemy of those angels and the god of the Jews"—a kind of private feud within the camp of the lower powers (*loc. cit.* 24. 1-2).

The larger systems on the other hand, as has been indicated, elaborate the descendance of the lower order from the highest principle in extensive and increasingly complicated genealogies—a kind of metaphysical "devolution" ending in the decadence that is this world. Thus, for instance, *Basilides* stretches the line of descent into an enormous chain which, via a number of spiritual figures like Nous, Logos, etc., leads through 365 successively generated heavens with their angelic populations, the last of which is the one we see, inhabited by the angels who made this world. Their leader is the god of the Jews. Here too the unnameable Father sends Christ, the eternal Nous, to liberate those who believe in him from the domination of the makers of the world. His passion was a deception, Simon of Cyrene dying on the cross in his shape (*loc. cit.* 24. 3-4; of the two other prominent examples of this type, the Barbeliotes and the Valentinians, we shall hear later).

In all these cases, the powers which are responsible for the world and against which the work of salvation is directed are more contemptible than sinister. Their badness is not that of the arch-enemy, the eternal hater of the Light, but that of ignorant usurpers who, unaware of their subaltern rank in the hierarchy of being, arrogate lordship to themselves and in the combination of feeble means with envy and lust for power can achieve only a caricature of true divinity. The world, created by them in illegitimate imitation of divine creativeness and as a proof of their own godhead, in fact proves their inferiority in both its constitution and its governance.

One recurring feature is the assertion that the prophecies and the Mosaic Law issued from these world-ruling angels, among whom the Jewish god is prominent.[3] This bespeaks a particular antagonism toward the Old Testament religion and toward its God, the reality of whom is by no means denied. On the contrary, after he had first in astrology lent his *names* to four of the seven planetary archons,[4] whom the Gnostics then promoted to world-

[3] Saturninus went so far as to say that the prophecies were spoken partly by the world-makers, partly by Satan.

[4] Iao, Sabaoth, Adonaios, Elohim; more rarely also Esaldaios = El-shaddai.

creators, his polemically drawn likeness emerged with increasing pre-eminence from their number as an unmistakeable caricature of the biblical God—not venerable indeed, but none the less formidable. Of the Seven, it is mostly Ialdabaoth who draws to himself this eminence and this likeness. In the system of the Ophites as related by Irenaeus, he is the firstborn of the lower Sophia or Prunikos and begets out of the waters a son called Iao, who in turn in the same way generates a son, Sabaoth, and so on to seven. Thus Ialdabaoth is mediately the father of them all and thereby of the creation. "He boasted of what was taking place at his feet and said, 'I am Father and God, and there is none above me'" (after the pattern of certain Old Testament formulas, such as Is. 45:5, "I am the Lord, and there is none else, there is no God beside me"); to which his mother retorts, "Do not lie, Ialdabaoth: there is above thee the Father of all, the *First Man,* and *Man* the Son of Man" (*loc. cit.* 30. 4-6).

The theme of the demiurgical conceit is frequent in gnostic literature, including the Old Testament allusions. "For there ruled the great Archon, whose dominion extends to the firmament, who believes that he is the only God and that there is nothing above him" (Basilides, in Hippol. VII. 25. 3, cf. 23. 4 f.). One step further in defamation of character goes the Apocryphon of John, where Ialdabaoth, for the sake of dominion, cheats his own angels by what he grants and what he withholds in their creation, and where his jealousy is taken to betray a knowledge rather than ignorance of the higher God:

He apportioned to them some of his fire, which is his own attribute, and of his power; but of the pure Light of the power which he had inherited from his Mother he gave them none. For this reason he held sway over them, because of the glory that was in him from the power of the Light of the Mother. Therefore he let himself be called "the God," renouncing the substance from which he had issued. . . . And he contemplated the creation beneath him and the multitude of angels under him which had sprung from him, and he said to them "I am a jealous god, besides me there is none"—thereby already indicating to the angels beneath him that there is another God: for if there were none, of whom should he be jealous?

(42:13 ff.; 44:9 ff., Till).

Mandaean speculations about the beginnings abound with the same theme, though here without manifest reference to the Old Testament God: "B'haq-Ziva regarded himself as a mighty one, and forsook the name which his Father had created [for him]. He said, 'I am the father of the Uthras, who have created sh'kinas for them.' He pondered over the turbid water and said, 'I will create a world'" (G 97 f.).

Typical also is the retort from on high which puts the creator in his place.[5] But even more humiliating is the same reprimand coming from the ascending soul of the pneumatic which flaunts its higher origin in the face of the lord, or lords, of the world:

> I am a vessel more precious than the woman that made ye. Your mother does not know her origin, but I know myself and know whence I come. I invoke the incorruptible Sophia who dwells in the Father and is the mother of your mother. . . . But a woman born of woman brought ye forth, without knowing her own mother and believing that she was from herself: but I invoke her mother.

(Iren. I. 21. 5)

Such formulas, of which there are many, forcibly express the confidence of the gnostic elect and his sovereign contempt for those lower powers even though they are the rulers of this world. This does not exclude a feeling of dread, which we find curiously blended with the daring of provocation. The soul's main concern is to *escape* the terrible archons, and rather than meet them face to face she likes to slip by them unnoticed if she can. Accordingly, the task of the sacraments is sometimes said to be that of making the souls in their future ascent invisible to the archons who would block their way, and especially to their prince, who in the role of judge

[5] E. g., the Ialdabaoth-Sabaoth of the "Gnostics" in Epiphanius is treated to exactly the same rebuke by his mother Barbelo (as the Sophia is called in that system) as was the Ialdabaoth of the Ophites in Irenaeus (Epiph. *Haer*. XXVI. 2. 3 f.). Basilides lets the correction issue, in the less harsh form of an enlightenment, from the "Gospel of the Sonship," which also finds a more satisfactory response than is elsewhere ascribed to the demiurge: "and the Archon learned that he was not the universal God but was begotten and had above him the treasure of the ineffable and nameless 'Non-Existent' [Basilides' paradoxical name for the First Cause] and of the Sonship; and he turned and was afraid, perceiving in what ignorance he had been . . . and he confessed the sin which he had committed in magnifying himself" (Hippol. VII. 26. 1-3). Cf. above p. 64, n. 18 on the "remorse of the creator."

would make them answerable for their deeds under his law. Since the gist of this law is "justice," the Gnostic's intended escape from its sanctions is part of the general antinomian attitude and expresses the repudiation of the Old Testament God in its moral aspect. We shall return to the subject in connection with gnostic libertinism; the relation to the Pauline antithesis of law and grace will come up presently.

In some of the Christian Gnostics, the figure of one world-god entirely absorbs the plurality of angels or archons and becomes, as he was represented in the Bible, the sole symbol of the creation and its law, so that the whole issue of salvation is narrowed down to one between him and the unknown God beyond. Of this quasi-monotheistic development, as far as the cosmic realm is concerned, we have several examples.[6] *Cerinthus* taught that "the world was made, not by the first God, but by a power which was far removed and separated from the source of being and did not even know of the God who is exalted above all things": Christ was the first to preach the unknown Father in the world (Iren. I. 26. 1).[7] In the same vein, *Cerdon* maintained that "the God whom Moses and the prophets preached is not the Father of Jesus Christ: the one is knowable, the other not, the one merely just, the other good" (*loc. cit.* 27. 1). Cerdon's doctrine, of which we possess nothing but this brief summary, leads into the closest neighborhood of *Marcion,* the greatest teacher of this group.

---

[6] Already the "Baruch" of Justin contrasts the one demiurgical *Elohim* with the supreme *Good* one, but has in the female *Edem* a third and still lower principle which is the cause of evil, though not plain evil in herself.

[7] As main Scriptural support for the doctrine of the Unknown Father first and solely revealed by Christ served Matt. 11:25-27 = Luke 10:21-22. In his general account of the Valentinians, Irenaeus relates: "As keystone of their thesis they adduce the following passage: 'I thank thee, Father, Lord of the heavens [sic] and the earth, that thou hast hid these things from the wise and prudent and hast revealed them unto babes . . . no one knows the Father but the Son, nor the Son but the Father and he to whomsoever the Son will reveal [this]' [thus quoted in slight deviation from our N.T. text]. With these words, they say, he has explicitly taught that the 'Father of Truth' newly invented by them had never been known to anybody before his [Christ's] appearance; and they wish to make out that the creator and maker of the world had always been known by all: those words, there-fore,—they say—the Lord has spoken about the Unknown-to-all Father whom they proclaim" (*adv. haer.* I. 20. 3).

(b) THE GOSPEL OF MARCION

Marcion of Sinope in Pontus occupies a unique position in gnostic thought, as well as in the history of the Christian Church. In the latter respect, he was the most resolutely and undilutedly "Christian" of the Gnostics, and for this very reason his was the greatest challenge to Christian orthodoxy; or more precisely, his challenge more than that of any other "heresy" led to the formulation of the orthodox creed itself. Within gnostic thought, the uniqueness of his position is such that his classification with the whole movement has been rejected by no less a student of Marcion than Harnack.

Marcion's Unique Position in Gnostic Thought

He is indeed the exception to many gnostic rules. He alone of them all took the passion of Christ seriously, although the interpretation he put on it was unacceptable to the Church; his teaching is entirely free of the mythological fantasy in which gnostic thought reveled; he does not speculate about the first beginnings; he does not multiply divine and semi-divine figures; he rejects allegory in the understanding of both Old and New Testaments; he does not claim possession of a superior, "pneumatic" knowledge or the presence in man generally of that divine element which could be its source or recipient; he bases his doctrine entirely on what he claims to be the literal meaning of the gospel; in this rigorous restriction he is entirely free of the syncretism so characteristic of Gnosticism in general; and lastly, like Paul, who was to him *the* apostle, he makes faith and not knowledge the vehicle of redemption. The last circumstance would seem to put Marcion squarely outside the gnostic area, if this is defined by the concept of gnosis. Yet the anti-cosmic dualism as such, of which Marcion is the most uncompromising exponent, the idea of the unknown God opposed to that of the cosmos, the very conception of an inferior and oppressive creator and the consequent view of salvation as liberation from his power by an alien principle are so outstandingly gnostic that anyone who professed them in this historical environment must be counted as one of the Gnostics, not merely by way of classification but in the sense that the gnostic ideas that were abroad had actually shaped his thinking. The same concept, however, that so strongly connects Marcion with the general gnostic stream, that of the "Alien," received in his teaching an entirely new twist.

In its briefest formulation, Marcion's gospel [8] was that "of the alien and good God, the Father of Jesus Christ, who redeems from heavy bonds to eternal life wretched mankind, who *yet are entire strangers to him*." The concept of the *alienness* of the true God Marcion shares with Gnosticism in general: that he is alien even to the objects of his salvation, that men even in their souls or spirits are strangers to him, is entirely his own. It actually cancels out one of the basic tenets of gnostic religion: that men are strangers in this world, that therefore their assumption into the divine realm is a return to their true home, or that in saving mankind the supreme God saves his own. According to Marcion, man in his complete constitution like all nature is a creature of the world-god and prior to the advent of Christ his rightful and unrestricted property, body and soul alike.[9] "Naturally," therefore, no part of him is alien in the world, while the Good God is alien in the absolute sense to him as to everything created. There is no sense in which the deity that saves from the world has anything to do with the existence of the world, not even the sense in which throughout gnostic speculation some part of it was drawn into the creation either by defection or by violence. Consequently no genealogy, or history of any kind, *connects* the demiurge with the Good God. The former is a divinity in his own right, expressing his nature in the visible universe his creation, and he is the antithesis to the Good God not as evil but as "just." Thus, however unsympathetically depicted, he is not the Prince of Darkness. In the elaboration of the antithesis between these two gods on the one

[8] The most extensive source is Tertullians' work in five parts, *Adversus Marcionem*. Of the comprehensive polemic of Origen, the other great critic of Marcion in the third century, only fragments are preserved. For the rest, all the heresiologists, beginning with the first of them, Justin Martyr (second century), dealt with Marcion or his followers, and the polemic continued into the fifth century, when whole Marcionitic communities, remnants of the church which Marcion had founded, were still extant in the East. In our summary of Marcion's teaching, we shall only occasionally indicate the particular source.

[9] Marcion accepts the Genesis account of the creation of man, with the consequence to him that the Good God had no hand in it at all.

hand and of the meaning of the redemption through Christ on the other consists the originality of Marcion's teaching.

Redemption According to Marcion

To begin with the second aspect, Harnack states: "The question as to what Christ saved us from—from the demons, from death, from sin, from the flesh (all these answers were given from the earliest days)—, Marcion answers radically: He has saved us from the world and its god in order to make us children of a new and alien God." [10] This answer prompts the question, What reason had the Good God for concerning himself in the destiny of man? To this the answer is, None except his goodness. He does not gather lost children from exile back into their home but freely adopts strangers to take them from their native land of oppression and misery into a new father's house. Accordingly, since they are not his but the world-god's original property, their salvation is a "buying free" on the part of Christ. Marcion here invokes Gal. 3:13, "Christ has purchased us" (and incidentally, by a change of two letters, read also Gal. 2:20, "purchased [$\dot{\eta}\gamma\dot{\omega}\rho\eta\sigma\epsilon$] me" for "loved [$\dot{\eta}\gamma\dot{\alpha}\pi\eta\sigma\epsilon$] me"—one of the textual emendations characteristic of Marcion), and argues, "evidently as strangers, for no-one ever purchases those who belong to him." The purchase price was Christ's blood, which was given not for the remission of sins or the cleansing of mankind from guilt or as a vicarious atonement fulfilling the Law—not, in brief, for any reconciliation of mankind with God—but for the cancellation of the creator's claim to his property. The legality of this claim is acknowledged, as is also the validity of the Law, to which as subjects of the world-lord, and as long as they are so, men owe obedience. In this sense Marcion understands the Pauline argument concerning the Law and generally interprets all those utterances of the apostle, otherwise inconvenient to his position, which stress the validity of the Old Testament revelation. This Marcion indeed acknowledges *qua* the authentic document of the world-god, and in its interpretation he sides with the Jewish exegesis against his Christian contemporaries in insisting on the

---

[10] Adolf von Harnack, *Marcion: Das Evangelium vom fremden Gott,* Leipzig, 1921, p. 31, n. 1. Harnack's book is a classic, by far the best monograph on any individual chapter of Gnosticism.

literal meaning and rejecting the allegorical method, which the Church applied to the Old Testament for the purpose of establishing its concordance with the New. Not only was he not interested in such concordance, he could not even concede it, seeing that the Old Testament declared itself to be the revelation of that god who created and governs the world. Accepting this claim, Marcion could accept in their literal sense statements which the Church could only by way of allegorical interpretation reconcile with the Christian revelation. Thus Marcion agreed with the Jews that their promised Messiah, the earthly one, son of the world-god, was really still to come and would establish his earthly kingdom just as the prophets had declared. Only this has nothing to do with the salvation brought by Christ, which is acosmic in its nature and does not change the course of worldly events, not even in the sense of amelioration: in fact it changes only the prospect for the future life of the redeemed soul and, through faith in this future, its present *spiritual* condition, but leaves the world to itself—i.e., to its eventual self-destruction. For the remainder of their earthly sojourn, the conduct of the believers is determined not so much by a positive concern of sanctifying life but by the negative one of reducing contact with the domain of the creator (see below). The future bliss can be anticipated here only by faith, and faith indeed is the only form in which the divine adoption offered by Christ is to be accepted, as by its withholding it can be rejected: those who remain under the sway of the creator do so by their own choice.[11] Thus no "pneumatic experience," no illumination of the elect by a "gnosis" transforming his nature or bringing forth the hidden divine element in him, intervenes in this strictly legal transaction among the Good God, the creator, and the souls *adopted* into the former's fatherhood. The saved ones are believers, not "gnostics," though faith with its *assurance* carries its own experience of blessedness.

So much about soteriology.

[11] In this connection Marcion has an original if somewhat facetious explanation for the alleged fact that, in contrast to Cain, the Sodomites, and their like, Abel, the patriarchs, and all the just men and prophets of biblical tradition were not saved when Christ descended to hell: knowing from long experience that their God liked to tempt them, they suspected a temptation this time too and therefore did not believe Christ's gospel (Iren. I. 27. 3).

The Two Gods

His *theology* Marcion elaborated in the form of "antitheses": this was the title of one of his lost books. Most of these antitheses were in terms of attributes of the two gods. One is "the craftsman" (*demiurgos*), the "God of creation" (or "generation"), the "ruler of this aeon," "known" and "predicable"—the other is "the hidden" God, "unknown," "unperceivable," "unpredicable," "the strange," "the alien," "the other," "the different," and also "the new." *Known* is the creator-God from his creation, in which his nature lies revealed. The world betrays not only his existence but also his character, and this as one of pettiness. One need only look at his pitiable product: "turning up their noses the utterly shameless Marcionites take to tearing down the work of the Creator: 'Indeed,' they say, 'a grand production, and worthy of its God, is this world!'" (Tertullian, *Contra Marc.* I. 13.) Elsewhere Tertullian mentions the expressions "these miserable elements" and "this puny cell of the Creator." [12] The same "pettinesses and weaknesses and inconsistencies" as in his creation show themselves in his dealings with mankind and even with his own chosen people. For this Marcion adduces evidence from the Old Testament, which is to him "true" in the sense indicated. His most revealing self-revelation is the Law, and this brings us to the final and to Marcion most important antithesis: that of the *"just"* God and the *"good"* God. From the Christian point of view this is the most dangerous aspect of Marcion's dualism: it sunders and distributes to two mutually exclusive gods that polarity of justice and mercy whose very togetherness in one God motivates by its tension the whole dialectic of Pauline theology. To Marcion, a lesser mind and therefore more addicted to the neatness of formal consistency, justice and goodness are contradictory and therefore cannot reside in the same god: the

[12] Generally Marcion determines the character of the world-god after that of the world, "for the made must be like unto the maker" (Hippol. *Refut.* X. 19. 2); his wisdom is identical with the "wisdom of this world" in the pejorative sense of transcendental religion. In the exegesis of certain passages in St. Paul, Marcion simply identifies the creator with the world, taking what is said of the latter as applying to the former; and according to him he finally perishes with the world by a kind of self-destruction, which shows that in the last analysis he is not genuinely a god but nothing but the spirit of this world.

concept of each god, certainly that of the true God, must be unequivocal—the fallacy of all theological dualism. The just god is
that "of the Law," the good god that "of the Gospel." Marcion,
here as elsewhere oversimplifying St. Paul, understands the "justice" of the Law as merely formal, narrow, retributive, and vin-
dictive ("an eye for an eye, a tooth for a tooth"): this justice, not
outright evilness, is the cardinal property of the creator-god. Thus
the god whom Christ has put in the wrong is not the Persian
Ahriman, not absolute darkness—Marcion left the devil in existence as a separate figure within the domain of the creator—nor
matter, but simply the world-god such as the Law and the prophets
had taught. Moral goodness under the Law, though by inner-
worldly standards preferable to licentiousness, is irrelevant from the
point of view of transcendent salvation.

As the creator-god is known, obvious, and "just," so the true
God is unknown, alien, and good. He is unknown because the
world can teach nothing about him. As he had no share in creation, there is no trace in all nature from which even his existence
could be suspected. As Tertullian sums up: "the God of Marcion,
naturally unknown and never except in the Gospel revealed" (*op.
cit.* V. 16). Being not the author of the world, including man, he
is also the alien. That is, no natural bond, no pre-existing relationship, connects him with the creatures of this world, and there is
no obligation on his part to care for the destiny of man. That he
takes no hand in the physical government of the world is self-
evident for Marcion: he had to eliminate from the gospel as Judaistic interpolation such of the Lord's sayings as that about the
Father's being mindful of sparrows and of each hair on one's head.
The Father whom Jesus Christ proclaimed could not have been
concerned with what is nature's affair or that of its god. This does
away with the whole idea of a divine providence within the world.
Only with one activity does the Good God intervene in the world,
and this is his sole relation with it: sending down his Son to redeem
man from the world and its god: "This *one* work suffices *our* God,
that he has liberated man by his supreme and superlative goodness, which is to be preferred to all grasshoppers[13]" (Tertullian *op.*

---

[13] Used as a contemptible symbol of the creation (or a reference to one of the
Egyptian plagues?).

cit. I. 17). We see that the goodness of the Good God is connected with his alienness in that the latter removes all other grounds for his concern with man. The goodness of his saving deed is the better for his being alien and dealing with aliens: "Man, this *work of the creator-god,* that better God chose to love, and for his sake he labored to descend from the third heaven into these miserable elements, and on his account he even was crucified in this puny cell of the creator" (*ibid.* 14).

"Grace Freely Given"

Thus the Good God's only relation to the world is soteriological, that is, directed against it and its god. With regard to man, this relation is entirely gratuitously entered into on the part of the alien God and is therefore an act of pure *grace.* Here again Marcion interprets in his own way a Pauline antithesis: that of the "grace freely given" and "justification through works." That the grace is freely given is to both men the whole content of the Christian religion; but whereas the "freely" in Paul means "in the face of human guilt and insufficiency," i.e., in the absence of all human merit, it means in Marcion "in the face of mutual alienness," i.e., in the absence of all obligating bonds. Neither the responsibility nor the fatherly attachment of a creator toward his creatures operates in this case, nor is the Good God in the usual gnostic manner mediately involved in the destiny of the souls (and the world) by the genealogical connections described: so that there is nothing for him to recover or restore. Finally, in the absence of any previous dealings the ideas of forgiveness and reconciliation cannot apply: if men have been sinners before, they certainly could not sin against Him. The point is that the very first relationship between this God and those creatures not his own was established through his act of a grace *without a past,* and the relation continues to exist in this mode entirely. It is for the Christian reader to ponder what has been done here to the Christian concept of divine love and mercy. The call to repent, the imminence of judgment, fear and trembling, atonement—all these are eliminated from the Christian message. But it may be noted here that while Marcion abolished the Pauline paradox of a God who is just *and* good and before whom man is guilty yet beloved, he stressed all the more the paradox of a grace given inscrutably, unsolicited, with no antecedents to prompt and to prepare it, an irreducible mystery of divine goodness as such. For this reason Marcion must be counted among the great protagonists of paradoxical religion.

Marcion's Ascetic Morality

No less uncompromising than in theological doctrine was Marcion in the precepts for conduct he deduced from it. There could of course be no qualifying for, or supplementing, divine grace through works, even less the perfecting of human nature through virtue in the pagan-classical manner. In principle, all positive morality, as a way of regulating and thereby confirming man's membership in the system of creation, was but a version of that Law through which the creator exercised his hold over man's soul and to which the saved were no longer beholden: to go on practicing it would be to consolidate a belonging to the cosmos which should on the contrary be reduced to the inevitable minimum pending the ultimate removal from its range. This last consideration defines the kind of morality which Marcion did enjoin. Its principle was: not to complete but to reduce the world of the creator and to make the least possible use of it. "By way of opposition to the Demiurge, Marcion rejects the use of the things of this world" (Clem. Alex. *Strom*. III. 4. 25).

The *asceticism* thus prescribed is strictly speaking a matter not of ethics but of metaphysical alignment. Much as the avoidance of worldly contamination was an aspect of it, its main aspect was to obstruct rather than promote the cause of the creator; or even, just to spite him: "[Marcion] believes that he vexes the Demiurge by abstaining from what he made or instituted" (Hippol. *Refut*. X. 19. 4). The "perpetual abstinence" in matters of food is "for the sake of destroying and contemning and abominating the works of the creator" (Jerome *Adv. Jovinian*. II. 16). Especially clear is the purpose of obstructing in the prohibition of sexual intercourse and marriage: "Not wishing to help replenish the world made by the Demiurge, the Marcionites decreed abstention from matrimony, defying their creator and hastening to the Good One who has called them and who, they say, is God in a different sense: wherefore, wishing to leave nothing of their own down here, they turn abstemious not from a moral principle but from hostility to their maker and unwillingness to use his creation" (Clem. Alex. *loc. cit.*). Here the pollution by the flesh and its lust, so widespread a theme in this age, is not even mentioned; instead (though not to its exclusion: cf. Tertullian, *op. cit.* I. 19, where marriage is called a "filthiness" or "obscenity" [*spurcitiae*]) it is the aspect of *reproduction* which disqualifies sexuality—that very aspect which in the eyes of the Church alone justifies it as its purpose under nature's dispensation. Marcion here voices a genuine and typical *gnostic* argument, whose fullest elaboration we shall meet in Mani: that the reproductive scheme is an ingenious archontic device for the indefinite retention of souls in the world.[14] Thus Marcion's asceticism, unlike that of the Essenes or later of Christian monasticism, was not conceived to further the sanctification of human existence, but was essentially negative in conception and part of the gnostic revolt against the cosmos.

Marcion and Scripture

In using his understanding of St. Paul as a yardstick for what is genuinely Christian and what not, Marcion subjected the New Testament writings to a rigorous sifting process to divide the true from what he had to regard as later falsifications. It was in this way that for the first time not only text-critical work, if in rather a high-handed manner, was applied to the early Christian documents but the very idea of a *canon* was conceived and executed in the Christian Church. The Old Testament canon had been established long before by Jewish theologians, but no body of authoritative or authentic books had been fixed so far as Holy Writ from the floating mass of Christian writings. The canon which Marcion laid down for the Church was understandably meager. That the Old Testament as a whole went by the board goes without saying. Of our present New Testament, only the Gospel according to Luke and the ten Pauline Letters were accepted, though even the latter with some emendations and excisions of what Marcion regarded as

[14] This incidentally provides a conclusive proof, against Harnack, of Marcion's dependence on prior gnostic speculation: for the argument makes real sense only where the souls are lost parts of the godhead to be retrieved—in that case reproduction prolongs divine captivity and by further dispersal makes more difficult the work of salvation as one of gathering-in.

Judaistic interpolations. The latter had in his view also invaded St. Luke's Gospel, which on the whole he considered the only authentic, i.e., God-given one (and therefore not by Luke), so that it needed careful expurgation: the birth story, for instance, with its Davidic reference, had to go, and much else (of which we have mentioned the elemination of 12:6). These major features are sufficient to illustrate the general character of Marcion's text-critical work. It was in answer to Marcion's attempt to thrust his canon and with it his whole interpretation of the Christian message upon the Church that the latter proceeded to establish the orthodox canon and the orthodox dogma. In fixing the former, the major struggle was about the retention or dropping of the Old Testament, and if "Holy Scripture" to this day means both Testaments, this is due to the fact that Marcionitism did not have its own way. In the parallel matter of the dogma, the anti-Marcionite emphasis is clearly discernible in its early formulations. The *regula fidei* with which Origen prefaced his main work, *De Principiis,* contains the emphatic statement,[15] "This God, just *and* good, the Father of our Lord Jesus Christ, has *himself* given the law and the prophets and the gospels, he who is the God both of the apostles and of the Old and the New Testament."

Yet in one way or another Marcionitism has remained an issue in Christianity to this day. And quite apart from all doctrinal controversy, Marcion's message of the new and alien God will never fail to touch the human heart.

[15] No less anti-Valentinian, of course, than anti-Marcionite.

Chapter 7. *The* Poimandres *of Hermes Trismegistus*

Throughout the last chapter we were moving in the Jewish-Christian orbit entirely, if in a highly aberrant sense of it and, as regards the Jewish aspect, related to it mainly by way of rebound. The doctrines concerning the world-creators just reviewed were shaped in particular antagonism to the Old Testament. Although it would be going too far to say that this antagonism was by itself the source of the gnostic tenets, it certainly expressed and colored them most forcefully in that whole group of systems. The subject of this chapter will show that there was abroad in the Hellenistic world gnostic thought and speculation entirely free of Christian connections. The Hermetic writings, composed in Greek from the first, not only are purely pagan but even lack polemical reference to either Judaism or Christianity, though the *Poimandres* treatise for one shows its author's acquaintance with the biblical story of creation which through the Septuagint translation had become widely known in the Greek world. The religion of the "Thrice-greatest Hermes" originated in Hellenistic Egypt, where Hermes was identified with Thoth. Not the whole Corpus can be regarded as a gnostic source: large parts of it breathe the spirit of a cosmic pantheism far removed from the violent denunciation of the physical universe so characteristic of the Gnostics. Other portions are predominantly moral, and their strong dualism of the sensual and the spiritual, of body and mind, though well agreeing with the gnostic attitude, would fit equally well, e.g., into a Christian or Platonic framework, since it expresses the general transcendental mood of the age. There are, however, unmistakably gnostic portions in this syncretistic whole, and especially the first treatise of the corpus, called *Poimandres,* is an outstanding document of gnostic cosmogony and anthropogony independent of the speculations of the Christian Gnostics. The system of the *Poimandres* is centered around the divine figure of Primal Man; his sinking into nature is the dramatic climax of the revelation and is matched by

147

the ascent of the soul, the description of which concludes the revelation. The antithesis of the creator and the highest God is absent here: the demiurge has been commissioned by the Father, and his creation seems to be (as it was still represented later in Manichaeism) the best way of coping with the existence of a chaotic darkness. Yet the unplanned inclusion of the divine Man in the cosmic system is distinctly tragic; and even the character of the most genuine product of the demiurge, the seven spheres and their governors, turns out to be much more problematic than one would expect from the account of their origin. There are considerable difficulties in integrating the different parts of the composition into a consistent doctrine, and perhaps a certain ambiguity, due to the combination of contradictory material, is of its very substance. We shall deal with these questions after having rendered the main body of the text.

(a) THE TEXT

(1) Once, when I had engaged in meditation upon the things that are and my mind was mightily lifted up, while my bodily senses were curbed . . . I thought I beheld a presence of immeasurable greatness that called my name and said to me: "What dost thou wish to hear and see and in thought learn and understand?" (2) I said, "Who art thou?" "I am," he said, "Poimandres, the Nous of the Absolute Power. I know what thou wishest, and I am with thee everywhere." (3) I said, "I desire to be taught about the things that are and understand their nature and know God. . . ." And he replied, "Hold fast in thy mind what thou wishest to learn, and I shall teach thee."

(4) With these words, he changed his form, and suddenly everything was opened before me in a flash, and I behold a boundless view, everything become Light, serene and joyful. And I became enamored with the sight. And after a while there was a Darkness borne downward . . . ,[1] appalling and hateful, tortuously coiled, resembling a serpent. Then I saw this Darkness change into some humid nature, indescribably

[1] "having originated in one part" or ". . . part by part," i.e., gradually (?).

agitated and giving off smoke as from a fire and uttering a kind of sound unspeakable, mournful. Then a roar [or: cry] came forth from it unarticulately, comparable to the voice of a fire. (5) From out of the Light a holy Word [*logos*] came over the nature, and unmixed fire leapt out of the humid nature upward to the height; it was light and keen, and active at the same time; and the air, being light, followed the fiery breath, rising up as far as the fire from earth and water, so that it seemed suspended from it; but earth and water remained in their place, intermingled, so that the earth was not discernible apart from the water; and they were kept in audible motion through the breath of the Word which was borne over them.

(6) Then Poimandres said to me: ". . . That light is I, Nous, thy God, who was before the humid nature that appeared out of the Darkness. And the luminous Word that issued from Nous is the Son of God. . . . By this understand: that which in thee sees and hears is the Word of the Lord, but the Nous [thy nous?] is God the Father: they are not separate from each other, for Life is the union of these. . . . Now then, fix your mind on the Light and learn to know it."

(7) Having said this, he gazed long at me intently, so that I trembled at his aspect; then when he looked up, I behold in my nous[2] the Light consisting in innumerable Powers and become a boundless Cosmos, and the fire contained by a mighty power and under its firm control keeping its place. . . .

(8) He again speaks to me: "Thou hast seen in the Nous the archetypal form, the principle preceding the infinite beginning."[3] . . . "Wherefrom then," I ask, "have the elements of nature arisen?" To which he replies: "From the Will[4] of God, who having received into herself the Word and beheld the beautiful [archetypal] Cosmos, imitated it, fashioning herself into a cosmos [or: ordering herself] according to her own elements and her progeny, i.e., the souls.

"(9) But the divine Nous, being androgynous, existing as Life and Light, brought forth by a word another Nous, the

[2] I.e., "in my own mind" as identical with the absolute Nous.
[3] Or, perhaps, "the infinite principle preceding the beginning"?
[4] *boulé,* a word of feminine gender.

GNOSTIC SYSTEMS OF THOUGHT

150

Demiurge, who as god over the fire and the breath fashioned seven Governors, who encompass with their circles the sensible world, and their government is called Heimarmene [Destiny]. (10) Forthwith the Word of God leapt out of the downward-borne elements upward into the pure [part of the] physical creation [the demiurgical sphere] and became united with the Nous-Demiurge, for he was of the same substance. And thus the lower elements of Nature were left without reason,[5] so that they were now mere Matter. (11) And together with the Word the Nous-Demiurge, encompassing the circles and whirling them with thunderous speed, set his creations circling in endless revolution, for it begins where it ends. And this rotation of the spheres according to the will of the Nous[-Demiurge] produced out of the lower elements irrational animals, for those elements had not retained the Word. . . . [air, water, earth— the last two now separated—each producing its own animals: androgynous ones, as appears later.]

"(12) Now the Nous, Father of all, being Life and Light, brought forth Man like to himself, of whom he became enamored as his own child, for he was very beautiful, since he bore the Father's image; for indeed even God became enamored of his own form, and he delivered over to him all his works. (13) And Man, beholding the creation which the Demiurge had fashioned in the fire [the celestial spheres], wished himself to create as well, and was permitted by the Father. When he had entered the demiurgical sphere where he was to have full authority, he beheld his brother's works, and they [the seven Governors] became enamored of him, and each gave him a share in his own realm.[6] Having come to know their essence and having received a share of their nature, he then wished to break through the circumference of the circles and to overcome [?][7] the power of him who rules over the fire. (14) And he [Man] who had full power over the world of things mortal

---

[5] "without *logos*," since the Logos (Word) had departed from them: *logos* meaning "word" and "reason," the argument is not fully apparent in the English rendering.

[6] Or: "of his own endowment."

[7] Or: "fully comprehend."

and over the irrational animals bent down through the Harmony[8] and having broken through the vault showed to lower Nature the beautiful form of God. When she beheld him who had in himself inexhaustible beauty and all the forces of the Governors combined with the form of God, she smiled in love; for she had seen the reflection of this most beautiful form of Man in the water and its shadow upon the earth. He too, seeing his likeness present in her, reflected in the water, loved it and desired to dwell in it. At once with the wish it became reality, and he came to inhabit the form devoid of reason. And Nature, having received into herself the beloved, embraced him wholly, and they mingled: for they were inflamed with love. (15) And this is why alone of all the animals on earth man is twofold, mortal through the body, immortal through the essential Man. For though he is immortal and has power over all things, he suffers the lot of mortality, being subject to the Heimarmene; though he was above the Harmony, he has become a slave within the Harmony; though he was androgynous, having issued from the androgynous Father, and unsleeping from the unsleeping one, he is conquered by love and sleep."

[There follows a circumstantial account of the origin of the present race of men (16-19), and a moral instruction (20-23),

[8] I stick to the astrological and dynamic meaning of the term. The most recent interpreters take *harmonia* here in the concrete sense it had in the language of the carpenter: "joint," "fitting together"; thus *Nock* proposes the translation "composite framework," *Festugière* translates *"armature des sphères."* Both these excellent scholars, though tentative as to the most suitable translation, are certain that the word throughout our treatise denotes a particular *material* structure and not, as I understand it, the general essence of a *power* system, viz., the law of the interrelated motions of the macrocosmos represented by the seven planets (the latter, however, considered mainly in their "psychological" aspect, as the subsequent account of the soul's ascent makes clear). Of the reasons I have against the newer interpretation, I indicate only two: that supplied by the phrase "[Man] having in himself the nature of the harmony of the Seven" (16), which makes sense only in connection with the *abstract* meaning first given to "harmony" by the Pythagoreans; and its additional support by the close correlation in which our text repeatedly (15; 19) puts "harmony" to "heimarmene" (destiny). In brief, *harmonia* stands for a totality of forces (the Governors) denoted by its unifying characteristic (the form of their collective government), and not just for a partitioning wall or any more complex entity of that kind, like a scaffolding. Incidentally, the spheric system was fashioned out of fire, which hardly goes well with a framework.

which we here summarize as follows. Since the Man, now intermingled with Nature, "had in himself the nature of the harmony of the Seven," Nature brought forth seven androgynous
men, corresponding to the natures of the seven Governors. We
pass over the details of the respective contributions of the elements earth, water, fire, and ether to the constitution of these
creatures. As to the contribution of Man as a part of the begetting mixture, he turned "from Life and Light into soul and
mind (*nous*), into soul from Life and into mind from Light"
(17). This condition of creation lasted to the end of a world-
era. The new world-era was initiated by the separation of all
the androgynous creatures, animals and men alike, into male
and female. And here occurs the only instance in which the
author shows his familiarity with the Greek Old Testament in
something like a direct quotation: on the model of Gen. 1:22,
28, God admonishes the new bisexual creation, "Be fruitful and
multiply," then continues in a very different vein: "And [man]
endowed with mind shall recognize that he is immortal and
that the cause of death is love" (viz., ultimately the love which
drew the Primal Man down into nature) (18). He who has
come thus to know himself has come into the supreme good;
he, however, who has cherished the body issued from the error
of love, he remains in the darkness erring, suffering in his
senses the dispensations of death. What then is the sin of those
ignorant ones, that they should be deprived of immortality?
The first cause of the individual body is the hateful darkness,
from which came the humid nature, from which was constituted the body of the sensible world, from which death draws
nourishment. Thus the lovers of the body actually are *in* death
and deserve death. On the other hand, he who knows himself
knows that the Father of all things consists of Light and Life,
therefore likewise the Primal Man issued from him, and by this
he knows himself to be of Light and Life, and will through this
knowledge return to the Life. The knowing ones, filled with
love for the Father, before they deliver the body to its own
death abhor the senses, whose effects they know; and the
Poimandres-Nous assists them in this by acting as a warder at
the gates and barring entrance to the evil influences of the body.

The unknowing ones are left a prey to all the evil passions, whose insatiability is their torment, always augmenting the flame that consumes them.]

[The last part of the instruction (24-26) is devoted to the soul's ascent after death. First at the dissolution of the material body you yield up to the demon your sensuous nature (?)[9] now ineffective, and the bodily senses return each to its source among the elements.] "(25) And thereafter, man thrusts upward through the Harmony, and to the first zone he surrenders the power to grow and to decrease, and to the second the machinations of evil cunning, now rendered powerless, and to the third the deceit of concupiscence, now rendered powerless, and to the fourth the arrogance of dominion, drained of [or: now impotent to achieve] its ambition, and to the fifth the impious audacity and the rashness of impulsive deed, and to the sixth the evil appetites of wealth, now rendered powerless, and to the seventh zone the lying that ensnares. (26) And then denuded of the effects of the Harmony, he enters the nature of the Ogdoas [i.e., the eighth sphere, that of the fixed stars], now in possession of his own power, and with those already there exalts the Father; and those present rejoice with him at his presence, and having become like his companions he hears also certain powers above the eighth sphere exalting God with a sweet voice. And then in procession they rise up towards the Father and give themselves up to the Powers, and having become Powers themselves, enter the Godhead. This is the good end of those who have attained gnosis: to become God."

(b) COMMENTARY

The composition of the treatise is clear. Its greatest part (1-26) is a report, in the first person, of a visionary experience and of the teachings conveyed in the course of it. The concluding paragraphs (27-32), omitted in our rendering, describe the subsequent missionary activity of the recipient among his fellow men. In the report of the revelation, with which alone we are dealing here, we discern

[9] The text has *ēthos* = "character," which in its meaning of moral character somehow clashes with the whole sequence, 25-26, as also do other statements in 24.

the following major divisions. Paragraphs 1 to 3 describe the *visionary situation* with the appearance of Poimandres ("Shepherd of Men"), who identifies himself as the Nous (Mind), i.e., the highest godhead. Paragraphs 4 to 11 propound the *cosmogony* up to the creation of irrational animals; paragraphs 12 to 19 the *anthropogony,* the central doctrine of the whole revelation. Paragraphs 20 to 23, drawing the moral conclusions from the preceding theoretical parts of the revelation, outline the two opposite types of *human conduct.* Paragraphs 24 to 26 complete the revelation by describing the *ascent* of the Gnostic's soul after death. We shall first comment on the central doctrine concerning the origin and essence of *man,* to which the cosmogonic part provides a background knowledge not absolutely necessary for its understanding. We shall then treat the *ascent of the soul,* which corresponds to the original descent of Primal Man, and whose details complement the account given of the latter. Only then shall we turn back to the *cosmogony* and make an attempt at disentangling the somewhat elusive and possibly not entirely homogeneous account of these opening phases of the drama.

The Origin of the Divine Man

Man is the third in the triad of successive divine creations or emanations: Word (Logos), Mind-Artificer (Nous-Demiurgos), Man (Anthropos). He can regard the Demiurge as his brother, but has the special analogy to the Logos that they both enter into close connection with the lower Nature which in due course is dissolved again. The Word and the Demiurge had to fulfill each a cosmogonic task, with which we shall deal later; whereas Man was begotten by the first God *after* the establishment of the cosmic system, though outside it, and with no apparent purpose except for God's enjoying his own perfection in a perfect image of himself untainted by the admixture of the lower world. In the traits of being created "in God's image" and only after the end of the cosmic creation, this version of the origin of the god Man shows a closer proximity to the biblical account than the version more generally current in Gnosticism according to which Man *precedes* creation and himself has a cosmogonic role. Rabbinical speculations about Adam based on the duplication of the report of his creation in

Gen. 1 and 2, which were referred to a celestial and a terrestrial Adam respectively, supply a link between biblical and gnostic doctrines concerning the First Man. Certain Zoroastrian teachings, either through the medium of those Jewish speculations or directly, may also have contributed to the conception of this supremely important figure of gnostic theology. The departure from the biblical model (if this really was the starting point of the development, which is much debated among modern scholars) is conspicuous in the following features: God does not "make" Man, but as an androgynous generative principle begets him and brings him forth, so that he is really an emanation of His own substance; he is not formed of clay, but is Life and Light purely; the "likeness" is one not of symbolic similitude but of a full sameness of form, so that in him God contemplates and loves His own adequate representation; he is extra-mundane, while even the Demiurge has his seat within the cosmic system, albeit in its highest and outermost sphere, the eighths; his dimensions are commensurate with those of the physical creation, as his later union with the whole of Nature shows; the mastery given to him is not as in Genesis over the terrestrial fauna merely, but over the astral macrocosmos as well.

The exercise of this power, however, was hardly the original purpose of his production by the Father: it accrued to him with the granting of his wish "himself to create as well." This motivation of divine descent and eventual involvement in the lower world is more often, and more logically, connected with the demiurgical principle itself and is to account for the very existence of the world.[10] But here the world is already created, and it is difficult to

[10] Thus in the Mandaean story of creation contained in the third book of the Right Ginza we read that first from the Great Mana issued the Life: "and this addressed a request to itself; and at its request there came forth the fast-grounded Uthra whom the Life called the Second Life. . . . That Second Life then created Uthras, established sh'kinas. . . . Three Uthras came forth who addressed a request to the Second Life; they *asked permission to create sh'kinas for themselves.* The [Second] Life granted it. . . . Then they said to it, 'Give us of thy splendor and of thy light, and we will go forth and descend beneath the streams of water. We will call forth unto thee sh'kinas, create unto thee a world, and the world be ours and thine.' This pleased [the Second Life], and it said, 'I will grant it to them'; but the Great [Mana] it did not please, and the [First] Life did not approve of it." It is in a countermove to this plan of the Uthras that the Great Mana creates Manda d'Hayye, who in this system most nearly corresponds to Primal Man, and charges him: " 'Do thou mount up above the Uthras and see what they are up to

see what the Man either in collaboration or in competition with the Demiurge has still left for him to do. Nor does the subsequent narrative provide an answer to this question: rather than a creative urge, his main motive in penetrating the demiurgical system seems to be curiosity. These inconsistencies suggest that we have here an adapted form of the Anthropos myth, with some traces of an original cosmogonic function of the figure faintly preserved.

The Descent of Man; the Planetary Soul

His entrance into the demiurgical sphere marks the beginning of his inner-worldly history. The tribute rendered him by the seven Governors' each giving him a share in his own realm appears to be in the nature of a positive accretion to his own being: he absorbs and henceforth has in himself the nature of the Harmony, i.e., the powers of the seven Governors in their respective spheres; and this, at least in the eyes of the lower Nature, seems to add to the attraction of the divine form when he shows himself to her. Yet it must not be forgotten that the Governors and their spheres were fashioned by the Demiurge out of fire, which, though the purest, is still one of the physical elements originating from the primal Darkness. Thus we may already at this point suspect that the gifts of the planetary powers might not have been wholly desirable to a being of pure divinity, and might even have their fatal aspects. The immediate context contains nothing to bear out such a suspicion, and would rather tend to dispel it, were it not for the subsequent

---

and what they intend, they who say, We will create a world' "; and later on " 'Thou hast seen, Manda d'Hayye, what the Uthras are doing and what they plan about this and that. Thou hast seen that they have forsaken the House of Life and turned their faces to the place of Darkness. . . . Who will bring order among them, who will deliver them from failure and error . . . that they brought upon themselves? Who will make them hear the call of the Great [Life]?' " In the sequence of this very ill-composed treatise an individual demiurgical figure becomes the executor of the cosmogonic plan of the Uthras—Ptahil-Uthra, who from his father (one of the Uthras, here called B'haq Ziva, elsewhere Abathur) receives the mandate, " 'Go, descend to the place without sh'kinas and without worlds. Create and make thyself a world like the sons of Blessedness whom thou hast seen' [here we have the motif of imitating an ideal world, widespread in gnostic speculation and also occurring in the *Poimandres*—possibly but not necessarily a distorted reminiscence of the Platonic Demiurge]. Ptahil-Uthra went forth and descended beneath the sh'kinas to the place where there is no world. He stepped into the filthy slime, he stepped into the turbid water . . . and the living fire in him was changed" (G 65 ff. 97 f.).

description of the *ascent* of the soul and for independent accounts, inside and outside of Hermetic literature, of its original descent through the spheres to its earthly abode. Here is indeed one of the instances, characteristic of the composite nature of Hermetic religion, in which it oscillates between the pre-gnostic and gnostic meaning of the same mythological theme. It is the theme of the planetary equipping of the soul. The conception belongs to the astrological range of ideas: each of the planetary powers makes its contribution to the equipment of the soul prior to its embodiment. In an affirmative cosmology these are useful gifts which fit man for his earthly existence. And by reason of having these psychical components in himself man is sympathetically connected with their astral sources, i.e., with the cosmos, in whose "harmony" he thus participates. Through this sympathy he is also subject to the *influences* of the stars and thus to the heimarmene—the basic premise of astrology—but as long as the cosmos is considered good there is nothing deleterious in this conception; indeed, it is the expression of cosmic piety.[11]

To this complex of ideas Gnosticism gave a new turn by conceiving the planetary constituents of the soul as *corruptions* of its original nature contracted in its descent through the cosmic spheres. The Christian Arnobius reports this as a Hermetic teaching:

While we slide and hasten downwards to the human bodies, there attach themselves to us from the cosmic spheres the causes by which we become ever worse.

(*Adv. nat.* II. 16)

A very close parallel (in inverse direction) to the *Poimandres* account of the soul's ascent is found in the following description of its descent:

As the souls descend, they draw with them the torpor of Saturn, the wrathfulness of Mars, the concupiscence of Venus, the greed for gain of Mercury, the lust for power of Jupiter; which things effect a confusion in the souls, so that they can no longer make use of their own power and their proper faculties.

(Servius *In Aen.* VI. 714)

---

[11] For this positive meaning of the gifts of the planets cf. Macrobius *In somn. Scip.* I. 12, Servius *In Aen.* XI. 51, and in the *Corpus Hermeticum* itself the *Korē Kosmou*.

The expressions make it clear that what attaches itself to the soul on its downward journey has the character of substantial though immaterial entities, and these are frequently described as "envelopments" or "garments." Accordingly the resultant terrestrial "soul" is comparable to an onion with so many layers, on the model of the cosmos itself, only in inverse order: what is outermost there is innermost here, and after the process is completed with incarnation, what is innermost in the spherical scheme of the cosmos, the earth, is as body the outer garment of man. That this *body* is a fatality to the soul had long ago been preached by the Orphics, whose teachings were revived in the era of Gnosticism. But now the *psychical* envelopments too are considered impairments and fetters of the transmundane spirit.

> Looking down from that highest summit and perpetual light, and having with secret desire contemplated the appetence of the body and its "life," so called on earth, the soul by the very weight of this its earthly thought gradually sinks down into the nether world. . . . In each sphere [which it passes] it is clothed with an etherial envelopment, so that by these it is in stages reconciled to the company of this earthen garment. And thus it comes through as many deaths as it passes spheres to what here on earth is called "life."
>
> (Macrobius *In somn. Scip.* II. 11)

Now, what are these foreign accretions? In their sum they are the empirical character of man, comprising all the faculties and propensities by which man relates himself to the world of nature and society; that is, they constitute what would normally be called his "psyche." And what is the original entity overlaid by these accretions? It is the transcendent acosmic principle in man, normally hidden and undiscovered in his earthly preoccupations, or only negatively betraying itself in a feeling of alienness, of not completely belonging, and becoming positive here only through the *gnosis'* giving it in the beholding of the divine light an acosmic content of its own and thereby restoring it to its original condition, now obscured. Frequently, as we have learned before, this secret principle is called "pneuma," while the term "psyche" is reserved for its manifest "cosmic" envelopment. The Hermetic writings avoid the term "pneuma" in the spiritual meaning,[12] replacing it by "nous"; but elsewhere the name "psyche" is also used, with appropriate qualifications, for *both* parts, and often, as in the above quotations, we read simply of the "soul" descending and undergoing the deteriorations described. In that case, where the traditional dignity of the term "soul" is retained, those deteriorations are called either spirits superadded to the original soul or outright a second soul containing the first one. For the first version we quote Clement of Alexandria:

> Those around Basilides are in the habit of calling the passions "appendages," which they say are in essence certain spirits appended to the rational soul in consequence of an original upheaval and confusion.
>
> (*Strom.* II. 20. 112)

In Basilides' school these "appendages" in their entirety were considered as themselves constituting a soul, as the title of a lost book by his son Isidorus shows, *On the Accreted Soul,* which treated of "the force of the appendages" (*ibid.*).[13] This results in a two-soul

[12] Where it occurs, it is in the sense of a physical element, agreeing with the Stoic use of the term.

[13] Already Plato uses the following telling simile for the present condition of the soul in relation to its true nature: "Our description of the soul is true of her present appearance; but we have seen her afflicted by countless evils, like the sea-god Glaucus, whose original form can hardly be discerned, because parts of his body have been broken off or crushed and altogether marred by the waves, and the clinging overgrowth of weed and rock and shell has made him more like some monster than his natural self. But we must rather fix our eyes on her love of wisdom [*philosophia*] and note how she seeks to apprehend and hold converse with the divine, immortal, and everlasting world to which she is akin, and what she would become if her affections were entirely set on following the impulse that would lift her out of the sea in which she is now sunken, and disencumber her of all that wild profusion of rock and shell whose earthy substance has encrusted her, because she seeks what men call happiness by making earth her food. Then one might see her true nature . . ." (*Republic* 611C-612A, tr. F. M. Cornford). It is remarkable how in this rather incidental simile Plato toys with several of the images which later were to become so deadly serious with the Gnostics: the symbolism of the sea and the foreign "accretions" to the soul. As regards the latter, Plato uses the same expression (*symphyein*—translated by Cornford with "overgrowth") as Isidorus has in the title of his book. Six hundred years after Plato, Plotinus refers to the passage in the *Republic* in his own most interesting discourse on the higher and lower soul (*Enn.* I. 1. 12), to which we shall have occasion to refer once more in connection with the symbol of the reflected image.

theory concerning terrestrial man, which we find explicitly stated as a Hermetic doctrine in a late Neoplatonic work.

Man has two souls: the one is from the First Mind and also shares in the power of the Demiurge, the other has been put in from the revolution of the heavens, and into this the God-seeing soul enters. Since this is so, the soul that has come down into us from the spheres (lit. "worlds") follows along with the revolutions of the spheres; but the one present in us as mind from the Mind is superior to the motion that works becoming, and it is through it that the liberation from the heimarmene and the ascent to the Intelligible Gods comes about.

(Iamblichus *De myst.* VIII. 6)

To give one more quotation, the Syrian Gnostic Bardesanes says:

There are hostile powers, stars and signs, a body from the Evil One without resurrection, a soul from the Seven.

(Ephraem, *Hymn.* 53)

We could multiply testimonies for the doctrine of the planetary soul (e.g., from the Mandaean literature and the *Pistis Sophia*), but our selection has made the essentials of the conception clear enough.

The Hermetic quotation from Iamblichus shows with singular distinctness what stands behind this mythological fantasy: not just a rejection of the physical universe in the light of pessimism, but the assertion of an entirely new idea of human freedom, very different from the moral conception of it which the Greek philosophers had developed. However profoundly man is determined by nature, of which he is part and parcel—and plumbing his own inwardness he discovers in layer after layer this dependence—there still remains an innermost center which is not of nature's realm and by which he is above all its promptings and necessities. Astrology is true of natural man, i.e., of every man as member of the cosmic system, but not of the spiritual man within the natural.[14] It is the first time in

---

[14] This supremacy is extended to the whole person of the Gnostic, in whom the "spirit" has become dominant: "Hermes asserts that those who know God not only are safe from the incursions of the demons but are not even under the power of fate" (Lactantius *Div. inst.* II. 15. 6; cf. Arnobius *Adv. nat.* II. 62—"not subject to the laws of fate"). Christian Gnostics thought similarly: "Prior to baptism fate

history that the radical ontological difference of man and nature has been discovered and the powerfully moving experience of it given expression in teachings strange and suggestive. This rift between man and nature was never to close again, and protesting his hidden but essential *otherness* became in many variations an abiding theme in the quest for truth concerning man.

The Union of Man with Nature; the Narcissus Motif

We now come to the other part of the Anthropos drama, the sinking of Man into lower Nature. Here our narrative is wonderfully clear and impressive: the revealing of his divine form from on high to terrestrial Nature is at the same time its mirroring in the lower elements, and by his own beauty thus appearing to him from below he is drawn downward. This use of the Narcissus motif is, at least in this explicitness, an original feature of the *Poimandres* and recurs only in indistinct indications elsewhere in the literature of the era. The Narcissus motif, however, gives merely a particular turn to a mythological idea of much wider currency in gnostic thought, whose original meaning had nothing to do with the Greek legend: the idea that either the cosmogonic process or the sinking of the Soul, or generally the downward movement of a divine principle, was initiated by a reflection of the upper Light in the Darkness below. If we analyze the *Poimandres* version carefully, we see that it adroitly combines three different ideas: that of the Darkness' becoming enamored of the Light and getting possession of a part of it; that of the Light's becoming enamored of the Darkness and voluntarily sinking into it; that of a radiation, reflection, or image of the Light projected into the Darkness below and there held fast. All three ideas have found independent representation in gnostic thought. The first ascribes the initiative toward the eventual intermingling to the nether forces, and this version is most completely expressed in the Manichaean system, with which we shall deal separately. The second version has been exemplified in the Hermetic quotation from Macrobius (p. 158). That it applied not only to the descent of the individual soul but first and foremost to the cos-

is real, after it the predictions of the astrologers are no longer true" (*Exc. Theod.* 87. 1).

mogonic descent of the primal Soul is shown by the Arabic account of the Harranites from which we have quoted before.[15]

The third version is to us strangest of all, as it implies the mythic idea of the substantiality of an image, reflection, or shadow as representing a real part of the original entity from which it has become detached. We have to accept this symbolism as convincing to those who used it for a crucial phase in the divine drama. In this role we find it used in the speculation of the Sethians (Hippol. V. 19), the Peratae (*ibid*. 12 ff.), the Gnostics Plotinus wrote against, and in a system recorded by Basilides not as his own but as that of certain "barbarians," by which most probably Persian thinkers are meant (*Act. Arch*. 67. 5). The general idea common to these doctrines is as follows. By its nature the Light shines into the Darkness below. This partial illumination of the Darkness either is comparable to the action of a simple ray, i.e., spreading brightness as such, or, if it issued from an individual divine figure such as the Sophia or Man, is in the nature of a *form* projected into the dark medium and appearing there as an image or reflection of the divine. In both cases, though no real descent or fall of the divine original has taken place, something of itself has become immersed in the lower world, and just as the Darkness treats it as a precious spoil, so the unfallen deity has become involved in the further destiny of this effluence. The Darkness is seized with greed for the brightness that has appeared in its midst or on the surface of the primordial waters and,

[15] See above, page 63. We give here the rest of the passage. "God, always concerned to turn everything to the best, joined her to Matter, of which he saw her so enamored, distributing in it a multitude of forms. Hence came about the composite creatures—the heaven, the elements [etc.: all of these are to be understood as receptacles of the "Soul"]. But unwilling to leave the Soul in her degradation with Matter, God endowed her with an intelligence and the faculty of perceiving, precious gifts which were intended to recall to her her high origin in the spiritual world, . . . to restore to her the knowledge of herself, to indicate to her that she was a stranger down here. . . . Since the Soul received this instruction through perception and intelligence, since she recovered the knowledge of herself, she desires the spiritual world, as a man transported to a foreign land sighs for his distant hearth. She is convinced that in order to return to her original condition she must disengage herself from the worldly bonds, from sensual desires, from all material things" (Chwolson, *Die Ssabier,* II, p. 493). Although the later part of the passage seems to refer to the human soul, and indeed does so, since it is in man that the fallen world-soul comes to be endowed with intelligence and perception, the earlier part unequivocally speaks of a universal Soul whose fall is the cause of the origination of the world.

trying to mingle with it thoroughly and permanently to retain it, drags it downward, engulfs it, and breaks it up into innumerable parts. From then on the higher powers are concerned in recovering these raped particles of Light. On the other hand, it is with the help of these elements that the lower forces are able to create this world. Throughout this creation is dispersed their original prey in the form of the "sparks," i.e., the individual souls. In a slightly more sophisticated version of the idea it is with the help of the projected *image* of the divine *form* that the lower forces make the world or man, i.e., as an *imitation* of the divine original; but since in this way the divine form also becomes embodied in the matter of Darkness and the "image" is conceived as a substantial part of the deity itself, the result is the same as in the cruder case of the swallowing and splitting up. In any case, this whole complex of imagery develops the divine tragedy without either a guilt from above or an invasion from below of the divine realm itself. That the mere and inevitable radiation of the Light and its reflection in the form of images creates new hypostases of its own being is still in Plotinus a metaphysical principle of the first order, affecting his general ontological scheme. As regards particularly the relation of the higher and lower soul, he explains, in the same context where he refers to Plato's simile of the sea-god (above, n. 13), that the turning downward of the Soul was nothing but illumining that which is beneath her, through which illumination there originated an *eidolon,* a reflection, and this is the lower soul subject to the passions; but the original Soul never really descended (*Enn.* I. I. 12). A surprisingly similar doctrine was held by the very same Gnostics who came under Plotinus' severe attack:

The Soul, they say, and a certain Wisdom [*sophia*—Plotinus is not sure whether she is different from or the same as the "Soul"] turned downward . . . and with her descended the other souls: these, as it were "members" of the Wisdom, put on bodies. . . . But then again they say that she on whose account they descended did in another sense not descend herself and somehow did not really turn downward, but only illumined the Darkness, and from this an "image" (*eidolon*) originated in Matter. Then they feign a further "image of the image" forming somewhere down here through Matter or Materiality . . . and let thus be generated him whom they call Demiurge and make him secede from his Mother, and from him they go on to derive the world down to the last of the "images" [16]

(Enn. II. 9. 10)

The main difference, and indeed a crucial one, between the Gnostics and Plotinus on this point is that the former deplore the "descent" by image-reflection as the cause of divine tragedy and passion, while Plotinus affirms it as the necessary and positive self-expression of the efficacy of the first source. But the vertical structure of this scale of unfolding, that is, the *downward* direction of all metaphysical generation which therefore cannot be but deterioration, is common to both.

Now, this appearing of the Light from on high in a reflection from down below could also be used as an explanation of divine error. The whole tragedy of the Pistis Sophia, all her wanderings, distress, and repentance in the world of darkness, followed from the one initial fact that she mistook the light she saw below for the "Light of Lights" for which she yearned, and went after it into the depths. We have furthermore, especially in Mani's speculation, the frequent use of a divine likeness as a bait used either by the archons to lure and entrap divine substance or by the messengers of the deity to extract captured light-substance from the hold of the archons. We now see that the Narcissus motif in the love-error of the Anthropos in the *Poimandres* is a subtle variation and combination of several of the enumerated themes. He is not as guilty as that primordial Soul which succumbs to a desire for the pleasures of the body, for it is the beauty of his own divine form, itself the perfect likeness of the highest God, that draws him downward. He is more guilty than the simply deceived Pistis Sophia, for he wished to act independently and could not mistake the reflection down below for the light of the Father from whom he had purposely departed. Yet he is half excused by his error, in that he was ignorant of the true

[16] Cf. the Mandaean passage "Abathur (one of the Uthras plotting the creation of a world) goes into that world [of darkness]. . . . He sees his face in the black water, and his likeness and son is formed unto him out of the black water." This son is Ptahil-Uthra, the actual demiurge of this world (G 173). This example from an area so far removed from the intellectual environment in which Plotinus met *his* Gnostics shows how persistently the act of mirroring is conceived in gnostic literature as the production of an *alter ego,* and at the same time how closely this is connected with cosmogony.

nature of the lower elements, clothed as they were in his own reflection. Thus the projection of his form upon earth and water has lost the character of a substantial event in itself, and in the hands of this Hellenistic author has become a means of motivating rather than constituting the submersion of a divine emanation in the lower world.

The Ascent of the Soul

We come now to the ascent of the knower's soul after death, the main prospect held out to the true Gnostic or pneumatic, in the anticipation of which he conducts his life. After what we have heard about the current doctrines connected with the astral descent of the soul, the description of the ascent in the *Poimandres* requires no further explanation: it is the reversal of the former. But some parallels and variations from other schools of gnostic speculation may emphasize the wide currency and great importance of this theme throughout the whole range of gnostic religion. The celestial journey of the returning soul is indeed one of the most constant common features in otherwise widely divergent systems, and its significance for the gnostic mind is enhanced by the fact that it represents a belief not only essential in gnostic theory and expectation, and expressive of the conception of man's relation to the world, but of immediate *practical* importance to the gnostic believer, since the meaning of *gnosis* is to prepare for this final event, and all its ethical, ritual, and technical instruction is meant to secure its successful completion. Historically there is an even more far-reaching aspect to the ascent doctrines than their literal meaning. In a later stage of "gnostic" development (though no longer passing under the name of Gnosticism) the external topology of the ascent through the spheres, with the successive divesting of the soul of its worldly envelopments and the regaining of its original acosmic nature, could be "internalized" and find its analogue in a psychological technique of inner transformations by which the self, *while still in the body,* might attain the Absolute as an immanent, if temporary, condition: an ascending scale of mental states replaces the stations of the mythical itinerary: the dynamics of progressive spiritual self-transformation, the spatial thrust through the heavenly spheres. Thus could transcendence itself be turned into immanence, the whole process become spiritualized and put within the power and the orbit of the subject. With this transposition of a mythological scheme into the inwardness of the person, with the translation of its objective stages into subjective phases of self-performable experience whose culmination has the form of ecstasis, gnostic myth has passed into mysticism (Neoplatonic and monastic), and in this new medium it lives on long after the disappearance of the original mythological beliefs.

In the *Poimandres* the ascent is described as a series of progressive subtractions which leaves the "naked" true self, an instance of Primal Man as he was before his cosmic fall, free to enter the divine realm and to become one again with God. We have encountered before an alternative version of the ascent, where not the stripping of the soul but its passage as such is the point of the journey. This version implies that what begins the ascent is already the pure pneuma disengaged from its earthly encumbrances, and furthermore that the rulers of the spheres are hostile powers trying to bar its passage with the aim of detaining it in the world. For both versions there is ample evidence in gnostic writings. Wherever we hear of the doffing of garments, the slipping of knots, the loosing of bonds in the course of the upward journey, we have analogies to the *Poimandres* passage. The sum of these knots, etc., is called "psyche": thus it is the soul that is put off by the pneuma (e.g., Iren. I. 7. 1; 21. 5). In this way the ascent is not only topological but also a qualitative process, that of putting off the worldly nature. It is noteworthy that in certain cults this ultimate process was anticipated by ritual enactments which in the way of sacraments were to effect the transformation provisionally or symbolically already in this life and guarantee its definitive consummation in the next. Thus the mysteries of Mithras had for their initiates the ceremonial of passing through seven gates arranged on ascending steps representing the seven planets (the so-called *klimax heptapylos,* Origen *Contra Celsum* VI. 22); in those of Isis we find a successive putting on and off of seven (or twelve) garments or animal disguises. The result achieved by the whole protracted and sometimes harrowing ritual was called rebirth (*palingenesia*): the initiate himself was supposed to have been reborn as the god. The terminology of "rebirth," "reformation" (metamorphosis), "transfiguration" was coined in the context of these rituals as part of the language of the mystery cults. The meanings and applications that could be given to these metaphors were wide enough to make them fit into various theological systems, their prima-facie appeal being "religious" in general rather than dogmatically specific. But though by neither origin nor validity bound to the gnostic frame of reference, they were eminently suited to gnostic purposes. In the context of the mystery cult, or in private and spiritualized substitutions for it inspired by its general model, the "celestial journey" might become an actual visionary experience attainable in the brief ecstatic state. The so-called Mithras Liturgy[17] gives a circumstantial description of such an experience, preceded by instructions on how to prepare for and induce the visionary state. (The theological system in this case is cosmic-pantheistic, not dualistic, the aim immortality by union with the cosmic principle, not liberation from the cosmic yoke.) The more specifically gnostic conception of the journey as a gradually subtractive ascent through the spheres had a long mystical and literary afterlife. A thousand years after the *Poimandres,* Omar Khayyám sings

> Up from earth's center through the seventh gate
> I rose, and on the throne of Saturn sate,
> And many a knot unravel'd by the road;
> But not the master-knot of human fate.
>
> There was the door to which I found no key;
> There was the veil through which I might not see:
> Some little talk awhile of Me and Thee
> There was—and then no more of Thee and Me.
>   (Rubā'īs 31-32 in Fitzgerald's translation)

The other version of the ascent, less spiritualized, has a more sinister aspect. It is with anxiety and dread that the soul anticipates its future encounter with the terrible Archons of this world bent on preventing its escape. In this case the gnosis has two tasks: on the one hand to confer a magical quality upon the soul by which it becomes impregnable and possibly even invisible to the watchful Archons (sacraments performed in this life may secure this end);

[17] Misleadingly so called since it is a literary product, not an actual cult document.

on the other hand by way of instruction to put man in possession
of the names and the potent formulas by which the passage can be
forced, and this "knowledge" is one meaning of the term "gnosis."
The secret names of the Archons have to be known, for this is an
indispensable means of overcoming them—the pagan author Celsus
who writes about these beliefs ridicules those who "have wretchedly
learned by heart the names of the doorkeepers" (Origen *Contra
Celsum* VII. 60). While this part of the "gnosis" is crude magic,
the formulas by which the Archons are to be addressed reveal significant aspects of the gnostic theology. We quoted one of them
before (p. 135) and add here a few more examples. Epiphanius
read in a gnostic Gospel of Philip:

> The Lord revealed to me what the soul must say when ascending
> into heaven, and how she must answer each of the upper powers: "I
> have come to know myself, and I have collected myself from every-
> where, and I have not sown children to the Archon but have uprooted
> his roots and have collected the dispersed members, and I know thee
> who thou art: for I am of those from above." And thus she is released.
> (Ephiph. *Haer*. 26. 13)

Origen in his precious account of the Ophites renders their complete
list of the answers to be given "at the eternally chained gates of the
Archons," of which we translate the following two. To Ialdabaoth,
"first and seventh":

> . . . I, being a word of the unmixed Nous, a perfect work to Son
> and Father, bearing a symbol imprinted with the character of Life—I
> open the world-gate which thou hast locked with thine aeon, and pass
> by thy power free again. May grace be with me, yea, Father, be it with
> me.

To Sabaoth:

> Archon of the fifth power, ruler Sabaoth, advocate of the law of
> thy creation, now undone by grace that is more powerful than thy
> fivefold power, behold the symbol impregnable to thine art[18] and let
> me pass by.
> (Origen *Contra Celsum* VI. 31)

[18] Tentative translation; alternatively: "impregnable symbol of thine art" (?).

It is obvious that these formulas have the force of passwords. What then is the interest of the Archons in opposing the exodus of the soul from the world? The gnostic answer is thus recounted by Epiphanius:

They say that the soul is the food of the Archons and Powers without which they cannot live, because she is of the dew from above and gives them strength. When she has become imbued with knowledge . . . she ascends to heaven and gives a defence before each power and thus mounts beyond them to the upper Mother and Father of the All whence she came down into this world.

(Epiph. *Haer.* 40. 2)

The First Beginnings

In the *Poimandres* we hear nothing about the Governors' being evil, though to be subject to their government, called Destiny, is clearly regarded as a misfortune of Man and a violation of his original sovereignty. This raises the question of the theological quality of the creation, and thus we come finally to the puzzling first part of the vision, dealing with the opening phases of cosmogony. The whole part of the revelation preceding the begetting of Man (4-11) shows the following subdivisions: direct vision of the first phase of cosmogony, preceding actual creation (4-5); explanation of its content by Poimandres (6); resumption and completion of the vision, revealing the intelligible world in God after which the sensible was fashioned (7). From here on the vision turns into audition, that is, the history of actual creation is verbally expounded by Poimandres to the now illumined understanding of the hearer. Paragraph 8 deals with the origin of the elements of nature: the relation of this instruction to the first visionary phase (4-5) presents the riddle with which we have now mainly to deal. Paragraphs 9-11 relate the begetting of the Demiurge by the first God, his fashioning the seven planetary powers and their spheres, the setting in motion of this system, and, in consequence of its revolution, the production of the irrational animals out of the lower elements of nature. Of the events following the appearance of the Demiurge in the theological scheme, only the leaping up of the Word from Nature into the uppermost sphere requires an explanation. For the rest, we are concerned with the pre-demiurgical phases only.

First we fix our attention upon the visual contents of the opening revelation, which makes the spectator an eyewitness of the first beginnings. The divine Light and the appalling serpent-like Darkness as first principles are now familiar to the reader of this book. Two features, however, must be noted in the presentation before us. The first is that the field of vision is to begin with made up of light alone, and that only "after a while" does there appear in one part of it a darkness which is borne downward: which leaves only the conclusion that this darkness is not an original principle coeval with the light but has somehow originated out of it. The other feature is the cryptic remark that a mournful or lamenting cry rises up from the agitated darkness. We shall presently take up the questions posed by both these statements.

As the first separate hypostasis of the supreme Nous, the *Word* issues from the divine Light and "comes over" the humid nature: from what happens later, this "coming over" has to be understood as an intimate union with the humid nature, in which the Word is kept until again disengaged by the work of the Demiurge. For the moment, the effect of the Word's presence in the dark nature is the latter's separating into lighter and heavier elements (incompletely with regard to earth and water, which are separated only later, in the demiurgical phase): this differentiating action upon chaotic matter is the chief cosmogonic function of the Logos (Word), but to maintain this differentiation pending its final consolidation by the work of the Artificer (Demiurge), the Logos has to stay *within* the nature thus parted. The Logos is here clearly in the Greek sense the principle of order, but at the same time a divine entity and as such substantially involved in what he affects.

In paragraph 7 the visionary, having been enjoined to look attentively at the light, discerns therein innumerable powers and discovers that it on its part is not a uniform expanse but is organized into a cosmos, which Poimandres tells him is the archetypal form; at the same time he sees the fire "contained by a mighty power," and this power can only be the Logos keeping the separated elements in their place from inside,[19] the fire being the outer circum-

[19] In spite of the term "encompass," suggesting an action from without.

ference constituted by its having leapt upward from the humid nature. According to this explanation, the beginning of the second vision presents not a new phase of the cosmogonic process but a recapitulation of the result of the first on a higher level of understanding; and this, if a correct hypothesis, is of decisive importance for the interpretation of the next, on any hypothesis mystifying, paragraph (8).

Just as in paragraph 7 the visionary learns something more about the light which he has seen before, so in this paragraph he asks for and receives instruction about something which had already formed the *visual* subject of the first vision: the origin of the elements of nature. To the question he asks, Wherefrom have they arisen? we expect the answer, From the humid nature by the separating action of the Word; and the humid nature, if the question is pushed farther, came from the odious darkness by the latter's changing into it; and then the remaining question would be, Whence came that, if it was not there from the beginning? which according to the first vision it was not: and this would be precisely the question of questions which all non-Iranian gnostic dualism must finally face and whose answer forms the main content of the ingenious speculations of the Valentinian type. Their common principle is that a break or darkening within the divinity must somehow account for the existing division of reality. Now, it is my tentative contention, seeing that all other explanations leave us even worse off, that the *Boulé* (Will) of God, introduced in this paragraph and dropped as suddenly, never to be mentioned again, is an alternative to the Stygian Darkness of the first vision, and as such an isolated rudiment of the Syrian type of speculation which has somehow found its way into this account. The main support of my argument is the role of the Logos in both instances. As the humid nature, after the Logos has "come over her," separates into the elements, so the female Will of God, having "received" into herself the Logos, organizes herself "according to her own elements." The additional feature in the latter case is that the Boulé orders herself "in imitation" of the archetypal order perceived by her through the Logos; that is, the Boulé is more of an independent agent than is the humid nature of the first vision. Also, beside the "elements" which were the subject of the question, a *psychical* "progeny" of the Boulé is mentioned, which supposedly is among her contributions to the future creation. Both traits give her a noticeable kinship with the Sophia figure of the Syrian gnosis. In other words, we would have in the Boulé a version of that problematical divine personage, capable of every degradation, which we first met in the Ennoia of Simon Magus.[20]

A crucial point in the proposed analogy of the Boulé to the "humid nature" is the meaning of the expression: she "received" the Logos. Fortunately this same expression recurs in the union of Nature with Man, where it not only carries a perfectly evident sexual meaning but also is elaborated into the description of how in this union Nature absorbs in his entirety him whom she thus "receives" (14). If this is what happened also to the Logos "received" by the Boulé, then he like the Anthropos after him is in need of a liberation from this immersion. And indeed we find that the first effect of the spheric organization of the macrocosmos by the Demiurge is the Logos' leaping upward from the lower Nature to the kindred spirit in the highest sphere. Now, this result of the Demiurge's work agrees perfectly with a doctrine most prominently represented in Manichaeism but also found elsewhere in Gnosticism, that the cosmic organization was undertaken with the *purpose* of extricating a divine principle fallen into the hold of the lower realm in the pre-cosmic stage. I cannot help feeling that all this puts the female "Will of God" into an interchangeable position with the "humid nature": it is into the former that the Logos had been "received" in the meaning of that term vouchsafed for our treatise; it is from the latter that he leaps upward to his true kin with the construction of the universe—which construction then was in the nature of a primordial "salvation."

The author of the *Poimandres* has permitted no more than traces of this doctrine to enter his composition. The liberation of

[20] The equation of the Boulé with the Sophia (via Isis) was first proposed by Reitzenstein (*Poimandres,* p. 45 f.), though with a "monistic" interpretation and therefore with conclusions different from ours. Festugière's arguments against it (*La Révélation d'Hermès Trismégiste,* IV, pp. 42 ff.) have not convinced me, especially since his alternative—the derivation from Pythagorean speculations on the issue of the (dark and female) dyad from the male-female monad—is not necessarily alternative but, in the give-and-take of syncretism, perfectly compatible with the Sophia hypothesis. I do agree with Festugière that there is no need to bring in Isis.

the Logos through the creation of the Demiurge is, on the terms of the *Poimandres* itself, perfectly explainable as a consequence of the fact that with the definite and stabilizing cosmic organization his presence in the lower Nature is no longer required for the purpose of keeping the elements apart, so that he might be said to be released from a task rather than from bonds. There still remains the fact that his communion with the Boulé terminologically parallels that of Man with Nature and that even an "offspring" of this union is mentioned: the "souls" as a product of the Boulé—a striking resemblance to what the Valentinians told of their Sophia (see p. 189). If we then look back to the two entities which we claim to be alternative versions of the same metaphysical principle, God's Boulé and the first Darkness, we observe of course the objection that some of the latter's attributes, such as frightfulness, hatefulness, and its resemblance to a serpent, fit only an original, anti-divine Darkness of the Iranian type and not a divine Sophia however obscured and estranged from its source. But it is equally noteworthy that this Darkness appears *after* the Light and must have arisen *out* of it (contrary to the Iranian type), and further that it "laments": both traits point more in the direction of the Sophia speculation than in that of a primary dualism. We have thus in the body of the *Poimandres,* more by way of an isolated interjection than as an autonomous theme of the composition, a faint reflex of that type of speculation to whose foremost representative we now turn.

Chapter 8. The Valentinian Speculation

(a) THE SPECULATIVE PRINCIPLE
OF VALENTINIANISM

Valentinus and his school represent the culmination of what for want of a better name we have been calling in this study the Syrian-Egyptian type of gnostic speculation. The distinguishing principle of the type is the attempt to place the origin of darkness, and thereby of the dualistic rift of being, *within* the godhead itself, and thus to develop the divine tragedy, the necessity of salvation arising from it, and the dynamics of this salvation itself, as wholly a sequence of inner-divine events. Radically understood, this principle involves the task of deriving not only such spiritual facts as passion, ignorance, and evil but the very nature of *matter* in its contrariety to the spirit from the prime spiritual source: its very existence is to be accounted for in terms of the divine history itself. And this means, in *mental* terms; and in view of the nature of the end-product more particularly, in terms of divine error and failure. In this way, matter would appear to be a function rather than a substance on its own, a state or "affection" of the absolute being, and the solidified external expression of that state: its stable externality is in truth nothing but the residual by-product of a deteriorating movement of *inwardness,* representing and as it were fixating the lowest reach of its defection from itself.

Now the religious significance, apart from the theoretical interest, of a successful discharge of this speculative task lies in this, that in such a system "knowledge," together with its privative, "ignorance," is raised to an *ontological* position of the first order: both are principles of objective and total existence, not merely of subjective and private experience. Their role is constitutive for reality as a whole. Instead of being, as generally in gnostic thought, a *result* of divine immersion in the lower world, "ignorance" here is rather the first cause of there being such a lower world at all, its begetting principle as well as its abiding *substance:* however numerous the intermediate stages through which matter, this seeming ultimate, is connected with the one supreme source, in its essence it is shown

174

to be the obscured and self-estranged form of that to which it appears to be the opposite—*just as ignorance,* its underlying principle, *is the obscured mode of its opposite, knowledge.* For knowledge is the original condition of the Absolute, the primary fact, and ignorance not simply the neutral absence of it in a subject unrelated to knowledge but a disturbance befalling a part of the Absolute, arising out of its own motivations and resulting in the negative condition still related to the original one of knowledge in that it represents the loss or perversion of it. It is thus a derivative state, therefore revocable, and so is its external manifestation or hypostatized product: materiality.

But if this is the ontological function of "ignorance," then "knowledge" too assumes an ontological status far exceeding any merely moral and psychological importance granted to it; and the redemptional claim made on its behalf in all gnostic religion receives here a metaphysical grounding in the doctrine of total existence which makes it convincingly the sole and sufficient vehicle of salvation, and this salvation itself in each soul a *cosmic event.* For if not only the spiritual condition of the human person but also the very existence of the universe is constituted by the results of ignorance and as a substantialization of ignorance, then every individual illumination by "knowledge" helps to cancel out again the total system sustained by that principle; and, as such knowing finally transposes the individual self to the divine realm, it also plays its part in reintegrating the impaired godhead itself.

Thus this type of solution of the theoretical problem of first beginnings and of the causes of dualism would if successful establish the absolute position of *gnosis* in the soteriological scheme: from being a qualifying condition for salvation, still requiring the co-operation of sacraments and of divine grace, from being a means among means, it becomes the adequate form of salvation itself. An original aspiration of all gnostic thought comes here to fruition. That knowledge affects not only the knower but the known itself; that by every "private" act of knowledge the objective ground of being is moved and modified; that subject and object are the same in essence (though not on the same scale)—these are tenets of a mystical conception of "knowledge" which yet can have a rational basis in the proper metaphysical premises. With the proud sense that their system did in fact represent the solution of the speculative task so understood and did provide the theoretical basis for the mystical sufficiency of "gnosis alone," the Valentinians could say, rejecting all mystery-ritual and sacraments:

One must not perform the mystery of the ineffable and invisible power through visible and corruptible things of creation, nor that of the unthinkable and immaterial beings through sensible and corporeal things. *Perfect salvation* is the *cognition* itself of the ineffable greatness: for since through "Ignorance" came about "Defect" and "Passion,"[1] the whole system springing from the Ignorance is dissolved by knowledge. Therefore knowledge is salvation of the inner man; and it is not corporeal, for the body is corruptible; nor is it psychical, for even the soul is a product of the defect and is as a lodging to the spirit: spiritual therefore must also be [the form of] salvation. Through knowledge, then, is saved the inner, spiritual man; so that to *us suffices* the *knowledge of universal being:* this is the true salvation.

(Iren. I. 21. 4)

This is the grand "pneumatic equation" of Valentinian thought: the human-individual event of pneumatic *knowledge* is the inverse equivalent of the pre-cosmic universal event of divine *ignorance,* and in its redeeming effect of the same ontological order. The actualization of knowledge in the person is at the same time an act in the general ground of being.

We have anticipated the result of Valentinian speculation and must now present the system itself as the argument supporting this result. We have met before in gnostic thought two different symbolic figures to represent in their fate the divine fall, the male Primal Man and the female Thought of God. In the typical systems of the Syrian-Egyptian Gnosis, it is the latter who personifies the fallible aspect of God, usually under the name of "Sophia," i.e., "Wisdom," a paradoxical name in view of the history of folly of which she is made the protagonist. A divine hypostasis already in post-biblical Jewish speculation, the "Wisdom" (*chokmah*) was there conceived as God's helper or agent in the creation of the world, similar to the alternative hypostasis of the "Word." How this figure, or at least its name, came to be combined in gnostic thought with the moon-, mother-, and love-goddess of Near Eastern

[1] All three nouns of this clause refer to the cosmogonic myth.

religion, to form that ambiguous figure encompassing the whole scale from the highest to the lowest, from the most spiritual to the utterly sensual (as expressed in the very combination "Sophia-Prunikos," "Wisdom the Whore"), we do not know and, lacking evidence of any intermediate stages, cannot even hypothetically reconstruct. As early as Simon the figure is fully developed in its gnostic sense. But the psychological elaboration of her destiny is there still rudimentary, the causation of her fall more in the nature of a mishap brought upon her by her offspring than in the nature of an inner motivation. In other systems leading over to the Valentinian form the tale of the Sophia is made the subject of more and more extensive elaboration, with her own psychological share in it becoming increasingly prominent.

The closest approximation to the Valentinian form is represented by the Barbeliotes described by Irenaeus (I. 29) and recently become more fully known through the *Apocryphon of John*. They, like the Ophites (*ibid.* 30), found it necessary, in view of the wide span of conditions to be represented by the female aspect of God, to differentiate this aspect into an upper and a lower Sophia, the latter being the fallen shape of the former and the bearer of all the divine distress and indignities following from the fall. In both systems the differentiation is expressed by separate names: the original female aspect of God is called by the Barbeliotes "Barbelo" (possibly "Virgin") and "Ennoia," by the Ophites "Holy Spirit" (this to the Barbeliotes is one of the names of the fallen form); the name "Sophia" is by both reserved for her unfortunate emanation, also called "Prunikos" and "The Left." This doubling of the Sophia is most fully worked out in the Valentinian system. The particular proximity of the Barbeliotes to the Valentinians consists in their having a developed doctrine of the Pleroma[2] and using the concept of emanation in pairs for its progressive production out of the divine unity of which its members are by their abstract names shown to be the different aspects.[3]

It is with the same formal means, but on a higher level of

---

[2] "Fullness," i.e., the spiritual world of "Aeons" around the godhead, expressing his inner abundance in particularized aspects through personal figures.

[3] See Appendix II to this chapter for the barbelo-gnostic doctrine as now known through the Apocryphon of John.

theoretical discipline and spiritual differentiation, that Valentinus and his followers undertook the treatment of the same speculative theme. Our analytical remarks at the beginning of this chapter have indicated the twofold task which the Valentinian speculation took upon itself: on the one hand to show the self-motivation of divine degradation without the intervention or even passive participation of an external agency, and on the other hand to explain matter itself as a spiritual condition of the universal subject. We do not claim that these two themes were the only theoretical concerns of the Valentinians (or even that to them the intellectual side in general, rather than the imaginative one, constituted the *religious* significance of their teaching); but the treatment of those particular themes is certainly the most original part of their thought, constituting that contribution to general gnostic doctrine which justifies our seeing in them the most complete representatives of a whole type.

Valentinus, the founder of the school, was born in Egypt and educated in Alexandria; he taught in Rome between about 135 and 160 A.D. He is the only one of the Gnostics who had a whole series of disciples known by name, of whom the most important ones were Ptolemaeus and Marcus. These were themselves heads of schools and teachers of their own versions of the Valentinian doctrine. The speculative principle of Valentinianism actually invited independent development of the basic ideas by its adherents; and in fact we know the doctrine better in the several versions and elaborations of the second generation than in the authentic teaching of Valentinus himself, of which very little has been preserved in the accounts of the Fathers.[4] How untrammeled and fertile the speculation of the school was, how great the wealth of its doctrinal differentiation, can be seen from the fact that of the development of the Pleroma alone we have in Irenaeus, Hippolytus, Epiphanius, and the Excerpts from Theodotus no fewer than seven versions (not counting that of Marcus), which in part diverge considerably and reveal great independence of individual thought. We hear of theoretical controversies about certain points on which the school divided into several branches. It is of the Valentinians that Irenaeus remarks,

---

[4] In the newly found *Gospel of Truth* we may possess in Coptic translation an original work of Valentinus himself.

"Every day every one of them invents something new, and none of them is considered perfect unless he is productive in this way" (I. 18. 5). We can well understand this from the very nature of the task posed by Valentinus' type of gnostic theory. It is probable that the fullness of the speculation was reached only in the work of the leading disciples. As regards the branches we mentioned, we hear of an Anatolian branch, mainly known to us through the Excerpts from Theodotus, besides the more fully documented Italic branch to which Ptolemaeus belonged, apparently the most prominent of the system builders. In the following abridged reconstruction we follow on the whole Irenaeus' general account (supplemented from that of Hippolytus) of "the Valentinians," meaning probably in the main Ptolemaeus, and shall only occasionally collate differing versions. Where appropriate, we shall insert quotations from the newly found *Gospel of Truth*[5] which in their succinctness lend new and sometimes poetic color to the doctrinal account. A full interpretation of the often cryptic and always profoundly symbolical material cannot be attempted here, as it would require a volume to itself.[6] We can only hope that the general pointers provided in our introductory remarks and occasional comments in the course of the account itself will help the reader to appreciate the relevant aspects of this ingenious and with all its strangeness fascinating system.

(b) THE SYSTEM

Development of the Pleroma

The mysteries of the first beginnings are introduced with these solemn words: "Indestructible Spirit greets the indestructible ones! To you I make mention of secrets nameless, ineffable, super-celestial, which cannot be comprehended either by the dominions or by the powers or the lower beings, nor by the entire mixture, but have been revealed to the Ennoia of the Immutable alone" (Epiph. *Haer*. 31. 5. 1 f.). And this is the secret doctrine itself.

In invisible and nameless heights there was a perfect Aeon

---

[5] Quoted GT, followed by page and line of the codex.

[6] See F. M. M. Sagnard, *La Gnose Valentinienne* (Paris, 1947), for a more complete synopsis and analysis of the various strands of the tradition.

pre-existent. His name is Fore-Beginning, Fore-Father, and Abyss. No thing can comprehend him. Through immeasurable eternities he remained in profoundest repose. With him was the Ennoia (Thought), also called Grace and Silence.[7] And once this Abyss took thought to project out of himself the beginning of all things, and he sank this project like a seed into the womb of the Silence that was with him, and she conceived and brought forth the Mind (*Nous:* male), who is like and equal to his begetter and alone comprehends the greatness of the Father. He is also called Only-Begotten, Father, and Beginning of all beings. Together with him Truth (*Aletheia:* female) was produced, and this is the first Tetrad: Abyss and Silence, then Mind and Truth.[8]

The Only-Begotten, perceiving with what intention he had been produced, on his part projected with his consort the pair Word (m.) and Life (fem.), respectively father of all things coming after him, and beginning and form-mother of the whole Pleroma. From them came forth Man and Church (*Ecclesia:* female), and

[7] All three names of feminine gender. As to whether the Fore-Father or Abyss was originally alone or was matched from the outset with Silence there was great difference of opinion among the Valentinians (cf. Iren. I. 11. 5, Hippol. VI. 29. 3).

[8] Already this first stage is variously expounded. The above version is one of those related by Irenaeus. Of the several alternatives we note that in Epiphanius: "As in the beginning the Self-Father encompassed within himself the All, which rested unconscious in him . . . the Ennoia within him, who is also called Grace . . . but most truly Silence . . . , once willed to break the eternal bonds, and moved the Greatness to the desire to lie with her. And uniting with him she brought forth the Father of Truth, whom the initiated rightly call 'Man,' because he is the image of the pre-existent Unbegotten. After that, the Silence brought forth Truth as the natural union of Light with Man" (Epiph., *loc. cit.*). The chief difference from the previous version is that here (as in Simon) the initiative to the creative process comes from the Ennoia and not from the Father.

And one more version: the followers of Ptolemaeus say that "the 'Abyss' has two consorts, whom they call also 'states,' namely 'Thought' and 'Will.' For at first he 'thought' to project something, then he 'willed' it. Thus from the mutual intermingling, as it were, of these two states and powers came about the projection, as a pair, of the 'Only-Begotten' and the 'Truth' " (identical in Iren. I. 12. 1, Hippol. VI. 38. 5 f.). These are far from being all the variants. Cf. also the abridged rendering GT 37.7-14: "When they [the Aeons] were still in the depth of His Mind, the Word (*logos*), which was the first to come forth, caused them to appear, joined to the Mind (*nous*) which pronounces the unique Word in Silent Grace, and which was called 'Thought' because they were in it before becoming manifest."

Regarding the term "projection," this is the literal Latin equivalent of the Greek *probolé* which is the constant term used in these texts for that creative activity more commonly translated as "emanating."

this is the original Ogdoad. These Aeons, produced to the glory of the Father, wished to glorify the Father by their own creations, and produced further emanations. From Word and Life issued ten additional Aeons, from Man and Church twelve, so that out of Eight and Ten and Twelve is constituted the Fullness (Pleroma) of thirty Aeons in fifteen pairs. We pass over the details of this generative process after the Ogdoad, and only observe that the names of the further twenty-two Aeons are all abstractions of the type of the first eight, that is, artificial constructions and not proper names from the mythological tradition. The last female Aeon in the chain of emanations is Sophia. "Pleroma" is the standard term for the fully explicated manifold of divine characteristics, whose standard number is thirty, forming a hierarchy and together constituting the divine realm. Mostly the Fore-Father or Abyss is counted in the number, but even this rule admits of exception.[9]

The Crisis in the Pleroma

The Pleroma is not a homogeneous assembly. The Only-Begotten Mind alone, having issued from him directly, can know the Fore-Father: to all the other Aeons he remains invisible and incomprehensible. "It was a great marvel that they were in the Father without knowing Him" (GT 22. 27 f.). So only the Nous enjoyed the contemplation of the Father and delighted in the beholding of his infinite greatness. Now he wished to communicate the Father's greatness also to the other Aeons, but the Silence restrained him by the will of the Father, who wanted to lead them all to pondering on their Fore-Father and to a desire to seek after Him. So the Aeons longed only secretly to behold the begetter of

[9] Thus Hippolytus (VI. 29. 5 ff.) has this version, exceptional also in that it omits the Silence or Ennoia and conceives of the first principle as without female counterpart: "The Father existed alone, unbegotten, without place, without time, without counsellor, and without any other property that could be thought of . . . solitary and reposing alone in himself. But as he had generative power, it pleased him once to generate and produce the most beautiful and perfect that he had in himself, for he did not love solitude. For he was all love, but love is not love if there is no object of love. So the Father, alone as he was, projected and generated 'Mind' and 'Truth' . . . [and so on]." The number of emanations is here first twenty-eight (the Father not being included in the count), and is brought up to thirty only after the crisis by the additional emanation of the pair Christ and Holy Spirit.

their seed and to search for the root without beginning. "Indeed the All [the world of Aeons = the Pleroma] was searching for Him from whom it came forth. But the All was inside of Him, that Incomprehensible, Inconceivable One who is superior to all thought" (GT 17. 4-9). (This is the beginning of a crisis in the Pleroma, since its harmony rests on its natural order, and this on the observation of their inherent limits by its members—which members yet, being spiritual subjects, cannot forgo the aspiration to know more than their limits permit and thus to abolish the distance separating them from the Absolute.) The last and youngest (and therefore outermost) of the Aeons, the Sophia, leapt farthest forward and fell into a passion apart from the embrace of her consort. That passion had originated and spread from the vicinity of the Mind and Truth but now infected the Sophia and broke out in her so that she went out of her mind, pretendedly from love, actually from folly or presumption, since she had no such community with the Father as the Only-Begotten Mind. "Oblivion did not come into existence close to the Father, although it came into existence because of Him" (GT 18. 1-3). The passion was a search for the Father, for she strove to comprehend his greatness. This, however, she failed to achieve, because what she attempted was impossible, and so she found herself in great agony; on account of the depth of the Abyss,[10] into which in her desire she penetrated more and more, she would in the end have been swallowed up by its sweetness and dissolved in the general being, had she not come up against the power that consolidates the All and keeps it off the ineffable Greatness. This power is called Limit (*horos*): by him she was stopped, consolidated, brought back to herself, and convinced that the Father is incomprehensible. Thus she abandoned her previous intention and the passion engendered by it.[11] These, however, now subsist by themselves as a "formless entity."

[10] For the "depth" of the Father as the very cause of the "Error" cf. GT 22. 23 ff.: "they had strayed (from their places) when they received Error because of the depth of Him who encircles all spaces."

[11] This is the first restoration and (incipient) "salvation" in the spiritual history of total being, and it occurs entirely inside the Pleroma, though as we shall see it is the cause of a chain of events outside it. The crisis itself is again differently described in the different versions. The Anatolian school in this case agrees with

Consequences of the Crisis. Function of the Limit

The passion and recovery of the Sophia have an effect reaching outside the Pleroma. The formless entity to which in her striving for the impossible she gave birth is the objectivation of her own passion; and at the sight of it, and reflecting upon her fate, she is moved by varying emotions: grief, fear, bewilderment and shock, repentance. These emotions too become embodied in the formlessness, and their complete series, developed in ever-new variations by the individual thinkers, plays an important ontological role in the system: "From here, from the ignorance, the grief, the fear and the shock, material substance took its first beginning" (Iren. I. 2. 3). "It was this ignorance concerning the Father which produced Anguish and Terror. Anguish became dense like a fog, so that no one could see. Therefore Error became fortified [i.e., assumed subsistence]. It elaborated its own Matter in the Void" (GT 17. 9-16). The actual transition to matter occurs only in the stage represented by the lower Sophia, when we shall deal with it. The first Sophia as we have heard was purified and steadied by the Limit and reunited with her consort, and thus the integrity of the Pleroma was restored. But her Intention, once conceived and having become effective, cannot be just undone: together with the Passion caused by it, it is separated from her and, while she herself remains within the Pleroma, is by the Limit cast outside it. As the natural impulse of an Aeon, this detached complex of mental states is now a hypostatized spiritual substance, but a formless and shapeless one, being an "abortion" brought forth without concep-

the version reproduced here, as the effectively condensed account in the *Exc. Theod.* shows: "The Aeon who wished to grasp what is beyond knowledge fell into ignorance and formlessness. Whence she brought into being the Void-of-knowledge, which is the Shadow of the Name" (31. 3 f.). Very different is the folly of the Sophia in Hippol. VI. 30. 6, here summarized: Rushing up to the depth of the Father, she perceives that whereas all the begotten Aeons generate by copulation, the Father alone generates out of himself (being in this version without consort, see note 9); in this she wants to emulate him and also generate out of herself without spouse, so that she may not fall short of the Father's achievement. She failed to perceive that this is the power solely of the Unbegotten One, and so she managed only to bring forth a formless entity. In this effect—the existence of a formless entity—all versions agree, and it is the important fact for the progress of the narrative, whether the guilty cause of it is presumption to imitate the Absolute, i.e., plain *hybris,* as here, or desire to know Him completely, i.e. trespassing love, as in the more prevalent versions.

tion. Therefore they call this also "strengthless and female fruit."

The Limit has thus a twofold function, a steadying and a separating: in the one he is called Cross, in the other, Limit. Both functions are exercised in two different places: between the Abyss and the rest of the Pleroma, in order to delimit the begotten Aeons from the unbegotten Father—it was in this capacity that he encountered the Sophia in her blind quest; and again, between the Pleroma as a whole and the outside, i.e., the expelled substance of passion, in order to secure the Pleroma against the re-entry of the disturbance from without.[12] In the sequence of the drama, only his role at the outer boundaries is emphasized: "He divides the cosmos from the Pleroma" (*Exc. Theod.* 42. 1). His more spiritual functions, such as restoring the Pleroma to its harmony, subsequently pass over to the Christos, leaving the role of the Limit mainly a preserving one. The meaning of this peculiar figure, which makes its appearance only with the error of the Sophia, not having been originated with the Pleroma itself, is precisely this, that through the aberration of the Sophia a decisive change has occurred in the divine order, which makes such a function necessary: it possesses its integrity no longer simply and unquestionably but only in contrast to a negativity posited without. This negativity is the residue of the disturbance which, *through* the conversion of the Sophia and the *separation* it involved, has become hypostatized as a positive realm by itself.[13] Only at this price could the Pleroma be rid of it. Thus the Limit was not planned in the original constitution of the Fullness, i.e., of the free and adequate self-expression of the godhead, but was necessitated by the crisis as a principle of consolidation and protective separation. The appearance of the figure itself is therefore a symbol of the beginning dualism as it dialectically arises out of original Being itself.

Restoration of the Pleroma

As ignorance and formlessness had appeared within the Pleroma, deep perturbation remained among the Aeons, who no

---

[12] For these two tasks Valentinus himself seems to have assumed two Limits, who were later contracted into one person.

[13] "This, then, was not a humiliation for Him. . . . For they were a Nothing, namely that Anguish and that Oblivion and that formation of Falsehood" (GT 17. 21 f.).

longer felt safe, fearing like happenings to themselves. Also, the continued existence of the product of the corrected ignorance, of the formlessness, though expelled, is in its present condition a constant reproach to the Sophia, who is full of grief about the "abortion" and disturbs the Aeons with her sighs. They therefore unite in prayer to the Father and obtain from him the emanation of a new pair of Aeons, Christos and Holy Spirit, who have this twofold office: within the Pleroma to restore true serenity; and, as a condition thereof, to take care of the residual formlessness and impart form to it. Thus Christos (as the male part representing the pair) is the first and only Aeon who has a role both this side and the other side of the Limit, whereas the Aeon Jesus, emanated still later, is already destined for the external mission entirely.

In this manner the development leads step by step outward under the necessity imposed by the failure which, once having occurred, now maintains reality and requires reparation. First to insure against any of the Aeons' suffering a similar fate, Christos establishes a new harmony in the Pleroma by enlightening the Aeons about the unknowability of the Father, i.e., bringing them the gnosis ("for of what was the All in need if not of the Gnosis of the Father?"—GT 19. 15 f.), and reconciling them to their apportioned ranks, so that the awareness of spiritual unity embracing their differences no longer lets individual aspirations arise. Thus they attain to perfect repose. As the fruit of their new unity, they all together, each contributing the best of his essence, produce an additional (and unpaired) Aeon, Jesus, in whom the Fullness is as it were gathered together and the regained unity of the Aeons symbolized. This "perfect fruit of the Pleroma," who contains all its elements, has later as Savior to carry in his person the Fullness out into the Void in which the residue of the past disturbance, meanwhile "formed" by Christos, still awaits salvation.[14]

Events Outside the Pleroma

At first it is Christos who takes care of the formless residue, for this still belongs to his proper task of restoring the peace of

[14] The report of Hippolytus introduces only at this point the figure of the Limit (Cross), produced "in order that nothing of the defect might come near the Aeons within the Pleroma" (VI. 31. 6).

the Pleroma, seeing that with the sad condition of the "abortion" and the despair of its guilty mother this peace could not last. A simple undoing of what has been done is not feasible: even in error the thought of an Aeon constitutes reality and lives on in its effects. Now, the Intention or Desire of the Sophia, hypostasized in its separation from her, is a new personal being: the lower Sophia or Achamoth.[15] We heard before that this Intention, together with the Passion, had to be "cast out into the spaces of the Shadow and the Void" and that she is now outside the Light and the Fullness, a shapeless and formless abortion. Christ, stretching out over the Cross,[16] imparted from his own power a first fashioning to her, a shaping of substance only, not yet the "informing" of knowledge, after which he withdrew back into the Pleroma within the Limit, leaving her with the awakened awareness of her separation from the Pleroma and the aroused longing for it. This initiates a re-demptional task whose accomplishment requires a long detour of suffering and successive divine interventions. Since Christos was not meant actually to leave the Pleroma, his main task being within it, and since on the other hand the imperfect female hypostasis could be made perfect only through a permanent spiritual pairing, her first formation over the Cross was all that Christos could do for her.[17]

[15] From the Hebrew *chokmah*, i.e., wisdom, the same as "Sophia," but in these speculations denoting her fallen form.

[16] It is highly significant that the first action from the Pleroma outward is in the sign of the Cross, though the latter has here little of the familiar Christian meaning. To understand the situation graphically, it has to be remembered that the Cross at that time was thought of as T-shaped. In its Valentinian symbolization, then, the horizontal bar is the Limit between the upper and the lower world over which Christos stretches himself out to reach the lower Sophia, while the vertical bar divides between the right and the left areas of the lower world, i.e., pneumatics and psychics, or between the "right" and "left" power of the psychical, or between the psychical and material.

[17] Valentinus himself offered a very different picture of the relation Christos-Sophia (from this stage on "Sophia" always means the lower one), and the Ana-tolian branch retained this form of the doctrine. According to it, "Christos did not issue from the Aeons in the Pleroma, but together with a shadow was brought forth according to the idea of the Better by the 'Mother' (Sophia) who had fallen outside the Pleroma. He, however, being male, cut off the shadow from himself and ascended to the Pleroma. The Mother, left behind with the shadow and emptied of the pneumatic element, brought forth another son: the Demiurge, who is also called All-Ruler of what is below" (Iren. I. 11. 1). The *Exc. Theod.* confirm this version as valid for the Anatolian branch (23. 2.; 32. 2; 39).

Sufferings of the Lower Sophia

Having become conscious through the formation imparted by Christos, the deserted Sophia impetuously sets out to seek after the vanished light, but cannot reach it, for the Limit obstructs her forward rush. She cannot penetrate through him, because of her admixture of the original Passion, and forced to remain alone in the outer darkness she falls prey to every kind of suffering that exists. In this she repeats on her own level the scale of emotions which her mother in the Pleroma underwent, the only difference being that these passions now pass over into the form of definitive states of being, and as such they can become the substance of the world. This substance, then, psychical as well as material, is nothing else than a self-estranged and sunken form of the Spirit solidified from acts into habitual conditions and from inner process to outer fact. How central to the Valentinians this point of their speculation was is shown by the mere number of variants in which the scale of emotions was developed and assigned its respective counterparts in terms of "substance." [18] The very fact that the correlation of emotions and elements is not fixed in detail but varies considerably from author to author, and probably even within the thought of one and the same author, illustrates how the subject was again and again pondered on. The account we are mainly using offers at this point the following series of emotions: *grief,* because she could not get hold of the light; *fear,* lest besides the light also life might leave her; *bewilderment,* added to these; and all of them united in the basic quality of *ignorance* (itself counted as an "affection"). And still another state of mind ensued: the *turning* (conversion) toward the Giver of Life. "This, then, became the composition and substance[19] of Matter, of which this world consists; from the turning back, all the Soul of the world and of the Demiurge took its origin; from fear and grief, the rest had its beginning." In numerical terms, which are about the only constant in this part of the speculation, we have five affections in all, four negative or

[18] See Irenaeus' gibe that "every one of them expounds differently in highsounding phrases from which emotions the elements of being took their origin" (4. 3).

[19] Or: This combination (of affections) became also the substance . . .

thoroughly dark ones ("passions" in the narrower sense), one positive or semi-bright. The latter, here called a "turning back," elsewhere (in Hippolytus) also "supplication" and "prayer," is the
origin of everything psychical in the world, which stands in rank
between matter and spirit. The four blind passions are of course
the sources of the traditional four elements of matter. How the
special position of "ignorance" as the common denominator of the
other *three* is rendered in this correlation we shall see later. As
regards these other three, "grief" and "fear" are most constantly
mentioned in the enumerations, "bewilderment" (*aporia*) is sometimes replaced by "consternation" or "shock" (*ekplexis*), and sometimes the triad becomes a tetrad by the addition of "laughter,"
whose physical correlate is the luminous substance in the universe
(e.g., that of the sun and the stars, which is conceived as different
from fire): "Now she wept and grieved because she was left alone
in the Darkness and the Void; now bethinking herself of the
Light which had left her she became cheerful and laughed; now she
again fell into fear, and otherwhiles she was bewildered and
amazed" (Iren. I. 4. 2).

Origination of Matter

After the Mother had thus passed through all the passions
and, barely emerged, had turned around in supplication to the
vanished light of Christos, the Aeons took pity on her, and since
Christos himself would not again leave the Pleroma they sent "the
common fruit" of the Pleroma, Jesus, to be the consort of the outer
Sophia (he being the only one of the Aeons produced without a
spouse) and to cure her of the passions from which she suffered
in her quest for Christos. Accompanying him were the angels
who had been emanated with him as his escort. Stepping outside
the Pleroma, he found the Sophia in the four primary passions:
fear, grief, bewilderment, and supplication, and he cured her of
them by now imparting to her the "informing" of knowledge (her
previous "forming" by Christos having been one of substance
only). Those passions he separated from her, but he did not leave
them to themselves as had been done with those of the upper
Sophia; on the other hand he could not simply annihilate them,
since they had already become "habitual and effective states," in

their own way eternal, and peculiar to the Sophia. Therefore he only detached them from the Sophia, that is, externalized and solidified them into independent substances. Thus, by the Savior's appearance, on the one hand is the Sophia freed of her passions and on the other hand are the things external founded;[20] and thereby the Savior "potentially" brings on (makes possible) the subsequent demiurgical creation. From incorporeal affection and accidence he turned the passions into matter, which was still non-corporeal; but then he imparted to them the capacity and natural tendency to enter into compounds and form bodies, so that two types of substance originated: the bad from the passions, the susceptible from the turning back. And the Achamoth, freed from her affections, joyfully "received" the sight of the lights around the Savior, i.e., of his escorting angels, and from this conception brought forth pneumatic fruit in their image. This is the origin of the pneumatic element in the lower world. (Compiled from Irenaeus, *Exc. Theod.,* and Hippolytus.)

Derivation of the Single Elements

As remarked before, the individual correlation of elements with passions varies greatly in the many versions of this part of the doctrine. Most generally agreed is that from the turning back or supplication resulted the "soul" of the world and of the Demiurge and everything psychical, and from the rest of the passions the material elements: e.g., from the tears the moist substance, from the laughter the luminous, from grief and shock the more solid elements of the cosmos; or, "from shock (terror) and perplexity as the more inarticulate condition, the corporeal elements of the cosmos—namely *earth* according to the stiffening of terror; then *water,* according to the movement of fear; *air,* according to the flight[21] of grief; the *fire,* however, is inherent in all of them as death and corruption, just as ignorance is hidden in the three passions" (Irèn. I. 5, 4).[22]

[20] Here John 1:3 "All things came into being through him [etc.]" is invoked!

[21] Reading πτῆσιν for πῆξιν, "hardening, congealing" (my tentative emendation).

[22] For the correlation of *fire* with "ignorance" and its special position in the "physical" system of the Valentinians, see Appendix I at the end of this chapter. Another rather subtle correlation is the following in Irenaeus: material substance

In sum, three essences originated from the experiences of the Sophia: from her passion, matter; from her turning back, soul; from her receiving the light of the Savior after her purification, the pneuma. This last essence, being the same as her own, she could not subject to any forming on her part. Thus she turned to the shaping of the psychical essence which had issued from her turning back.

Demiurge and Creation of the World

Out of the psychical substance, the lower Sophia shapes the father and king of all things psychical and material, for he created everything that comes after him, though without his knowledge guided by his mother. He is called "father" of the right-hand things, i.e., the psychical, "artificer" (demiurge) of the left-hand things, i.e., the material, and "king" of them all, i.e., of all things outside the Pleroma.

Error elaborated its own Matter in the Void, without knowing Truth. It applied itself to the fashioning of a formation, trying to produce in beauty a substitute of Truth. . . . Not having any root, it remained immersed in a fog with regard to the Father while it was engaged in preparing Works and Oblivions and Terrors in order to attract, with their help, those of the Middle and to imprison them.

(GT 17. 15-35)

He creates seven heavens, which are at the same time angels, above which he resides. Therefore he is also called "Heptad," and the Mother above him, "Ogdoad." In this position he is "the Place of the Middle," [23] beneath the Sophia and above the material world

stems from the three passions fear, grief, and bewilderment; the psychical, from fear and turning back combined; and within the latter combination the element of turning back accounts for the Demiurge, that of fear, for all other psychical substance in beasts and men. Here fear participates in the origination of material *and* psychical substance and thus mediates between the upper and lower extremes of the extra-spiritual scale; it does however not replace "ignorance" as the underlying principle of the whole scale. Very different is the following correlation from Hippolytus: from fear came psychical substance, from grief, physical; from bewilderment, demonic; and from the turning back, the so-called "right power" of the psychical (as opposed to the "left," which issued from fear), namely, ascent and repentance. The Demiurge issues here from the affection of fear, and thus belongs entirely to the "left power" of the soul (VI. 32. 6 f.).

[23] In *Exc. Theod.* also simply "Place" (*topos*), which in the Jewish tradition served as a circumlocution for God.

which he has fashioned. In another respect the Mother, the Ogdoad, is in the middle, namely, above the Demiurge but beneath the Pleroma, outside of which she is kept "until the consummation."

The ontological relation of Sophia and Demiurge is best expressed in the statement "the Sophia is called 'pneuma,' the Demiurge, 'soul'" (Hippol. VI. 34. 1). For the rest, we meet in the Demiurge of the Valentinians all the traits of the world-god with which we have by now become familiar and can therefore deal here very briefly: his *ignorance* first, which the Valentinians stress emphatically and which in the first place relates to things above him. These, including his mother, remain entirely unknown to him; but also concerning his own fashioning beneath himself he "is unthinking and foolish, and knows not what he does and effects" (Hippol. VI. 33)—which permits his mother to slip her own designs into what he believes he does on his own.[24] On his ignorance then is based the second major trait which he shares with the general gnostic conception of the Demiurge: the *conceit* and presumption in which he believes himself to be alone and declares himself to be the unique and highest God. Thus in need of correction, he is finally enlightened by the Sophia and by her instruction brought to the knowledge and acknowledgment of what is above him; however, he keeps to himself the great mystery of the Father and the Aeons into which the Sophia has initiated him[25] and divulges it to none of his prophets—whether at the will of the

[24] Cf. the "Platonizing" description in Iren. I. 5. 3 and *Exc. Theod.* 49. 1: "The Demiurge, his nature given to action, believed that he manufactured these things by himself, unaware that the Achamoth worked through him. He made a heaven without knowing 'the heaven'; he formed a man without knowing about 'the man'; he made appear an earth without knowledge of 'the earth': throughout he was ignorant of the *ideas* of whatever he created and of the Mother herself and believed himself alone to be everything." This, of course, consciously *revises* Plato's picture of the Demiurge, who does know the ideas.

[25] This doctrinal item which has its almost literal parallel in the older *Book of Baruch* of Justin the Gnostic (Hippolyt. V. 26 f.) is quite possibly a foreign intruder in the body of Valentinian teaching. For as consistent as it is with the system of the *Baruch* (where the "Elohim" [= Demiurge] is pneuma), as inconsistent with the main Valentinian doctrine is it that the very principle and representative of everything "psychical," the Demiurge, could be the recipient of the higher gnosis: on the human plane the Valentinians very definitely deny this possibility to the *psychikos;* and generally the only possible organ of "knowledge," the subject to be "formed" by it, is the *pneuma.*

Sophia or his own is not stated, but most probably because the pneumatic message and illumination cannot be properly transmitted through a psychical agent. To communicate the saving gnosis to the pneumatic elements in the creation, the Sophia must therefore resort to an agent of her own, the incarnation of the Aeons Jesus and Christos from the Pleroma in the person of the historical Jesus. His advent is in a paradoxical way prepared for by the prophets, who were those of the Demiurge but through whose mouth the Mother, unknown to him, frequently conveyed her messages, which therefore are embedded in those of the world-god. The prophets are not always treated so tolerantly, and in one place they and the Law are rather rudely called "ignorant fools speaking for a foolish God" (Hippol. VI. 35. 1).

A more moderate and thoughtful attitude toward the Mosaic Law, on the other hand, comes to word in Ptolemy's *Letter to Flora,* written to allay the scruples of an educated Christian Lady. The writer is at pains to make it clear from the outset that the Law of Moses, though certainly not from the perfect Father, is neither from Satan; nor is the world: both are the work of a god of justice. Those who attribute creation and legislation to an evil god are as much in error as those who ascribe the Law to the supreme God: the former err because they do not know the god of justice, the latter, because they do not know the Father of All. From the middle position of the legislator-god follows a middle attitude toward his Law—which however is not identical with the whole body of the pentateuch. The latter contains three elements: ordinances from "God," from Moses, and from the elders. Those from "God" again are threefold: the pure legislation unmixed with evil, which the Savior came not to abolish but to make full, because it was still imperfect (e.g., the decalogue); the legislation tainted with badness and injustice, which the Savior abolished because it was alien to his nature and that of the Father (e.g., "an eye for an eye"); and the legislation symbolic of things pneumatic and other-worldly, which the Savior translated from the literal and sensible to the spiritual meaning (the ritual laws). The "God" who ordained this Law, being neither the perfect Father nor the devil, can only be the Demiurge, the maker of this universe, different in substance from either, holding median rank between them and therefore called the "middle principle." He is inferior to the ungenerated perfect God, superior to the adversary, neither good like the first nor evil and unjust like the second, but properly called "just" and the arbiter of his kind of justice (a kind inferior to that of the Father).

This is the most charitable view taken of the Creator in all the Sophia-gnosis, inside and outside the Valentinian school. The sinister Ialdabaoth of the Barbeliotes, for instance, comes much closer to merging with the figure of the adversary. Yet in the last analysis these are no more than variations of mood [26] in the development of a basic theme, and by and large the traits we have met all along in connection with the gnostic "theology" of the world-god are those of the Valentinian demiurge too.

Generally with the creation of the world the Valentinian speculation merges with the stream of common gnostic ideas, with only minor features peculiar to the school. Two of these, connected with the Demiurge, may be mentioned here. As the Demiurge is a creature of the Mother from the psychical substance, so the Devil, also called "Cosmocrator," is a creature of the Demiurge from the "spiritual substance of wickedness," which in turn originated from the "grief" (elsewhere: from the "perplexity"): and here we have the rather puzzling teaching that Satan (with the demons), being the *spirit* (*pneuma*) of wickedness, *knows* about the things above, whereas the Demiurge, being only psychical, does not (Iren. I. 5. 4). If the reader fails to see how a "spirit" of *wickedness* enjoying the genuine spirit's privilege of knowledge is compatible with the ontological position of pneuma in the system, and a higher gnosis without sanctification of the knower with the salvational conception of gnosis as such, he is in no worse a position than this writer.

Another original feature in the Valentinian account of creation is instructive regarding the much-debated question of the "Platonism" of the Gnostics.[27] The world was created after the image of the invisible world of the Pleroma by a Demiurge carrying out unwittingly his mother's intention. His ignorance, however, was

[26] Or of policy: the *Letter to Flora* is a decidedly exoteric writing.

[27] See above, p. 191, note 24.

not complete, as is shown in the following quotation, which implies on his part at least an inadequate and distorted idea of the higher world:

When the Demiurge further wanted to imitate also the boundless, eternal, infinite and timeless nature of the upper Ogdoad (the original eight Aeons in the Pleroma), but could not express their immutable eternity, being as he was a fruit of defect, he embodied their eternity in times, epochs, and great numbers of years, under the delusion that by the quantity of times he could represent their infinity. Thus truth escaped him and he followed the lie. Therefore his work shall pass away when the times are fulfilled.

(Iren. I. 17. 2)

This of course is a parody of the famous passage in the *Timaeus* (37 *C* ff.) where Plato describes the creation of time as "the moving image of eternity." The vast gulf that divides the spirit of *this* imitation from *its* original will be evident to anyone who takes the trouble to compare the two passages.

Salvation

The speculation about the beginnings, which provides the ontology upon which all the other parts of the Valentinian teaching are based, is the essential aspect of Valentinianism. The Valentinian theory of man and of ethics will appear later in a different context. Regarding the doctrine of salvation, we have given the principal idea in the introduction to this chapter and indicated its connection with the essence of the speculation itself. It will now have become intelligible in the concrete how the Valentinians grounded the metaphysical sufficiency of *gnosis* with respect to salvation in the very nature of universal being, deriving as they did the existence and condition of the lower world, and with it the existence and condition of the composite entity "man," from the *ignorance* of an Aeon and reducing the whole physical system to spiritual categories. The Valentinian speculation itself, understood in its own spirit, recapitulates the journey of the fall, the odyssey of ignorance, in the form of knowledge, and thereby raises the existence which is the victim of the one and the agent of the other out of the depth whose origination it describes. How "perfect salvation" is defined as "the cognition itself of the ineffable greatness" was shown in the passage from Irenaeus quoted on p. 176. We can now supplement this with some lines from the Gospel of Truth whose elliptic rendering of the idea, addressed to the initiates, would by itself hardly be understood in its full speculative implications. "Since Oblivion [the lower world] came into existence because they [the Aeons] did not know the Father, therefore if they attain to a knowledge of the Father, Oblivion becomes at that very instant non-existent. That, then, is the Gospel of Him whom they seek and which [Jesus] revealed to the Perfect" (GT 18. 7-14). We have only left to say something about why there are men to be saved.

We go back to the statement that of the three substances, matter, soul, and spirit, which had come into being, the Sophia could "form" only the first two but not the pneuma, because it was of the same essence as herself. This fruit of hers had therefore to pass into and through the world to be "informed" in its course. The Demiurge is an unwitting instrument in this process. As part and in completion of his own creation he fashions the earthly man and breathes into him the psychical man. The pneumatic element, which the Mother brought forth from the sight of the angels, he did not perceive because it was of the Mother's essence, and so it could be secretly deposited in his creature. Thus through his unknowing agency the spiritual seed was implanted in the human soul and body, to be carried there as if in a womb until it had grown sufficiently to receive the Logos. The pneuma sojourns in the world in order to be pre-formed there for the final "information" through the gnosis. This was the secret aim which the Mother had in mind with the demiurgical creation. The gnosis itself is finally brought down to a sufficiently readied mankind by Jesus unified with Christos, descending upon the human Jesus at his baptism in the Jordan and departing from him before his passion so that Death was deceived. The suffering of the mortal Jesus had no other significance than that of a stratagem.[28] The real

[28] This statement has to be qualified as far as the Gospel of Truth is concerned. Here, where possibly Valentinus speaks himself, we encounter genuinely Christian tones in the passage on Jesus' suffering: "For this reason, Jesus, the merciful and faithful, patiently accepted the endurance of suffering until such time as he should have taken possession of that Book, since he knew that his death meant life for many. . . . He was nailed to a wood, and he attached the deed of disposition of

"passion" was the pre-cosmic one of the upper and lower Sophia, and it was what made salvation necessary, not what brought salvation. Nor was there ever an "original sin" of man, a guilt of the human soul: there was, instead, the time-preceding guilt of an Aeon, a divine upheaval, whose reparation in its course required the creation of the world and that of man. Thus the world, unbeknown to its immediate author, is for the sake of salvation, not salvation for the sake of what happened within creation and to creation. And the real object of salvation is the godhead itself, its theme the divine integrity.

The spirits transformed by knowledge rest in the middle region of the Ogdoad, where their Mother the Sophia clothed with them awaits the consummation of the world. Her own final salvation takes place when all the pneumatic elements in the world have been "formed" by knowledge and perfected. Then the spirits, stripped of their souls, with their Mother enter the Pleroma, which becomes the bridal chamber in which takes place the marriage of Sophia with Jesus and that of the spirits with their bridegrooms, the angels around Jesus. With this, the Fullness is restored in its integrity, the original breach finally repaired, the pre-temporal loss retrieved; and matter and soul, the expression of the fall, with their organized system, the world, cease to exist. Once more, and in conclusion, we let the Gospel of Truth speak.

The Father . . . reveals that of Himself which was hidden (that of Himself which was hidden was His Son) so that, through the compassions of the Father, the Aeons may know Him and cease their strivings in search of the Father, reposing in Him, knowing that repose consists in this: having filled Deficiency, He abolished Shape. Its Shape is the Cosmos, to which he (the Son?) had been subjected,

---

the Father to the cross. Oh! great, sublime teaching. He abases himself even unto death though clothed with immortal life" (GT 20:10-30). The sentiment of these lines cannot be undone by the later, more docetic statement "He came *in a similitude* of flesh, although nothing could obstruct its course, because it was incorruptible and uncoerceable" (31.4 ff.). About the theological meaning of Christ's suffering we hear only that it was due to the anger of "Error," and have the feeling that this does not quite exhaust the religious significance resounding in the quoted passage, whatever this significance may be (and certainly nothing remotely Pauline is hinted at). But even with this new evidence it remains true that in the total theology of the Valentinians the suffering of the Sophia, not that of Christ, is the central fact, doctrinally and emotionally.

For the place in which there is envy and dissension, is Deficiency, but the place which is Unity, is Plenitude. Since Deficiency came into existence because they did not know the Father, so when they know the Father, Deficiency, at that same instant, disappears. As a person's ignorance, at the moment when he comes to know, disappears of its own accord; as darkness dissolves at the appearance of light; so also Deficiency is dissolved in the fact of Plenitude. Therefore, from that moment on, Shape is no longer apparent, but disappears in fusion with Unity—for now their works have' become equal one to the other—at the moment when Unity perfected the spaces.

(GT 24:11-25:10)

Appendix I to Chapter 8

The Position of Fire Among the Elements

We have seen that the elements of matter were derived from the successive emotions through which the Sophia passed in her suffering. The number of these emotions is standardized to either four or three, depending on whether or not "ignorance" is counted in with them. The basic condition of the erring Sophia, prior to its differentiation into a plurality of affections, is ignorance. On the other hand, in enumerations of the complete series of the affections, ignorance sometimes, heading the list and joined by a simple "and" to the rest, seems to be one, though the first, in their co-ordinated number. Yet ignorance is never just one of them, but, as it preceded them in their genesis, it is also explicitly stated to persist as their common *genus* and principle rather than as a separate condition. In fact there are only three affections or passions properly speaking—grief, fear, bewilderment (or shock)—and of them it is said that "they all are *in ignorance*," or that "ignorance is immanent in all three of them." This explains how the healing of the Sophia of her affections can take place through the communication of knowledge, her "forming in knowledge," since this repairs their underlying condition. Now, since the elements of matter were to be correlated one by one to the affections as their originating principles, and the traditional number of elements was four, ignorance was needed as a *particular* principle to make up that number, yet must not lose by this correlation its unique status as *general* principle of them all. This apparent difficulty the Valentinians turned into an eminent occasion for emphasizing the fundamental role of ignorance in their ontological system: to ignorance in the mental realm corresponds in the physical realm the fire, which like its archetype is not so much an element among elements, as a force active in all of them. Thus we quoted on p. 189 the correlation of earth to shock, water to fear, air to grief, ending: "the fire, however, is inherent in all of them as death and corruption, just as ignorance is hidden in the three passions." Not interested in a physical theory for its own sake, the Valentinians elaborated the eminent position of fire among the elements solely for the sake of that spiritual correlation. Such an elaboration of the physical side we find in the *Excerpts from Theodotus* 48.4: "In the three elements there plays and is spread abroad and lies concealed the fire; from them it is kindled and with them it dies, for it has no separate character of its own like the other elements out of which the composite things are fashioned." This of course recalls the position of fire in Heraclitus, which was taken over and developed by the Stoics in their cosmology. In the Stoic version the doctrine was so widely known at the time that the fundamental role of fire in the Valentinian system of nature must be counted among those intentional borrowings which combine with the acceptance of a cosmological scheme its radical revaluation by the anti-cosmic spirit. This is how the Stoics viewed the cosmic position of fire: "This warm and fiery essence is so poured out in all nature that in it inheres the power of procreation and the cause of becoming" (Cicero *Nat. deor.* II. 9. 28); to them it is "rational fire," "the fiery Mind of the universe," the most truly divine element in the cosmos. But what to the Stoics is thus the bearer of cosmic Reason, to the Valentinians is with the *same* omnipresence in all creation the embodiment of Ignorance. Where Heraclitus speaks of "the ever-living fire," they speak of fire as "death and corruption" in all elements. Yet even they would agree that as far as *cosmic* "life" so-called and *demiurgical* "reason" so-called are concerned these are properly symbolized in fire, as indeed in many gnostic systems the Demiurge is expressly called the god of the fire; but since that kind of "life" and of "reason" are in their true nature death and ignorance, the agreement in effect amounts to a subtle caricature of the Heraclitean-Stoic doctrine. We observe here the transition to the conception of fire as the hellish element: as such we shall meet it in the "burning fire of darkness" which the Manichaeans regarded as one of the properties of "Matter."

Appendix II to Chapter 8

The System of the Apocryphon of John

For comparison, we give here a résumé of this chief work of the Barbelo-gnosis recently published from a Coptic papyrus-codex (58 pages). With a cast no less numerous than that of the Valentinian myth, it represents in certain respects the closest parallel to the latter's system, albeit on a more primitive intellectual level in general, and in particular lacking those profundities of conception which constitute the unique originality of Valentinian thought. For this very reason we may regard it as more nearly an expression of the common thought of the Syrian-Egyptian or Sophia-gnosis at large.

The First God

Like all gnostic speculation, the revelation of the Apocryphon (the revelatory stage first having been set) starts with a dissertation on the ultra-transcendent First Principle; and here we meet with the kind of emphatic and pathetic verbosity which the "ineffable" seems to have incited in many of its professors: the over four pages of effusive description devoted to the very indescribability of the divine Absolute—expatiating on the theme of His purity, boundlessness, perfection, etc., being beyond measure, quality, quantity, and time; beyond comprehension, description, name, distinction; beyond life, beatitude, divinity, and even existence—are a typical example of the rising "negative theology," whose spokesmen did not tire for centuries of the self-defeating nature of their task. Justly more reticent, the Valentinians contented themselves on this point with a few telling symbols (as "Abyss," "Silence").

Barbelo and Aeons (Pleroma)

The Spirit-Father is surrounded by the "pure [also: living] water of His light;"[1] and how through His reflection in this the

[1] Similar in Mandaean teachings.

first spontaneous reduplication of divinity comes about, resulting in
the hypostatizing of His Thought, the First Ennoia, has been related before (see quotation on p. 104, note 4). She is also "First
Man" (a name further on applied to the Father Himself), "original
spirit," "male-female," and is called Barbelo. Hence proceeds the
generation of the Pleroma. "The Barbelo asked of Him to give her
a 'First Knowledge'; this He granted: after He had granted it, the
First Knowledge became manifest [came forth into appearance, i.e.
passed from immanence into separate being]," [2] and in a like manner further Aeons—personified abstracts who join in exalting the
Invisible and the Barbelo—are produced until the Pleroma is complete; save the Only-Begotten Son (Christos) who in a more sexual
manner is "borne" by the Ennoia from her having "intently" contemplated the Father. Not found here is the emission of the Aeons
in pairs which as such become the source for further emission (the
Valentinian scheme, by Irenaeus also vouchsafed for the Barbeliotes). But the pair-principle is suddenly mentioned where it is
violated: at the aberration of the Sophia.

Sophia and Ialdabaoth

Herewith the narrative comes to the crucial event of trespass
and crisis from which the lower order originated. "But our (youngest) sister,[3] Sophia, being an Aeon, conceived a Thought out of
herself; and by thinking the Spirit [Father] and the First Knowledge she willed to make the likeness appear out of herself, even
though the Spirit had not consented nor granted it; nor had her
pair-companion consented with her.[4] . . . She found her consort
no more as she proceeded to grant without the Spirit's consent and
without the knowledge of her own consort, swelling out [?] because of the prurience in her. Her thought could not remain latent
[inactive] and her work came forth, imperfect and ugly of aspect,
because she had made it without her pair-companion. And it did
not resemble its Mother, as it was of a different form . . . [*sc.* of
serpent- and lion-shape]. . . . She pushed it away from her, outside
those places so that none of the Immortals might see it, because she

[2] Similar in Mandaean teachings.

[3] "Christ" is the speaker.

[4] We found this explanation of the fault of the Sophia also as a dissenting
version in the Valentinian school, listed by Hippolytus (see above, p. 182, note 11).

had borne it in ignorance. She joined a light-cloud to it lest anyone see it . . . and she called it Ialdabaoth. This is the First Archon. He extracted much power from his Mother. He withdrew from her and turned away from the place where he was born. He took possession of a different place. He created himself an aeon which blazes with shining fire where he dwells even now."

The Archons and Angels

"And he joined himself with the Unreason that was with him, and he called forth the powers that are beneath him . . . [angels, after the numerical pattern of the incorruptible Aeons, multiplied by a none too clear number-play to the total of 360]. . . . They came forth into appearance out of the Archbegetter, the First Archon of the Darkness, out of the Ignorance of him who begot them. . . ." The chief powers are twelve, of which seven are set over the heavens, five over the chaos of the nether world (no more mentioned further on). The names of the seven are, with one exception, names of the Hebrew God or corruptions thereof, and their beast-cognomens (e.g., Eloaios the ass-faced, Iao the serpent-faced, Adoni the ape-faced) show the depth of contempt or revulsion to which the world-rulers have sunk for the Gnostics. They all personify "appetite and wrath."

But the real counterpart of the Old Testament God is their master and begetter Ialdabaoth. We have related before how he secured his mastery over these creatures of his by withholding from them the power he had drawn from his Mother (see quotation on p. 134). The dark picture is somewhat brightened by his joining to each of the seven a better power (some of them apparently copies of corresponding Aeons, as "providence," "understanding," "wisdom"): whether these are in earnest what their names purport, or a mockery of the "real thing," the text does not here allow us to decide; but in view of the later role of the "counterfeit spirit" as the most characteristic life-expression of the archons, the second alternative is more probable.

Repentance, Suffering, and Correction of Sophia

At the boasting of Ialdabaoth, who was ignorant of the existence of anything higher than his Mother, the latter became sorely agitated: the evilness and apostasy of her son, the "imperfect abortion of darkness," made her realize her own guilt and deficiency, incurred through her acting without the consent of her pair-companion. "She repented and wept violently and, moving to and fro in the darkness of ignorance, she was ashamed of herself and dared not return." This is the "suffering of the Sophia" in this system: it comes *after* the facts that arose from her aberration and is thus a mere emotional episode compared to the crucial, literally "substantial" role it plays in the Valentinian system.

In response to her repentant prayer and the intercession of her "brothers" the Aeons, the supreme Spirit let her pair-companion descend to her in order to correct her deficiency; but because of the excessive ignorance that had appeared in her she had to remain in the "Ninehood," i.e., above the cosmic Ogdoad outside the Pleroma, until her restoration was complete. In furtherance of this goal a voice came to her: "The Man exists, and the Son of Man" (the first God and the Only-begotten).

Archontic Creation of Man (*Psychic Adam*)

Now Ialdabaoth heard this voice too, and apparently (lacuna in text) it also produced in the water an image of the perfect Father, the "First Man," in the shape of "a man." [5] This inspired Ialdabaoth (as it does also the King-Archon of Mani) with a creative ambition to which all the seven archons consented. "They saw in the water the appearance of the image and said to each other 'Let us make a man after the image and the appearance of God.'" Thus the puzzling plural form of the famous Bible verse, which has invited many a mystical interpretation in Judaism itself and outside it, is here exploited for the gnostic ascription of man's creation to the archons. The imitation, illicit and blundering, of the divine by the lower powers is a widespread gnostic idea: sometimes a feature already of demiurgical activity as such (Valentinian), it culminates in the creation of natural man—in this connection we shall meet it again at greater detail in Mani's myth.

The tale continues: "Out of themselves and all their powers they created and formed a formation. And each one created from [his] power the *soul:* they created it after the image they had seen,

[5] Cf. the Poimandres myth and the discussion of the mirror-image, pp. 162 ff.

and by way of an imitation of Him who exists from the fore-beginning, the Perfect Man." This is as yet the creation of the *psychical* Adam only: "out of themselves" means out of their substance which is "soul," not matter. Each archon contributes his share to the "soul," which is thus sevenfold, the different parts being related to different parts of the body: a "bone-soul," a "sinew-soul," etc.; and the rest of the 360 angels compose the "body." [6] But a long time the creature remained immobile and the powers could not make it rise.

The Injection of Pneumatic Man

Now, the presumption as well as the bungling of the archons' work played into the hands of the Mother, who wished to recover the power which in her state of ignorance she had passed on to her son, the First Archon. At her entreaty the Light-God sent Christos with his four "Lights" (Aeons), who in the shape of angels of Ialdabaoth (!—the highest God is not considered above this piece of deception) gave the latter the advice, calculated to make him part with the "power of the Mother" in him: "Breathe in his face some of the spirit [*pneuma*] which is in thee, and the thing will arise." He did so, and Adam began to move. Thus pneumatic man came to be inserted into psychic man. We may note here that in general there are two gnostic explanations of the presence of pneuma in created man: one, that it marks a discomfiture of the Light—whether due to its own downward inclination (e.g., Poimandres) or to archontic design (Mani); one, that on the contrary it is a stratagem of the Light in its contest with the archons (as here and in the Valentinian myth). But the latter version must not be supposed to be more "optimistic" than the former, since the stratagem only makes the best of a basic evil, viz., this divine substance having become divorced from the world of Light in the first place.

Move and Counter-Move

With dismay the archons perceived that the creature which bore their powers and souls excelled them in wisdom, and they carried him down to the region at the bottom of all Matter. Again

---

[6] Which at this stage must be considered as immaterial, a form of psychical substance.

the Father intervened, for the sake of the "power from the Mother" now enclosed in the creature, and sent down the Good Spirit, the Thought of Light called by him "Life" (fem.), who hid herself within him, so that the archons would not be aware of her. "It is she who works at the creature, exerts herself on him, sets him in his own perfect temple, enlightens him on the origin of his deficiency, and shows him his [way of] ascent." Adam shone from the light within him and his thought rose above that of his creators.

Man Fettered in a Material Body

These thereupon made a new decision, in concert with all the angels and powers. "They caused a great upheaval [of the elements]. They brought him into the shadow of death. They made again a formation, out of earth [= 'matter'], water [= 'darkness'], fire [= 'desire'], and wind [= 'counterspirit']. . . . This is the fetter, this is the tomb of the body with which man was clothed so that it be [for him] the fetter of Matter." Thus earthly man is complete and is set by Ialdabaoth in paradise. (About this, and the distinction of the two trees, see quotation on p. 92.)

Creation of Eve

Ialdabaoth, to extract from Adam the hidden power which the Darkness pursued but was unable to reach, let insensibility (impotence to know) down upon Adam, and "out of his rib" he embodied the Thought of Light (contained therein?) in a female form. But she took the veil from his senses, and he, "sobering from the intoxication of the Darkness," recognized his essence in her.[7] Through the Epinoia in Eve, Christ taught Adam to eat of the tree of Knowledge, which Ialdabaoth had forbidden him "lest he look upward to his perfection and notice his nakedness concerning it." But the serpent (at a later stage—see below) taught him the lust of procreation which serves the Archon's interest.

The Struggle for Man: Spirit and Counter-Spirit

When Ialdabaoth perceived that Adam and Eve, with the knowledge they had acquired, were turning away from him, he

[7] My rendering is here conjectural, the text being obscure.

cursed them and expelled them from "paradise" into black darkness. Then he became inflamed with lust for the virgin Eve, ravished her and begot with her two sons: Javē the bear-faced, and Eloim the cat-faced, among men called Cain and Abel to this day. Eloim "the just" he set over fire and wind (the upper elements), Javē "the unjust" over water and earth (the nether elements): together they rule over the "tomb" (i.e., the body)—quite a feat of Old Testament exegesis! Furthermore he implanted in Adam the lust of begetting (i.e., the Demiurge is the "serpent"), and Adam begot with Eve Seth, thus starting the chain of procreation. The Mother sent her Spirit down to the generations of man, to awaken the kindred essence in them from the impotence of knowledge and the evil of the "tomb." This continuing activity of the maternal spirit is to prepare them for the coming of the Spirit from the holy Aeons themselves who will bring the perfection.

The archons counter this action with the equally continuous one of their "Counterfeit Spirit," [8] which enters the souls, overgrows, hardens, closes them, weights them down, leads them astray to works of evil, and thus makes them impotent to know. Through it also all carnal procreation is carried on.

Institution of the Heimarmene

One other move of Darkness in the grand struggle must be mentioned: the ordaining of the *heimarmene,* the Archon's diabolic invention. Beholding the success of the Spirit's efforts in the thinking of men, "he wished to get possession (control) of their faculty of thought. . . . He made a decision with his powers: they let Fate come into being, and through measure, periods and times they fettered the gods of the heavens [planets and stars], the angels, the demons, and men, so that all should come under its bond and it [Fate] should be lord over them all: an evil plan, and a perverse one!"

In the long run all this, though impeding and delaying the work of salvation, is in vain. The further incidents we may omit and here close our account.

[8] *Antimimon pneuma,* known also from the *Pistis Sophia* (later): a term apparently of wide currency in one branch of gnosticism.

Chapter 9. *Creation, World History, and Salvation According to Mani*

(a) MANI'S METHOD; HIS VOCATION

In the Valentinian system we learned to know the crowning achievement of the Syrian-Egyptian type of gnostic speculation. Its counterpart for the Iranian type is the system of Mani. Originating a century later, it yet represents, by reason of the type as such, and in spite of its highly wrought elaborateness, in its theoretical substance a more archaic level of gnostic thought. For the simple and straightforward "Zoroastrian" dualism of two co-eternal opposite principles, which Mani takes for a point of departure, obviates that theoretical task of developing dualism itself in a transcendental inner history which called forth all the subtleties of Valentinian speculation. On the other hand, and perhaps for this very reason, Mani's is the only gnostic system which became a broad historical force, and the religion based on it must in spite of its eventual downfall be ranked among the major religions of mankind. Mani indeed, alone among the gnostic system-builders, *intended* to found, not a select group of initiates, but a new universal religion; and so his doctrine, unlike the teaching of all other Gnostics with the exception of Marcion, has nothing esoteric about it. The Valentinians regarded themselves as an elite of the knowing ones, the "pneumatics," divided by the very gulf of knowledge from the mass of the Christians of simple faith; and their pneumatic exegesis of Scripture stressed the difference between the manifest meaning open to the "psychics" and the hidden one accessible to themselves. Mani's work was not to penetrate the secret aspects of a given revelation and to establish a minority of higher initiation within an existing church but to supply a new revelation himself, a new body of Scripture, and lay the foundation for a new church that was meant to supersede any existing one and to be as ecumenical as ever the Catholic Church conceived itself to be. Indeed, Manichaeism was a real and for a time quite serious rival of the Catholic Church in the novel attempt at an organized mass-religion concerned with the salvation of mankind and with systematic missionary activity to promote this end. In brief, it was a church after the incipient Catholic model.

In one respect Mani's "catholicity" went beyond the Christian model: whether for the sake of universal appeal or because of his own many-sided affinities, he made the doctrinal basis of his church as syncretistic as was compatible with the unity of the central gnostic idea. In principle he recognized the genuineness and provisional validity of the great earlier revelations;[1] in practice, in the first attempt of this kind in recorded history, he deliberately fused Buddhist, Zoroastrian, and Christian elements with his own teaching, so that not only could he declare himself to be the fourth and concluding prophet in a historical series and his teaching the epitome and consummation of that of his predecessors,[2] but his mission could in each of the three areas dominated by the respective religious traditions emphasize that aspect of the Manichaean synthesis which was familiar to the mind of the hearers. The success seemed at first to vindicate this eclectic approach. Manichaeism stretched from the Atlantic to the Indian Ocean and deep into central Asia. In the East its missionaries ranged far beyond the areas penetrated by Christianity, and there some branches of the church lasted centuries after its Western branches had been suppressed by the victorious Christian Church.

Yet it must not be supposed because of Mani's syncretistic method that his system itself was a syncretistic one. It was on the contrary the most monumental single embodiment of the gnostic

---

[1] Of his open-mindedness in this respect the Coptic *Kephalaia* give evidence in a beautiful passage. Speaking of his predecessors, or the "Churches chosen" by them, Mani introduces the simile of royal couriers: "The countries and the tongues to which they are sent are different from one another; the one is not like the other. So it is likewise with the glorious Power which sends out of itself all the Apostles: the revelations and the wisdom which it gives them, it gives them in different forms, that is, one is not like the other, for the tongues to which they are sent do not resemble each other" (*Keph.* Ch. 154).

[2] As did Mahomet after him, and the gnostic "Book of Baruch" more vaguely before him—the latter already with a tetrad of historic revelations, though a very different one from that recognized by Mani (Jesus being the only member of the series common to both—Jonas, *Gnosis,* I, p. 285, n. 1). The omission of Moses and the prophets from Mani's list of authentic "Apostles" is, of course, no accident.

208   GNOSTIC SYSTEMS OF THOUGHT

religious principle, for whose doctrinal and mythological representation the elements of older religions were consciously employed. This is not to deny that Mani's thought was actually influenced by the three religions whose founders—Buddha, Zoroaster, Jesus—he recognized as his precursors. If we try to apportion this influence, we might say that that of Iranian religion was strongest on his cosmogony, that of Christian religion on his eschatology, and that of Buddhism on his ethical and ascetic ideal of human life. The heart of Manichaeism, however, was Mani's own speculative version of the gnostic myth of cosmic exile and salvation, and this version showed an amazing vitality: as an abstract principle stripped of most of the mythological detail with which Mani had embroidered it, it again and again reappeared in the sectarian history of mediaeval Christendom, where often "heretical" was identical with "neo-Manichaean." Thus, while in profundity and subtlety of thought certainly inferior to the best creations of the Syrian-Egyptian gnosis, which by their very sophistication addressed themselves to select groups, from the point of view of the history of religions Manichaeism is the most important product of Gnosticism.

Mani was born, probably of Persian parents, about 216 A.D. in Babylonia, then belonging to the Parthian kingdom. His father seems to have been connected with a "baptist" sect, by which we may quite possibly understand the Mandaeans (more probably the closely related Elkesaites or Sabians), as indeed Manichaean hymn-poetry shows the distinct influence of Mandaean models. In his childhood falls the reconstitution of the Persian kingdom under the Sassanids. His main activity as teacher and organizer of a new religion took place under Shapur I (241-272), and he was crucified under his successor Bahram I about 275 A.D. He received his "call" in the reign of Ardashir I, the founder of the Sassanid dynasty, who died in 241. He himself described this event in his life in the following words:

In the years of Ardashir King of Persia I grew up and reached maturity. In that particular year when Ardashir . . . ,[3] the Living Paraclete came down to me and spoke to me. He revealed to me the

[3] The condition of the manuscript does not permit identification of the event in Ardashir's reign referred to as the date of the vocation.

hidden mystery that was hidden from the worlds and the generations: the mystery of the Depth and the Height: he revealed to me the mystery of the Light and the Darkness, the mystery of the conflict and the great war which the Darkness stirred up. He revealed to me how the Light [turned back? overcame?] the Darkness by their intermingling and how [in consequence] was set up this world . . . he enlightened me on the mystery of the forming of Adam the first man. He instructed me on the mystery of the Tree of Knowledge of which Adam ate, by which his eyes were made to see; the mystery of the Apostles who were sent out into the world to select the churches [i.e., to found the religions]. . . . Thus was revealed to me by the Paraclete all that has been and that shall be, and all that the eye sees and the ear hears and the thought thinks. Through him I learned to know every thing, I saw the All through him, and I became *one* body and *one* spirit.

(*Keph.* Ch. 1, 14:29-15:24)

Already this autobiographical report of his call (not rendered in full here) contains in abridgment all the major topics and tenets of Mani's developed doctrine. That doctrine undertook to expound "beginning, middle and end" of the total drama of being, where the triad designates the three major divisions of the teaching: "The foundation of Mani's teaching is the infinity of the *primal principles;* the middle part concerns their *intermingling;* and the end, the *separation* of the Light from the Darkness." [4]

(*b*) THE SYSTEM

The following reconstruction of the detailed system follows in the main the Syriac account of Theodore bar Konai, supplemented by whatever pieces of material from parallel texts fit into a particular passage and contribute to the fuller presentation of the idea

---

[4] Cf. West, *Pahlavi Texts,* III, p. 234. In the short outlines of the doctrine used in catechisms, this division appears under such headings as "the doctrine of the three times," or "three days," or "three moments," as in the following example: "Since we have learned to know the true God and the sacred doctrine, we know . . . the doctrine of the three times; . . . we know (1) what is said to have been before there was earth and heaven; we know (2) why God and Satan fought, how Light and Darkness mingled, and who is said to have created earth and heaven; we know further (3) why eventually earth and heaven shall pass away, and how Light and Darkness shall be separated from each other, and what shall happen thereafter" (*Chuastuanift,* ed. Bang, p. 157).

treated. Those parallel versions are taken from the *Acta Archelai* (quoted as "Hegemonius"), Alexander of Lycopolis, Titus of Bostra, Severus of Antiochia, Theodoret, St. Augustine, and the Mohammedan En-Nadim. Since this is not a study of the source material addressed to scholars, we spare the reader the ascription of individual passages in the body of our presentation as this moves back and forth among the sources. The mosaic method employed is not meant as the reconstruction of a hypothetical original but merely as a synoptic utilization of the dispersed remnants for the convenience of the non-specialist reader.

The Primal Principles

"Before the existence of heaven and earth and everything in them there were two natures, the one good and the other evil.[5] Both are separate each from the other. The good principle dwells in the place of Light and is called 'Father of Greatness.' Outside him dwelt his five Sh'kinas:[6] Intelligence, Knowledge, Thought, Deliberation, Resolution. The evil principle is called 'King of Darkness,' and he dwells in his land of Darkness surrounded by his five Aeons (or, 'Worlds'), the Aeons of Smoke, of Fire, of Wind, of Water, and of Darkness. The world of Light borders on that of Darkness without a dividing wall between the two" (bar Konai).

This is the "foundation" of the teaching, and with the contraposing of the two arch-principles all accounts of Mani's teaching begin. The Persian Manichaeans, following their Zoroastrian tradition, called the personified Darkness Ahriman, the Arabic sources, Arch-Devil or Iblis (corrupted from the Greek *diabolos*). The Greek sources almost unanimously attach to it the term *Hyle,* i.e., Matter; and the Greek word is even used in Syriac and Latin renderings of the doctrine, to say nothing of its use in the Coptic Manichaean texts. There can be no doubt that Mani himself in his writings (mostly Syriac) used this Greek term for his principle of evil; but it is equally certain that "Matter" has here always the

---

[5] "Natures": also "principles," "substances," "beings," "roots." In the Gathas of Zoroaster, which here served as a model, they were called "the two initial spirits," and "twins." "Good and evil": also "light and darkness," "God and matter."

[6] See explanation in Glossary, p. 98. In the non-Syriac sources they are called "members of God," also "powers" and "aeons."

function of a mythological figure and not that of a philosophical concept. Not only is it personified, but it has an active spiritual nature of its own without which it could not be "evil": and positive evilness is its essence, not passive materiality, which is "bad" only by privation, i.e., by the absence of good. We thus understand the seeming contradiction that the Darkness is called in the same breath "matter" and "immaterial and intellectual" (Severus); and of this Matter it is said that it "once gained the faculty of thought" (Ephraem).[7] The most articulate distinction of Mani's *hyle* from that of Plato and Aristotle is set forth in the account of the philosophically versed Alexander, who points out that Mani ascribes to it powers, movements, and strivings of its own which differ from those of God only by being evil: its movements are "disorderly motion," its strivings "evil lust," and its powers are symbolized in the "dark consuming fire." So far is Matter here from being the passive substratum of the philosophers that the Darkness with which it is identical is even alone the originally active of the two opposed principles, and the Light in its repose is forced into action only by an initial attack of the Darkness.

The two realms are co-eternal as regards the past: they have no origin but are themselves the origins, though it is sometimes said that Satan as the *personal* embodiment of Darkness was procreated out of its pre-existing elements.[8] At any rate, the two realms as such exist side by side completely unconnected, and the Light, far from considering the existence of Darkness as a challenge, wants nothing but the separateness and has neither benevolent nor ambitious tendency to enlighten its opposite. For the Darkness is what it is destined to be, and left to itself it fulfills its nature as the Light fulfills its own. This self-sufficiency of the Light, which wishes to shine only for itself and not also for what is devoid of

[7] Cf. the older doctrine of the Sethians "The Darkness, however, is not without understanding but is quite knowing and aware that, if the Light should be withdrawn from the Darkness, it would be left barren, dark, powerless, inert, strengthless. Therefore it exerts all its cunning and intelligence to forcibly retain the Light [etc.]" (Hippol. *Refut.* V. 19. 6).

[8] A Christian formula of abjuration lists as Manichaean the teaching that "the Devil was procreated from the world of darkness" and opposes to it as the teaching of the Church that "he was created a good angel by God and changed afterwards by his own perversity" (Anathema XI of Milan, about 600 A.D.).

it, and which by its own counsels could last untempted through
the eternities, demonstrates the profound difference of Manichaean
from Christian sentiment,[9] but also from the Syrian gnosis, which
lets a downward movement start in the Light itself and thus makes
it responsible for the given dualism. There is an aristocratic element, preserving something of the original spirit of Iranian religion, in Mani's belief in the inner changelessness of the Light,
which in its self-content furnishes no motive of becoming and can
accept as the natural state of things the profound split of being
with the existence of a Darkness raging within itself, so long as it
only rages within itself. Also in the manner in which the threatened Light subsequently responds to the necessity of battle and
accepts the prospect of defeat and sacrifice, the courageous spirit of
the older Iranian dualism survives, if in gnostic, i.e., anti-cosmic,
transformation.

Now, if the dualistic separation is the normal and satisfactory
state for the Light, then instead of a drift from above downward
an uprising from below must set destiny in motion. The beginning,
therefore, lies in the depth and not in the height. This idea of an
original initiative of the depth forcing the height to relinquish its
repose again separates the Iranian from the Syrian gnosis. Nevertheless, these two different modes of causation are to explain the
same gnostically valid effect—the entrapment of Light in the Darkness—and thus the Light's way into the deep, i.e., a downward
movement, however caused in the first place, is in both cases the
cosmogonic theme.

[9] Severus (123rd Homily), dealing with Mani's teaching that the "Tree of
Life" (the world of Light) prudently conceals its "fruits" (its light and goodness)
and encloses itself within its glory "so as not to furnish an occasion for desire to
the Evil Tree," objects in the Platonic spirit that it would be more befitting the
goodness of God to transform the bad Matter by letting it participate in his superior
nature, and that God could justly be accused of jealousy for hiding himself instead
of by his own splendor attracting his enemy toward the good. However, Severus'
own report suggests that the self-concealment of the Light may have been prompted
by charity as much as by prudence, for the statement about "not furnishing an occasion" goes on to quote "lest this might become for the evil tree a cause of excite-
ment, torment and danger." In fact, since the Darkness, by Manichaean ideas
incapable of reformation, cannot possibly profit from the perception of the Light,
Severus' alternative concerning the conduct of the good God lacks point, and the
real point at issue between the Christian and the Manichaean is, not the nature of
divine goodness, but precisely the idea of eternally unredeemable badness.

The Attack of the Darkness

What caused the Darkness to mount up and fight against the Light? In terms of external occasion: the perception of the Light, which heretofore had been unknown to it. To get to such a perception, the Darkness had first to reach its own outer limits, and to these it was pushed at some time in the course of the internal warfare in which the destructive passion of its members was ceaselessly engaged. For the nature of Darkness is hate and strife, and it must fulfill this nature against itself until the encounter with the Light presents an external and better object. We render this piece of doctrine in the following compilation from Severus, Theodoret, and Titus.

The Darkness was divided against itself—the tree against its fruits and the fruits against the tree. Strife and bitterness belong to the nature of its parts; the gentle stillness is alien to them who are filled with every malignity, and each destroys what is close to him.

Yet it was their very tumult which gave them the occasion to rise up to the worlds of Light. For truly, these members of the tree of death did not even know one another to begin with. Each one had but his own mind, each knew nothing but his own voice and saw but what was before his eyes. Only when one of them screamed did they hear him and turned impetuously towards the sound.

Thus aroused and mutually incited they fought and devoured one another, and they did not cease to press each other hard, until at last they caught sight of the Light. For in the course of the war they came, some pursued and some pursuing, to the boundaries of the Light, and when they beheld the Light—a sight wondrous and glorious, by far superior to their own—it pleased them and they marvelled at it; and they assembled—all the Matter of Darkness—and conferred how they could mingle with the Light. But because of the disorder of their minds they failed to perceive that the strong and mighty God dwelt there. And they strove to rise upward to the height, because never a knowledge of the Good and the Godhead had come to them. Thus without understanding, they cast a mad glance upon it from lust for the spectacle of these blessed worlds, and they thought it could become theirs. And carried away by the passion within them, they now wished with all their might to fight against it in order to bring it into their power and to mix with the Light their own Darkness. They united the whole dark pernicious Hyle and with their innumerable forces rose all together, and in desire for the better opened the attack. They attacked in one body, as it were without knowing their adversary, for they had never heard of the Deity.

This forceful fantasy was not in all its parts of Mani's own invention. Orthodox Zoroastrianism furnished the original model, and already at least a century before Mani the Iranian model had been adapted for gnostic purposes.[10] But, that it is the fratricidal strife of Darkness that inevitably leads to its first beholding of Light, and that this beholding in turn leads to the terrible union of its divided forces, seems to be Mani's original and ingenious contribution to the doctrine.[11] Apart from this, it is in the general Iranian pattern that the perception of the Light excites in the Darkness envy, greed, and hate, and provokes its aggression. Its first onrush is wild and chaotic, but in the progress of the war it develops devilish intelligence, and in the fashioning of man and the device of sexual reproduction it later achieves a stroke of Mephistophelian ingenuity: all this for the purpose of possessing and holding the Light and escaping from the odiousness of its own company. For the hate is paradoxically mixed with recognition of and desire for the envied superiority and is thus at the same time self-hate of the Darkness in the light of the better.[12] The phrase "desire

[10] Basilides around 140 A.D. records as a doctrine existing before him that "there are two beginnings of all things, to which they [the thinkers in question] ascribe good and evil. . . . As long as these kept to themselves, each of them pursued its own proper life. . . . However, after they had come to perceive each other and the Darkness had contemplated the Light, it was seized as by a lust for the better and pursued it and longed to mingle with it and take part in it." Thereupon follows a rape of portions of the Light, or rather of a reflex and image of Light (see above, Ch. 7, p. 162 f.), and the fashioning of the world with the help of this spoil (Hegemonius 67).

[11] He thus made speculative use of the idea, probably current before him and following naturally from the older conception of a primal chaos as soon as this becomes spiritualized, that the Darkness is in a constant turmoil of internecine war. Cf. the Mandaean passage: "The King of this Aeon put on a sword and crown of darkness. . . . A sword he took in his right hand, he stands there and kills his sons, and his sons kill one another," effectively contrasted by: "The King of outside the worlds put on a crown of light. . . . The Kushta he took in his right hand, and he stands there and instructs his sons, . . . and his sons instruct one another" (J 55).

[12] Cf. again a Mandaean parallel: "The King of Darkness caught sight of the world of Light from afar on the border between the Darkness and the Light, as a fire on the summit of high mountains, as stars shining in the firmament. . . . He

for the better" which repeatedly occurs in this connection permits a neat confrontation of Iranian and Greek conceptions. In Plato's *Symposium* it is precisely the "eros" of the deficient for the better that animates the striving of all things toward participation in immortality and in the case of man is the eminent agent of his rise toward knowledge and perfection. The naturalness with which in the Manichaean context the "desire for the better" on the part of the Darkness is taken as perverse presumption and sinful craving points out the gulf that separates this world of thought from that of Hellas no less than from Christianity. The "desire" is not for being but for possessing the better;[13] and its recognition is one not of love but of resentment.

The threatened attack of the Darkness stirs the realm of Light out of its repose and forces it to something that would not otherwise have occurred to it, namely, "creations."

The Pacifism of the World of Light

"As the King of Darkness was planning to mount up to the place of Light, fear spread through the five Sh'kinas. Then the Father of Greatness considered and said:

> Of these my Aeons, the five Sh'kinas,
> I shall send none forth to battle,
> For I created them for peace and blessedness.
> I myself will go instead
> And will wage war against the enemy."

(Theodore bar Konai)

About the inability of the world of Light to wage war, i.e., to do anything injurious, we read at greater length: "God had nothing evil with which to chastise Matter, for in the house of God there is nothing evil. He had neither consuming fire with

---

pondered in his heart, fell into a rage . . . and said, 'If there is such a world, what is to me this habitation of darkness? . . . I will rise up to that luminous earth and make war upon its King' " (G 279).

[13] However, in the first Psalm of Thomas, a disciple of Mani, we read, "Where did the Son of Evil see them—the poor one who has nothing, no riches in his treasure, no Eternity in his possession? He rose up saying 'May I be one like them' " (Man. Psalm-Book. p. 203. 25 ff.; the phrase "may I be one like them" is there repeated over and over again).

which to hurl thunder and lightning, nor suffocating water with which to send a deluge, nor cutting iron nor any other weapon; but all with him is Light and noble substance [lit. "place"], and he could not injure the Evil One." [14] This radical conception of the peaceableness of the world of Light leads sometimes to the version that the new divine hypostasis called forth by God for the encounter with the forces of Darkness is from the outset created not for battle but for a saving sacrifice,[15] and in this case it is called Soul rather than Primal Man, who is a fighting figure.[16] Since by the weight of testimony as well as by the total construction of the system the pre-cosmic struggle of Primal Man with the arch-enemy is the prevalent conception, our account will follow mainly the sources rendering this version. Sometimes we find even the opposite assurance: "His hosts would have been strong enough to overwhelm the enemy, but he wished to accomplish this by his own might alone" (En-Nadim).[17] What matters for the progress of the myth is the fact common to all versions that the godhead, to meet the aggressor, had to produce a special "creation" representing his own self—for this is the meaning of "I myself will go forth"—and that in response to the ensuing fate of this divine hypostasis the further multiplication of divine figures out of the supreme source comes about. This is the general gnostic principle of emanation, here combined with the idea of an external rather than internal necessity provoking it.

The First Creation: Primal Man

"The Father of Greatness called forth the Mother of Life, and the Mother of Life called forth the Primal Man, and the

[14] Compiled from Severus and Theodoret.

[15] The Greek Simplicius at this point raises against the Manichaean God the reproach of cowardice (see below, note 23). Without joining the argument one might point out that there is at least some truth in the idea that the Light cannot meet Darkness, or the spirit brute force, with its own weapons, and only circuitously can prevail against it.

[16] Cf. Man. Psalm CCXIX: "The Warrior, the strong one of manifold activities, who subdued the rebels by his power, our Father, the First Man of glory" (1.25f.).

[17] Cf. Man. Psalm CCXXIII: "There was a multitude of angels in the Land of Light, having the power to go forth to subdue the enemy of the Father, whom it pleased [however] that by his Word whom he would send he should subdue the rebels" (9.26-29).

Primal Man called forth his five Sons, like a man who girds on his armor for battle. The Father charged him with the struggle against the Darkness. And the Primal Man armed himself with the five kinds, and these are the five gods: the light breeze, the wind, the light, the water, and the fire. He made them his armor . . . [we pass over the detailed description of how he clothes himself in these elements one by one, lastly taking the fire for a shield and lance] and plunged rapidly from the Paradises downward until he came to the border of the area adjoining the battlefield. Before him advanced an angel, who spread light ahead of the Primal Man." [18]

The "first creation" produces at the very beginning of the divine history the central soteriological figure of the system: Primal Man. Created to preserve the peace of the worlds of Light and to fight their battle, through his defeat he involves the deity in a long-drawn-out work of salvation, as part of which the creation of the world comes about. The figure occurs widely throughout gnostic speculation: we have seen one instance in the Hermetic *Poimandres*. We cannot here go into its antecedents in older oriental speculation. To the Gnostics the existence of a pre-cosmic god "Man" expressed one of the major secrets of their Knowledge, and some sects even went so far as to call the highest godhead himself "Man": "This [according to one branch of the Valentinians] is the great and hidden secret, that the name of the power that is above all things, the forebeginning of everything, is Man." [19] It is significant that the Persian Manichaeans called the Primal Man "Ormuzd": this in Zoroastrianism was the name of the God of Light himself (Ahura Mazda), to whom the God of Darkness, Ahriman, was opposed. He is now identified with the Primal Man, an *emanation* of the highest godhead—evidence on the one hand of the enormous religious enhancement of the idea of man and, on the other, of the heightening of divine transcendence, which no longer permitted that direct involvement of the First God in the metaphysical struggle which was such a prominent trait of the Iranian Ormuzd. Also the defeat which in the gnostic version befell the fighter against

---

[18] Compiled from Theodore bar Konai and En-Nadim.

[19] Iren. I. 12. 4: similarly the Ophites (*ibid*. 30.1), the Naassenes of Hippolytus, and the Apocryphon of John.

the Darkness was not compatible with the status of the highest godhead. Thus to the Manichaeans Ormuzd as the equivalent of Primal Man becomes the executive organ of the original Gods of Light: "Ormuzd came with the Five Gods to fight at the behest of all Gods against the Devil. He descended and fought with the godless Arch-demon and the Five Devils" (*Chuastuanift* Ch. 1). The five elements of Light which the Primal Man puts on as an armor are as it were denser representations of the original five hypostases of the deity, the Sh'kinas; in spite of their rather material names, they are, as later becomes obvious, spiritual natures, and as such the origin of all "soul" in the universe.

The Defeat of Primal Man

"The Arch-devil too took his five kinds, namely the smoke, the consuming fire, the darkness, the scorching wind, and the fog, armed himself with them, and went to meet the Primal Man. As the King of Darkness beheld the light of the Primal Man, he took thought and spoke: 'What I sought afar I found near by.' After they had struggled long with one another, the Arch-devil overcame the Primal Man. Thereupon the Primal Man gave himself and his five Sons as food to the five Sons of Darkness, as a man who has an enemy mixes a deadly poison in a cake and gives it to him. The Arch-devil devoured part of his light [viz., his five sons] and at the same time surrounded him with his kinds and elements. As the Sons of Darkness had devoured them, the five luminous gods were deprived of understanding, and through the poison of the Sons of Darkness they became like a man who has been bitten by a mad dog or a serpent. And the five parts of Light became mixed with the five parts of Darkness." [20]

From now on the metaphysical interest passes over to the "Five Gods," the armor or escort of the Primal Man, as the most

[20] Compiled from Theodore bar Konai and En-Nadim. See also the dramatic version of the *Chuastuanift* Ch. 1. "God and Devil, Light and Darkness, were intermingled at that time. The escorts of Ormuzd, the Five Gods, [i.e.] our souls, fought for a while with the Devils and were injured and wounded. And mingling with the badness of the Lord of all Devils and of the insatiable, shameless Demon of Greed . . . [and so on], they were deprived of thought and sense: [they] who were self-born and self-originated wholly forgot the eternal land of the Gods and became separated from the Gods of Light."

thoroughly involved victims of his defeat, and of them we most frequently hear wherever the religiously relevant aspect of the divine fate is expressed: "that luminosity of Gods which from the beginning of all things was beaten by Ahriman, the Demons [etc.], and which they hold captive even now";[21] "from the five elements, the bodyguard of the God Ormuzd, he took as booty the fair Soul and fettered it in the impurity. Since he had made it blind and deaf, it was unconscious and confused, so that at first it did not know its true origin" (Salemann: see correction p. 341). Here we have the reason for the importance of the destiny of the "armor": from its substance came our souls, and our condition is a consequence of what happened to it. As it is most simply stated in Hegemonius, "The Archons of Darkness ate of his armor—*that is, the soul.*" This equivalence is one of the pivotal points of the system.

The Sacrifice and Adulteration of the Soul

The devouring has also an effect on the devourer. Not only does it deflect the Darkness from its original objective, the world of Light itself, but within it the devoured substance acts like a soothing poison, and whether its desire has been satisfied or dulled, its attack has by this means been stopped. Both substances are poison to each other, so that some versions make the Primal Man not so much be defeated as in anticipation of the effect voluntarily give himself to be devoured by the Darkness. At any rate, the surrender of the Soul to the Darkness not only averts the immediate threat from the endangered world of Light but at the same time provides the means by which in the end the Darkness is conquered. The former, short-term aim is expressed in the idea of the "enticement" and the "soothing poison"; the long-term aim of the ruse (for the sacrifice is one, even though forced upon the deity) lies in the idea that the eventual re-separation means the "death" of the Darkness, i.e., its final reduction to impotence. This is how it is put in the sources which concentrate on the Soul and pass over the Primal Man: "He sent forth against Matter a force which we call Soul, a part of his own light and substance, to protect the borders, but in truth as a bait,[22] so that it should lull Matter against its will and

[21] Andreas-Henning, p. 179.
[22] Severus: "like an enticement of flattery and deceit."

wholly mix with it; for if at a later time this power should part again from Matter it would mean the latter's death. And so it happened: as Matter perceived the power that had been sent forth, it was drawn towards it by passionate desire, and in a more violent onrush caught and devoured it, and was as it were bound like a wild beast or (as they also say) put to sleep as by a spell. Thus by the providence of God the Soul mingled with Matter, unlike with unlike. By the mixing, however, the Soul became subject to the affections of Matter and against its true nature was degraded to sharing in evil." [23]

The most impressive rendering of this phase of the struggle, combining First Man the warrior and Soul the weapon and victim, is found in four stanzas of Psalm CCXXIII of the Manichaean Psalm-Book, which in spite of the inevitable duplications should not be withheld from the reader of this account.

Like unto a shepherd that sees a lion coming to destroy his sheep-fold: for he uses guile and takes a lamb and sets it as a snare that he may catch him by it; for by a single lamb he saves his sheep-fold; and after these things he heals the lamb that has been wounded by the lion:

This too is the way of the Father, who sent his strong son; and he [the son] produced from himself his Maiden equipped with five powers, that she might fight against the five abysses of the Dark.

When the Watcher [?] stood in the boundaries of Light, he shewed to them his Maiden who is his soul; they bestirred themselves in their abyss, desiring to exalt themselves over her, they opened their mouth desiring to swallow her.

He held her power fast, he spread her over them, like nets over fishes, he made her rain down upon them like purified clouds of water, she

---

[23] Compiled from Alexander and Titus; cf. Severus' account: "And because of this attack which was being prepared from the Deep against the Land of Light, a part of the Light had to mix itself into these evil [substances], in order that by means of the mixture the enemies would be fettered, quietude would be brought about for the Good ones and the nature of the Good would be preserved." To this part of the doctrine refers the criticism of the Neoplatonist Simplicius: "They make God out to be contemptible, since when the Evil had come close to his borders he was afraid lest it might invade his territory; and out of this cowardice he unjustly and unfittingly cast to the evil power the souls, parts and members of himself, that had done no wrong, so that he might save the remainder of the good beings" (In Encheir. Epict. 27).

thrust herself within them like piercing lightning. She crept in their inward parts, she bound them all, they not knowing it.

(9:31-10:19)

The reader will note in the shifting imagery of this passage that the "armor" of most texts is replaced by the "maiden" as symbol of the soul (surely to our taste a more suitable image), and that the latter is deliberately, and most effectively, *employed* by the Primal Man as a means of offensive warfare: there is no mention of defeat. This is one example of the freedom with which Manichaean thinking handled its symbolism. Yet even here, the Primal Man, apparently so victorious, has afterwards to be "helped out of the abyss" by "his brother" (the Living Spirit—see below), which brings us back to the leading theme of the doctrine.

To take up the narrative, then, the emissary of Light—Primal Man with his fivefold armament the Soul—in spite of his success in stopping the enemy is caught in the Darkness, "hard pressed," benumbed and unconscious, and "thereby God was compelled to create the world," for the sake of unmixing what had been mixed.

The Second Creation: The Living Spirit; Liberation of Primal Man

"The Primal Man regained consciousness and addressed seven times a prayer to the Father of Greatness. The Father heard his prayer and called forth as the second creation the Friend of Lights, and the Friend of Lights called forth the Great Architect, and the Great Architect called forth the Living Spirit. And the Living Spirit called forth his five sons [one from each of the five spiritual natures of God; we pass over their names]. And they betook themselves to the Land of Darkness and from the boundary looked down into the abyss of the deep Hell and found the Primal Man swallowed up in the Darkness, him and his five sons. Then the Living Spirit called with a loud voice; and the voice of the Living Spirit became like to a sharp sword and laid bare the form of the Primal Man. And he spoke to him:

> Peace be unto thee, good one amidst the wicked,
> luminous one amidst the darkness,
> God who dwells amidst the beasts of wrath,
> who do not know his honor.

Thereupon Primal Man answered him and spoke:

> Come for the peace of him who is dead,
> come, oh treasure of serenity and peace!

and he spoke further to him:

> How is it with our Fathers,
> the Sons of Light in their city?

And the Call said unto him: It is well with them. And Call and Answer joined each other and ascended to the Mother of Life and to the Living Spirit. The Living Spirit put on the Call and the Mother of Life put on the Answer, her beloved son. The Primal Man was freed from the hellish substances by the Living Spirit who descended and extended to him his right hand, and ascending he became a God again. But the Soul he left behind [for these parts of the Light were too thoroughly mingled with those of the Darkness]." [24]

"Soul" is thus the power which the Primal Man, himself already freed and restored before the beginning of the world, had lost to Matter. For the sake of these lost and thoroughly engulfed parts, the cosmos had to be created as a great mechanism for the separation of the Light. As regards the pre-temporal liberation of the divine Man, it has to the Manichaean a significance analogous to that of the resurrection of Christ to the Christian: it is not an event merely of the past (in the eschatological time-view there is no "mere past"), but the symbolic archetype and the effective guarantee of all future salvation. For the believer it has essential reality, because in suffering and redemption it is the exemplar of his own destiny: it is not for nothing that this God bears the name "Man." Therefore what in the external time of the myth seems to be a mere episode, unnecessary for its objective progress, almost interfering with it (as this progress turns on the very continuance of the mixed state), belongs by its analogical inner significance to the immediate actuality of salvation. A proof of this, apart from the hauntingly human appeal of the mythical scene itself, is the ceremony of daily life in which the Manichaeans related themselves to the archetypal liberation of Primal Man by repeating the crucial gesture: "On that

---

[24] Compiled from Theodore bar Konai, Hegemonius, and En-Nadim.

account the Manichaeans when meeting one another grasp right hands in sign that they themselves are of those saved from the Darkness" (Hegemonius). "The first 'right hand' is that which the Mother of Life gave to Primal Man when he was about to go forth to the war. The second 'right hand' is that which the Living Spirit gave to Primal Man when he led him up out of the war. In the image of the mystery of that right hand originated the right hand that is in use among men in giving it to one another" (*Keph.* pp. 38. 20; 39. 20-22).[25] Another proof is the role which the two hypostases Call and Answer (or alternatively for the latter, "Hearing") play throughout the historical process of salvation, and pre-eminently at the final consummation at the end of time. We shall give the relevant passage from the Kephalaia at the end of the chapter, but wish to quote here the excellent observation of its first commentator: "Herewith the myth of the raising up of the Primal Man by the Living Spirit is brought into relation to the salvation at the end of time as its prototype and precondition: the 'Call' of the Living Spirit and the 'Hearing' in which the Primal Man responded to it live on in the Light-portions he left behind as the disposition and ability to effect by themselves the return to the realm of Light at the end of the world." [26] Without this mystical "presence," the many pre-cosmic "salvations" in gnostic speculation would not be understandable.[27]

[25] Cf. also Epiph. *Haer.* 66.25. 7-8.—Clasping hands had been in use in antiquity as a symbolic act on certain *legal* occasions (conclusion of contracts), but not as a salutation. Also in Gal. 2:9, "giving the right hand of fellowship" seals a compact (between the apostles, concerning the mission among Gentiles and Jews respectively). The salutation between the early Christians was the kiss of brotherhood, which relatively soon ceased to be practiced. Whether as a form of salutation the handclasp spread through the European and mid-Eastern peoples from Manichaean or from Christian custom I am unable to say; except that the *Acta Archelai*, a Christian writing of the early fourth century (here quoted as "Hegemonius") notes it as a Manichaean peculiarity. It was shared by the Mandaeans; see Glossary to Ch. 3 p. 97: "Kushta," "to pass Kushta" — to this day with them part of the baptismal rites.

[26] H. J. Polotsky in C. Schmidt und H. J. Polotsky, "Ein Mani-Fund in Agypten," *Sitzungsberichte d. Preuss. Akad.* 1933, vol. I. p. 80.

[27] The archetypal significance of the pre-cosmic episode is clearly stated, e.g., in the *Book of Baruch* when it is said of the rehabilitated "Elohim" after his separation from "Edem," i.e., the lower Nature, that "by ascending to the Good one he showed the way to all those who wish likewise to ascend" (Hippol., *Refut.* V. 27).

Creation of the Macrocosmos

In the following account of the creation we can pass over many mythological details that are more fantastic than significant. As a first step, the Living Spirit and his entourage of gods separate the "mixture" from the main mass of Darkness. Then "the King of Light ordered him to create the present world and to build it out of these mixed parts, in order to liberate those Light-parts from the dark parts." To this end the Archons who had incorporated the Light (and thereby become weakened) are overcome, and out of their skins and carcasses heaven and earth are made. Though it is said that the Archons are fettered to the firmament (still fastened to their outstretched skins which form the heavens?), and though on the other hand earth and mountains are said to have been formed from their flesh and bones, the sequence makes it clear that by all this neither have they lost their demonic life nor has the Darkness in general lost its power to act. But Manichaean pessimism has here devised the extreme imaginative expression of a negative view of the world: all the parts of nature that surround us come from the impure cadavers of the powers of evil.[28] As one Persian-Manichaean text briefly puts it, "the world is an embodiment of the Arch-Ahriman." It is also a prison for the powers of Darkness who are now confined within its scope; and again it is a place of re-purification for the Soul:

He spread out all the powers of the abyss to ten heavens and eight earths, he shut them up into this world (*cosmos*), he made it a prison for all the powers of Darkness. It is also a place of purification for the Soul that was swallowed in them.

(Man. Ps. CCXXIII. 10. 25-29)

After this, that part of the devoured Light which is least sullied is extracted [29] from the Hyle, purified to "light" in the physical sense, and from the purest part are formed sun and moon—the two "ships"—and from the rest the stars. Thus the stars, with the exception of the planets, which belong to the archons, are "remnants of the Soul." But with this macrocosmic organization only a small

[28] See Cumont, *Recherches*, pp. 26 f.
[29] By a strange stratagem which we shall describe at its repetition later on.

portion of Light is saved, "all the rest still imprisoned, oppressed, sullied," and the celestials lament it.

The Third Creation: The Messenger

"Then arose in prayer the Mother of Life, the Primal Man, and the Living Spirit, and besought the Father of Greatness: 'Create a new god, and charge him that he go and see that dungeon of the Demons, and that he establish annual revolution and protective escort for sun and moon, and that he be a liberator and savior for that luminosity of gods which from the beginning of all things was beaten by Ahriman, the Demons [etc.], and which they hold captive even now, and also for that luminosity which is retained in the cosmic realms of heaven and earth and there suffers, and that he prepare for the wind, the water and the fire a way and a path to the Most High.' And the Father of Greatness heard them, and called forth as the third creation the Messenger. The Messenger called the Twelve Virgins (according to their names, personified virtues and divine properties), and with them set up an engine of twelve buckets." [30] The Messenger betakes himself to the ships of Light, which up to now have been stationary, and sets them in motion and starts the revolution of the spheres. This revolution becomes the vehicle of the *cosmic* process of salvation, as distinct from that enacted through the minds of men, since it functions as a mechanism for the separation and upward transportation of the Light entrapped in nature.

Origin of Plants and Animals

First, however, the Messenger tries a shorter way: "As the ships moved and came to the middle of the heavens, the Messenger revealed his forms, the male and the female, and became visible to all the Archons, the children of the Darkness, the male and the female. And at the sight of the Messenger, who was beautiful in his forms, all the Archons became excited with lust for him, the male ones for his female appearance and the female ones for his male appearance. And in their concupiscence they began to release

[30] The Zodiac, envisioned as a kind of water-wheel. The whole passage is compiled from Theodore bar Konai, Hegemonius, and a Turfan fragment which furnishes the text of the prayer (Andreas-Henning, p. 179 f.).

the Light of the Five Luminous Gods which they had devoured"
(Bar Konai). This is a strangely naturalistic way of extracting the
Light from its captors, a mythical theme which Gnostics before
Mani had already embodied in their systems.[31] The escaping Light
is received by the angels of Light, purified, and loaded onto the
"ships" to be transported to its native realm. But the dubious trick
of the Messenger is double-edged in its success, for together with
the Light and in the same quantity Dark substance ("sin") also
escapes from the Archons and, mingled with the Light, endeavors
also to enter the ships of the Messenger. Realizing this, the Messenger conceals his forms again and as far as possible separates out the
ejaculated mixture. While the purer parts rise upward, the con-
taminated parts, i.e., those too closely combined with the "sin," fall
down upon the earth, and there this mixed substance forms the
vegetable world. Thus all plants, "grain, herbs and all roots and
trees are creatures of the Darkness, not of God, and in these forms
and kinds of things the Godhead is fettered." A similarly miserable
origin, only more so, is assigned to the animal world, which springs
from abortions of the daughters of Darkness at the sight of the
Messenger and similarly keeps Light-substance imprisoned.[32]

Creation of Adam and Eve

The brief revealing of the forms of the Messenger, in addition
to leading to these new kinds of imprisonment of the Light, also
inspires the Darkness with the idea of a last and most effective
means of keeping its threatened spoil, namely, by binding it in the
form most adequate to it. That form is suggested to it by the
divine form itself which it has seen.[33] Anticipating the eventual
loss of all Light through the continual separating effect of the
heavenly revolutions; seized by the ambition to create out of himself something equal to that vision; reckoning by this means to
devise the safest prison for the alien force; and finally, wishing to
have in his world a substitute for the otherwise unattainable divine

---

[31] For the full material concerning the origin and gnostic use of this motholog-
ical motif, see the Appendix, "La Séduction des Archontes," in Cumont's *Recherches,*
pp. 54 ff.

[32] The sources for this paragraph are Theodore bar Konai and Augustine.

[33] Again a widespread gnostic theme: the counterfeiting of the divine by the
Archons.

figure, over which to rule and through which to be sometimes freed from the odious company of his kind, the King of Darkness produces Adam and Eve in the image of the glorious form, and pours into them all the Light left at his disposal. This procreation is described with much repulsive circumstance, involving copulations between the male and female demons, devouring of the progeny by their King, et cetera. The main doctrinal point in this fantasy is that, whereas the genesis of plants and animals was unplanned, the miscarriage of a tactical maneuver of the Light, the creation of man is a deliberate counter-move, in fact the grand counter-move, of the Darkness against the strategy of Light. And by using the divine form itself for its purpose, it ingeniously turns the most dangerous threat to its dominion into the main weapon of defense. This is what has become of the Biblical idea of man's being created in the image of God! The "image" has become a device of the Darkness, the copying not only a kind of blasphemy in itself but a devilish trick directed against the original. For all sources agree in this: as generally the aim of the Darkness is "the non-separation of the Light from the Darkness," so in the likeness of the divine form a particularly *large* part of the Light could as "soul" be fettered and *more effectively* be retained than in any other form. From now on the struggle between Light and Darkness concentrates upon man, who becomes the main prize and at the same time the main battlefield of the two contending parties. In him both sides have almost all their stakes: Light that of its own restoration, Darkness that of its very survival. This is the metaphysical center of the Manichaean religion, and it enhances the deeds and destiny of individual man to an absolute importance in the history of total existence.

The human body is of devilish substance and—in this trait exceeding the general derogation of the universe—also of devilish *design*. Here the Manichaean hostility to body and sex, with its vast ascetic consequences, is provided with a mythological foundation. This hostility and this asceticism have their general rationale in the gnostic view of things, whatever the particular mythological arguments; but rarely have they been so thoroughly and so unyieldingly underpinned as in the Manichaean myth. In the context of this theoretical underpinning, the dwelling on the especially re-

pulsive details of man's begetting by the demons merely adds an
element of the nauseous to an otherwise "rationally" supported
enmity.

The creation of Eve had a special purpose. She is more thoroughly subject to the demons, thus becoming their instrument
against Adam; "to her they imparted of their concupiscence in order
to seduce Adam"—a seduction not only to carnal lust but through
it to reproduction, the most formidable device in Satan's strategy.
For not only would it indefinitely prolong the captivity of Light,
but it would also through the multiplication so disperse the Light
as to render infinitely more difficult the work of salvation, whose
only way is to awaken every individual soul. For the Darkness,
therefore, everything turned on the seduction of Adam, as for the
celestials, on awakening him in time to prevent his seduction.

Mission of the Luminous Jesus; the Jesus Patibilis

"As the five angels saw the Light of God in its defilement,
they begged the Messenger of Good Tidings, the Mother of Light
and the Living Spirit that they send someone to this primal creature to free and save him, reveal to him knowledge and justice,
and liberate him from the devils. So they sent Jesus. The Luminous Jesus approached the innocent Adam. . . ." Here follows the
scene whose full text is given on p. 86. Jesus is here the god with
the mission of revelation to *man*, a more specialized hypostasis or
emanation of the Messenger, whose mission was to the captive
Light in general and preceded the creation of man. That it is he
who makes Adam eat from the Tree of Knowledge explains the
Christian accusation that the Manichaeans equated Christ with the
serpent in Paradise.[34] Of the content of his revelation, the doctrine
concerning "his own self cast into all things" requires comment. It
expresses the other aspect of this divine figure: in addition to
being the source of all revelatory activity in the history of mankind,
he is the personification of all the Light mixed into matter; that
is, he is the suffering form of Primal Man. This original and
profound interpretation of the figure of Christ was an important
article of the Manichaean creed and is known as the doctrine of the

[34] Cf. in this connection the section on "Gnostic Allegory," p. 92 ff.

Jesus patibilis, the "passible Jesus" who "hangs from every tree," "is served up bound in every dish," "every day is born, suffers and dies." He is dispersed in all creation, but his most genuine realm and embodiment seems to be the vegetable world, that is, the most passive and the only innocent form of life.[35] Yet at the same time with the active aspect of his nature he is transmundane Nous who, coming from above, liberates this captive substance and continually until the end of the world collects it, *i.e., himself,* out of the physical dispersal.

The various aspects of this redeemed-redeeming principle are beautifully set forth in a psalm:

Come to me, my kinsman, the Light, my guide . . .

Since I went forth into the darkness I was given a water to drink . . . I bear up beneath a burden which is not my own.

I am in the midst of my enemies, the beasts surrounding me; the burden which I bear is of the powers and principalities.

They burned in their wrath, they rose up against me . . .

Matter and her sons divided me up amongst them, they burnt me in their fire, they gave me a bitter likeness.

The strangers with whom I mixed, me they know not; they tasted my sweetness, they desired to keep me with them.

I was life to them, but they were death to me; I bore up beneath them, they wore me as a garment upon them.

I am in everything, I bear the skies, I am the foundation, I support the earths, I am the Light that shines forth, that gives joy to the souls.

I am the life of the world: I am the milk that is in all trees: I am the sweet water that is beneath the sons of Matter. . . .

I bore these things until I had fulfilled the will of my Father; the First Man is my father whose will I have carried out.

Lo, the Darkness I have subdued; lo, the fire of the fountains I have extinguished, as the Sphere turns hurrying round, as the sun receives the refined part of life.

O soul, raise thy eyes to the height and contemplate thy bond . . . lo, thy Fathers are calling thee.

[35] "What is 'the soul that is slaughtered, by being killed, oppressed, murdered in the enemy'?—What has been called 'the slaughtered, killed, oppressed, murdered soul' is the [life] force of the fruits, the cucumbers and seeds, which are beaten, plucked, torn to pieces, and give nourishment to the worlds of flesh. Also the wood, when drying up, and the garment, when getting old, will die: they too are a part of the total 'murdered, slaughtered soul'" (*Keph. p.* 176. 23; 178. 5 ff.).

Now go aboard the Ship of Light and receive thy garland of glory and return to thy kingdom and rejoice with all the Aeons.

(Man. Ps. CCXLVI. 54. 8-55. 13)

The revelation of Jesus to Adam includes a warning against approaching Eve. Adam at first obeys, but with the help of the demons is later seduced by her, and so starts the chain of reproduction, the temporal perpetuation of the kingdom of Darkness. This makes necessary a temporal history of revelation, which in periodic repetition leads via Buddha, Zoroaster, and the historical Jesus to Mani himself and in essence merely renews again and again the original revelation of the Luminous Jesus, accommodated to the historical progress of religious understanding.

From aeon to aeon the apostles of God did not cease to bring here the Wisdom and the Works. Thus in one age their coming [i.e., that of "the Wisdom and the Works"] was into the countries of India through the apostle that was the Buddha; in another age, into the land of Persia through Zoroaster; in another, into the land of the West through Jesus. After that, in this last age, this revelation came down and this prophethood arrived through myself, Mani, the apostle of the true God, into the land of Babel.[36]

In this prophetology Mani takes up an older gnostic teaching, most distinctly expounded in the Pseudo-Clementines, of the one "true Messenger who from the beginning of the world, altering his forms with his names, courses through the Aeon until he shall have reached his time and, anointed by God's mercy for his labor, attained to eternal rest" (*Homil.* III. 20).

When we look back at the cosmogony, we perceive the following divisions. Three "creations" were forced upon the deity by the aggression of the Darkness and its consequences: that of Primal Man for battle and sacrifice; of the Living Spirit (also called Demiurge) for the champion's liberation and, because this remains incomplete, for the construction of the universe from the

---

[36] From the "Shahpurakan" by Mani, quoted in Al-Biruni's *Chronology.* When Mani also calls himself "the apostle of Jesus Christ," it is in the sense in which the historical Jesus too was an apostle, viz., of the eternal "Light-Jesus," and implies no subordination to this predecessor, either in person, or in message, or in the status of the church "selected"; in the last two respects, Mani on the contrary claims the superiority of the concluding and most universal form.

intermingled substance; of the Messenger (also called Third Messenger) for the setting in motion of the universe and the liberation of the Light embodied in it. This third mission is countered by the Darkness with the creation of man, which in its turn necessitates the mission of the Luminous Jesus to Adam. Through the latter's seduction and the ensuing fact of reproduction, the drama and with it the mission of "Jesus" is protracted into the history of mankind. This world history in the narrower sense of the word belongs as a whole to the division of divine history represented by the emanation of the Messenger: it is his changing hypostases who act as deities of revelation in human religious history, namely, "Jesus" for Adam in the beginning, the Paraclete for Mani at the height, and the Great Thought at the apocalyptic end of history. To the last apocalyptic act we shall turn later.

Practical Conclusions; Mani's Ascetic Morality

The practical conclusions from this cosmo-soteriological system are extremely clear-cut, all of them amounting to a rigorous asceticism. "Since the ruin of the Hyle is decreed by God, one should abstain from all ensouled things and eat only vegetables and whatever else is non-sentient, and abstain from marriage, the delights of love and the begetting of children, so that the divine Power may not through the succession of generations remain longer in the Hyle. However, one must not, in order to help effect the purification of things, commit suicide" (Alexander). The abstinence in matters of food is ruled by two points of view besides the general ascetic attitude: not unnecessarily to incorporate and thereby bind additional Light-substance; and, as this cannot be wholly avoided (plants also containing it), at least to avoid *hurting* Light in its sentient form in animals.[37] Furthermore, from the maxim of keeping contact with the substance of Darkness at a minimum and of not feeling at home in a world whose very purpose is to promote the "separation" follows the commandment of poverty, which involves among other things the prohibition or counsel against building a house. Finally, the pan-psychism which follows from the idea of

---

[37] The "wounded" condition of "soul" in the physical creation, ultimately dating back to the primordial struggle, explains the frequent appellation "Jesus, the Physician of the wounded" in the Manichaean psalms.

the mingling and assumes the presence of vulnerable Light-substance everywhere (even in "inanimate" nature) leads to the most
exaggerated idea of sin that has ever been conceived: "When someone walks on the ground he injures the earth [i.e., more accurately,
the Light mixed in with it]; he who moves his hand injures the
air, for this is the soul of men and beasts . . . [and so on]" (Hegemonius). "It behooves man that he look down at the ground when
walking on his way, lest he tread under his foot the cross of the
Light and destroy the plants" (*Keph*. p. 208. 17). The sin thus *ipso
facto* involved in all action is of course unavoidable and was as
such intended by the Darkness in creating man, but sin it is nonetheless and has to be included in the regular confession.[38] Turned
into a principle of practice, this conception engenders an extreme
quietism which strives to reduce activity as such to what is absolutely necessary.

However, the full rigorism of the Manichaean ethics is reserved
for a particular group, the "Elect" or "True," who must have led
a monastic life of extraordinary asceticism, perhaps modeled on
Buddhist monasticism and certainly a strong influence on the formation of Christian monasticism. The great mass of the believers,
called "Hearers" or "Soldiers," lived in the world under less rigorous rules, and to their meritorious deeds belonged the caring for the
Elect that made their life of sanctification possible. In all we have
therefore three categories of men: Elect, Soldiers, and sinners, an
obvious parallel to the Christian-gnostic triad of pneumatics, psychics, and sarkics ("fleshly men"). Accordingly there are three
"ways" of the souls after death: the Elect comes to the "Paradises
of Light"; the Soldier, the "guardian of religion and helper of the

---

[38] The *Chuastuanift*, a manual of confession, systematically deduces this category of sin from the cosmogonic doctrine. After first relating the fate of the "Five
Gods," the sons of Primal Man, it enumerates the types of sins induced by this basic
condition: with fingers and teeth; by eating and drinking; in relation to earth,
plants, and animals. The different acts are named as "breaking," "violating," "injuring," "tormenting" of the Five Gods. In the formulary of confession itself we
read: "My Lord! We are full of defects and sins, we are deep in guilt: because of
the insatiable shameless demon of greed we always and incessantly, in thought, word
and deed, and in seeing with our eyes, in hearing with our ears, in speaking with
our mouths, in grasping with our hands, and in walking with our feet, torment
the Light of the Five Gods, the dry and the wet earth, the five kinds of animals,
the five kinds of herbs and trees" (Ch. 15).

Elect," must return into the "world and its terrors" so often and so long "until his light and his spirit shall be freed and after long wandering back and forth he attains to the assembly of the Elect"; the sinners fall into the power of the Devil and end up in Hell. (En-Nadim)

The Doctrine of the Last Things

Thus the history of the world and of man is a continual process of the freeing of Light, and all the arrangements of the universe like all events of history are considered from this point of view. Instruments of salvation in history are the calls of the apostles, the founders of the "churches" (religions), with their effect of awakening, instruction, and sanctification. The universe's instrument of salvation is the cosmic revolution, especially that of the sun, which "circling the heavens collects with its rays the members of God even out of the sewers" (Augustine). That is, the sun automatically, as a process of nature, extracts, attracts, and purifies Light from the Hyle, and like a ship transports it to the wheel of the Zodiac, whose rotation brings it to the world of Light.[39] The two instruments of salvation supplement each other: "The liberation, separation and raising up of the parts of Light is helped by the praise, the sanctification, the pure word, and the pious works. Thereby the parts of Light [i.e., the souls of the dead] mount up by the pillar of dawn to the sphere of the moon, and the moon receives them incessantly from the first to the middle of the month, so that it waxes and gets full, and then it guides them to the sun until the end of the month, and thus effects its waning in that it is lightened of its burden. And in this manner the ferry is loaded and unloaded again, and the sun transmits the Light to the Light above it in the world of praise, and it goes on in that world until it arrives at the highest and pure Light. The sun does not cease to do this until nothing of the parts of Light is left in this world but a small part so bound that sun and moon cannot detach it [this the final conflagration will free]."[40]

[39] The "astronomical" details of the conception are variously elaborated in the sources, and except for the role of the moon are of no particular interest here.
[40] Compiled from Shahrastani, En-Nadim, and Hegemonius.

> Smaller and smaller from day to day
> grows the number of souls [on earth]
> while they rise upward, purified.
>   (Ephraem, s. Mitchell I 109)

There is something undeniably grandiose in this cosmic vision, and to the Manichaeans it was so convincing that they could say, "this matter is obvious even to the blind" (Alexander). We shall hardly concur in this but may readily agree that the image of a moon waxing and waning with a freight of souls, of a sun continually separating out and refining divine Light, of a Zodiac like a water-wheel ceaselessly scooping and transporting upward, has a fascinating quality about it and that it gives to the order of the universe a religious meaning which the sinister "spheres" of other gnostic systems lack.

Thus in the sequence of times, of calls, and of revolutions, "all parts of Light ascend incessantly and mount up to the height, and the parts of Darkness incessantly descend and sink down into the depth, until the one are freed from the other and the mixture is nullified and the compounds are dissolved and each has come to its whole and to its world. And this is the resurrection and the restitution" (Shahrastani). When this has been completed down to that most closely mingled remainder, then "the Messenger manifests his image, and the angel who supports the earth throws off his burden, and the great fire from outside the cosmos breaks out and consumes the whole world, and does not cease to burn until what Light still remains in the creation is released" (compiled from Hegemonius[= Epiphanius] and En-Nadim).

The end-apocalypse of what the preceding quotation summarily termed "the Messenger" [41] is more fully described in two pieces of the *Kephalaia* (Ch. 5; 16), the first entitled "On the four Hunters of the Light and the four of the Darkness," where the fourth and final Hunter (or Fisher) of Light [42] is called the "Great Thought"; to these a passage from the Psalm-Book supplies a fitting conclusion.

---

[41] According to the convincing emendation of πρεσβύτης to πρεσβευτής in *Act. Arch.* 13 and Epiph. *Haer.* 66. 31 (*et al.*) (Flügel, Bousset, Cumont).

[42] The three preceding Hunters of the Light: the first is the Primal Man, his "net"—the Soul spread over all the Children of Darkness (see above, p. 220 f.), the "sea"—the Land of Darkness (cf. p. 117 f.); the second Hunter is the Third

At the end, when the cosmos is dissolved, this same Thought of Life shall gather himself in and shall form his Soul [i.e., his Self] in the shape of the Last Statue. His net is his Living Spirit, for with his Spirit he shall catch the Light and the Life that is in all things and build it onto his own body.

The Call and the Hearing, the Great Thought who came to the intermingled elements . . . and stood there in silence . . , till that time . . . when he wakes up and takes his stand in the great fire and gathers in his own Soul unto himself and forms himself in the shape of this Last Statue. And thou shalt find him as he sweeps out of himself and casts out the impurity which is alien to him, but yet gathers in to himself the Life and the Light that is in all things and builds it onto his body. Then when this Last Statue is perfected in all its members, then it shall escape and be lifted up out of that great struggle through the Living Spirit, its father, who comes and . . . fetches the members out of . . . the dissolution and the end of all things.

And [43] the counsel of death too, all the Darkness, he will gather together and make a likeness of its very self . . .

In a moment the Living Spirit will come . . . he will succour the Light. But the counsel of death and the Darkness he will shut up in the dwelling that was established for it, that it might be bound for ever.

There is no other means to bind the Enemy save this means; for he will not be received to the Light because he is a stranger to it; nor again can he be left in his land of Darkness, that he may not wage a war greater than the first.

A new Aeon will be built in the place of the world that shall dissolve, that in it the powers of the Light may reign, because they have performed and fulfilled the will of the Father entire, they have subdued the hated one . . .

This is the Knowledge of Mani, let us worship him and bless him.

Messenger, his "net"—his Light-form which he showed to the Deep and with which he ensnared the Light in all things, his "ship"—the sun (see above, p. 225); the third Hunter is the Light-Jesus, his "net"—the Wisdom of the Light with which he ensnares the souls, his "ship"—the Holy Church (rather, Churches, see above, p. 230).

[43] From here on Ps. CCXXIII, 11. 10 ff.; the two lines there preceding read "All Life, the relic of Light wheresoever it be, he will gather to himself and of it depict an image" (*andrias,* translated above as "statue")—which clearly connects this passage with that of the *Kephalaia.*

Thus, while of the end-condition it may sometimes be said briefly that "the two natures are restored and the Archons shall henceforth dwell in their nether regions, but the Father in the upper regions after he has taken back unto himself his own" (Hegemonius), the real idea is that the power of the Dark, though not Darkness itself, will be destroyed forever, and in contrast to the wild turmoil of the beginning it now lies in deathly stillness. By a long route the initial sacrifice of Light has found its reward and achieved its goal: "The Light is henceforth safe from the Darkness and from injury by it" (En-Nadim).

(c) RECAPITULATION: TWO TYPES OF DUALISM IN GNOSTIC SPECULATION

After this long journey through the maze of gnostic thought and fantasy in which the reader may easily have lost sight of the main contours of the landscape, he may welcome a re-statement of certain bird's-eye viewpoints of general orientation, even at the cost of some outright repetitions.

The Gnostics were the first speculative "theologians" in the new age of religion superseding classical antiquity. Their task was set by the basic gnostic experience which sustained a general view of existing reality somehow *a priori* valid for the sharers of that experience. This view comprised as main tenets the ideas of an antidivine universe, of man's alienness within it, and of the acosmic nature of the godhead. Reality being such, it presupposes a history in which it assumed its present "unnatural" condition. The task of speculation was to tell this history, i.e., to account for the present state of things by recounting the successive stages of its genesis from first beginnings, thereby to lift the vision of reality into the light of gnosis and give grounded assurance of salvation. The manner of doing so was invariably mythological; but the resulting myths, with their personifications, hypostases, and quasi-chronological narrative, are consciously constructed symbols of metaphysical theory.

Two types of system, called here for short (and without undue commitment to a theory of actual genetics) the Iranian and the Syrian, were evolved to explain essentially the same facts of a dislocated metaphysical situation—both "dualistic" as concerns this, their common result: the existing rift between God and world, world and man, spirit and flesh. The Iranian type, in a gnostic adaptation of Zoroastrian doctrine starting from a dualism of two opposed principles, has mainly to explain how the original Darkness came to engulf elements of the Light: i.e., it describes the world-drama as a war with changing fortunes, and the divine fate, of which man's is a part and the world an unwilled consequence, in terms of mixing and unmixing, captivity and liberation. The Syrian speculation undertakes the more ambitious task of deriving dualism itself, and the ensuing predicament of the divine in the system of creation, from the one and undivided source of being—by means of a genealogy of personified divine states evolving from one another, which describe the progressive darkening of the original Light in categories of guilt, error and failure. This inner-divine "devolution" ends in the decadence of complete self-alienation that is this world.

Both dramas start with a disturbance in the heights; in both, the existence of the world marks a discomfiture of the divine and a necessary, in itself undesirable, means of its eventual restoration; in both, the salvation of man is that of the deity itself. The difference lies in whether the tragedy of the deity is forced upon it from outside, with Darkness having the first initiative, or is motivated from within itself, with Darkness the product of its passion, not its cause. To divine defeat and sacrifice in the one case, corresponds divine guilt and error in the other; to compassion for the victimized Light—spiritual contempt of demiurgical blindness; to eventual divine liberation—re-formation through enlightenment.

Our division is typological and therefore not much affected by what is made of the geographic and ethnic intimations of the names chosen for it. The Valentinian and Manichaean systems exemplify the two types. The difference of speculative principle signifies, on the common gnostic ground, an important difference in religious attitude; and whereas the Iranian type permits the more concrete and gripping dramatization, the Syrian type is profounder, and alone of the two, by according metaphysical status to knowledge and ignorance as modes of the divine life itself, can do full justice to the redemptional claim made on behalf of knowledge throughout gnostic religion.

PART III

Gnosticism and the Classical Mind

So far we have considered the gnostic world of ideas by itself, without more than an occasional reference to the cultural background against which it stands out. Account was taken of its relations to the Jewish and Christian environment, which itself was a new-comer in the world of Graeco-Roman civilization. Unorthodox and subversive as Gnosticism was in relation to these more kindred systems of thought, its revolutionary character comes fully to light only in a confrontation with the *classical-pagan* world of ideas and values, which it met in a head-on clash. This world, as we pointed out in the introductory chapter, represented in its Hellenistic version the cosmopolitan, secular culture of the age, looking back upon a long and imposing history. Compared with it, the gnostic movement in addition to being a stranger was an upstart, with no legitimate parentage: what heritage it did carry from its own several oriental antecedents it made free with to the point of controverting its meaning. This alone testifies to its being non-traditional. Yet the true background to its novelty in the dimension of universal history is supplied by the larger world into which it emerged and to whose long-established mental and moral attitudes it seemed to be the almost intentional antithesis. Those attitudes were sustained by an ideological tradition, Greek in origin and venerable by its intellectual achievements, which acted as the great conservative agency in an era of increasing spiritual tension and threatening

239

dissolution. The gnostic challenge was one expression of the crisis which the general culture experienced. To understand Gnosticism as such a challenge is part of understanding its essence. To be sure, the insights which its message propounded for the first time stand in their own right. But without the Hellenic counter-position upon which it burst, Gnosticism would not have been of that significance in the world history of ideas which it assumed as much by historical configuration as by its intrinsic content. The stature of what it challenged gives it some of its own historic stature. And its being "first" with those insights, and "different," and filled with the intoxication of unprecedentedness, colors its views no less than their utterance.

The following confrontation, by placing Gnosticism in its proper contemporary setting, will bring out with greater clarity what was new in it, what it challenged, and what it stands for in the history of man's understanding of himself.

Chapter 10. *The Cosmos in Greek and Gnostic Evaluation*

(a) THE IDEA OF "COSMOS" AND MAN'S PLACE IN IT

The Greek Position

To compare the two worlds, the new and the old, the attacker and the attacked, there is no more prominent symbol in which the essence of each reveals itself than the concept of "cosmos." By a long tradition this term had to the Greek mind become invested with the highest religious dignity. The very word by its literal meaning expresses a positive evaluation of the object—any object— to which it is accorded as a descriptive term. For *cosmos* means "order" in general, whether of the world or a household, of a commonwealth or a life: it is a term of praise and even admiration. Thus when applied to the universe and becoming assigned to it as to its eminent instance, the word does not merely signify the neutral fact of all-that-is, a quantitative sum (as the term "the All" does), but expresses a specific and to the Greek mind an ennobling quality of this whole: that it is order. And indissoluble as this assignment of the term became in time, and much as the emphatic form *"the* comos" could denote only the universe, it yet never came to monopolize the meaning of the word and to oust its other uses.[1] Had these withered away, the name in isolation from its original semantic range might have paled to the indifference of the English "world." "Cosmos" never suffered this fate. A manifold of application to objects and situations of daily life—applications ranging from general to special, from moral to aesthetic, from inner to outer, from

---

[1] Here are some of these. For things of all kinds: arrangement, structure, rule; conformity to rule, i.e., regularity. In the public sphere: political or legal constitution; conformity to that, i.e., lawful conduct or condition. In the military sphere: discipline, battle order. In the private sphere: decency, propriety, decorum (the adjective *cosmios* means well-behaved, its negative, unruly). As the social reflection of quality: honor, fame. As form of convention: etiquette, ceremonial. As form of display: ornament, decoration, especially in dress—hence, finery.

spiritual to material quality—remained in currency side by side with the exalted use, and this co-presence of familiar meanings, all of them laudatory, helped to keep alive the value-consciousness which had first prompted the choice of so qualitative a name for this widest and in a sense remotest of all objects.

But more than merely the widest instance, the universe was considered to be the perfect exemplar of order, and at the same time the cause of all order in particulars, which only in degrees can approximate that of the whole. Again, since the sensible aspect of order is beauty, its inner principle reason, the All as perfect order must be both beautiful and rational in the highest degree. Indeed this bounded physical universe denoted by the name "cosmos" was considered·a divine entity and often called outright a god, finally even *the* God. As such, it was of course more than merely a physical system in the sense in which we have come to understand the term "physical." As the generative, life-begetting powers of nature bespeak the presence of soul, and the eternal regularity and harmony of the celestial motions the action of an ordering mind, the world must be considered as one animated and intelligent whole, and even as wise. Already Plato, though not regarding the cosmos as the highest being itself, called it the highest sensible being, "a god," and "in very truth a living creature with soul and reason." [2] It is superior to man, who is not even the best thing within the world: the heavenly bodies are his betters, both in substance and in the

[2] *Timaeus* 30B; 34A. We render some of Plato's argument. "[The creator] was good; and in the good no jealousy in any matter can ever arise. So, being without jealousy, he desired that all things should come as near as possible to being like himself. . . . Desiring, then, that all things should be good and, so far as might be, nothing imperfect, the god took over all that is visible . . . and brought it from disorder into order, since he judged that order was in every way the better. . . . He found that . . . no work that is without intelligence will ever be better than one that has intelligence, . . . and moreover that intelligence cannot be present in anything apart from soul. In virtue of this reasoning, when he framed the universe, he fashioned reason within soul and soul within body, to the end that the work he accomplished might be by nature as excellent and perfect as possible. This, then, is how we must say . . . that this world came to be, by god's providence, in very truth a living creature with soul and reason" (29D-30C; tr. F. M. Cornford, *Plato's Cosmology,* London, 1952). The reader will note that the reasoning which in the Genesis account of creation implicitly applies to man here applies to the cosmos.

purity and steadiness of the intelligence that activates their motion.[3]

Stoic monism led to a complete identification of the cosmic and the divine, of the universe and God. Cicero, in the second book of "The Nature of the Gods," gives eloquent expression to this theological status of the visible universe. Since his argument, compounded of elements from Stoic sources, is supremely instructive, we quote it here almost in full, indicating the main logical stages by interpolated headings.

(General statement)

There is then a nature [heat] which holds together and sustains the universe, and it possesses both sensibility and reason. For everything which is not separate and simple but joined and connected with other things must have within it some governing principle. In man it is mind, in beasts something similar to mind [sense], from which the appetites arise. . . . In each class of things nothing can be or ought to be more excellent than this its governing principle. Hence that element wherein resides the governing principle of Nature as a whole must be the best of all things and most worthy of power and dominion over all things. Now we see that in certain parts of the cosmos—and there is nothing anywhere in the cosmos which is not *a part of the whole*—sensibility and reason abide. In that part, therefore, in which the governing principle of the cosmos resides, these same qualities must of necessity be present—only keener and on a grander scale. Therefore the cosmos must also be wise, for that substance which encompasses and holds all things must excel in the perfection of its reason; and this means that the cosmos is God and that all its particular powers are contained in the divine nature. . . .

(Special arguments: a. sensibility and soul)

Seeing that men and beasts are quickened by this warmth and that by its agency they move and feel, it is absurd to say that the cosmos is devoid of sensibility, he who is quickened by a warmth that is whole and free and pure and also most keen and agile. . . . Since that heat

[3] "It would be strange to think that the art of politics, or practical wisdom, is the best knowledge, since man is not the best thing in the world. . . . But if the argument be that man is the best of the animals, this makes no difference; for there are other things much more divine in their nature even than man, e.g., most conspicuously, the bodies of which the heavens are framed" (Aristotle *Eth. Nic.* VI. 7. 1141 a 21 f.; 33 f.; tr. W. D. Ross).

is moved not by an external impulse but spontaneously of itself [and since according to Plato self-motion is of the soul only], the conclusion is that the cosmos is animate.

(b. intelligence)

Then, that the cosmos is endowed with intelligence, is also evident from the consideration that the cosmos [as the whole] must be superior to any particular entity. For, as every separate member of our bodies is of less worth than we ourselves are, so the totality of the cosmos is necessarily of greater worth than any part of it. If this is true, then the universe must be intelligent;[4] for if it were not, man, who is a part of the universe and who partakes in reason, would have to be of higher worth than the whole cosmos.

(c. wisdom)

Moreover, if we begin with the first and inchoate beings and proceed to the last and perfected ones, we shall inevitably arrive at the order of the gods. . . . [The ascent goes from plants through animals to man.] . . . But the fourth and highest order is that of those beings who are born naturally good and wise and to whom right and constant reasoning is innate from the beginning, a quality which must be deemed superhuman and can be attributed only to *God, that is to say to the cosmos,* in which that consummate and absolute reason necessarily must reside.

Furthermore, it cannot be denied that for every ordered whole there is a state representing its ultimate perfection. In the case of vines or of cattle we can perceive how Nature, unless thwarted by some sort of violence, pursues her own straight course toward fulfilment. . . . Even so for Nature as a whole, but in a far higher degree, there must be something which makes it complete and perfect. Now, there are many external circumstances to prevent the perfection of other beings; but nothing can impede universal Nature, because she herself encompasses and contains all particular natures. Therefore it is necessary that there is this fourth and highest order which no extrinsic force can interfere with; and it is this order in which universal Nature must be placed.

(Conclusion from whole argument)

Now since she is such that she excels all other things and no thing can obstruct her, it is necessary that the cosmos is intelligent and even

---

[4] *Sapiens,* elsewhere translated by "wise," must in this particular phase of the argument (if Cicero was consistent) stand for "intelligent" in general.

wise. What can be more foolish than to deny that that Nature which comprehends all things is the most excellent, or, if this is granted, to deny that it is firstly animate, secondly rational and reflective, and thirdly wise? How else could it be the most excellent? For if it were like plants or beasts, it would have to be considered the lowest rather than the highest of beings. Again, if it were rational but not from the beginning wise, the state of the cosmos would be inferior to that of man; for man can *become* wise, but if the cosmos during the infinite aeons of the past has been lacking in wisdom, it will certainly never attain it, and will thus be *inferior to man*. Since *this is absurd* [!], it must be held that from the beginning the cosmos has been both wise and God. And there is naught else except the cosmos which lacks nothing and which is in all particulars and parts fit and perfect and complete.

(The position of man)

Chrysippus aptly observes that, as the shield-casing exists only for the shield and the scabbard for the sword, so everything save the universe was brought into being for the sake of something else . . . [plants for the benefit of animals, animals for the benefit of man]. Man himself, however, was born *to contemplate the cosmos* and *to imitate* it; he is far from being perfect, but he is a little part of the perfect.[5]

The concluding statement about the purpose of human existence in the scheme of things is of profoundest significance. It establishes the connection between cosmology and ethics, between the apotheosis of the universe and the ideal of human perfection: man's task is the theoretical one of contemplating and the practical one of "imitating" the universe, the latter being explained in a fuller statement as "imitating the *order of the heavens* in the manner and constancy of one's life" (Cicero, *Cato Major* XXI. 77). To the Christian reader the reminder may not be out of place that it is the *visible* heavens (not the spiritual "heaven" of faith) which provides the paradigm of human existence. No more telling contrast to the gnostic attitude can be imagined. Let us state the points which Cicero emphasizes. This world is the All, and there is nothing beside it; it is perfect, and there is nothing equaling it in

[5] Cicero *De Natura Deorum* II. 11-14. The translation is based in part on that of H. M. Poteat, University of Chicago Press, 1950. I have italicized such statements or phrases that are especially revealing for the purposes of our confrontation.

perfection; it is perfect as the whole of its parts, and the parts participate in degrees in its perfection; as a whole it is ensouled, intelligent, and wise, and something of these attributes is also exhibited in some ·of its parts; the evidence of its wisdom is the perfect order of the whole (especially the eternal harmony of the celestial motions); the parts are necessarily less perfect than the whole: this applies also to man, who, though sharing in the highest cosmic attributes of soul and mind, is not the most perfect of beings, since he is not by nature but only potentially wise, while the intelligence of the cosmos is perpetually in the state of wisdom; but man in addition to the natural share he has as a *part* in the perfection of the divine universe has also the capacity to perfect himself by assimilating his being to that of the whole through contemplating it in his understanding and imitating it in his conduct.

The veneration of the cosmos is the veneration of the whole of which man himself is a part. The recognition of and compliance with his position as a part is one aspect of man's proper relation to the universe in the conduct of his life. It is based on the interpretation of his existence in terms of the larger whole, whose very perfection consists in the integration of all its parts. In this sense man's cosmic piety *submits* his being to the requirements of what is better than himself and the source of all that is good.[6] But at the same time man is not just a part like other parts making up the universe, but through the possession of a mind a part that enjoys *identity* with the *ruling principle* of the whole. Thus the other aspect of man's proper relation to the universe is that of *adequating*

[6] The classical statement of this position is found in Plato's *Laws.* "The ruler of the universe has ordered all things with a view to the excellence and preservation of the whole, and each part, as far as may be, has an action and passion appropriate to it. Over these, down to the last fraction of them, ministers have been appointed to preside, who have wrought out their perfection with infinitesimal exactness. And one of these portions· of the universe is thine own, unhappy man, which, however little, contributes to the whole; and you do not seem to be aware that this and every other creation is for the sake of the whole, and in order that the life of the whole may be blessed; and that you are created for the sake of the whole, and not the whole for the sake of you. For every physician and every skilled artist does all things for the sake of the whole, directing his effort towards the common good, executing the part for the sake of the whole, and not the whole for the sake of the part. And you are annoyed because you are ignorant how what is best for you happens to you and to the universe, as far as the laws of the common creation admit" (*Laws* X. 903 B-D; tr. Jowett).

his own existence, confined as it is as a mere part, to the essence of the whole, of reproducing the latter in his own being through understanding and action. The understanding is one of reason by reason, cosmic reason by human reason, i.e., of like by like: in achieving this knowing relation, human reason assimilates itself to the kindred reason of the whole, thereby transcending the position of a mere part.[7] In the calm and order of the moral life conducted on this intellectual basis the cosmos is "imitated" also practically, and thus the whole is once more appropriated by the part in the role of an exemplar.

We are spectators and actors alike of the grand play, but we can be the latter successfully and to our own happiness only if we are the former in an ever more comprehensive sweep—encompassing our own acting itself.

Nature did not destine us for a base and ignoble existence but introduced us into life and the universe as if into a great festive gathering,[8] that we might be spectators of their contending for the prices of victory and assiduous contenders with them ourselves. . . . [If someone could look at the world from on high and behold the wealth of beauty in it] he would soon know what we were born for.[9]

Cosmos-Piety as a Position of Retreat

Grand and inspiring as this conception is, it must not be overlooked that it represented a position of retreat inasmuch as its appeal was addressed to a human subject that was no longer a part of anything *except the universe*. Man's relation to the cosmos is a special case of the part-whole relationship which is so fundamental a theme in classical thought. Philosophy and political science alike had ever anew discussed its problems, which in the last analysis led back to the most fundamental problem of ancient ontology, that

[7] According to the pseudo-Aristotelian treatise "On the Cosmos" (by an unknown author of the first century A.D.) this is the very definition of the task of *philosophy*: in contemplating the All, philosophy "recognizes that which is akin to itself and with divine eye beholds the divine" (Ch. 1. 391 a 14). Combined with Cicero's statement that "man was born to contemplate the All," this means: man was born to be a philosopher! The work, to which we shall refer again, is among the noblest documents of late-classical cosmos-piety.

[8] Like the Olympic games.

[9] "On the Sublime" (first century A.D.), 25. 2.

of the Many and the One. According to classical doctrine, the whole is prior to the parts, is better than the parts, and therefore that for the sake of which the parts are and wherein they have not only the cause but also the meaning of their existence. The living example of such a whole had been the classical *polis,* the city-state, whose citizens had a share in the whole and could affirm its superior status in the knowledge that they the parts, however passing and exchangeable, not only were *dependent* on the whole *for* their being but also *maintained* that whole *with* their being: just as the condition of the whole made a difference to the being and possible perfection of the parts, so their conduct made a difference to the being and perfection of the whole. Thus this whole, making possible first the very life and then the good life of the individual, was at the same time entrusted to the individual's care, and in surpassing and outlasting him was also his supreme achievement.

Now this justifying complement of the primacy of the whole in socio-political terms—the part's vital and self-fulfilling function in the whole—had lapsed in the conditions of later antiquity. The absorption of the city-states into the monarchies of the Diadochi and finally into the Roman Empire deprived the polis intelligentsia of its constructive function. But the ontological principle survived the conditions of its concrete validation. Stoic pantheism, and generally the physico-theology of post-Aristotelian thought, substituted for the relation between citizen and city that between the individual and the cosmos, the larger living whole. By this shift of reference the classical doctrine of whole and parts was kept in force even though it no longer reflected the practical situation of man. Now it was the *cosmos* that was declared to be the great "city of gods and men," [10] and to be a citizen of the universe, a *cosmopolites,* was now considered to be the goal by which otherwise isolated man could set his course. He was asked, as it were, to adopt the cause of the universe as his own, that is, to identify himself with that cause directly, across all intermediaries, and to relate his inner self, his *logos,* to the *logos* of the whole.

[10] It is characteristic, however, that the treatise "On the Cosmos" in elaborating the comparison between the universe and a commonwealth uses the model of monarchy rather than of republic: see in ch. 6 the circumstantial treatment of the rule of the Persian Great King and its parallel in the divine rule of the universe.

The practical side of this identification consisted in his affirming and faithfully performing the *role* allotted to him by the whole, in just that place and station in which cosmic destiny had set him. Wisdom conferred inner freedom in shouldering the tasks, composure in facing the whims of fortune besetting their execution, but did not set or revise the tasks themselves. "To play one's part"— that figure of speech on which Stoic ethics dwells so much—unwittingly reveals the fictitious element in the construction. A role played is substituted for a real function performed. The actors on the stage behave "as if" they acted their choice, and "as if" their actions mattered. What actually matters is only to play well rather than badly, with no genuine relevance to the outcome. The actors, bravely playing, are their own audience.

In the phrase of playing one's part there is a bravado that hides a deeper, if proud, resignation, and only a shift in attitude is needed to view the great spectacle quite differently. Does the whole really care, does it concern itself in the part that is I? The Stoics averred that it does by equating *heimarmene* with *pronoia,* cosmic fate with providence. And does my part, however I play it, really contribute, does it make a difference to the whole? The Stoics averred that it does by their analogy between the cosmos and the city. But the very comparison brings out the tenuousness of the argument, for—in contrast to what is true in the *polis*—no case can be made out for my relevance in the cosmic scheme, which is entirely outside my control and in which my part is thus reduced to a passivity which in the *polis* it did not have.

To be sure, the strained fervor by which man's integration in the whole was maintained, through his alleged affinity to it, was the means of preserving the dignity of man and thereby of saving a sanction for a positive morality. This fervor, succeeding that which had formerly been inspired by the ideal of civic virtue, represented a heroic attempt on the part of the intellectuals to carry over the life-sustaining force of that ideal into fundamentally changed conditions. But the new atomized masses of the Empire, who had never shared in that noble tradition of *areté,* might react very differently to a situation in which they found themselves passively involved: a situation in which the part was insignificant to the whole, and the whole alien to the parts. Yet the idea of order as something divine and of the universe as such an order retained a pervading public validity and represented something like the religion of the intellectuals.

The Gnostic Revaluation

The gnostic attack upon the classical position singled out this most valued concept of the cosmos for its most radical revaluation. It had against it the full force of the tradition we described, not the least of it embodied in the very name "cosmos." In retaining this name for the world, the Gnostics retained the idea of order as the main characteristic of what they were set on depreciating. Indeed, instead of denying to the world the attribute of order (which theoretically a cosmic pessimism could choose to do), they turned this very attribute from one of praise into one of opprobrium, and in the process if anything increased the emphasis on it. As we shall see when we treat the concept of fate, it is the very features of order, rule, and law which are not only left to the gnostically reinterpreted world but even enhanced in their power and their impact on man —but in their spiritual quality, their meaning, their value, radically changed. It is almost by exaggeration that the divinity of cosmic order is turned into the opposite of divine. Order and law is the cosmos here too, but rigid and inimical order, tyrannical and evil law, devoid of meaning and goodness, alien to the purposes of man and to his inner essence, no object for his communication and affirmation. A world emptied of divine content had its own order: an order empty of divinity. Thus, the metaphysical devaluation of the world extends to the conceptual root of the cosmos-idea, that is, the concept of order itself, and includes it with its quality perverted in the now debased concept of the physical universe. In this manner the term "cosmos," endowed with all its semantic associations, could pass over into gnostic use and could there, with its value-sign reversed, become as symbolic as it had been in the Greek tradition.

"Cosmos" thus becomes in the newly appearing view of things an emphatically negative concept, perhaps more strongly because more emotionally charged than it had been a positive concept in the Greek view. This negative conception is of course counterbalanced by a new positive one, that of the transmundane deity. In the passage from Cicero we found that the cosmos is the All, i.e., that there is nothing beside it and nothing which is not a part of it, and that this all-embracing whole is God. This is the specific position of Stoic pantheism; but also in the Aristotelian scheme the relation of Nature to the divine Nous, though the latter is not itself immanent in the world, leads essentially to the same result of making the world a manifestation of the divine; and even the supreme transcendentalism of Plotinus left this relation intact. The gnostic God is not merely extra-mundane and supra-mundane, but in his ultimate meaning contra-mundane. The sublime unity of cosmos and God is broken up, the two are torn apart, and a gulf never completely to be closed again is opened: God and world, God and nature, spirit and nature, become divorced, alien to each other, even contraries. But if these two are alien to each other, then also man and world are alien to each other, and this in terms of feeling is very likely even the primary fact. There is a basic experience of an absolute rift between man and that in which he finds himself lodged, the world. Greek thought had been a grand expression of man's belonging to the world (if not unreservedly to mere terrestrial life) and through knowledge that breeds love had striven to heighten the intimacy with the kindred essence of all nature: gnostic thought is inspired by the anguished discovery of man's cosmic solitude, of the utter otherness of his being to that of the universe at large. This dualistic mood underlies the whole gnostic attitude and unifies the widely diversified, more or less systematic expressions which that attitude gave itself in gnostic ritual and belief. It is on this primary human foundation of a dualistic mood, a passionately felt experience of man, that the articulated dualistic doctrines rest.

The dualism between man and world posits as its metaphysical counterpart that between the world and God. It is a duality not of complementary but of contrary terms, a polarity of incompatibles, and this fact dominates gnostic eschatology. Gnostic doctrine explicates the duality, or rather the feeling underlying it, in its different objective aspects. The theological aspect holds that the divine has no part in the concerns of the physical universe: that the true God, strictly transmundane, is not revealed or even indicated by the world, and is therefore the Unknown, the totally Other, unknowable in terms of any worldly analogies. Correspondingly, the cosmological aspect holds that the world is the creation not of God but of some inferior principle, whose inferiority is a perversion of the divine, and whose main traits are dominion and power. And the anthropological aspect holds that man's inner self is not part of the world, of the demiurge's creation and domain, but is within that world as totally transcendent and as incommensurate to all cosmic modes of being as is its transmundane counterpart, the unknown God without.

The new vocabulary reflects the revolution of meaning as an established semantic fact: "cosmos" and such derivative expressions as "cosmic," "of the cosmos," etc., figure as detractive terms in gnostic speech, and this with the force of a fixed terminology. But it is to be noted that the negativity of the concept "cosmos" is not merely that of the absence of divine values in the universe: its combination with such terms as "darkness," "death," "ignorance," and "evil" shows it to be possessed of a counter-quality of its own. That is, contrary to the modern analogue, the withdrawal of the divine from the cosmos leaves the latter not as a neutral, value-indifferent, merely physical fact but as a separatistic power whose very self-positing outside God betrays a direction of *will* away from God; and its existence is the embodiment of that will. Thus the darkness of the world denotes not only its being alien to God and devoid of his light but also its being a *force alienating* from God. In short, it denotes ultimately a spiritual, not merely physical, fact, and in its paradoxical way the gnostic cosmos is as much a theo-logical entity as that of the Stoics. Accordingly, the world has its own spirit, its god—the prince of this world. But it is no longer the All that it was to the Greeks: it is limited and transcended by that which is essentially non-world and the negation of everything that is world. To gnostic piety the true God is chiefly defined by this contraposition. As the world is that which alienates from God, so God is that which alienates and liberates from the world. God as the negation of the world has a nihilistic function with regard to all inner-worldly attachments and values. But the world is none the less real for this nihilistic exposure. In other words, the removal of true divinity from the world does not deprive it of reality and make it a mere shadow or illusion (as in certain teachings of Indian mysticism). As theologically seriously as the Stoic cosmos was an object of love, veneration, and confidence, so seriously is the gnostic cosmos an object of hate, contempt, and fear. And here we remind once more of the role of the idea of order. As already stated, the universe of the gnostic vision, though having none of the venerability of the Greek cosmos, is still cosmos, that is, an order, but order with a vengeance. It is called that now with a new and fearful emphasis, an emphasis at once awed and disrespectful, troubled and rebellious: for that order is alien to man's aspirations. The blemish of nature lies not in any deficiency of order but in the all-too-pervading completeness of it. Far from being chaos, the creation of the demiurge, that antitype of knowing, is a comprehensive system governed by law. But cosmic law, once regarded as the expression of a reason with which man's reason can communicate in the act of cognition and which it can make its own in the shaping of conduct, is now seen only in its aspect of compulsion which thwarts man's freedom. The cosmic *logos* of the Stoics is replaced by *heimarmene,* oppressive cosmic fate. Of this special feature we shall presently have to say more. As a general principle, the vastness, power, and perfection of order evoke no longer contemplation and imitation but aversion and revolt.

The Greek Reaction

In the eyes of antiquity, this was not merely a strange view but plain blasphemy, and wherever it took explicit notice of it, it characterized it as such—as a sacrilegious attitude of which only a profoundly irreligious and impious soul is capable. Plotinus's treatise against the Gnostics (*Enn.* II. 9) is an eloquent testimony of this reaction. Even the title declares it to be a polemic against the detractors of the world, and the work throughout breathes the indignation which ancient cosmos-piety felt at the folly and arrogance of such teachings.

Denying honor to this creation and to this earth, they pretend that a new earth was made for them, to which they will depart from here [Ch. 5]. They blame this All . . . and denigrate its governor and identify the demiurge with the Soul and attribute to him the same passions as those of the particular souls [Ch. 6]. One must instruct them, if only they have the grace to accept instruction, as to the nature of these things, so that they desist from frivolously slandering things which deserve honor [Ch. 8]. This cosmos too is from God and looks towards him [Ch. 9]. He then who blames the nature of the cosmos knows not what he does nor where this his audacity carries him [Ch. 13]. Once more, not by despising the cosmos and the gods it contains and the other beautiful things in it can one become good. . . . How can it be pious to deny that Providence penetrates into this world and into every thing? . . . Who of those that are so unreasonably arrogant is as well-ordered and sagacious as the All? [Ch. 16]

A similar protest was voiced by the rising Church, which in spite of Christianity's own acosmic tendencies was yet an heir of antiquity in face of the excesses of anti-cosmic dualism. Instead of the Greek immanence of the divine in the universe, it was the biblical doctrine of creation and of God's government of the world which provided the argument against the gnostic antithesis of God and world. Here too the slander of the world is rejected as blasphemy: "To say that the world is a product of fall and ignorance is the greatest blasphemy" (Iren. *Adv. Haer.* II. 3. 2). The worst provocation came from Marcion's pitiless contempt of the creator and his work, and we have listed from Tertullian some of the dicta which outraged him most (see p. 141). The sneering tone adopted by Marcion against the world is unequaled even in gnostic literature. But only in this epoch was it possible to speak about the world so rebelliously and contemptuously. Never before or after had such a gulf opened between man and the world, between life and its begetter, and such a feeling of cosmic solitude, abandonment, and transcendental superiority of the self taken hold of man's consciousness.

(b) DESTINY AND THE STARS

That aspect of the cosmos in which to the Gnostics its character was pre-eminently revealed is the *heimarmene,* that is, universal fate. This heimarmene is dispensed by the planets, or the stars in general, the mythical exponents of the inexorable and hostile law of the universe. The change in the emotional content of the term "cosmos" is nowhere better symbolized than in this depreciation of the formerly most divine part of the visible world, the celestial spheres. The starry sky—which from Plato to the Stoics was the purest embodiment of reason in the cosmic hierarchy, the paradigm of intelligibility and therefore of the divine aspect of the sensible realm—now stared man in the face with the fixed glare of alien power and necessity. Its rule is tyranny, and not providence. Deprived of the venerability with which all sidereal piety up to then had invested it, but still in possession of the prominent and representative position it had acquired, the stellar firmament becomes now the symbol of all that is terrifying to man in the towering factness of the universe. Under this pitiless sky, which no longer inspires worshipful confidence, man becomes conscious of his utter forlornness, of his being not so much a part of, but unaccountably placed in and exposed to, the enveloping system.

Forms of Sidereal Piety in the Ancient World

Let us again consider what this development means in the context of ancient religion and cosmology. The deification of the heavens or of the chief heavenly bodies is for the most natural and universally operative reasons an element in all ancient religions (except the Jewish one). The abode of light and, in its greatest star, source of the warmth that nourishes all life on earth; by its movement causing the change of seasons which governs the rhythm of terrestrial existence; itself immediately majestic by the spectacle of its magnitude, beauty, and remoteness; incorruptible and pure; uniting sublimity, infinity, and law in visible form—the heaven was the natural object of all higher piety as it rose above the worship of the chthonic forces. Aristotle went so far as to declare the spectacle of the starred sky to be one of the two origins of religion (the other being dreams; fr. 14, Cicero *Nat. deor.* II. 37. 95); and the author of "On the Cosmos" adduces (Ch. 6) the testimony of mankind: don't we all in prayer raise our hands to heaven?

Solar Monotheism. In the primary form of the cults of the heaven, sun and moon occupy a natural eminence, with the rest of the heavenly host, especially the five other planets and the twelve signs of the Zodiac, added in various roles. A hierarchy is thus suggested from the outset, and one line of development is that the obvious eminence of the sun is increasingly emphasized. Under certain conditions this can lead to a kind of solar monotheism or pantheism, which, briefly realized already in the sun-religion of

Amenhotep IV, at the time of the Roman Empire with which we are dealing rose in the shape of the Syrian sun-religion to great prominence and for a time even became something like the state religion of the Caesars.

Astrological Pluralism. Another line along which sidereal piety developed is represented by the late-Babylonian religion, the most pronounced star-worship of antiquity. In the speculations of a priest caste which, since the fall of the Babylónian monarchy, was no longer the theological guardian of a political system calling for a celestial monarchy, a peculiar leveling of the original hierarchy of celestial powers took place, with the preservation however of their plurality: sun and moon figure as equals among the rest of the planets; the chief deities of the older Babylonian pantheon, divested of their concrete personal character, are assigned to firmly defined causal functions and in these functions identified with the seven planets as the sole powers left. In connection with this depersonalization, the aspect of law and calculable regularity in their operation comes ever more into the foreground. Scientific astronomy, of long standing in Babylon, joined with its prestige and its lore in this religious process. Thus originated the conception of an interplay of a fixed number of impersonal powers which together constitute a system of rule to which all occurrence is subject. This system of cosmic rule has its counterpart in a systematized body of human knowledge concerning this rule. In other words, religion became astrology.

From the time of the Diadochi, the Babylonian astrological religion advanced powerfully westward. Everywhere in Hellenism, especially in Egypt, astrological ideas and astrological practice gained influence, and they furnished the framework, though not the ultimate content, of the gnostic heimarmene concept. The process here described is of great general importance. For the first time in the history of mankind, the world is considered as at every moment the necessary result of a plurality of cosmic powers which simply by virtue of their given quality and the rules of their movements, i.e., non-spontaneously, influence each other and together determine the course of things down to the most particular events on earth. Here theoretical abstraction has traveled a long way from the original intuition of astral nature-religion. That efficacy of the celestial powers which is either directly experienced or in mythical imagination easily associated with their visible properties has given way to defined roles in a system of destiny in which the original objects figure no longer with their sensible features but merely as signs for the general law they impose. The sun, for instance, is no longer the sun of concrete experience and of nature-religion, the god which dispenses light, warmth, life, growth, and also scorching, pestilence, and death, who victoriously rises out of night, puts to flight the winter, and renews nature: it is now one of a number of co-ordinated forces, almost a cipher in a calculable set of determinants. It is its allotted cipher-value and not its original phenomenal quality that now matters.

This evanescence of natural quality removed what would have been the strongest obstacle to a pejorative revaluation of the astral pantheon. As a mere representation of abstract destiny, divorced from the immediate, naïve appeal of the heavenly spectacle, the system could be freely assimilated to opposite world-views. In fact, the world-view of astrology was already ambiguous; and to some extent the fatalistic consciousness of subjection to a rigid necessity as such, and the passivity to which it seemed to condemn man, played into the hands of the gnostic revolution in the total attitude to the world. But astrology is not by itself this revolution. A new active principle of evaluation was needed to fill the value-emptied forms of astral symbolism with a new specific meaning and make them subservient to the expression of a more than cosmic view. This Gnosticism did by transcending the cosmic system as such and from this transcendence looking back upon it.

Philosophic Star-Religion. Finally, we have to mention a third development of sidereal piety in antiquity: the valuation of the stars in Greek philosophy. Here it is not, as in nature-religion, the empirical role of the celestial bodies in sustaining life, nor, as in astrology, their role in human destiny, but their paradigmatic existence in themselves, which made them objects of veneration. The purity of their substance, the perfection of their circular motion, the unimpededness with which in thus moving they follow their own law, the incorruptibility of their being and the immutability of their courses—all these attributes make them in the sense of Greek philosophy "divine," which is here an impersonal ontological predicate pertaining to an object in virtue of such qualities as generally make for eminence of being. Among these constancy of being and immortality of life are paramount. Divine, therefore, are the stars, primarily not by their action but by the rank which they occupy in the hierarchy of things according to their immanent properties. And these are just the properties of order, eternity, and harmony which constitute the "cosmos" character of the All in general: this they represent most purely and completely.[11] To man, therefore, they are over against all the restrictions and impairments of terrestrial processes the convincing manifestation of cosmos as such, the visible evidence of its divinity, whose spectacle assures the onlooker of what is so often obscured here below.[12] Beyond this ideal significance, their perfection is also the real guarantee of the duration of the whole, i.e., of the eternity of cosmic movement and life.[13] Thus they are the most powerful assurance which the Greek affirmation of the world had been able to conceive.

Here again it is the seven planets, or rather the seven spheres in which they are thought to be located, encompassed by the outermost sphere of the fixed stars, which with their mutually attuned movements make up this system that keeps the universe going. They move according to law, or, which is the same, according to *reason*,

[11] Cf. *De mundo*, Ch. 5, 397 a 8 f.: "Which of the individual things could equal the order that sun, moon and stars exhibit in their heavenly revolution, moving in perfectly accurate measure from eternity to eternity? And which could achieve the unfailing rule that the Horae observe, the fair ones, begetters of all things, who in appointed order bring on day and night, summer and winter, so as to make months and years grow full? Truly, of all things the cosmos [here = the heavens] is surpassing in greatness, in movement swiftest, in splendor brightest; his power is unaging and never passes away."

[12] *Ibid.,* Ch. 6, 397 b 27 f.: "The sphere nearest to God enjoys most of his power, then the one beneath it, and so on down to the regions inhabited by us. Therefore the earth and things terrestrial, being farthest from God's influence, appear to be unsteady, disjointed, and full of confusion." This version of the argument fits the monotheism of *De mundo* which places God (as Aristotle placed Mind) above the Sphere: with a slight modification of statement, the argument holds in Stoic pantheism as well.

[13] Cf. Aristotle, *Metaphysics* IX, 8, 1050 b 23 f.: "And so the sun and the stars and the whole heaven are ever active, and there is no fear that they may sometime stand still, as the natural philosophers fear they may. Nor do they tire in this activity; for movement is not for them, as it is for perishable things, connected with the potentiality for opposites, so that the continuity of the movement should be laborious; for it is that kind of substance which is matter and potency, not actuality, that causes this" (tr. Ross).

for the intelligibility of their law implies intelligence in their activation.[14] The degree of intelligibility, considered to rest in intrinsic rationality, is the measure of the grade of being; and by the inference just mentioned, it is also the measure of the intelligence residing in the object itself. (According to the modern view, it is a measure of the intelligence of the cognizing subject merely.) The apprehending of the rationality of the stellar motions by mathematical reason, therefore, is nothing less than the communion of human intelligence with divine intelligence.

The Pythagoreans had found in the astral order the proportions of the concordant musical scale, and accordingly had called this system of the spheres in operation a *harmonia,* that is, the fitting together of a many into a unified whole. Thereby they created the most enchanting symbol of Greek cosmic piety: "harmony," issuing in the inaudible "music of the spheres," is the idealizing expression for the same fact of irrefragable order that astrology stresses less optimistically in its own context.[15] Stoic philosophy strove to integrate the idea of destiny as propounded by contemporary astrology with the Greek concept of harmony: heimarmene to the Stoics is the practical aspect ·of the harmony, i.e., its action as it affects terrestrial conditions and the short-lived beings here. And since the stellar movements are actuated by the cosmic logos and this logos functions in the world-process as providence (*pronoia*), it follows that in this wholly monistic system *heimarmene* itself is *pronoia,* that is, fate and divine providence are the same. The understanding of and willing consent to this fate thus interpreted as the reason of the whole distinguishes the wise man, who bears adversity in his individual destiny as the price paid by the part for the harmony of the whole.

The existence of the whole as such, however, is the ultimate and no further questionable, self-justifying end in this teleological scheme: for the sake of the cosmos its constituent parts exist, as

[14] Cf. Plato, *Laws* X. 898 C: ". . . there would be impiety in asserting that any but the most perfect soul, or souls, carries around the heavens" (tr. Jowett). The idea was elaborated by Aristotle.

[15] "They all together, singing in symphony and moving round the heaven in their measured dance, unite in one harmony whose cause is one (God) and whose end is one (cosmos): it is this harmony which entitles the All to be called 'order' and not disorder" (*De mundo* Ch. 6, 399 a 12 f.).

the members exist for the sake of the whole organism. Man is such a member, and is by his reason called to fit consciously into the whole; but his is by no means the highest mode of being, he is not the end of nature, and the cosmos is not for his sake.

From the time of Poseidonius (one of the philosophic teachers of Cicero, second to first century B.C.), the elevation of the intellect to the stellar regions becomes tinged with an enthusiasm betraying oriental influence and assumes sometimes the characteristic of a mystical escape from the misery of terrestrial conditions. An astral mysticism developed within the Stoa, yet without breaking the confines of cosmic monism.

The Gnostic Revaluation

Over this whole complex of sidereal piety, gnostic dualism comes as a new principle of meaning, appropriates the elements which it can use for its purposes, and subjects them to a radical reinterpretation. Especially the astrological scheme left by the depersonalization of Babylonian religion invited gnostic use and permitted the transposition into a new context of values. As a symbol of general cosmic law, the realm of astral objects had become so formalized that it could be filled at will with very different qualitative content. This content would ultimately be a function of what the world was conceived to be in its basic theological quality. Thus gnostic dualism, taking over the planets in the role in which it had found them, namely, that of rigid cosmic government, makes them on account of this very role the extreme expression of everything anti-divine which the world as such now represented. With all dependence on the material of tradition, no development but only a radical break leads from the position of sidereal religion to the gnostic conception of astral rule. The inescapable law of cosmic dominion, which even in the mixture of worship and fear characteristic of astrological fatalism had made the stars the highest deities, now provoked the violent revolt of a new consciousness of acosmic freedom, which transferred them in a body to the enemy side. For whatever reasons, the experience of this "order" had turned from a worshipful to a terrifying one. The all-encompassing necessity of its rule became an opprobrium of the powers that exercised it. The new dualism as it were "bracketed" the whole universe with all its gradation of lower and higher levels and shifted it as a whole to one side of the duality. The spheric architecture as it had been elaborated by traditional cosmology was retained; but whereas it had included the divine, it now became closed against the divine, which was irrevocably placed outside it. And whereas the heavenly spheres had represented the divinity of the cosmos at its purest, they now most effectively separated it from the divine. Enclosing the created world, they made it a prison for those particles of divinity which had become entrapped in this system.

We can imagine with what feelings gnostic men must have looked up to the starry sky. How evil its brilliance must have looked to them, how alarming its vastness and the rigid immutability of its courses, how cruel its muteness! The music of the spheres was no longer heard, and the admiration for the perfect spherical form gave place to the terror of so much perfection directed at the enslavement of man. The pious wonderment with which earlier man had looked up to the higher regions of the universe became a feeling of oppression by the iron vault which keeps man exiled from his home beyond. But it is this "beyond" which really qualifies the new conception of the physical universe and of man's position in it. Without it, we should have nothing but a hopeless worldly pessimism. Its transcending presence limits the inclusiveness of the cosmos to the status of only a part of reality, and thus of something from which there is an escape. The realm of the divine begins where that of the cosmos ends, i.e., at the eighth sphere. The total gnostic view is neither pessimistic nor optimistic, but eschatological: if the world is bad, there is the goodness of the outer-worldly God; if the world is a prison, there is an alternative to it; if man is a prisoner of the world, there is a salvation from it and a power that saves. It is in this eschatological tension, in the polarity of world and God, that the gnostic cosmos assumes its religious quality.

We have seen in previous chapters that in this polarity the cosmic powers undergo a new mythological *personification*. The frightening features of the Archons are a far cry from a mere symbolism of abstract cosmic necessity: they are willful, anti-divine figures and exercise their rule with all the purpose and passion of a selfish cause. Thus, after the philosophical and astrological abstraction of the Hellenistic speculation, the star-gods gain a new

concreteness in mythical imagination—not in return to but at a yet
farther remove from the "natural" view of earlier mythology. This
is just one example of the fact that in the Hellenistic environment
Gnosticism acted as a source of new myth-creation. But it must be
noted that this new mythology, despite some genuinely "first" creations, was a secondary one in that it supervened upon an older
mythological tradition and constructed its new object-system out of
the consciously reinterpreted elements of a complex heritage. In
this connection the eminence accorded to the astral powers is not
so much an authentic choice on the part of the gnostic myth-makers
as a conversion of their pre-given role to the function which the
new value-system required. Their eminence is to the same extent
negative as it had been positive before.

The Greek Reaction; the Brotherhood of Man and Stars

Plotinus again bears witness to the resistance which Greek
piety offered to this detraction of the stellar world; again we meet
the tone of indignation that we found directed against the detraction of the world in general.

They should desist from the horror-stories of the frightful things
which allegedly take place in the cosmic spheres, those spheres which
in truth are the givers of everything beneficial. What have they frightful in them by which to frighten those who are inexperienced in reason
and have never heard of the well-ordered knowledge [*gnosis*] acquired
by education? If their bodies are of fire, that is no reason to fear them,
for they are in proper proportion to the All and to the earth; but one
must rather consider their souls—after all, do not the Gnostics themselves claim their own value according to theirs? . . . If men are
superior to the other living creatures, how much more superior are
they (the spheres), which are in the All not for tyrannical rule but to
confer on it order and harmony [*Enn.* II. 9. 13]. The stars too have
souls, which far surpass ours in intelligence, goodness, and contact with
the spiritual world [*ibid.* 16].

Obviously Plotinus' argument is conclusive only on the common Greek assumption (tacitly presupposed by him) of the general
homogeneity of all cosmic existence, which permits comparison
between all parts by a uniform standard of evaluation. The standard is that of "cosmos," i.e., order itself, and by this standard man

indeed must rank far below the stars, which achieve undeviatingly and for the whole what man may at best achieve passingly and on his small scale, namely, ordered activity. The argument as to worth is hardly convincing to us. How much farther Plotinus as the representative of the classical mind is here from our own position than the Gnostics are with all their mythological fancy, the following quotation will make evident.

> Even the basest men they deem worthy to be called brothers, while with frenzied mouth they declare the sun, the stars in the heavens, and even the world-soul, unworthy to be called by them brothers. Those who are base have indeed no right to claim that kinship, but those who have become good [have acquired the right].
>
> (*ibid.* 18)

Here the two camps confront each other with inimitable clearness. Plotinus maintains the unity of all being in the universe, with no essential separation of the human and the non-human realm. Man is in his essence kindred to the whole cosmos, even to the macrocosmic entities, which are like himself ensouled; only they are incomparably better than he, superior in strength and purity of that which is also the best in him, namely, reason, and in this feature imitable by him. The better he is, the more he actualizes his kinship with the cosmic powers, that is, the more he increases the original generic community of his being and that of the total cosmos.

Gnosticism, on the contrary, removes man, in virtue of his essential belonging to another realm, from all sameness with the world, which now is nothing but bare "world," and confronts him with its totality as the absolutely different. Apart from his accessory outer layers contributed by the world, man by his inner nature is acosmic; to such a one, all the world is indifferently alien. Where there is ultimate otherness of origin, there can be kinship neither with the whole nor with any part of the universe. The self is kindred only to other human selves living in the world—and to the transmundane God, with whom the non-mundane center of the self can enter into communication. This God must be acosmic, because the cosmos has become the realm of that which is alien to the self. Here we can discern the profound connection which exists between the discovery of the self, the despiritualizing of the world, and the positing of the transcendent God.

The Acosmic Brotherhood of Salvation

The pantheistic or panlogistic confidence of antiquity is shattered in Gnosticism. The self is discovered as incommensurable with all things of nature. This discovery at first makes the self emerge in its utter solitude: the self is discovered by a break with the world. At the same time, this recoil from cosmic alienness leads to a new emphasis on the fellowship of man as the only realm of kinship left, united not only by the community of origin but also by the community of the situation of aliens in the world. But this fellowship refers not to the natural and social concerns of men, that is, to man's worldly existence, but only to the acosmic inner self and its concern of salvation. Thus is founded the new brotherhood of the elect, or the believers, or the knowers, to which even those who by the standard of worldly virtue are the "basest" belong if they are bearers of the pneuma. That these "basest" are superior to the sun and all the stars is self-evident with the new evaluation of selfhood and nature. It is equally evident that the mutual concern of the eschatological brotherhood cannot consist in furthering the integration of man into the cosmic whole, as far as feeling is concerned, nor in making him "play his proper part," as far as action is concerned. He is no longer a part of this whole, except in violation of his true essence. Instead, the mutual concern of the brotherhood, thrown together by the common cosmic solitude, is to deepen this very alienation and to further the other's redemption, which to each self becomes a vehicle of his own.

About the ethical implications of the anti-cosmic orientation we shall hear more in the next chapter. Here, in our confrontation of the gnostic with the classical concept of cosmic law as especially connected with the status of the stars, we have to appreciate the symbolic significance of Plotinus' polemic. What arouses his ire—that the basest of men are acknowledged as brothers but even the highest elements of the universe (and even "our sister the world-soul") are denied this honor—is a precise expression of a profoundly new attitude whose heirs at a far remove we are still today. The gnostic attitude which here assumes an absolute difference of being, not merely a difference of value, strikes us as somehow more "modern" than the Greek position taken by Plotinus which in the comprehensive orders of the objective world recognizes a more perfect instance of our own being and grants to the wise and virtuous a kinship with these closer than that connecting him with the imperfect of his own race. Ranged in this opposition, in which it shares common ground with Christianity, Gnosticism becomes visible as what it truly is: one factor in the historic turning of the collective mind which we often hear described merely negatively as the decline of antiquity, but which is at the same time the rise of a new form of man. In what he criticizes, Plotinus shows us one of the roots of our world.

Chapter 11. *Virtue and the Soul in Greek and Gnostic Teaching*

(a) THE IDEA OF VIRTUE: ITS ABSENCE IN GNOSTICISM

Among the reproaches which Plotinus raises against the Gnostics (all of which relate to what is typically un-Hellenic in them) is that they lack a theory of virtue; and he maintains that it is their contempt of the world that prevents them from having one.

This point must least escape our attention: what influence their teachings have on the souls of their hearers and of those who are persuaded by them to despise the world and the things in it. . . . Their doctrine, even more audacious than that of Epicurus [who only *denied* providence], by *blaming* the Lord of providence and providence itself, holds in contempt all the laws down here and virtue which has risen among men from the beginning of time, and puts temperance to ridicule, *so that nothing good may be discovered in this world*. Thus their doctrine nullifies temperance and the justice inborn in the human character and brought to fulness by reason and exercise, and in general everything by which a man can become worthy and noble. . . . For of the things here *nothing* is to them noble, but only something "different," which they will pursue "hereafter." But should not those who have attained "knowledge" [*gnosis*] pursue the Good already here, and in pursuing it first set right the things down here, for the very reason that they [the Gnostics] claim to have sprung from the divine essence? For it is of the nature of this essence to regard what is noble. . . . But those who have no share in virtue have nothing to transport them from here to the things beyond.

It is revealing that they conduct no inquiry at all about virtue and that the treatment of such things is wholly absent from their teaching: they do not discourse on what virtue is and how many kinds there are, nor do they take notice of the many and precious insights which can be found in the writings of the ancients, nor do they indicate how virtue originates and how it is acquired, nor how to tend and to purify the soul. For simply saying "Look towards God" is of no avail without teaching *how* to look. What prevents one, somebody might say, from

266

looking towards God without abstaining from any pleasure and curbing violent emotion? or from remembering the name of God and yet remaining in the grip of all passions? . . . In fact only virtue can reveal God to us, as it progresses and becomes real in the soul together with insight. Without true virtue, God remains an empty word.

(*Enn.* II. 9. 15)

The polemic is exceedingly instructive. It exposes more than a mere omission on the part of the Gnostics. The absence of a doctrine of virtue in gnostic teaching is connected with the anticosmic attitude, that is, the denial of any worth to the things of this world and consequently also to man's doings in this world. Virtue in the Greek sense (*areté*) is the actualization in the mode of excellence of the several faculties of the soul for dealing with the world. By doing the right things in the right way at the right time, man not only fulfills his duty toward his fellow men and the city but also furthers the good of his soul by keeping it in the shape of excellence, much as running keeps a racehorse in shape, while at the same time being that for which it is to be in shape. Thus is "action according to virtue" means and end at the same time. The good of the racehorse and the good of man are vastly different, but they both are the good of their subjects in basically the same sense: each represents in terms of *activity* the most perfect *state* of its subject according to its inborn nature. In man's case this nature involves a hierarchy of faculties, of which the highest one is reason. Its being "naturally" superior to the other faculties in man does not assure its being accorded this superiority in the actual life of a person. Virtue, therefore, though bringing "nature" understood as the true human nature into its right, is not itself present by nature but requires instruction, effort, and choice. The right shape of our actions depends on the right shape of our faculties and dispositions, and this on the actual prevailing of the "naturally" true hierarchy. To perceive what is the natural hierarchy and the position of reason therein is itself a feat of reason; therefore the cultivation of reason is part of virtue. In other words, it is up to man to transform his inchoately given nature into his true nature, for in his case alone nature does not automatically realize itself. This is why virtue is necessary both *toward* the full realization and *as* the full realization of man's being. Since this being is a being in the world with fellow beings, in the context of the needs and concerns determined by this setting, the exercise of virtue extends to all the natural relations of man as part of the world. He is most perfect in himself when he is most perfectly the part he was meant to be; and we have seen before how this idea of self-perfection is connected with the idea of the cosmos as the divine whole.

It is obvious that Gnosticism had no room for this conception of human virtue. "Looking towards God" has for it an entirely different meaning from the one it had for the Greek philosophers. There it meant granting the rights of all things as graded expressions of the divine within the encompassing divinity of the universe. The self-elevation in the scale of being through wisdom and virtue implies no denial of the levels surpassed. To the Gnostics, "looking towards God" means just such a denial: it is a jumping across all intervening realities, which for this direct relationship are nothing but fetters and obstacles, or distracting temptations, or at best irrelevant. The sum of these intervening realities is the world, including the social world. The surpassing interest in salvation, the exclusive concern in the destiny of the transcendent self, "denatures" as it were these realities and takes the heart out of the concern with them where such a concern is unavoidable. An essential mental reservation qualifies participation in the things of this world, and even one's own person as involved with those things is viewed from the distance of the beyond. This is the common spirit of the new transcendental religion, not confined to Gnosticism in particular. We remind the reader of St. Paul's saying:

> But this I say, brethren, the time is short: it remaineth, that both they that have wives be as though they had none; and they that weep, as though they wept not; and they that rejoice, as though they rejoiced not; and they that buy, as though they possessed not; and they that use this world, as not abusing it: for the fashion of this world passeth away.
> (I Cor. 7:29-31)

The world and one's belonging to it are not to be taken seriously. But virtue *is* seriousness in the execution of the different modes of this belonging and the taking seriously of oneself in meeting the demands of the world, i.e., of being. If as in Platonism the world is not identical with true being, it is yet a stepping stone to it. But "this world" of gnostic dualism is not even that. And as a dimension of existence it does not offer occasion to the perfectibility of man. The least, then, that the acosmic attitude must cause in the relation to inner-worldly existence is the mental reservation of the "as-though-not."

But gnostic dualism goes beyond this dispassionate position. For it regards the "soul" itself, the spiritual organ of man's belonging to the world, as no less than his body an effluence of the cosmic powers and therefore as an instrument of their dominion over his true but submerged self. As the "terrestrial envelopment of the pneuma," the "soul" is the exponent of the world within man—the world is *in* the soul. A profound distrust, therefore, of one's own inwardness, the suspicion of demonic trickery, the fear of being betrayed into bondage inspire gnostic psychology. The alienating forces are located in man himself as composed of flesh, soul, and spirit. The contempt of the cosmos radically understood includes the contempt of the *psyche*. Therefore what is of the psyche is incapable of being elevated to the condition of virtue. It is either to be left to itself, to the play of its forces and appetites, or to be reduced by mortification, or sometimes even extinguished in ecstatic experience.

The last statement indicates that the negative attitude to the world, or the negative quality of the world itself, though it does not give room to virtue in the Greek sense, still leaves open the choice between several modes of conduct in which the negativity is turned into a principle of praxis. Insofar as such forms of conduct are put forward as norms and express a gnostic "ought," they embody what can be called gnostic morality. In its context, even the term "virtue" may re-emerge; but the meaning of the term has then radically changed, and so has the material content of particular virtues. We shall give some examples of types of gnostic morality and of the rather paradoxical kind of "virtue" it admitted; and we shall occasionally take our evidence from beyond the strictly "gnostic" realm, since the dissolution and controversion of the classical *areté*-concept is a broader phenomenon connected with the rise of acosmism or transcendental religion in general.

(b) GNOSTIC MORALITY

The negative element we have so far emphasized represents of course one side only of the gnostic situation. Just as the cosmos is no longer the All but is surpassed by the divine realm beyond, so the soul is no longer the whole person but is surpassed by the acosmic pneuma within—something very different from the "reason" and "intellect" of Greek teaching. And just as the profound cosmic pessimism is set off against the optimism of the eschatological assurance, so the profound psychological pessimism, despairing of the soul as a slave of the cosmos, is set off against the overweening confidence in the ultimately unassailable freedom of the pneuma. And if the contra-position of the cosmos to that which is not cosmos means that from the prison of the former there is an escape, so the inner duality of "soul" and "spirit," i.e., the inner presence of a transcendent principle, indefinable as it is in its difference from everything "worldly," holds out the possibility of stripping off one's own soul and experiencing the divinity of the absolute Self.

Nihilism and Libertinism

The purest and most radical expression of the metaphysical revolt is moral nihilism. Plotinus' critique implied moral indifference in the Gnostics, that is, not only the absence of a doctrine of virtue but also the disregard of moral restraints in real life. The polemic of the Church Fathers tells us more about the theory or metaphysics of what is known as gnostic libertinism. We quote from Irenaeus:

Psychical men are instructed in things psychical, and they are steadied by works and simple faith and do not possess the perfect knowledge. These (according to them) are we of the Church. To us, therefore, they maintain, a moral life is necessary for salvation. They themselves, however, according to their teaching, would be saved absolutely and under all circumstances, not through works but through the mere fact of their being by nature "spiritual." For, as it is impossible for the earthly element to partake in salvation, not being susceptible of it, so it is impossible for the spiritual element (which they pretend to be themselves) to suffer corruption, whatever actions they may have indulged in. As gold sunk in filth will not lose its beauty but preserve its own nature, and the filth will be unable to impair the gold, so nothing can injure them, even if their deeds immerse them in matter, and nothing can change their spiritual essence. Therefore "the most perfect" among them do unabashed all the forbidden things of which Scripture assures us "that they which do such things shall not inherit the kingdom of God." . . . Others serve intemperately the lusts of the flesh and say you must render the flesh to the flesh and the spirit to the spirit.

(*Adv. Haer.* I. 6. 2-3)

There are several important arguments contained in this report. One is based on the idea of invariable natures or substances, and according to this argument the pneumatic is "naturally saved," i.e., saved by virtue of his nature. The practical inference from this is a maxim of general license which permits the pneumatic the indiscriminate use of the natural realm. The inner-worldly difference of good and evil has been submerged in the essential indifference of everything cosmic to the destiny of the acosmic self. But indifference is not the whole story of gnostic libertinism. Already the last sentence in the passage from Irenaeus suggests a positive enjoinder to excess. Before we turn to this strange doctrine of immoralism on a religious basis, we may state the position of indifference more fully.

The only thing the pneumatic is committed to is the realm of the transmundane deity, a transcendence of the most radical kind. This transcendence, unlike the "intelligible world" of Platonism or the world-Lord of Judaism, does not stand in any positive relation to the sensible world. It is not the essence of that world, but its negation and cancellation. The gnostic God as distinct from the demiurge is the totally different, the other, the unknown. In him the absolute beyond beckons across the enclosing cosmic shells. And as this God has more of the *nihil* than of the *ens* in his concept, so also his inner-human counterpart, the acosmic Self or pneuma, otherwise hidden, reveals itself in the negative experience of otherness, of non-identification, and of protested indefinable freedom. For all purposes of man's relation to existing reality, both the hidden God and the hidden pneuma are nihilistic conceptions: no *nomos* emanates from them, that is, no law either for nature or for human conduct as a part of the natural order. There is indeed a law of creation, but to him who created the world the alien in man owes no allegiance; and neither his creation, though incomprehensibly encompassing man, nor his proclaimed will offers the standards by which isolated man can set his course. Thus ensues the antinomian argument of the Gnostics, so far as it is merely *negative*: as such, it states no more than that the norms of the non-spiritual realm are not binding on him who is of the spirit.

In this connection we sometimes meet in gnostic reasoning the *subjectivist* argument of traditional moral skepticism: nothing is naturally good or bad, things in themselves are indifferent, and "only by human opinion are actions good or bad." Spiritual man in the freedom of his knowledge has the indifferent use of them all (Iren. *op. cit.* I. 25. 4-5). While this reminds one of nothing more than the reasoning of certain classical Sophists, a deeper gnostic reflection upon the *source* of such "human opinions" transforms the argument from a skeptical to a metaphysical one, and turns indifference into opposition: the ultimate source is found to be not human but demiurgical, and thus common with that of the order of nature. By reason of this source the law is not really indifferent but is part of the great design upon our freedom. Being law, the moral code is but the psychical complement to the physical law, and as such the internal aspect of the all-pervading cosmic rule. Both emanate from the lord of the world as agencies of his power, unified in the double aspect of the Jewish God as creator and legislator. Just as the law of the physical world, the heimarmene, integrates the individual bodies into the general system, so the moral law does with the souls, and thus makes them subservient to the demiurgical scheme.

For what is the law—either as revealed through Moses and the prophets or as operating in the actual habits and opinions of men—but the means of regularizing and thus stabilizing the implication of man in the business of the world and worldly concerns; of setting by its rules the seal of seriousness, of praise and blame, reward and punishment, on his utter involvement; of making his very will a compliant party to the compulsory system, which thereby will function all the more smoothly and inextricably? Insofar as the principle of this moral law is justice, it has the same character of constraint on the psychical side that cosmic fate has on the physical side. "The angels that created the world established 'just actions' to lead men by such precepts into servitude." [1] In the normative law man's will is taken care of by the same powers that control his body. He who obeys it has abdicated the authority of his self. Here we have, beyond the mere indifference of the "subjectivist" argument and beyond the merely permissive privilege of freedom, a positive metaphysical interest in repudiating allegiance to all objective norms and thus a motive for their outright violation. It is the double interest in asserting the authentic freedom of the self by daring the Archons and in injuring their general cause by individually thwarting their design.

Even this is not the whole story of gnostic libertinism. Beyond the motive of defiance, we find sometimes the freedom to do everything turned into a positive *obligation* to perform every kind of action, with the idea of rendering to nature its own and thereby exhausting its powers. The doctrine, briefly indicated in the quoted passage from Irenaeus (I. 6. 2-3), is more fully stated by him in his report on Carpocrates and the Cainites. In the former it is combined with the doctrine of transmigration, and in this combination amoralism is the means by which freedom is to be attained rather than the manner in which it is possessed.

The souls in their transmigrations through bodies must pass through every kind of life and every kind of action, unless somebody has in one coming already acted everything at once. . . . According to their writings, their souls before departing must have made use of every mode of life and must have left no remainder of any sort still to be performed: lest they must again be sent into another body because there is still something lacking to their freedom. This Jesus indicated with the words, ". . . I tell thee, thou shalt not depart thence, till thou hast paid the very last mite" (Luke 12:59). . . . This means that he shall not get free from the power of the angels that made the world, but has always to be reincarnated until he has committed every deed there is in the world, and only when nothing is still lacking will he be released to that God who is above the world-creating angels. Thus the souls are released and saved . . . after they have paid their debt and rendered their due.

(Iren. I. 25. 4; cf. Eusebius, *Hist. eccl.* IV 7)

[1] Simon Magus: compare the complete passage as given on p. 108.

And again, of the Cainites Irenaeus reports,

> Not otherwise can one be saved than by passing through every action, as also Carpocrates taught. . . . At every sinful and infamous deed an angel is present, and he who commits it . . . addresses him by his name and says, "O thou angel, I use thy work! O thou Power of such-and-such, I perform thy deed!" And this is the perfect knowledge, unafraid to stray into such actions whose very names are unmentionable.
> (Iren. I.31.2)

The idea that in sinning something like a program has to be completed, a due rendered as the price of ultimate freedom, is the strongest doctrinal reinforcement of the libertinistic tendency inherent in the gnostic rebellion as such and turns it into a positive prescription of immoralism. Sin as the way to salvation, the theological inversion of the idea of sin itself—here is one of the antecedents of mediaeval Satanism; and again an archetype of the Faustian myth. On the other hand, the combination of this doctrine with the theme of transmigration in Carpocrates represents a curious adaptation of Pythagorean teachings and perhaps also of the Indian karma-doctrine, where the release from the "wheel of birth" is also, though in a very different spirit, the governing concern.

We may doubt with Irenaeus whether the preachers of these views lived up to their own professions. To scandalize has always been the pride of rebels, but much of it may satisfy itself in provocativeness of doctrine rather than of deeds. Yet we must not underrate the extremes to which revolutionary defiance and the vertigo of freedom could go in the value-vacuum created by the spiritual crisis. The very discovery of a new vista invalidating all former norms constituted an anarchical condition, and excess in thought and life was the first response to the import and dimensions of that vista.

Asceticism, Self-Abnegation, the New "Virtue"

Libertinism had its alternative in asceticism. Opposite as the two types of conduct are, they yet were in the gnostic case of the same root, and the same basic argument supports them both. The one repudiates allegiance to nature through excess, the other, through abstention. Both are lives outside the mundane norms.

Freedom by abuse and freedom by non-use, equal in their indiscriminateness, are only alternative expressions of the same acosmism. Libertinism was the most insolent expression of the metaphysical revolt, reveling in its own bravado: the utmost of contempt for the world consists in dismissing it even as a danger or an adversary. Asceticism acknowledges the world's corrupting power: it takes seriously the danger of contamination and is thus animated more by fear than by contempt. And even in the extreme of negativism, the ascetic life may conceive itself as productive of a positive quality —purity—and as thereby already *realizing* something of the future state of salvation in the present condition. This is especially the case where the asceticism is practiced as an almost technical method with a view to preparing the soul for the reception of a mystical illumination in which the ultimate consummation of the hereafter is as it were pre-experienced. Here asceticism serves the cause of sanctification, and the qualities which it confers upon the subject, be they the mystical ones just mentioned or merely moral ones, are considered valuable in themselves; i.e., asceticism has a relation to "virtue," if in a new sense determined by the acosmic frame of reference. That this positive meaning, however, is by no means a necessary aspect of gnostic asceticism, Marcion shows with abundant clarity: his moral argument, as we have seen (Ch. 6, *b*), is based entirely on the theme of contempt and enmity toward the world and does not entrust to the abstention from its works the task of perfecting the subject. The abstention is essentially a matter of rejection and thus is as much an expression of the revolt against the creator as is the libertine indulgence.

We encountered the ascetic attitude in much of the material presented in earlier chapters and need not repeat the evidence here. For Marcion we refer to pp. 144 f., for Mani, to pp. 231 ff. These two are the most outstanding examples of a rigorous asceticism following from the very core of doctrine. In the case of Mani we found it connected with the theme of compassion, which enjoins sparing the particles of Light dispersed in the creation. But the idea of the impurity of the cosmic substance is present with at least equal force, so that again, whatever the part of "sympathy," rejection is an essential factor in the ascetic life.

Not everywhere does the ascetic mood go to such grim lengths as in these cases. The acosmic attitude may express itself in a general toning-down of all relations to the things of this world, in reducing their hold upon the soul and keeping a cautious distance from them. "Love ye not gold and silver and the possessions of this world"; "Be not a son of the house . . . love not pleasant-smelling garlands, and take not pleasure in a fair woman . . . love not lust nor deceiving shadows"— so we read in the Mandaean sources quoted above, p. 84, and the general rationale of these enjoinders is expressed in the words, "Thou wert not from here, and thy root was not of the world" (G 379). Thus the acosmic position comes to express itself in a general morality of withdrawal, which develops its own code of negative "virtues."

It is no accident that, whereas the libertinistic version of gnostic morality was represented by decidedly esoteric types, our examples for the ascetic version are taken from what we may call exoteric types of Gnosticism. Both Marcion and Mani intended to found a general church, not a minority group of initiates; and Mandaeism, numerically small as it remained, was a community religion of popular complexion. Anarchy is incompatible with institution as such, and any religious establishment will lead in the direction of discipline. To some extent the church takes over the functions of the polis; ideally it aspires to being an all-embracing *civitas* itself, in this world though not of this world, replacing the secular *civitas* in regulating the lives of its members. This must necessarily give rise to a canon of "virtues" appropriate to the aim of these new societies. In short, institutionalized salvation, that is, the very idea of "church," favors the discipline of ascetic morality over a literal understanding of the ideal of pneumatic freedom, which the anti-cosmic position as such suggests. The. literal conclusions were drawn by sectarians only who emphatically considered themselves to be such. The Christian Gnostics listed by Irenaeus as holding libertine views regarded their "freedom" as an exclusive privilege never meant for the ordinary members of the Church, those of "simple faith." And even among the sects, there were probably as many who, like the Encratites and the Ebionites, had with all emphasis on the difference between the knowers and the common crowd decided for the ascetic alternative of the anti-cosmic position. Generally we may surmise that, except for a brief period of revolutionary extremism, the practical consequences from gnostic views were more often in the direction of asceticism than of libertinism. After all, rebellion (and gnostic libertinism was the brazen expression of a rebellion no less against a cultural tradition than against the demiurge) is not a state that can be maintained indefinitely. It is over when the new vision has created its own tradition.

Areté and the Christian "Virtues"

The denial of man's natural stature, and therewith of the "excellence" (virtue) attainable through its development, is universal in the acosmic climate of opinion. In this respect the Gnostics are part of a much broader tide which undermined and finally engulfed the classical position. The Christian reader is here on familiar ground: he will readily recall the kind of "virtues," and of corresponding vices, which can be extracted from New Testament admonitions. Lowliness, meekness, long-suffering, patience, even fear and sorrow, are praised; pride, vainglory, imaginations, "everything high that exalteth itself against the knowledge [*gnosis*] of God," are warned against.[2] I John 2:15-16 (see above, p. 73) clearly shows the anti-cosmic framework of the ethical orientation. Those modes of conduct, the common quality of which is humility, we may call virtues of self-abnegation: the self so abnegated is that of natural man. They have, it is true, their positive complement in faith, hope, and charity. But though these three were later actually termed "virtues" and as such joined to the four "cardinal virtues" of the ancients, it is obvious that, judged by the original meaning of the term, they can be thus called only in a very paradoxical sense. For far from confirming selfhood in its autonomous worth, they presuppose man's radical inability to achieve his own perfection and include the acknowledgment of this insufficiency— that is to say, the self-negating position of humility—in their very meaning. They are, in truth, like the former, the denial of *areté*.[3]

[2] E.g., Eph. 4:1-2; Phil. 2:3; II Cor. 10:5; Rom. 5:3-4; II Cor. 7:10; Ep. Barnab. 2:2.

[3] The word itself is hardly used in the New Testament. In all the Pauline epistles, with their rich exhortatory vocabulary, it occurs only once, and there without particular significance (Phil. 4:8; the only other occurrence in connection with man is II Pet. 1:5). The silence itself is telling: the word did not suit the intentions of the first Christian writers.

The other-worldly reference of all these "virtues" and their depreciation of natural values, including personal autonomy, are familiar enough to obviate elaboration. Lest it should appear, however, that this reflects solely the Christian position and is necessarily bound up with the doctrines of original sin and salvation through the Cross, we shall by way of digression introduce the less well-known case of Philo Judaeus, in whom we can observe the transformation of the classical *areté*-concept in the stage of actual discourse joining issue with the philosophical tradition. We shall then see that it is the impact of transcendental religion in general which leads to this reinterpretation of the ethical world.

Virtue in Philo Judaeus

Philo was enough heir to the Stoic and Platonic tradition to accord to the concept and name of areté an important place in his thought. But how does this virtue look in his presentation? For one thing, Philo never tires of emphasizing that the virtues originate in the soul not from ourselves but from God: they enter the soul "from outside," as he says, or "from above," by divine grace and without contribution from the self. God alone is their author. The soul has no excellence of its own, and can only long for it.[4] Not even this longing, nor the effort which it devotes toward the attainment of virtue, must the soul ascribe to itself: they too have to be attributed to God, who "gives" the *eros,* i.e., the tendency toward virtue.[5] Philo uses various images to describe this relation of divine activity and human receptivity, notably that of sowing and begetting. This image points to the idea, widespread in the gnostic world also, of a quasi-sexual relation in which the soul is the female and conceiving part and is impregnated by God. "God alone can open the wombs of the souls, sow virtues in them, make them pregnant, and cause them to give birth to the Good." [6] The idea is very un-Greek, when we remember what the original meaning of

[4] Cf. *Mut. nom.* 141. 258 f.

[5] Cf. *Leg. all.* III. 136.

[6] *Ibid.,* 180. In the following paragraph the image changes: there it is the "virtue" in its turn whose womb God opens in order to sow in it the good actions. This duplication of divine activity emphasizes the passivity of the soul to the point of exaggeration; cf. *Cherub.* 42 ff.; *Post. Cai.* 133 f.; *Deus immut.* 5.

areté as self-activity implied. And the image concerns not merely the *genesis* of virtue in the soul but the very mode of its possession. For, according to Philo, the *consciousness* of this its origin should (and this "should" is a new ethical imperative), precisely in its negative aspect, i.e., the non-attribution to the self, become an essential element of virtue itself—to the extent that this reflection in fact constitutes the virtuousness of the virtue, which possessed otherwise would not be virtue at all. The reflection in question is that upon man's *nothingness*.[7] This creates a highly paradoxical situation for the meaning of virtue. The several primary virtues of the ethical tradition, notwithstanding Philo's praise of them in the Stoic manner, no longer stand on their own intrinsic content, since this content has become ambiguous. It is rather the way in which the self determines its relation to their presence that becomes the true dimension of virtue and vice in a new sense. The subject may impute the virtue to itself as its own achievement (and this is the original meaning of areté as excellence): to Philo this self-imputation consumes, as it were, the moral value of those "virtues" and perverts them into vices; rather than modes of self-perfection, they are temptations by the fact that they can be taken as such. "Selfish and godless is the nous who thinks himself equal to God and believes he is acting where in truth he is suffering. Since it is God who sows and plants the goods in the soul, it is impious of the nous to say, I plant" (*Leg. all.* I. 49 f.; cf. III. 32 f.). Alternatively, the self may renounce the claim to its own authorship and acknowledge its essential insufficiency—and this secondary reflection, or rather the general attitude it expresses, becomes the real object of the moral command and is *itself considered as "virtue,"* although it is the denial of there being any virtue of the self. Thus the very meaning of areté is withdrawn from the positive faculties of the person and placed in the knowledge of nothingness. Confidence in one's own moral powers, the whole enterprise of self-perfection based on it, and the self-attribution of the achievement—integral aspects of the Greek conception of virtue—this entire attitude is here condemned as the vice of self-love and conceit. Recognition and confession of one's own incapacity, confidence alone

[7] *Sacr. Ab. et Cai.* 55; *Somn.* I. 60.

in God's granting what the soul cannot attain by itself, and acknowledgment of the divine source of what has been granted—this whole attitude is that of "virtue" as such.[8]

It is characteristic of Philo's position of compromise between the Greek and the "new" viewpoints that he adds the thus defined "virtue" to the list of the traditional virtues which he retains in name, putting it at the head of these as if it were of the same order, whereas in truth it invalidates the independent status of them all and becomes the sole condition of their worth; and the same with the corresponding vice. Thus, "queen of the virtues," "the most perfect among the virtues," is faith,[9] which combines the turning to God with the recognition and contempt of one's own nothingness.[10] In acquiring this "virtue," man acquires all the other virtues as its fruit. On the other hand, "the vice most odious to God" is vainglory, self-love, arrogance, presumption—in brief, the pride of considering oneself as one's own lord and ruler and of relying on one's own powers.[11]

This complete disintegration of the Greek ideal of virtue implies that of its anthropological foundations: "In ourselves are the treasures of evil, with God those of good alone" (*Fug. et inv.* 79). While to the Hellenes from Plato to Plotinus man's way to God led through moral self-perfection, for Philo it leads through self-despair in the realization of one's nothingness. "Know thyself" is an essential element of both ways. But to Philo self-knowledge means "to know the nothingness of the mortal race" (*Mut. nom.* 54), and through this knowledge one attains to the knowledge of God: "For then is the time for the creature to encounter the Creator, when it has recognized its own nothingness" (*Rer. div. her.* 30). To know God and to disown oneself is a standing correlation in Philo.[12] Among the impressive images which he coins

---

[8] Symbolized in Cain and Abel, cf. *Sacr. Ab. et Cai.* 2 ff.

[9] *Abrah.* 270; *Rer. div. her.* 91.

[10] *Mut. nom.* 155.

[11] *Somn.* I. 211; *Rer. div. her.* 91.

[12] What we here render by "disown" is in the Greek original a compound from the verb "to know"—a play on words which is lost in English translation. The following is a good example of Philo's frequent variations on this theme: "When Abraham knew most, he most disowned himself, that he might attain the perfect knowledge of the Truly Existent. This is the natural course: he who comprehends himself wholly, wholly lets go of the nothingness which he discovers in all creation, and he who lets go of himself comes to know the Existent" (*Somn.* I. 60.)

in this connection (by way of Scriptural allegory) is that of "defecting from oneself"; and the favorite one, "to fly from oneself and flee to God." "He who runs away from God flees to himself . . . he who flies from his own nous flees to that of the All" (*Leg. all.* III. 29; cf. *ibid.* 48).

This fleeing from oneself can, besides the ethical meaning which we have so far been considering, assume also a mystical meaning, as in the following passage: "Get thee out,[13] not only from thy body . . . ["country"] and from sense-perception . . . ["kindred"] and from reason . . . ["father's house"], but escape even thyself, and pass out of thyself, raving and God-possessed like the Dionysian Corybantes" (*Rer. div. her.* 69; cf. *ibid.* 85). With this mystic version of the abandonment of the self we have to deal in the context of gnostic psychology.

(c) GNOSTIC PSYCHOLOGY

The Demonological Interpretation of Inwardness

After this digression into the broader spiritual environment, we return to the area of Gnosticism proper. The deprecation of man's natural status and powers which we found as a general feature under the new dispensation of transcendental religion is in Gnosticism connected with the dualistic metaphysics and the problematical status of the soul in its system. Where Philo's monotheism with its doctrine of divine creation lacked a real theory of the derogation, and Christianity devised one in the theory of original sin, Gnosticism based the dubious character of the soul and the profound moral helplessness of man on the cosmic situation as such. The subservience of the soul to the cosmic powers follows from its very origination from those powers. It is their effluence; and to be afflicted with this psyche, or to be housed in it, is part of the cosmic situation for the spirit. The cosmos is here by itself a demonic system—"there is no part of the cosmos empty of demons" (*C.H.* IX. 3); and if the soul represents the cosmos in the inwardness of man, or through the soul "the world" is in man himself, then man's inwardness is the natural scene for demonic activity and his self is

[13] The passage is an exegesis of Gen. 12:1: "Now the Lord had said unto Abram, Get thee out of thy country, and from thy kindred, and from thy father's house, unto a land that I will shew thee."

exposed to the play of forces which it does not control. These forces may be considered as acting from outside, but they can act so because they have their counterpart in the human constitution itself, ready to receive their influence. And they have a powerful head start against the divine influence, shut off as the cosmic system is from the transcendent realm and enveloped as the inner spirit is by the psyche. Therefore it is the natural condition of man to be a prey of the alien forces which are yet so much of himself, and it requires the miraculous supervening of gnosis from beyond to empower the imprisoned pneuma to come into its own. "Those who are enlightened in their spiritual part by a ray from the divine light—and they are but few—from these the demons desist . . . all the others are driven and carried along in their souls and their bodies by the demons, loving and cherishing their works. . . . All this terrestrial rule the demons exercise through the organs of our bodies, and this rule Hermes calls 'heimarmene'" (*C.H.* XV. 16). This is the interiorized aspect of cosmic destiny, denoting the power of the world as a moral principle: in this sense heimarmene is that government which the cosmic rulers exercise over us through our selves, and its manifestation is human vice of any kind, whose common principle is nothing but the abandonment of the self to the world. Thus inner-worldly existence is essentially a state of being *possessed* by the world, in the literal, i.e., demonological, sense of the term. In a rather late source[14] we even encounter, as the contrast-term to spiritual man, the expression "demonic man" instead of the usual "psychic" or "sarkic" (fleshly). Each man, so the text explains, is from birth possessed by his demon, which only the mystical power of prayer can expel after the extinction of all passions. In this voided state the soul unites with the spirit as bride with bridegroom. The soul which does not thus receive Christ remains "demonic" and becomes the habitation of "the serpents." To appreciate the wide gap between this and the Greek position, one need only recall the Greek doctrine of "the guardian daimon with us from our birth," [15] and generally compare the depraved

---

[14] The *Asceticon* of the Messalians, a heretical monastic sect mentioned in heresiological literature from the fourth century A.D. onward: see reconstruction and analysis of their views in Reitzenstein, *Historia Monachorum,* pp. 197 ff.

[15] "Everyone has with him from his birth a daimon as the good mystagogue of his life" (Menander in Ammian. Marcell. *Rer. gest.* XXI. 14. 4).

concept of "demon" in Gnosticism and Christianity with the classical one, which denoted a being superior to man in the divine hierarchy. The gap is as great as that between the two conceptions of the cosmos, of which the concept of "demon" is the direct function.

There is little left of the classical idea of the unity and autonomy of the person. Against the proud and somewhat superficial confidence of Stoic psychology in the self as complete master in its own house, enjoying complete knowledge of what is and what occurs therein, the terrified gnostic glance views the inner life as an abyss from which dark powers rise to govern our being, not controlled by our will, since this will itself is instrument and executor of those powers. This is the basic condition of human insufficiency. "What is God? unchanging good; what is man? unchanging evil" (Stob. *Ecl.* I. 277. 17). Abandoned to the demonic whirl of its own passions, the godless soul cries, "I burn, I blaze . . . I am consumed, wretch that I am, by the evils that possess me" (*C.H.* X. 20). Even the opposite experience of spiritual freedom is one of receptivity rather than activity: "the spiritual part of the soul is immune against enslavement by the demons and is fit to receive God into itself" (*C.H.* XV. 15).

The Soul as Female

It is in keeping with this general conception of the inner life that the soul is often regarded as a receptacle occupied by the different spiritual forces that battle for its possession. Valentinus compares the human heart to an inn where all comers lodge, and says, "In this manner the heart, so long as it has not met with providence, is impure, being the habitation of many demons" (Clem. Alex. *Strom.* II. 20. 114). Basilides calls man "an encampment of many different spirits" (*ibid.* 113); and even Porphyry the Neoplatonic philosopher expresses himself in this vein: "Where ignorance of God obtains, there must necessarily dwell the evil demon; for, as thou hast learned, the soul is a receptacle for either gods or demons" (*Ad Marc.* XXI). We have seen in Philo how this concept of the soul's receptivity leads to the image of its female function in a dual relationship. In Philo this image refers only to the soul's intercourse with God, since his biblical-Jewish theology did not acknowledge demons as an alternative to God. In the Gnostic use of the image, good and bad thoughts are both considered as (respectively) divine and demonic "conceptions" by the soul. "The spirit gives birth to all thoughts, good ones when it has received the seeds from God, contrary ones when from one of the demons, as there is no part of the universe empty of some demon . . . which entering into the soul may there sow the seed of his own works" (*C.H.* IX. 3). Beyond this pessimistic aspect of the concept, we find the sexual soul-imagery throughout the language of later Hellenistic piety, which is saturated with the spirit of supranatural religiosity. The "sacred marriage" of the mystery-cults is an example; and many Christian descriptions of the action of grace and the diffusion of the Holy Spirit in the soul belong to the same circle of metaphors.

Ecstatic Illumination

The enlightenment by a ray of the divine light (see p. 282) which transforms the psychic nature of man may be an article of faith, but it may also be an experience. Such superlative experience is sometimes claimed and even described (more often probably aspired to and set as a goal) in the religious literature of the age, inside and outside Gnosticism. It involves an extinction of the natural faculties, filling the vacuum with a surpassingly positive and at the same time in its ineffability negative content. Annihilation and deification of the person are fused in the spiritual ecstasis which purports to experience the immediate presence of the acosmic essence.

In the gnostic context, this transfiguring face-to-face experience is *gnosis* in the most exalted and at the same time most paradoxical sense of the term, since it is knowledge of the unknowable. Hitherto we have found "gnosis" to mean one of these things: knowledge of the secrets of existence as related in the gnostic myth, and these comprise the divine history from which the world originated, man's condition in it, and the nature of salvation; then, more intellectually, the elaboration of these tenets into coherent speculative systems; then, more practically, knowledge of the "way" of the soul's future ascent and of the right life preparing for this event; and, most technically or magically, knowledge of the sacraments, effective formulas, and other instrumental means by which the passage and liberation can be assured. All these interrelated kinds of "knowledge," theoretical or practical, convey information *about* something and are thus different from their object, from what they are to promote.[16] The mystical *gnosis theoû*—direct beholding of the divine reality—is itself an earnest of the consummation to come. It is transcendence become immanent; and although prepared for by human acts of self-modification which induce the proper disposition, the event itself is one of divine activity and grace. It is thus as much a "being known" by God as a "knowing" him, and in this ultimate mutuality the "gnosis" is beyond the terms of "knowledge" properly speaking. As beholding of a supreme object it may be said to be theoretical—hence "knowledge" or "cognition"; as being absorbed in, and transfigured by, the presence of the object it may be said to be practical—hence "apotheosis" or "rebirth": but neither the mediacy of knowledge-about . . . , nor that of praxis instrumental-for . . . applies where the knower's being merges with that of the object—which "object" in truth means the obliteration of the whole realm of objects.

The "experience" of the infinite in the finite cannot but be a paradox on any terms. By its own testimony throughout mystical literature it unites voidness and fullness. Its light illuminates and blinds. With an apparent, brief suspension of time, it stands within existence for the end of all existence: "end" in the twofold, negative-positive sense of the ceasing of everything worldly and of the goal in which the spiritual nature comes to fulfillment. To this extent the ecstatic experience exhibits the double-edged character of the true *eschaton* of eschatological transcendental religion, which it draws—illegitimately, as we think—into the range of temporal life and the possibilities open to it. We may call it an anticipation of death—as it is indeed often described in the metaphors of dying.

We have seen (pp. 165 ff., "The Ascent of the Soul") how the mythical eschatology describes the future ascent of the soul as its progressive denudation while passing upward through the cosmic spheres. And we indicated at the time that this process, thought to take place in the outer dimension of the mythological objectivity,

---

[16] This indeed does not apply to the speculative "knowledge" of the Valentinians when taken by their own *speculative claims*—see pp. 174 ff. But it does apply to it by the actual facts of theoretical knowledge as such.

was capable of an interiorization by which the mythical scale becomes transformed into an inner mystical one. It is this transposition of eschatology into the inwardness which yields the surpassing concept of gnosis here discussed. The culminating experience itself is professedly ineffable, though it can be symbolically circumscribed. The process leading up to it admits of description. Thus the Hermetic treatise of rebirth (*C.H.* XIII) describes the stages by which in the mystical situation the astral soul is dissolved and the spiritual self generated: one by one, the demonic powers (hailing from the Zodiac[17]) are ousted from the subject and replaced by "powers of God" descending into it by grace and with their entrance progressively "composing" the new person. The initiate, ascetically prepared, is throughout receptive rather than active. With the dissolving of the former self he passes outside and beyond himself into a different being. The process is climaxed and closed by the ecstatic experience of deification.

Much of the imagery and the psychological terms of such descriptions (which are understandably rare) derives from the ritual of the mystery-religions. As was the case with the subject of "virtue," we are here again dealing with a phenomenon which Gnosticism shared with the broader religious tide of the age. In fact, the real *conceptual* elaboration of the whole idea of an inner ascent ending in mystical ecstasis, and its articulation into psychologically definable stages, was the work of no other than Plotinus and the Neoplatonic school after him—anticipated to some extent by Philo—i.e., of a "philosophy" turned mystical; and, slightly later, of the monastic mystics of eastern Christianity (where the theoretical basis was derived from Origen). In a less refined way, however, the experience or idea of pneumatic illumination was older and at least in part a gnostic phenomenon. The very concept of a saving power of gnosis as such, surpassing that of mere faith, suggests a resort to some kind of inner evidence which through its exalted nature puts the event of transformation and the possession of a higher truth beyond doubt. And with the disposi-

---

[17] In Egyptian astrology the twelve signs of the Zodiac tend to take the place of the seven planets (Babylonian astrology) as the symbols of cosmic rule—in the gnostic version, of cosmic corruption.

tion as widespread and intense as it was, there will not have lacked the actual occurrence, in all degrees, of such experiences that by their own testimony could be taken as direct encounter with the transcendent absolute itself. Henceforth the subject "knew" God and also "knew" himself to be saved.

It is the aftermath rather than those elusive "experiences" themselves—what was felt to be their lasting effect on a "reformed" life —which can speak to us, and there is no doubting the fervor and profound emotion of the two Hermetic prayers of thanks that follow.

We thank thee, with our whole soul and our whole heart stretched out to thee, ineffable Name . . . that thou hast shown to all of us fatherly goodness, love and kindness, and an even sweeter power in bestowing on us by thy grace mind, speech, gnosis: mind, that we think thee, speech, that we praise thee, gnosis, that in thy knowledge we rejoice.

Saved by thy light, we rejoice that thou hast shown thyself to us whole, we rejoice that thou hast made us gods while still in our bodies through the vision of thee.

Man's only thank-offering to thee is to know thy greatness. We came to know thee, O light of human life, we came to know thee, O light of all gnosis, we have come to know thee, O womb impregnated by the seed of the Father . . .

In adoration of thy grace, we ask no other grace but that thou shouldst preserve us in thy gnosis and that we shall not stumble from the life so gained.

(Final prayer of the *Logos Teleios:* pseud-Apuleius, *Asclepius* 41)

Holy is God the Father of the All, holy is God whose will is accomplished by his own powers, holy is God who wills to be known and is known to his own.

Holy art thou who by thy word hast created all things. Holy art thou of whom all nature was born an image, holy art thou whom nature has not expressed in its form.

Holy art thou who art mightier than all power, holy art thou who surpassest all sublimity, holy art thou who art above all praise.

Receive pure spiritual sacrifices from a heart and soul stretched out to thee, thou ineffable, inexpressible, nameable by silence.

Grant my prayer that I may not lose hold of the gnosis fit for our nature, and give me the strength thereto; and with the same grace enlighten those of the race, my brothers and thy children, who are in ignorance.

Therefore I trust in thee and bear witness that I shall come into life and light. Praised be thou, Father, thy Man desires to be holy [or: do holy work] with thee, as thou hast granted him the full power.

(C.H. I. 31-32)

(d) CONCLUSION: THE UNKNOWN GOD

The beginning and end of the paradox that is gnostic religion is the unknown God himself who, unknowable on principle, because the "other" to everything known, is yet the object of a knowledge and even asks to be known. He as much invites as he thwarts the quest for knowing him; in the failure of reason and speech he becomes revealed; and the very account of the failure yields the language for naming him. He who according to Valentinus is the Abyss, according to Basilides even "the non-being God" (Hippol., *Refut.* VII. 20); whose acosmic essence negates all object-determinations as they derive from the mundane realm; whose transcendence transcends any sublimity posited by extension from the here, invalidates all symbols of him thus devised; who, in brief, strictly defies description—he is yet enunciated in the gnostic message, communicated in gnostic speech, predicated in gnostic praise. The knowledge of him itself is the *knowledge of his unknowability;*[18] the predication upon him as thus known is by negations: thus arises the *via negationis,* the negative theology, whose melody, here first sounded as a way of confessing what cannot be described, hence swells to a mighty chorus in Western piety.

> Thou art the alone infinite
> and thou art alone the depth
> and thou art alone the unknowable
> and thou art he after whom every man seeks
> and they have not found thee
> and none can know thee against thy will
> and none can even praise thee against thy will . . .
> Thou art alone the non-containable

---

[18] Even to the Aeons of the Pleroma: see the Valentinian teaching, pp. 181 f.

and thou art alone the non-visible
Thou art alone the non-subsistent

> (Gnostic hymn, preserved in Coptic; see
> C. Schmidt, *Koptisch-gnostische Schriften,* 1905, p. 358)

O thou beyond all things
    what else can it be meet to call thee?
How can speech praise thee?
    for thou art not expressible by any speech.
How can reason gather thee?
    for thou art not comprehensible by any mind.
Thou that art alone ineffable
    while thou engenderest all that is open to speech.
Thou that alone art unknowable
    while thou engenderest all that is open to thought. . . .
End of all things art thou
    and one and all and none,
Not being one nor all, claiming all names
    how shall I call thee?

> (Opening lines of a hymn by Gregorius the
> Theologian; see E. Norden, *Agnostos Theos,* p. 78)

In the voice of these professions the message of the alien God, freed from the polemical reference to a deposed Demiurge, rings across the centuries. Its mysterious beckoning may still, and ever again, haunt the god-seeking heart of man.

Chapter 12. *The Recent Discoveries in the Field of Gnosticism*

The discovery, about 1945, at Nag Hamadi in Egypt (the ancient Chenoboskion), of what was probably the complete sacred library of a gnostic sect, is one of those sensational events in the history of religious-historical scholarship which archeology and accident have so lavishly provided since the beginning of this century. It was preceded (speaking of written relics only) by the enormous find, early in the century, of Manichaean writings at Turfan in Chinese Turkestan; by the further unearthing, about 1930 in the Egyptian Fayum, of parts of a Manichaean library in Coptic; and was closely followed by the discovery of the Dead Sea scrolls in Palestine. If we add to these new sources the Mandaean writings, whose progressive coming to light since the latter part of the last century is owed, not to the digging of archeologists or the scavenging of shepherds and peasants, but to contacts with the still living, long forgotten sect itself, we find ourselves now in possession of a massive literature of "lost causes" from those crucial five or so centuries, from the first century B.C. onward, in which the spiritual destiny of the Western world took shape: the voice of creeds and flights of thought which, part of that creative process, nourished by it and stimulating it, were to become obliterated in the consolidation of official creeds that followed upon the turmoil of novelty and boundless vision.

Unlike the Dead Sea finds of the same years, the gnostic find from Nag Hamadi has been beset from the beginning and to this day by a persistent curse of political roadblocks, litigation and, worst of all, scholarly jealousies and "firstmanship"—the combined upshot of which is that fifteen years after the first recognition of the nature of the documents, only two of the 46 (49)[1] writings have been

[1] One writing occurs twice, and one occurs three times in the collection.

properly edited,[2] three more have been translated in full;[3] and another two (4)[4] are available from a different papyrus also containing them and published not long ago in its gnostic parts, after having been in the Berlin Museum for sixty years.[5] For all the rest, about which fragmentary information has been seeping out over the years, we have now,[*] and probably for some time, to be content with the provisional descriptions, excerpts and summaries offered in J. Doresse's book *The Secret Books of the Egyptian Gnostics*.[6] It is the purpose of this chapter to take such account of the whole body of new evidence as it presently yields and as is pertinent to our general treatment of the gnostic problem.

[2] *Evangelium veritatis* . . . eds. M. Malinine, H.-Ch. Puech, G. Quispel. Zurich, 1956; *The Gospel according to Thomas,* eds. A. Guillaumont, H.-Ch. Puech, G. Quispel, W. Till, Y. 'Abd al Masïh. Leiden, 1959. The first could just be utilized to some extent in the first edition of this book. [See end of note 3.]

[3] The *Hypostasis of the Archons,* the *Gospel according to Philip,* and an untitled cosmogony (no. 40 of the collection by Doresse's counting, no. 14 by Puech's)— all three translated into German by H. M. Schenke: see supplementary bibliography. These translations were made from a photographic reproduction of the texts in Pahor Labib, *Coptic Gnostic Papyri in the Coptic Museum at Old Cairo,* Vol. I. Cairo, 1956 (the beginning of a planned, provisional publication of all the manuscripts). For the missing title of the cosmogony (no. 40), Schenke proposes "Discourse on the Origin of the World," which we shall here adopt in a shortened form: *Origin of the World.* [Since this was written and set, the complete text of the treatise was published, with translation and commentary, by A. Böhlig and P. Labib: see supplementary bibliography. Schenke's translation, it now appears, covers only the first half of the writing, which he took for the whole.]

[4] *The Sophia of Jesus* and *The Secret Book of John* (quoted later as *Apocryphon of John*).

[5] W. Till, *Die gnostischen Schriften des koptischen Papyrus Berolinensis* 8502. Berlin, 1955. The codex will be quoted as BG.

[6] (Subtitle, *An Introduction to the Gnostic Coptic Manuscripts discovered at Chenoboskion.*) New York, 1960. The French original appeared in 1958. Its author, a French Egyptologist, happened to be on the spot when, in 1947, the first of the thirteen papyrus codices comprising the find was acquired by the Coptic Museum in Cairo. He recognized its significance and was from then on intimately connected with the unfolding story of further acquisition—and the aforementioned intramural feuds. Having had access, if for brief times only, to all of the twelve Cairo codices (one codex found its way to Europe and was acquired by the Jung Institute in Zurich), he has catalogued the writings composing them and taken notes—sometimes hurried—of their contents. These, as embodied in his book, are at the moment a major evidence beyond the fully published or translated writings cited above.

[*] This was written in 1962 and no longer holds (1970). For present condition, including numeration of codices and writings, see Addendum on p. 319.

I. OBSERVATIONS ON THE CHENOBOSKION LIBRARY

With the obvious reservations dictated by the state of affairs, let us ask: What do the new finds[7] add to our knowledge and understanding of Christian gnosticism? It is, of course, simply not the case that our evidence hitherto was scanty. The patristic testimony is rich and stands vindicated with every test by newly recovered originals (i.e., texts preserved on their own and not through doxography). Also, as regards the question of authentic information in general, the reminder is not out of place that nothing in the new sources, being translations one and all (from Greek into Coptic), equals in directness of testimony the direct quotations in the Greek fathers (such as, e.g., Ptolemy's *Letter to Flora*), which render the Greek originals themselves—even if a longer line of copyists then intervenes between them and our oldest manuscript. This aspect is easily forgotten in the elation over the mere physical age of the writing which happens to come into our hands. But of such complete or extensive verbatim renderings (see above, p. 38) there are not many in the Church writers, while the original Coptic works which hitherto constituted our independent evidence (sc., of "Christian" gnostic literature) were not from the classical period of heretical growth (second and third centuries A.D.), with which the Church writers dealt. It is of this period that we now possess a whole library:[8] with it we are truly "contemporaneous" with the Christian critics, and this is an inestimable advantage.

A priori, and quite apart from questions of doctrine, it is obvious that so large an accretion of original writings will afford us a much more full-blooded, full-bodied experience of the authentic flavor of gnostic literary utterance, a more intimate view of the working and manner of self-communication of the gnostic mind, than any doxographic excerpts or rendering of doctrinal substance can convey. As has happened before in the case of the Manichaean documents, the form and tone of statement in all its profusion now add their undimmed voice to the object "content," the "themes" as it were,

---

[7] I include in these the writings of the Berlin papyrus, whose publication at long last, in 1955, was indeed prompted by the Nag Hamadi discovery.

[8] The manuscripts are probably from the 4th century, but the contents are older, and some can be dated with fair certainty in the 2nd century.

which the heresiologists could for purposes of debate detach from the din of their polyphonous treatment: and the latter is of the substance, even if it should not show it to advantage. If the picture becomes more blurred instead of more clear, this would be part of the truth of the matter.

Further, we learn what was the reading matter of a gnostic community[9] of the fourth century, probably typical for the Coptic area and possibly well beyond it. From the relative weight of *Sethian* documents in the total we may conclude that the community was Sethian. But the presence of many writings of quite different affiliations[10] shows the openmindedness, the feeling of solidarity, or the mutual interpenetration, which must have been the rule among the Gnostics at large. Really surprising in this respect is the inclusion of five *Hermetic* treatises in an otherwise "Christian" gnostic collection—which proves a greater proximity, or at any rate feeling of proximity at this time, between the two streams of speculation than is usually conceded. On the other hand, as Doresse has pointed out (*op. cit.,* p. 250), none of "the great heretical teachers" of patristic literature "makes any explicit appearance in the writings from Chenoboskion," i.e., none is either named as author of a writing or mentioned in a writing. From this, however, it does not follow, especially in an age of revelatory literature, which favors anonymous authorship or outright pseudepigraphy, that some of the texts might not be by one or the other of the known teachers. Some conjectures, involving the authorship of Valentinus and Heracleon, have indeed been advanced in connection with the strongly Valentinian parts of the Jung Codex; and Doresse believes to recognize "Simon Magus" in two treatises (*op. cit.,* Appendix I). In any case, the absence of the "great names" of the second century must not be taken to detract from the importance which patristic testimony ascribes to them (and thereby from the value of that testimony in general)—it merely reflects the intellectual level and literary habits of the Chenoboskion group and its likes in the fourth century.

[9] It is, of course, possible that the collection was that of a wealthy individual, but he too must have belonged to some kind of group, whatever its form of coherence.

[10] E.g., the *Apocryphon of John, Hypostasis of the Archons, Origin of the World* are barbelo-gnostic, the *Gospel of Truth, Letter to Reginos, Gospel of Philip* are Valentinian, etc.

To the Sethians no historical teacher is attributed by the heresi-ologists anyway. Their teaching itself is now richly documented. The (Iranian) doctrine of "three roots," i.e., of a third primordial principle intermediate between Light and Darkness—which they shared with the Peratae, Justin, the Naassenes, and others—stands forth clearly and in full accord with Hippolytus' account. Of course, the relative prominence of this cosmogonic feature in the Chenobo-skion collection—a consequence of its Sethian emphasis—is no reason for now seeing in it more than the quite specific feature, peculiar to one group of teachings, as which it appeared before. The ema-nation-, aeon- and Sophia-speculation of the whole "Syrian-Egyptian" gnosis has no room for it; the "Iranian" gnosis itself, to which it belongs, can do without it (as not only Mani, but long before him the system cited by Basilides proves—see above, p. 214, n. 10); and even in the Sethian case the speculative role of the intermediate principle is in fact slight: the real meaning is dualistic, and in gen-eral the third principle either affords—as "Space"—the mere topolog-ical meeting ground for the opposites, or in its substantial descrip-tion—as "Spirit"—is an attenuated form (notwithstanding the assurance of co-primacy) of the higher principle, susceptible of inter-mingling. As the various alternatives show, this susceptibility, for which gnostic speculation calls, does not really require a separate aboriginal principle. Because of this relative systematic unimpor-tance—as distinct from the importance for questions of historic affiliations—no example of this type was included in our selection of gnostic myths.[11] However, a full publication of the *Paraphrase of Shem*, the main Sethian cosmogony in the collection (and the longest of the "revelations" in the whole library) may in time prompt a new evaluation of this point.[12]

I turn to some general doctrinal observations which can be

[11] In my more detailed German work, a special section is devoted to the "three roots" systems: *Gnosis und spaetantiker Geist, I*, pp. 335-344.

[12] Apropos of the *Paraphrase of Shem*, Doresse has called attention (*op. cit.*, p. 150) to its close resemblance with what Hippolytus reports of a "Paraphrase of Seth" (*Refut.* V. 19-22). There is, however, this important difference: the first speaks in the Manichaean manner of a rising up of the primordial Darkness to the Light, whereas the latter speaks of the Light's being attracted to the Darkness. We see how much wavering—or shall we say, free play of variation—there was on such cardinal points.

provisionally gleaned from the new material and related to the older evidence. By way of confirmation, and in part reinforcement, of the latter, one is struck by the impressively persistent recurrence of certain motifs which, well documented as they were before, now receive added accreditation as basic articles of faith from the sheer weight of numerical and even verbal constancy.

1. Prominent among them is the theme—familiar to the reader of this book—which for short I will call "the pride of the demiurge," i.e., the story of his ignorance, perversity, and conceit. The ubiquity of this theme, with an almost stereotyped repetition of its formulae throughout the cosmogonic writings of the Chenoboskion collection, is a striking though not surprising fact of the new evidence: it agrees with the patristic testimony down to the literal phrasing of (a) the demiurge's thinking that he alone exists and there is nothing above him, (b) his boasting about his creation, issuing in the cry "I am God and there is no other God than I," (c) his humbling by the retort from on high "Thou art mistaken (or, "do not lie") . . . ! There is above thee . . ." This nearly invariant cluster of features, already familiar from Irenaeus,[13] Hippolytus,[14] Epiphanius,[15] and attributed by them to a variety of gnostic sects, is found in no less than the following writings of the "library": No. 27,[16] *Paraphrase of Shem* (Doresse, p. 149); no. 39, *Hypostasis of the Archons;*[17] no. 40, *Origin of the World;*[18] nos. 2-7, *Sacred Book of the invisible Great Spirit,* or *Gospel of the Egyptians* (Doresse, p. 178); no. 4, *Sophia of Jesus;*[19] nos. 1-6-36, *Apocryphon of John.*[20] These, if I am not mistaken, are all the cosmogonic tractates of the collection which Doresse has summarized.

Some particulars are worth mentioning. Concerning (b): The assertion by the demiurge of his arrogant claim always takes the form of an "exclamation" in the unmistakeably Old Testament style

[13] E.g., *Adv. Haer.* I. 30. 6.
[14] E.g., *Refut.* VII. 25. 3.
[15] E.g., *Panar.* 26. 2.
[16] I use throughout the counting introduced by Doresse. [See Addendum, p. 319.]
[17] 134:27-135:4; 142:21-26; 143:4-7 (Schenke, cols. 664; 667; 668).
[18] 148:29-33; 151:3-28; 155:17-34 (Schenke, cols. 249; 251; 253).
[19] BG 125:10-126:5 (Till, pp. 290-293): the Nag-Hamadi manuscript has a lacuna here.
[20] BG 44:9-16, cf. 45:11 f.; 45:20-46:9 (Till, pp. 128-133).

of divine self-predication (recalling, e.g., Is. 45:5, 46:9, LXX), some-times adding to the profession of uniqueness that of jealousy.[21]

Except for the special psychological twist in the *Apocryphon,* the trait is familiar from patristic reports and is now shown to be one of the true invariants of that whole type of gnostic cosmogony in which the "lower" represents a defection from the "higher." [22] The anti-Jewish animus of these transparent identifications of Ialdabaoth (etc.) with the Judaic god is one of the elements one has to con-sider in forming any hypothesis on the origins of Gnosticism.

Concerning (c): The rebuke from on high, mostly by his mother Sophia, reveals to the demiurge, and to the lower powers at large, the existence of the higher God "who is above the All" (*Sophia of Jesus,* BG 126:1-5), thus undeceiving him and humbling his pride; but its most telling form is "*Man* exists [above thee = before thee] and so does the Son of Man." [23] This formula, too, which shows "Man" elevated to a supracosmic deity, is known from patristic testimony (e.g., Iren. I. 30. 6), and there some of the systems listed even go so far as to equate him outright with the first and supreme God himself,[24] as do some (or all?) of the passages in the new sources. Now this elevation—whether going that far or not—of 'Man' to a transmundane deity, prior and superior to the creator of the universe, or, the assigning of that name to such a deity, is one of the most significant traits of gnostic theology in the general history of religion, uniting such widely divergent speculations as

[21] E.g., in nos. 2=7 "I am a jealous God and there is no other beside me!"; identical in nos. 1=6=36 (*Apocryphon of John*) — where the exclamation is neatly turned into proof of his awareness "that there is another God: for if there were none, of whom should he be jealous?" (see above, p. 134).

[22] It is not, however, confined to that type: in the *Paraphrase of Shem* the trait appears in a context which the doctrine of 'three roots' puts squarely within the Iranian type. Doresse's summary does not show how in this case the demiurge (as also Sophia) originated. But from other instances it appears that Ialdabaoth could also be conceived as a wholly evil power rather than the son of the fallen Sophia. Mythographically, the figure is indeed independent of the latter and became sec-ondarily combined with her.

[23] Nos. 2=7 (Doresse, p. 178); no. 40, 151:19 f. "An Immortal Man of Light"; *Apocryphon of John,* in all versions—there apparently as a voice coming to Sophia herself from above, but also heard by Ialdabaoth.

[24] Cf., e.g., Iren. I. 12. 4 for one branch of the Valentinians (see above, p. 217); cf. *ibid.* 30. 1 for the Ophites: the primal Light in the Abyss, blessed, eternal and infinite, is "the Father of all, and his name is First Man"; cf. also the Naassenes and the Arab Monoimos in Hippolytus' report, *Refut.* V. 7, VIII, 12.

those of the Poimandres and of Mani. It signifies a new metaphysical status of man in the order of things; and by being advised of it
is the creator of the world put in his place. Join to the theological
concept the fact which the very name ensures, viz., that terrestrial
man can identify his innermost being ("spirit," "light," etc.) with
this supracosmic power, can therefore despise his cosmic oppressors
and count on his ultimate triumph over them—and it becomes visible
that the doctine of the god Man, and in the creation story specifically: the humiliation of the demiurge in his name, mark the
distinctly *revolutionary* aspect of gnosticism on the cosmic plane,
which on the moral plane shows itself in the defiance of antinomianism, and on the sacramental plane in the confidence of defeating
Fate and outwitting the archons. The element of revolt, with its
affective tone, will be discerned only when taken together with the
element of oppression and the consequent idea of liberation, i.e., of
reclaiming a freedom lost: we must remember that the role of the
demiurge is not exhausted in his feat of creation, but that, through
his "Law" as well as through cosmic Fate, he exercises a despotic
world rule aimed mainly at enslaving man. In the *Revelation of
Adam to his son Seth* (no. 12, Doresse, p. 182), Adam tells how,
after he had learnt (from Eve?) about "the eternal angels" (aeons),
who "were higher than the god who had created us . . . the Archon,
in anger, cut us off from the aeons of the powers . . . The glory
that was in us deserted us . . . the primordial knowledge that had
breathed in us abandoned us . . . It was then that we knew the
gods who had created us . . . and we were serving him in fear and
humility:" [25] what relish, then, to learn that, even before, the Archon
himself had been humiliated by the disclosure that above him is
"Man!" [26]

---

[25] Cf. also *Gospel of Philip*, 102:29 f. "They (the Archons) wanted to take
the free one and make him their slave in eternity" (Schenke, col. 7).

[26] In both the *Hypostasis of the Archons* and the *Origin of the World*, the
demiurge Ialdabaoth, when rebuked by Sophia for his boasting, is addressed with the
alternative name of *Samael*, which is said to mean "the blind god" (*Hypostasis*,
134:27-135:4; 142:25 f.; *Origin*, 151:17 f.). The plausible but secondary (Aramaic)
etymology explains the appellation "the blind one" for the demiurge in Hippolytus'
account of the Peratae, where it is merely based on an allegory of the Esau story
(*Refut.* V. 16. 10—see above p. 95): we now learn that the predicate "blind" was
more than an *ad hoc* exegetical improvisation. Indeed, the very description of the
archons in the *Hypostasis* begins thus: "Their lord is blind. Because of his power,

2. Practically coextensive in occurrence with the "pride of the demiurge" is the theme I will briefly call *"the folly of Sophia,"* i.e., the story of her aberration and fall from the higher divine order, of which she is and continues to be a member even during her exile of guilt. In the sequence of the myth this topic, as we have seen, precedes the pride of the demiurge—in fact, Sophia's fall is the generative cause of the demiurge's existence and of his *ab initio* inferior nature. But historically the figure is of different provenance. The Jewish reference, and thus the anti-Judaic sting, are absent;[27] and in spite of the genealogical connection and even culpability, the affective tone of the symbol is different: she evokes tragic "fear and compassion," not revolt and contempt. The presence of this theme is an infallible sign that we deal with the "Syrian-Egyptian" type of gnostic speculation, in which the cosmogonic process, engulfing parts of divinity, is originated by a self-caused descensus from the heights, and not, as in the "Iranian" type, by the encroachment of a primordial darkness from without. One of the new texts, the *Origin of the World,* provides by its polemical opening telling proof that the proponents of the Sophia myth were well aware of this doctrinal point: "Since everybody, the gods of the world and men, contend that nothing existed before the Chaos, I will prove that they all are mistaken, for they never knew the origin of Chaos, nor its root . . . The Chaos originated from a Shadow and was called 'Darkness'; and the Shadow in turn originated from a work that exists since the beginning": this primordial work was undertaken by Pistis Sophia outside the realm of the "Immortals"—who at first existed alone and whence she strayed (145:24-146:7). Thus the very existence of darkness is here the consequence of a divine failing. Sophia, "Wisdom," is the agent and vehicle of this failing (not the least of the paradoxes in which Gnosticism delighted); her soul-drama before time prefigures the predicament of man within creation (though

---

ignorance, and conceit, he says in the midst of his creation 'I am God . . .'" (134:27-31; cf. also *Sophia of Jesus,* BG 126:1-3).—Another (Hebrew) etymology, found in the *Origin of the World,* is "Israel = the man-that-sees-God" (153:24 f.). This is very well known from Philo, with whom it assumes great doctrinal significance (cf. *Gnosis und spätantiker Geist.* II, 1, p. 94 ff.). A concordance pairing the educated Hellenist with the obscure sectarian testifies to a common background of well established Jewish exegesis.

[27] The first in spite of the name Achamoth = Hebr. *chokma:* a pagan female deity, as Bousset has shown, provided the mythological substratum for the figure.

it has preempted "guilt" for the precosmic phase alone); and the various possibilities of motivation open to choice make for considerable freedom in the actual psychological evolution of the transcendental adventure tale. Of this freedom, the number of variations found in the literature bears witness: even for the one Valentinian school, two alternative conceptions of the first cause and nature of Sophia's fault are recorded. Thus we have here, with all sameness of the basic idea, not the same rule of stereotype as in the "demiurge" theme. We list a few instances from the new sources and relate them to their counterparts in the old.

The *Hypostasis of the Archons* and the *Origin of the World* both tell us that Pistis Sophia (a) desired to produce alone, *without her consort,* a work that would be like unto the first-existing Light: it came forth as a celestial image which (b) constituted a *curtain* between the higher realms of light and the later-born, inferior aeons; and a *shadow* extends beneath the curtain, that is, on its outer side which faces away from the light. The shadow, which was called "Darkness," becomes *matter;* and out of this matter comes forth, as an abortion, the lion-shaped Ialdabaoth. Comments:

a) Nature of the fault. "Without consort" (*Hypostasis* 142:7): the same motif occurs in the *Apocryphon of John* (BG 36:16-37:4; see above, p. 200), also in the *Sophia of Jesus,*[28] and is fully explained in Hippolytus' version of the Valentinian myth, viz., as impossible imitation of the Father's mode of creativity "out of himself," which requires no sexual partner (see above, p. 182, n. 11). Thus Sophia's fault is here presumption, *hybris,* leading directly to failure, but indirectly, in the further chain of consequences (via the demiurge, in whom the *hybris* reappears compounded by ignorance and *amor dominandi*) to the becoming of the material world: this, therefore, and with it our condition, is the final fruit of the abortive attempt of an erring sub-deity to be creative on her own. The student of Valentinianism knows from Irenaeus (Ptolemy: Italian school) and the *Excerpts from Theodotus* (Anatolian school) of a different and more sophisticated motivation of Sophia's error: excessive desire for complete knowledge of the Absolute (see above, p. 181 f.). To this variant there seems to be no parallel in the new documents, anymore than there was in the older ones. And in the light of the Coptic testi-

[28] "Without her male partner," cf. Till, p. 277, footnote to BG 118:3-7.

mony it is now safe to assume what internal evidence by the criterion of subtlety and crudity always suggested: that Hippolytus' version, which agrees so well with the now attested gnostic Vulgate, represents within Valentinian literature an archaism, preserving currency from the established gnostic Sophia mythology, whereas the version prevalent within the school itself represents a uniquely Valentinian refinement.

b) Consequence of the fault. The "curtain," in the above examples obviously a direct effect of Sophia's work as such, is in the *Sophia of Jesus* a creation of the Father in response to this "work": he spreads a separating screen "between the Immortals and those that came forth after them," so that the "fault of the woman" may live and she may join battle with Error (BG 118:1-17).[29] This recalls the "limit" (*horos*) of the Valentinians, in the second of his roles.[30] In this version, then, the "curtain" or "limit" was ordained with the intent of separation and protection: while in the other version, where it arises with Sophia's work itself, it becomes the unintended cause of the "darkness" beneath itself—which becomes "matter," in which Sophia then carries on her "work": in this unintended aspect it rather recalls the "fog" of the *Gospel of Truth*,[31] which in its turn recalls the Valentinian doctrine that Sophia, falling into ignorance and formlessness, "brought into being the Void-of-Knowledge, which is the Shadow [i.e., the cone of darkness produced by her blocking the light] of the Name" (*Exc. Theod.* 31. 3 f.). Thus, where the "curtain" is not spread by the Father but directly results from Sophia's error, it forms a link in the genealogical deduction of darkness from that primordial error, if by a somewhat extraneous kind of causality. We have here the incipient or cruder form of that derivation of matter from the primal fault[32] whose perfected

[29] Cf. also the eschatological speculation on the "renting of the curtain" in the *Gospel of Philip*, 132:22 ff. (cf. 117:35 ff.).

[30] See above, p. 184; the "second" role of the limit is that between the Pleroma and the outside—cf. e.g., Hippol. VI. 31. 6 "that nothing of the deficiency might come near the Aeons within the Pleroma."

[31] 17:11-16 "The Anguish condensed like a fog, so that no one could see. Because of this, Error gained strength and set to work upon her own matter in the void."

[32] Cf. *Hypostasis* 142:10-15 "And a Shadow formed below the curtain, and that shadow turned into matter and . . . was cast into an (outer) part . . . comparable to an abortion"; *Origin* 146:26-147:20 "Its outer side is Shadow which was called Darkness. From it a Power came forth . . . The Powers that arose after it

form we encounter in the Valentinian doctrine of the origin of psychic and hylic substance *out* of—not merely in consequence of—the *mental* affections of Sophia herself. In the *Gospel of Truth*, this subtle doctrine seems presupposed.[33] Again the new texts permit us to measure the step which Valentinianism took beyond the more primitive level of its general group.

c) The passion of Sophia. This step is also apparent in the meaning given the *suffering* of Sophia, i.e., in whether it is incidental (however movingly told) or, as a second phase, crucial to the cosmogonic process. As that process was initiated by the "error" which somehow gave rise, in the first phase, to a darkness and chaos that were not before (thus providing the monistic turn in the theory of dualism), there was ample cause, without further purpose, for distress, remorse and other emotions on the part of the guilty Sophia. It is obvious that these formed part of the story before their speculative use was seized upon. What do the Coptic sources tell us in this respect? In the *Apocryphon of John,* Sophia's distress arises over the creative doings of the demiurge, her son[34]—a comment on, not an originative factor in the cosmogonic process, by now well under way (though a factor in her own conversion and provisional redemption). In the *Pistis Sophia,* let us remember, the long drawn out, dramatic epic of this suffering is wholly for its own emotional sake (cf. p. 68 above). But in the *Origin of the World,* noted before for its awareness of the theoretical implications of the Sophia theme, a substantive and originative role is assigned to her very distress, which accordingly there precedes the demiurgical stage: Sophia, beholding the "boundless darkness" and the "bottomless waters" (= Chaos), is dismayed at these products of her initial fault; and

called the Shadow 'the boundless Chaos.' From it the race of the gods sprouted . . . so that a race of abortions followed from the first work . . . The Deep (Chaos) thus stems from the Pistis . . . As when a woman gives birth, all her redundancy (afterbirth) is wont to fall off, thus did Matter come forth from the Shadow." This comes very close indeed to the Valentinian doctrine: the barbelo-gnosis, to which both writings (as also the *Apocryphon of John*) belong, is generally of all varieties of Gnosticism the one most akin to Valentinianism in the speculation on the beginnings (see *Gnosis und spätantiker Geist* I, p. 361).

[33] See above, n. 31, and 24:22 ff: the world is the "shape" (*schema*) of the "deficiency" [thus "deficiency" its matter], and "deficiency" arose because of the primordial Ignorance about the Father.

[34] "She saw the wickedness and the apostasy which clung to her son. She repented . . ." (etc.): see above, p. 201 f.

her consternation turns into the apparition (upon the waters?)[35] of a "work of fright," which flees away from her into the Chaos (147:23-34): whether this is the male-female Archon, later mentioned, himself or his first adumbration, the future creator of the world is either mediately or directly a projection of the despair of "Wisdom." This comes closest to the hypostasizing role which the "affects" of Sophia assume in Valentinian speculation; also the two-step development (first chaos, then demiurge) adumbrates the differentiation into a higher and a lower Sophia.[36] Yet it is still a marked step hence to the definite derivation of the several psychic and hylic elements of the universe from those passions; and nothing so far in the new texts suggests the existence of something as subtle outside the Valentinian circle: the latter's originality stands forth again and again.

The particular cosmogonic importance of the two barbelo-gnostic writings translated by H.-M. Schenke, viz., the *Hypostasis of the Archons* and (according to his title-suggestion) the *Discourse on the Origin of the World,* warrants the reproduction here, in English, of the main cosmogonic passages fom both. Schenke[37] has summarized the very close relationship between the two writings in the following points of agreement: fall of Pistis Sophia by the creation of a curtain before the world of light; formation of a shadow and of matter; origin of the male-female Ialdabaoth and his male-female sons; pride and punishment of Ialdabaoth; elevation of his penitent son Sabaoth; origin of Death and his sons. The *Origin* offers the more circumstantial description, and the name "immortal Man" for the highest God occurs only there. In the following selection, passages are rearranged to fit the order of the cosmogonic process.

1. *The Hypostasis of the Archons* (Cod. II, 4)

Above, in the limitless Aeons, there exists the Incorruptibility. The Sophia, who is called Pistis, wished to accomplish a Work by herself,

[35] For the begetting of the demiurge through a reflection upon the waters of the abyss, see above p. 164, n. 16; cf. the general remarks on the motif of the mirror image, pp. 62 ff.

[36] The differentiation is fully present in the *Gospel of Philip,* 108:10-15 "Another is Ekhamoth, and another is Ekhmoth. Ekhamoth is the Sophia simply, but Ekhmoth is the Sophia of Death . . . who is called 'the little Sophia.' " The *Gospel of Philip* is by all accounts a Valentinian composition—cf. H.-M. Schenke in *Theologische Literaturzeitung* 84 (1959) 1, col. 2 f.

[37] *Theologische Literaturzeitung* 84 (1959), 4, col. 246 f.

without her consort. And her work became a celestial image, so that a curtain exists between the upper ones and the aeons that are below. And a shadow formed below the curtain, and that shadow turned into matter and . . . was cast into an (outer) part. And its shape became a work in matter, comparable to an abortion. It received the impression (*typos*) from the shadow and became an arrogant beast of lion shape (Ialdabaoth). . . . He opened his eyes and beheld matter great and boundless; he became haughty and said: "I am God, and there is none other besides me." Saying this, he sinned against the All. A voice came from the height of the Sovereignty . . . "Thou art mistaken, Samael," that is, the blind god or, god of the blind (142:4-26). His thoughts were blind (135:4). He bethought himself to create sons to himself. Being male-female, he created seven male-female sons and said to them "I am the God of the All" (143:1-5). [Zoe, daughter of Pistis Sophia, has Ialdabaoth bound and cast into Tartarus at the bottom of the Deep by a fiery angel emanating from her (143:5-13).]

When his son Sabaoth saw the power of this angel, he repented. He dissembled his father and his mother, Matter; he felt loathing for her . . . Sophia and Zoe carried him upward and set him over the seventh heaven, beneath the curtain between above and below (143:13-22). When Ialdabaoth saw that he was in this great glory . . . he envied him . . . and the envy begot death, and death begot his sons . . . (144:3-9).

The Incorruptibility looked down upon the regions of the water. Its image revealed itself in the water and the powers of darkness fell in love with it (135:11-14). The archons took counsel and said "Come, let us make a man from dust . . ." (135:24-26). They formed (their man) after their own body and after the image of God which had revealed itself in the water. . . . "We will equal the image in our formation, so that it (the image) shall see this likeness of itself, [be attracted to it,] and we may trap it in our formation (135:30-136:1). [We omit the ensuing story of Adam, Eve, paradise, serpent, Norea, etc.]

2. *Discourse on the Origin of the World* (Cod. II, 5)

When the nature of the Immortals had perfected itself out of the Boundless, an image flowed out from Pistis who was called Sophia. She wished it to become a work like unto the Light that existed first. And forthwith her will came forth and appeared as a celestial image . . . which was in the middle between the Immortals and those who arose after them according to the celestial model, which was a curtain that separated men and the upper ones. The Aeon of Truth has no shadow inside[38] himself . . . But his outside is shadow, which was called "Darkness." From it came forth a power (to rule) over the Darkness. But the powers who came into being after him called the Shadow "boundless Chaos." From it, the race of the gods sprouted . . . so that a race of abortions followed from the first work. The Deep (Chaos), therefore, stems from the Pistis (146:11-147:2).

The Shadow then became aware that there was one stronger than himself. He became envious, and having forthwith become pregnant from himself gave birth to Envy . . . That Envy was an abortion devoid of Spirit. It arose like shadows (cloudiness) in a watery substance. Thereupon the Envy was cast . . . into a part of Chaos . . . As when a woman gives birth all her redundancy (afterbirth) is wont to fall off, thus did Matter come forth from the Shadow (147:3-20).

After these happenings, Pistis came and revealed herself over the Matter of the Chaos which had been cast (there) like an abortion . . . : a boundless darkness and a bottomless water. When Pistis saw what had come forth from her transgression she was dismayed; and the dismay turned into the apparition of a work of fright, which fled away from her into the Chaos. She turned to it to breathe into its face, in the deep beneath the heavens [of Chaos] (147:23-148:1).

When Sophia wished this (abortion) to receive the impression (*typos*) of an image and to rule over matter, there first came forth from the water an Archon with lion shape . . . who possessed great power but knew not whence he had come (Ialdabaoth) . . . When the Archon beheld his own magnitude . . . seeing only himself, and nothing else except water and darkness, he thought that he existed alone. His thought came forth and appeared as a spirit which moved to and fro upon the water (148:1-149:2).

[149:10-150:26: creation by Ialdabaoth of six male-female "sons" (archons); their male and female names (among them Sabaoth); creation of a heaven for each, with thrones, powers, archangels, etc.]

When the heavens (after a helping intervention by Pistis) were firmly established, with their powers and all their dispositions, the Archbegetter became filled with pride. He received homage from all the host of the angels . . . and he boasted . . . and said "I am God . . ." (etc., with Pistis' rejoinder here expanded beyond the stereotype:) "Thou art mistaken, Samael"—that is, the blind god. "An immortal Man of Light exists before thee, who will reveal himself in your creation (*plasma*). He will tread thee underfoot . . . and thou with thine

---

[38] The ms. has "outside": an obvious error.

will descend to thy mother, the Deep.[39] For at the end of your works the whole Deficiency which has come forth from the Truth will be dissolved: it will pass, and it will be as if it had never been." Having spoken thus, Pistis showed the form of her greatness in the water, and then returned to her light (151:3-31).

After the Archbegetter had seen the image of Pistis in the water he became sad . . . and was ashamed of his transgression. And when he recognized that an immortal Man of Light existed before him, he became greatly agitated, having said before to all the gods "I am God, and there is none beside me," for he was afraid they might discover that there was one before him, and disown him. But being without wisdom . . . he had the insolence to say "If there is one before me, may he reveal himself!" Forthwith a light came out of the upper Ogdoad. It passed all the heavens of earth . . . and in it the form of a Man appeared . . . When the Pronoia (the consort of Ialdabaoth) saw this angel, she fell in love with him; but he hated her because she was of the Darkness. She wanted to embrace him but could not . . . (155:17-156-18).[40]

After Sabaoth, the son of Ialdabaoth, had heard the voice of Pistis (sc. in her threatening speech to Ialdabaoth) he exalted her and disowned his father. He exalted her for having taught about the immortal Man and his Light. Pistis Sophia . . . poured over him light from her light . . . and Sabaoth received great power over all the forces of Chaos . . . He hated his father, the Darkness, and his mother, the Deep. He loathed his sister, the Thought of the Archbegetter who moves to and fro above the water . . . When Sabaoth had, as reward for his repentance, received the place of rest (in the seventh heaven), Pistis also gave him her daughter Zoe (Life) . . . in order that she instruct him on all (the Aeons) that exist in the Ogdoad (151:32-152:31).

When the Archbegetter of Chaos beheld his son Sabaoth in his

---

[39] Schenke (*op. cit.* 251, n. 39) observes to this passage that the teaching of this (and the preceding) treatise, according to which *Ialdabaoth* indeed arises from Chaos, brilliantly confirms the explanation which already Hilgenfeld proposed for the puzzling name of the demiurge: *yalda bahuth* (Son of Chaos).

[40] To this appearance of the heavenly Man and its sequence in our text, which leads to the origin of earthly man, of Eros, and of plant life, Schenke suggests two parallels from widely divergent provinces of the gnostic realm: *Poimandres* § 12-17, where the female *Physis* who is seized with love for the divine *Anthropos* would correspond to the Pronoia here (*op. cit.* col. 254, n. 57—see above pp. 150 f.; 161 ff.; 172 f.); and from Mani's doctrine, the role of the "Third Messenger" in causing the origin of plants, animals, and man, by arousing the lust, with pollutions and abortions, of the male and female archons (*op. cit.* col. 247—see above pp. 225 ff.).

glory . . . he envied him. And when he got angry he begot Death from his own death (etc.) (154:19-24). (End of translation)

The favorable treatment of Sabaoth in these two, closely related writings betrays a streak of sympathy for Judaism strangely contrasting with the antijudaic animosity which the selfsame writings show in the transparent identification of the hateful Ialdabaoth with the Old Testament God.

Having dealt with some of the larger and pervading features, let us also list a few more particular observations. The *Apocryphon of John,* which we have summarized from the Berlin version (above, pp. 199-205), occurs three times in the codices fom Chenoboskion, two of them giving longer versions (nos. 6 and 36). Among the amplifications is an ending tacked on to them, which shows the ease with which heterogeneous material was accepted into gnostic compositions of well established literary identity. The appended ending is a self-account by a saving deity of her descent into the depth of Darkness, to awaken Adam: its particular gnostic parentage is readily identified by such passages as "I penetrated to the midst of the prison . . . and I said 'Let him who hears wake up from heavy slumber!' Then Adam wept and shed heavy tears . . . : 'Who called my name? And from whence comes this hope, while I am in the chains of the prison?' . . . 'Stand up, and remember that it is thyself thou hast heard, and return to thy root . . . Take refuge from . . . the demons of Chaos . . . and rouse thyself out of the heavy sleep of the infernal dwelling' " (Doresse, p. 209). The close parallels in Manichaean (also Mandaean) writings (see above, pp. 86 ff.) tell that we have here an intrusion of "Iranian" gnosis into an otherwise "Syrian" context.

No. 12, *Revelation of Adam to his son Seth,* presents the (originally Iranian?) doctrine of a succession (thirteen, or more?) of Enlighteners coming down into the world in the course of its history, through the miraculous births of prophets. Variations of this theme occur in the Pseudo-Clementines, Mani and elsewhere in Gnosticism (see above, p. 230; 207, n. 2)—the first conception of one "world history" as a divinely helped progress of gnosis. The author of our treatise is unaware of a clash between this idea of intermittent revelation and that of a continuous secret transmission of the "secrets of Adam" through Seth and his descendants, which he professes in the same breath (Doresse, p. 183). To the latter doctrine Doresse adduces (p. 185) a parallel from a later Syriac *Chronicle*,[41] which we will rather use for a confrontation of standpoints. In the Christian rendering of the *Chronicle*, Adam, when imparting revelations to his son Seth, shows him his original greatness before his transgression and his expulsion from Paradise and admonishes him never to fail in justice as he, Adam, had done: in the gnostic rendering of the *Revelation*, Adam is not the sinner, but the victim of archontic persecution—ultimately of the primordial Fall to which the world's existence and his own are due. Here is one simple criterion for what is "Christian" (orthodox) or "gnostic" (heretical): whether the *guilt* is Adam's or the Archon's, whether human or divine, whether arising in or before creation. The difference goes to the heart of the gnostic problem.

As a curiosity let us note that no. 19 (title missing)—which is also interesting by a polemic of Marcionic vehemence against the Law—launches a startling attack upon the baptism of John: "The river Jordan . . . is the strength of the body, that is, the essence of pleasures, and the water of Jordan is the desire for carnal cohabitation"; John himself is "the archon of the multitude"! (Doresse, p. 219 f.). This is entirely unique. Could it be a retort to the Mandaeans and their option for John against Christ? the other side of the bitter quarrel, of which we have the Mandaean side in their writings? A tempting idea. The available account is too sketchy to permit more than suggesting it as a possibility.

To return once more from intra-gnostic doctrinal matters to the subject of "foreign relations," of which we had an instance in the inclusion of Hermetic writings in the Nag Hamadi collection, it is almost irresistible to ask the question whether there are any links between the Nag Hamadi codices and the Dead Sea scrolls, between "Chenoboskion" and "Qumran"—the two groups whose relics, by one of the greatest coincidences imaginable, have come to light at almost the same time. Indeed there may have been, according to a fascinating suggestion by Doresse (*op. cit.* p. 295 ff.), whose gist, in all brevity, is this: *Qumran* could be *Gomorrha*—a hypothesis first suggested by F. de Saulcy on linguistic and topo-

---

[41] From the Zuqnin monastery near Amida, finished about 774 A.D.: quoted in U. Monneret de Villard, *Le leggende orientali sui Magi evangelici*, p. 27 f.

graphical grounds; Gomorrha and Sodom are named by ancient writers as places of Essenian settlements, and in this connection the Biblical connotations of the two names seem not to matter; no. 2 of the Nag Hamadi texts, the *Sacred Book of the invisible Great Spirit,* or *Gospel of the Egyptians,* has the following passage: "The great Seth came and brought his seed, and sowed it in the aeons that have been engendered and of which the number is the number of Sodom. Some say: 'Sodom is the dwelling place of the great Seth, which [or: who?] is Gomorrha.' And others say: 'The great Seth took the seed of Gomorrha, and he has transplanted it to the second place which has been called Sodom'" (Doresse p. 298). The suggestion is that, late as the text is relative to the date of the cessation of the Qumran community, it may refer to it (or else, to some neighboring group) as "the seed of the great Seth" and even allude to its reconstitution farther south, at Sodom, after the catastrophe that overtook Qumran. There would then be some kind of continuity between the disappearing Essenian movement and an emerging Sethian gnosis. Pending more data, it is impossible to assess the merits of this bold conjecture. Certainly, the implications of such a linkage between Essenes and Gnostics, as here intimated by a mythologized "historical" memory, would be vast and intriguing.

My comments so far have ranged over the whole of the Chenoboskion library for much of which the information is still fragmentary. Of the two fully edited and translated writings (see above, n. 2), I bypass the *Gospel according to Thomas,* a collection of "secret sayings of the living Jesus" allegedly taken down by Didymus Judas Thomas (about 112[42] of them), the relation of which to the Sayings of the Lord in the four gospels (thus to the whole problem of the synoptic tradition) is the subject of intensive study by New Testament scholars. Suffice it to say that of these "sayings" some (over 20) are almost identical with or very close to canonical ones, others (nearly 30) are looser parallels, with only partial agreement in word and content; another group (about 25) are but faint echoes of known logia; and the very substantial remainder (about 35) has no counterpart at all in the New Testament: the largest body so far of "unknown sayings of Christ." The gnostic character of the collec-

[42] The counting by different scholars varies somewhat.

tion (if it has that as a whole) is not readily recognizable: only in a few cases does it show unmistakably, often it may be guessed from the slant given a saying in the deviant version, and the meaning of many is veiled and elusive—or as yet so. While this text, because of its far-reaching implications for the question of the original substance and history of the Jesus tradition, is probably to the New Testament scholar the most exciting single writing of the whole Nag Hamadi find, the student of Gnosticism finds his richest reward so far in the so-called *Gospel of Truth* (*Evangelium Veritatis*), which has been published from the Jung codex. I shall devote the remainder of this chapter to some observations on this fascinating document.[43]

II. THE GOSPEL OF TRUTH (GT — Cod. I, 2)

The composition has no title in the codex, but begins with the words "The gospel of truth . . ." This, and the emphatically Valentinian character of language and content, have led the first editors to see in this meditation on the secrets of salvation and of the savior that "Gospel of Truth" with whose fabrication Irenaeus (*Adv. haer.* III. 11. 9) charges the Valentinians. The identification is entirely plausible, though of course not demonstrable. That the writing is very different in type from what a "gospel" should be according to the New Testament usage, viz., a record of the life and the teaching of Christ, is no objection. The extreme latitude with which the hallowed title was bestowed in gnostic circles has just been tellingly demonstrated by Nos. 2-7 of the Chenoboskion collection itself: with not the faintest likeness to a "gospel" in our sense (it deals not even with Jesus but with the Great Seth) it has for its second title, besides *Sacred Book of the invisible Great Spirit: Gospel of the Egyptians*. If our text is the "Gospel of Truth" denounced by Irenaeus, its authority among the Valentinians must have been well established by his time, which would place its origin in the previous, i.e.,

[43] For a somewhat fuller presentation of the argument rendered on the following pages see my two articles: "Evangelium Veritatis . . .", *Gnomon* 32 (1960), 327-335 [German], and "Evangelium Veritatis and the Valentinian Speculation," *Studia Patristica*, vol. VI (*Texte u. Unters. z. Gesch. d. Altchr. Litr.*, 81). Berlin: Akademie-Verlag, 1962, pp. 96-111.

the first Valentinian generation (about 150 A.D.) and indeed the authorship of Valentinus himself must not be ruled out. Its form is that of a homily or meditation; its style an allusive and often elusive mystical rhetoric with an ever shifting wealth of images; the emotional fervor of its piety is for once responsive to the mystery of incarnation and the suffering of Christ (see above, p. 195, n. 28): especially in this last respect, the GT adds a new voice to the gnostic chorus as we heard it before. As to doctrinal content, I shall single out one train of thought which constitutes something of an argument—that argument, in fact, which without exaggeration can be termed the hub of the Valentinian soteriology.

In the opening lines the Gospel of Truth is declared to be "a joy for those who have received from the Father of Truth the gift of knowing Him through the power of the Word (*Logos*) who has come from the Pleroma . . . for the redemption of those who were in ignorance of the Father"; the name "gospel" (*evangelium*) itself is then explained as "the manifestation of hope" (i.e., of the hoped-for). In other words, *evangelium* has here the original and literal meaning of "glad tidings" that hold out a hope and give assurance of the fulfillment of that hope. Accordingly, two salient themes in what follows are: the content or object of the hope, and the ground of the hope. Merged with these two is a third theme, viz., the role which the "tidings" themselves play in the realization of the hope.

The object of the hope, of course, is salvation, and accordingly we find large parts of the book devoted to expounding the nature or essence of salvation, which is by preference called "perfection"; and this being a gnostic treatise, we are not surprised to find the essence of perfection intimately related to *gnosis,* knowledge. The term "gnosis" specifies the content of the hope and itself calls for further specification as to the content of the knowledge.

It is the grounding of the hope which involves an argument: for the connection of ground and consequence is of the form "because this is (or was) so, therefore this is (or will be) so," which is the form of reasoning. Its content is determined by the particular doctrine in the given case: if our writing is Valentinian we must meet here with the speculative reasoning peculiar to Valentinian theory; and a conformity on this point is indeed the crucial test for the Valentinianism of the whole document.

Now, it is Valentinian, as generally gnostic, doctrine that the ground of eschatological hope is in the beginnings of all things, that the first things assure the last things as they have also caused the need for them. The task, then, of furnishing a ground to the eschatological hope is to establish a convincing nexus between what is proclaimed to be the means and mode of salvation, viz., knowledge, and the events of the beginning that call for this mode as their adequate complement. That nexus alone provides an answer to the question why knowledge, and just knowledge, can be the vehicle and even (in the Valentinian version) the essence of salvation. The cogency of that nexus, which is part of the very truth that the gospel has to reveal, and therefore part of the saving knowledge itself, indeed constitutes the gladness of the glad tidings. For it makes what otherwise might be a personal goal merely by subjective preference—the psychological state of knowledge—objectively valid as the redemption of the inner man and even (again in the Valentinian version) as the consummation of Being writ large. In this direction, then, we have to look when asking what not only *evangelium* in general—"a manifestation of hope"—but what the *evangelium veritatis* of our determinate message may be.

To this, our text gives a formal and concise answer, coming at the end of a brief account of the first beginnings: "*Since* 'Oblivion' came into being *because* they did not know the Father, *therefore if* they come to know the Father, 'Oblivion' becomes, at that very instant, non-existent" (18:7-11). Of this bald proposition it is then emphatically asserted that *it* represents the gist of the revelation of truth, the formulation as it were of its logic: "That, then, is the Gospel of Him whom they seek, which Jesus the Christ revealed to the Perfect, thanks to the mercies of the Father, as a hidden mystery" (18:11-16). More expressly could an author not declare what he regarded as the statement of the innermost secret of his gospel.

The proposition, in its bald formality far from self-explanatory and thus calling for the speculative context from which it receives meaning, has in fact the quality of a formula: it is twice more on record, with the identical grammatical structure of "since-therefore" and the reference to past history: once more within the GT itself, and once prominently in the Valentinian quotations of Irenaeus. This recurrence alone would show it to be an important and as such stereotyped item of the doctrine in question—a Valentinian doctrine, by the testimony of Irenaeus. In the GT, the formula reappears in the same brevity but with a slight variation of expression: "Since 'Deficiency' came into being because they did not know the Father, therefore when they know the Father, 'Deficiency' becomes, at that same instant, non-existent" (24:28-32). From this version we learn that "oblivion" (of the first version) is interchangeable with "deficiency"; and this very term "deficiency" leads us to the fullest extant statement of the formula, which was known before and by some recognized as the all-important Valentinian proposition as which it is now explicitly confirmed by the GT. It is quoted by Irenaeus in the famous passage *Adv. haer.* I. 21. 4, which we have rendered in full on p. 176 and from which we here repeat only the "formula" itself: "*Since* through 'Ignorance' came about 'Deficiency' and 'Passion,' *therefore* the whole system springing from the Ignorance is dissolved by Knowledge." This slightly fuller version of the formula adds one important item to the elliptic versions offered in the GT: it does not simply state that, since Deficiency (or Oblivion: mere negative terms) came into being through not-Knowing, it will cease with the advent of Knowledge, but it speaks of a "whole system" (*systasis*—a positive term) originating from the Ignorance and of *its dissolution* by Knowledge. This sounds much less tautological than the elliptic version. The reader of Irenaeus, of course, knows from what went before in his grand account of Valentinian speculation that the "system" in question is nothing less than this world, the cosmos, the whole realm of matter in all its elements, fire, air, water, earth, which only seem to be substances in their own right but are in truth by-products and expressions of spiritual processes or states: knowing this *he* can understand the argument of the formula which otherwise, by the mere terms of its language, would not be understandable even in this fuller version. The reader of Irenaeus knows further (which is equally indispensable for understanding the formula) that the Ignorance and Passion here named are not ordinary ignorance and ordinary passion as in us, but Ignorance and Passion writ large, on a metaphysical scale and at the origin of things: that far from being mere abstracts they denote concrete events and entities of the cosmogonic myth: that the subjective states they apparently name, being those of divine powers, have objective efficacy, and an efficacy on the scale of the inner life whereof they are states—the inner life of divinity—and therefore can be the ground of such substantive, total realities as cosmos and matter. In short, the premise of the formula, presupposed by it and required for the understanding of it, is the complete Valentinian *mythos,* of which the formula is in fact the epitome—that speculation on the beginnings of things that was developed in the tale of the Pleroma, the Sophia, and the Demiurge. Of this premise, even of several versions of it, the reader of Irenaeus is possessed when he comes to the passage in question.

Is the reader of the GT in the same position—assuming that he has nothing but the GT itself to go by? To ask thus amounts to asking whether the *tale* of the beginnings to which the formula makes reference is spelled out in the Gospel itself. The answer is "yes and no." The tale is offered and withheld at the same time, its essentials are recounted for those who already know but tantalizingly veiled for those who do not. The following is a quotation, in their order of occurrence, of the several passages in the GT that deal with the primordial past and—employing the argument of the "formula"—with the eschatological future as its counterpoint.[44]

The All was searching for Him from whom it had come forth, . . . that incomprehensible, unthinkable one who is superior to all thought. The Ignorance concerning the Father produced Anguish and Terror. And the Anguish became dense like a fog so that no one could see. Thus Error (*plane*) gained strength. It set to work on its own matter (*hyle*) in the void, not knowing the Truth. It applied itself to the fashioning of a formation (*plasma*) exerting itself to produce in beauty (fair appearance) a substitute for Truth (17:5-21). . . . They were a Nothing, that Anguish and that Oblivion and that formation of Falsehood (17:23-25). . . . Not having thus any root Error was immersed in a fog concerning the Father while engaged in producing works and oblivions and terrors in order to attract, by their means, those of the Middle and to imprison them (17:29-35). . . . Oblivion did not originate close to (or: with) the Father although it did originate because of

[44] Parts of these passages have been quoted by us before, on pp. 60, 181, 182, 183, 185, 190, 196 f. Other quotations from the GT are found on pp. 70, 71, 75, 76, 78, 89, 94, 180 (n. 8), 195.

Him. On the contrary, what originates in Him is the Knowledge, which was revealed so that the Oblivion should be dissolved and they might know the Father. Since Oblivion came into being because they did not know the Father, therefore if they attain to a knowledge of the Father, Oblivion becomes, at that same instant, non-existent. That, then, is the Gospel of Him whom they seek, which Jesus the Christ revealed to the Perfect, thanks to the mercies of the Father, as a hidden mystery (18:1-16). . . . The All is in want (of the Father) for He retained in Himself their perfection which He had not accorded to the All (18:35-38). . . . He retained their perfection in Himself, according it to them (later) in order that they should return to Him and should know Him through a knowledge unique in perfection (19:3-7). . . . For of what was the All in want if not of the knowledge of the Father? (19:15-17) . . . Since the perfection of the All is in the Father, it is necessary for the All to reascend towards Him (21:8-11) . . . They had strayed (from their places) when they received Error because of the Depth of Him who encompasses all spaces . . . It was a great marvel that they were in the Father without knowing Him and that it was possible for them to escape outside by their own will because they could not understand and know Him in whom they were (22:23-33) . . . Such is the Knowledge of this living Book which He revealed to the Aeons in the end (22:37-23:1) . . . (The Father) reveals that of Himself which was hidden—that of Himself which was hidden was His Son—so that, through the mercies of the Father, the Aeons may know Him and cease their toiling in search of Him, reposing in Him (and) knowing the repose to consist in this that by filling Deficiency he (the Son?) has abolished Shape (*schema*): its (Deficiency's) Shape is the world (*cosmos*), to which he (the Son?) had been subjected (24:11-24) . . . Since Deficiency came into being because they did not know the Father, therefore when they know the Father, Deficiency, at that same instant, will cease to exist. As a person's ignorance, at the moment when he comes to know, dissolves of its own accord: as darkness dissolves at the appearance of light: so also Deficiency is dissolved with the advent of Perfection. Surely from there on Shape is no longer apparent but will dissolve in fusion with Unity . . . at the moment when Unity shall perfect the Spaces (= Aeons?). (So also)[45] through Unity shall each one (of us) receive himself back. Through knowledge he shall purge himself of diversity towards Unity, by consuming the matter within himself like a flame, darkness by light, and death by life (24:28-25:19).

[45] Here is a transition from the macrocosmic to the microcosmic scene, from universal to individual salvation—for all the foregoing referred to the Aeons and not to terrestrial man.

This, then, is the account of the beginnings as our writing offers it, and the spelling-out of the ground of hope that is to lend meaning and conclusiveness to the proposition condensed in the "formula." But is that account, destined to support a proposition not otherwise intelligible, itself intelligible as it stands? The answer, I think, must be "No": suggestive it surely is and intriguing, adumbrating a world of meaning which yet eludes our grasp unless we have the benefit of extraneous help. We must, of course, try to forget whatever we know of the Valentinian myth from other sources and consult the language of the text alone. Now what can a reader thus unprepared make of the information that "Anguish" became dense like a fog, that "Error" elaborated "its matter" in the void, that "it" fashioned a formation, produced works, became angry, etc.? that "the All" was searching, that "they" did not know the Father? that "Oblivion" originated "because" of the Depth of the Father? that "Deficiency" has a "shape" and is "dissolved" with the coming of Plenitude, when "they" know the Father?

What scanty explanation of this cryptic language the text supplies it drops almost inadvertently by the way, and at that mostly so late in the account that we have to read it from the end backwards to profit by those cues. Thus we do finally learn that it is "the Aeons" that search for Him, lack knowledge and attain to a knowledge of Him: but this we learn on p. 24, when for once the noun is used after all previous statements from p. 18 on had over and over again the unexplained pronoun "they" [46]—which in turn replaced the expression "the All" with which the account opened on p. 17. As far as the evidence of the GT itself goes, we might not have known until then that "the All" is not the world, and "they" are not people, but that both refer to the Pleroma of the divine Aeons that antedate creation. Or, to take another example, we do encounter at last, on that same p. 24, the key-word *cosmos,* which retroactively secures the meaning of a host of earlier terms which in themselves have no cosmological reference: for *cosmos* is said to be the "shape" (*schema*) of "Deficiency"; Deficiency we could equate with the "Oblivion" on p. 18 (because it takes the latter's place in the formula), Oblivion in turn is there related to "Error"

[46] This in Coptic also serves to express an impersonal passive—thus "they do not know the Father" = "the Father is unknown."

(*planē*) and its "formation" (*plasma*), this in turn to "Anguish" and "Terror," they again to "Ignorance"—and so the whole chain of apparently psychological and human concepts, through which the mysterious tale moves, has almost by accident its cosmic meaning authenticated, which up to that moment the uninitiated reader could at best divine. He will still find himself at a loss how to picture, in the concrete, those abstracts of mind and emotion as actors in cosmogonic roles. With not so much as a mention of the chief *dramatis personae* like Sophia and demiurge the account remains elliptic and allusive. Even those sparing cues which we were able to glean from the text are not offered there as cues at all, as a dénouement for which the reader had been kept waiting. He is obviously expected to have known this all along: the terms in question occur where they do as a matter of course.

In other words, the intended reader of the GT must be supposed to have been on familiar ground when meeting, abruptly in our text, with those opaque terms like "Anguish," "Terror," and so on, his familiarity stemming from prior acquaintance with some complete version[47] of the Valentinian myth which enabled him to read the speculative passages of the GT as a mere condensed repetition of well-known doctrine.

Now this finding is of some importance for a true evaluation of our document. For one, it means that it is not a systematic or doctrinal treatise—which is anyway obvious from its general, homiletic style. Further, it is esoteric, addressed to initiates: it can therefore, in the speculative parts, largely work with "code" words, each an abstraction with a somewhat indefinite range as to the concrete mythical entities covered by it.[48] Lastly, the reductive picture it thus

---

[47] It does not matter which: the GT reflects the central principle of Valentinianism as such and in this common denominator agrees with any version of it. It may well also reflect a particular version, and an unknown one at that. We must not forget what Irenaeus has said about the individual freedom of invention rampant in the school (*Adv. haer.* I. 18. 5).

[48] "Anguish" and "Terror" seem not to be persons, but must be states of persons or of a person, and here one thinks of Sophia, out of whose "affects," in Valentinian teaching, the elements of matter condense: and the "affects" in turn are products of "ignorance." "Error" definitely is a person, and here one thinks of the demiurge. The "formation" which it fashions out of matter as an "equivalent" or "substitute" (i.e., in imitation?) of "Truth" could by general gnostic analogies be either the universe or man, but in the progress of the GT the cosmic reference preponderates. What Error fashions is "its own hyle": why "its own"? Is it the

offers of the "system" (with no mention of Sophia and demiurge, of the number and names of Aeons, etc.) does not justify the inference that it represents an incipient, still undeveloped, as it were embryonic stage of that speculation.[49] It rather represents a symbolism of the second degree. But it is indeed significant that the inner meaning of the doctrine *could* be expressed, at least to the "knowing" ones, in such abstaction from the lavish personal cast with which it was presented on the mythological stage. And this contains the answer to the question: what does the GT contribute to our knowledge of Valentinian theory?

In the field of universal speculation, with which alone I am here concerned, the GT may or may not add a new variant of the Valentinian doctrine to the several ones known from patristic testimony: any reconstruction of it from the sparse hints which the language of the text yields must at best remain highly conjectural. Not conjectural is the concordance in outline and spirit with the general *eidos* of Valentinian speculation, and here the GT is extremely valuable for an *understanding* of that very speculation which is so much more fully documented in the older reports. For the speculative passages of the GT are not merely an abridgment or summary of some fuller version: they point up, in their symbolic contraction, the essence of the doctrine, stripped of its vast mythological accessories and reduced to its philosophical core. Thus, as

---

"fog" to which "anguish" condensed? From its darkening effect (blotting out the light and thus visibility) Error originally "gained strength"—a negative strength, viz., "oblivion." But besides being the source, the "fog" (or a further condensation of it?) may also be the material (*hyle*) for the activity of this strength: if so, one could say that "matter" is the external, "oblivion" the internal aspect of the "deficiency" in which Error objectified itself. In the final product, the "deficiency" is the world as fashioned by Error in a "shape" (*schema*), in which the force of oblivion that lies at its root lives on.

[49] This thesis has been advanced by van Unnik (H.-C. Puech, G. Quispel, W. C. van Unnik, *The Jung Codex*, London 1955, 81-129): it is critically dealt with in my articles named above, n. 43. The tenor of my argument is that it is more plausible for the abstraction to come after than before the concrete imagination. Accordingly the GT would be a kind of "demythologized" expression of Valentinianism (it could still, as such, be by Valentinus himself or a contemporary). It must be conceded that the inverse sequence: a pre-mythological, quasi-philosophical beginning which then becomes clothed in mythology, is not impossible *per se*. But that the GT, with its free play of mystical variations on an underlying theological theme, its rich but loosely associated and ever blending imagery, should belong to an immature stage of Valentinianism is utterly implausible to me.

the GT can only be read with the help of the circumstantial myth, so the myth receives back from such reading a transparency as to its basic spiritual meaning which the density of its sensuous and necessarily equivocal imagery somehow disguises. In this role the GT acts like a pneumatic transcription of the symbolic myth. And what is truly inestimable: since its discovery we have it on their own authority *what* the Valentinians themselves considered as the heart of their doctrine: and that the heart of that heart was the proposition expressed in the "formula."

That formula, we found, had been known before (though not recognized as a formula) from the famous passage in Irenaeus which we quoted. Irenaeus himself gives no particular emphasis to it: the passage occurs at the tail-end of his comprehensive reports on Valentinian doctrine, among sundry supplementary information which is packed into (or rather, as I believe, follows upon[50]) the chapters dealing with the Marcosian heresy—which inclined students to see in it a tenet peculiar to one variety of this particular branch of the Valentinian tree and not central to Valentinianism as such. Nevertheless, the passage has for a long time impressed students of Gnosticism with its intrinsic significance.[51] Unexpectedly, this impression is now confirmed by the most authentic testimony. For the GT (whose authority with the Valentinians must have been great, if it is the "Gospel of Truth" assigned to them by Irenaeus) does nothing less than state in so many words that the truth condensed in the "formula" is—the gospel of truth! That the sentence in question had the currency of a formula we learn only now from its repetitious use in our text. That it was used by Valentinians we knew from Irenaeus. And only Valentinians could use it legitimately, for none but Valentinian speculation provided its validating context. To realize this, the reader is referred to the general characterization of "the speculative principle of Valentinianism" at the beginning of Chapt. 8 (pp. 174-176), which terminates in the exposition of what I call there the "pneumatic equation"—namely: that the human-individual event of pneumatic *knowledge* is the inverse equiv-

---

[50] I have never persuaded myself that from chapt. 19 on Irenaeus still deals with the Marcosians in particular, and not with Valentinian teachings in general.

[51] See, e.g., my treatment in *Gnosis und spätantiker Geist,* I (1934), 206, 2; 374 f; cf. II, 1 (1954), 162 f.

alent of the pre-cosmic universal event of divine *ignorance,* and in its redeeming effect of the same ontological order; and that thus the actualization of knowledge in the person is at the same time an act in the general ground of being. The "formula" is precisely a shorthand expression of that pneumatic equation—which thus is the Gospel of Truth.

Addendum to Chapter 12

In the above chapter, which was added to this book for its Second Edition in 1963, I used J. Doresse's numeration of the Nag Hammadi writings. This, as well as the different numeration by H.-Ch. Puech, has meanwhile been superseded by that of Martin Krause, which is based on a detailed inventory of the thirteen Codices.[1] In Krause's numeration, Roman numerals indicate the Codex (in the sequence adopted by the Coptic Museum in Cairo), followed by Arabic numerals for the individual Tractates as counted from number 1 in each Codex. The following concordance will enable the reader to convert Doresse's numbers, insofar as they appear in my presentation, into what now has become the standard reference system.

1=III,1; 2=III,2; 4=III,4; 6=IV,1; 7=IV,2; 12=V,5;
19=IX,3; 27=VII,1 and 2; 36=II,1; 39=II,4; 40=II,5

The complete inventory now counts fifty-three or more Tractates (as against forty-nine counted by Doresse and Puech) on an estimated original number of 1350 or more pages, of which about 1130 (plus a number of fragments) are preserved. The progress made in the study and publication of this vast material since the above chapter was written is reflected to some extent in the revised Supplementary Bibliography (pp. 351ff), which was prepared for the third printing of this edition.

---

[1]M. Krause. "Der koptische Handschriftenfund bei Nag Hammadi: Umfang und Inhalt," *Mitteilungen d. Dt. Archäol. Instituts, Abtl. Kairo* 18 (1962).

13. Epilogue: *Gnosticism, Existentialism, and Nihilism*

In this chapter I propose, in an experimental vein, to draw a comparison between two movements, or positions, or systems of thought widely separated in time and space, and seemingly incommensurable at first glance: one of our own day, conceptual, sophisticated, and eminently "modern" in more than the chronological sense; the other from a misty past, mythological, crude—something of a freak even in its own time, and never admitted to the respectable company of our philosophic tradition. My contention is that the two have something in common, and that this "something" is such that its elaboration, with a view to similarity and difference alike, may result in a reciprocal illumination of both.

In saying "reciprocal," I admit to a certain circularity of procedure. My own experience may illustrate what I mean. When, many years ago, I turned to the study of Gnosticism, I found that the viewpoints, the optics as it were, which I had acquired in the school of Heidegger, enabled me to see aspects of gnostic thought that had been missed before. And I was increasingly struck by the familiarity of the seemingly utterly strange. In retrospect, I am inclined to believe that it was the thrill of this dimly felt affinity which had lured me into the gnostic labyrinth in the first place. Then, after long sojourn in those distant lands returning to my own, the contemporary philosophic scene, I found that what I had learnt out there made me now better understand the shore from which I had set out. The extended discourse with ancient nihilism proved—to me at least—a help in discerning and placing the meaning of modern nihilism: just as the latter had initially equipped me for spotting its obscure cousin in the past. What had happened was that Existentialism, which had provided the means of an historical analysis, became itself involved in the results of it. The fitness of its categories to the particular matter was something to ponder about.

320

They fitted as if made to measure: *were* they, perhaps, made to measure? At the outset, I had taken that fitness as simply a case of their presumed general validity, which would assure their utility for the interpretation of any human "existence" whatsoever. But then it dawned on me that the applicability of categories in the given instance might rather be due to the very kind of "existence" on either side—that which had provided the categories and that which so well responded to them.

It was the case of an adept who believed himself in possession of a key that would unlock every door: I came to this particular door, I tried the key, and lo! it fitted the lock, and the door opened wide. So the key had proved its worth. Only later, after I had outgrown the belief in a universal key, did I begin to wonder *why* this one had in fact worked so well in this case. Had I happened with just the right kind of key upon the right kind of lock? If so, *what* was there between Existentialism and Gnosticism which made the latter open up at the touch of the former? With this turnabout of approach, the solutions in the one became questions to the other, where at first they had just seemed confirmations of its general power.

Thus the meeting of the two, started as the meeting of a method with a matter, ended with bringing home to me that Existentialism, which claims to be the explication of the fundamentals of human existence as such, is the philosophy of a particular, historically fated situation of human existence: and an analogous (though in other respects very different) situation had given rise to an analogous response in the past. The object turned object-lesson, demonstrating both contingency and necessity in the nihilistic experience. The issue posed by Existentialism does not thereby lose in seriousness; but a proper perspective is gained by realizing the situation which it reflects and to which the validity of some of its insights is confined.

In other words, the hermeneutic functions become reversed and reciprocal—lock turns into key, and key into lock: the "existentialist" reading of Gnosticism, so well vindicated by its hermeneutic success, invites as its natural complement the trial of a "gnostic" reading of Existentialism.

More than two generations ago, Nietzsche said that nihilism, "this weirdest of all guests," "stands before the door."[1] Meanwhile the guest has entered and is no longer a guest, and, as far as philosophy is concerned, existentialism is trying to live with him. Living in such company is living in a crisis. The beginnings of the crisis reach back into the seventeenth century, where the spiritual situation of modern man takes shape.

Among the features determining this situation is one which Pascal was the first to face in its frightening implications and to expound with the full force of his eloquence: man's loneliness in the physical universe of modern cosmology. "Cast into the infinite immensity of spaces of which I am ignorant, and which know me not, I am frightened."[2] "Which know me not": more than the overawing infinity of cosmic spaces and times, more than the quantitative disproportion, the insignificance of man as a magnitude in this vastness, it is the "silence," that is, the indifference of this universe to human aspirations—the not-knowing of things human on the part of that within which all things human have preposterously to be enacted—which constitutes the utter loneliness of man in the sum of things.

As a part of this sum, as an instance of nature, man is only a reed, liable to be crushed at any moment by the forces of an immense and blind universe in which his existence is but a particular blind accident, no less blind than would be the accident of his destruction. As a thinking reed, however, he is no part of the sum, not belonging to it, but radically different, incommensurable: for the *res extensa* does not think, so Descartes had taught, and nature is nothing but *res extensa*—body, matter, external magnitude. If nature crushes the reed, it does so unthinkingly, whereas the reed —man—even while crushed, is aware of being crushed.[3] He alone

[1] *Der Wille zur Macht*, (1887), § 1.

[2] *Pensées*, ed. Brunschvicg, fr. 205.

[3] *Op. cit.* fr. 347 "A reed only is man, the frailest in the world, but a reed that thinks. Unnecessary that the universe arm itself to destroy him: a breath of air, a drop of water are enough to kill him. Yet, if the All should crush him, man would still be nobler than that which destroys him: for he knows that he dies, and he knows that the universe is stronger than he; but the universe knows nothing of it."

in the world thinks, not because but in spite of his being part of nature. As he shares no longer in a meaning of nature, but merely, through his body, in its mechanical determination, so nature no longer shares in his inner concerns. Thus that by which man is superior to all nature, his unique distinction, mind, no longer results in a higher integration of his being into the totality of being, but on the contrary marks the unbridgeable gulf between himself and the rest of existence. Estranged from the community of being in one whole, his consciousness only makes him a foreigner in the world, and in every act of true reflection tells of this stark foreignness.

This is the human condition. Gone is the *cosmos* with whose immanent *logos* my own can feel kinship, gone the order of the whole in which man has his place. That place appears now as a sheer and brute accident. "I am frightened and amazed," continues Pascal, "at finding myself here rather than there; for there is no reason whatever why here rather than there, why now rather than then." There had always been a reason for the "here," so long as the cosmos had been regarded as man's natural home, that is, so long as the world had been understood as "cosmos." But Pascal speaks of "this remote corner of nature" in which man should "regard himself as lost," of "the little prison-cell in which he finds himself lodged, I mean the (visible) universe." [4] The utter contingency of our existence in the scheme deprives that scheme of any human sense as a possible frame of reference for the understanding of ourselves.

But there is more to this situation than the mere mood of homelessness, forlornness, and dread. The indifference of nature also means that nature has no reference to ends. With the ejection of teleology from the system of natural causes, nature, itself purposeless, ceased to provide any sanction to possible human purposes. A universe without an intrinsic hierarchy of being, as the Copernican universe is, leaves values ontologically unsupported, and the self is thrown back entirely upon itself in its quest for meaning and value. Meaning is no longer found but is "conferred." Values are no longer beheld in the vision of objective reality, but are posited as feats of valuation. As functions of the will, ends are solely my own creation.

[4] *Op. cit.* fr. 72.

Will replaces vision; temporality of the act ousts the eternity of the "good in itself." This is the Nietzschean phase of the situation in which European nihilism breaks the surface. Now man is alone with himself.

> The world's a gate
> To deserts stretching mute and chill.
> Who once has lost
> What thou hast lost stands nowhere still.

Thus spoke Nietzsche (in *Vereinsamt*), closing the poem with the line, "Woe unto him who has no home!"

Pascal's universe, it is true, was still one created by God, and solitary man, bereft of all mundane props, could still stretch his heart out toward the transmundane God. But this god is essentially an unknown God, an *agnostos theos,* and is not discernible in the evidence of his creation. The universe does not reveal the creator's purpose by the pattern of its order, nor his goodness by the abundance of created things, nor his wisdom by their fitness, nor his perfection by the beauty of the whole—but reveals solely his power by its magnitude, its spatial and temporal immensity. For extension, or the quantitative, is the one essential attribute left to the world, and therefore, if the world has anything at all to tell of the divine, it does so through this property: and what magnitude can tell of is power.[5] But a world reduced to a mere manifestation of power also admits toward itself—once the transcendent reference has fallen away and man is left with it and himself alone—nothing but the relation of power, that is, of mastery. The contingency of man, of his existing here and now, is with Pascal still a contingency upon God's will; but that will, which has cast me into just "this remote corner of nature," is inscrutable, and the "why?" of my existence is here just as unanswerable as the most atheistic existentialism can make it out to be. The *deus absconditus,* of whom nothing but will and power can be predicated, leaves behind as his legacy, upon leaving the scene, the *homo absconditus,* a concept of man characterized solely by will and power—the will for power,

[5] Cf. Pascal, *loc. cit.* "In short, it is the greatest sensible sign of God's omnipotence that our imagination loses itself in this thought (*sc. of* the immensity of cosmic space)."

the will to will. For such a will even indifferent nature is more an occasion for its exercise than a true object.[6]

The point that particularly matters for the purposes of this discussion is that a change in the vision of nature, that is, of the cosmic environment of man, is at the bottom of that metaphysical situation which has given rise to modern existentialism and to its nihilistic implications. But if this is so, if the essence of existentialism is a certain dualism, an estrangement between man and the world, with the loss of the idea of a kindred *cosmos*—in short, an anthropological acosmism—then it is not necessarily modern physical science alone which can create such a condition. A cosmic nihilism as such, begotten by whatever historical circumstances, would be the condition in which some of the characteristic traits of existentialism might evolve. And the extent to which this is found to be actually the case would be a test for the relevance which we attribute to the described element in the existentialist position.

There is one situation, and one only that I know of in the history of Western man, where—on a level untouched by anything resembling modern scientific thought—that condition has been realized and lived out with all the vehemence of a cataclysmic event. That is the gnostic movement, or the more radical ones among the various gnostic movements and teachings, which the deeply agitated first three centuries of the Christian era proliferated in the Hellenistic parts of the Roman empire and beyond its eastern boundaries. From them, therefore, we may hope to learn something for an understanding of that disturbing subject, nihilism, and I wish to put the evidence before the reader as far as this can be done in the space of a brief chapter, and with all the reservations which the experiment of such a comparison calls for.

The existence of an affinity or analogy across the ages, such as is here alleged, is not so surprising if we remember that in more than one respect the cultural situation in the Greco-Roman world of the first Christian centuries shows broad parallels with the modern

[6] The role of Pascal as the first modern existentialist, which I have here very roughly sketched as a starting point, has been more fully expounded by Karl Löwith in his article on "Man Between Infinities," in *Measure, A Critical Journal* (Chicago) vol. 1 (1950).

situation. Spengler went so far as to declare the two ages "con-temporaneous," in the sense of being identical phases in the life cycle of their respective cultures. In this analogical sense we would now be living in the period of the early Caesars. However that may be, there is certainly more than mere coincidence in the fact that we recognize ourselves in so many facets of later post-classical antiquity, far more so, at any rate, than in classical antiquity. Gnosticism is one of those facets, and here recognition, difficult as it is rendered by the strangeness of the symbols, comes with the shock of the unexpected, especially for him who does know something of Gnos-ticism, since the expansiveness of its metaphysical fancy seems ill to agree with the austere disillusionment of existentialism, as its religious character in general with the atheistic, fundamentally "post-Christian" essence by which Nietzsche identified modern nihilism. However, a comparison may yield some interesting re-sults.

The gnostic movement—such we must call it—was a widespread phenomenon in the critical centuries indicated, feeding like Chris-tianity on the impulses of a widely prevalent human situation, and therefore erupting in many places, many forms, and many lan-guages. First among the features to be emphasized here is the radically dualistic mood which underlies the gnostic attitude as a whole and unifies its widely diversified, more or less systematic expressions. It is on this primary human foundation of a passionately felt experience of self and world, that the formulated dualistic doc-trines rest. The dualism is between man and the world, and con-currently between the world and God. It is a duality not of sup-plementary but of contrary terms; and it is one: for that between man and world mirrors on the plane of experience that between world and God, and derives from it as from its logical ground—unless one would rather hold conversely that the transcendent doc-trine of a world-God dualism springs from the immanent experience of a disunion of man and world as from its psychological ground. In this three-term configuration—man, world, God—man and God belong together in contraposition to the world, but are, in spite of this essential belonging-together, in fact separated precisely by the world. To the Gnostic, this fact is the subject of revealed knowledge, and it determines gnostic eschatology: *we* may see in it the projection of his basic experience, which thus created for itself its own revelatory truth. Primary would then be the feeling of an absolute rift between man and that in which he finds himself lodged—the world. It is this feeling which explicates itself in the forms of objective doctrine. In its theological aspect this doctrine states that the Divine is alien to the world and has neither part nor concern in the physical universe; that the true god, strictly transmundane, is not revealed or even indicated by the world, and is therefore the Unknown, the totally Other, unknowable in terms of any worldly analogies. Correspondingly, in its cosmological aspect it states that the world is the creation not of God but of some inferior principle whose law it executes; and, in its anthropological aspect, that man's inner self, the *pneuma* ("spirit" in contrast to "soul" = *psyche*) is not part of the world, of nature's creation and domain, but is, within that world, as totally transcendent and as unknown by all worldly categories as is its transmundane counterpart, the unknown God without.

That the world is created by some personal agency is generally taken for granted in the mythological systems, though in some an almost impersonal necessity of dark impulse seems at work in its genesis. But whoever has created the world, man does not owe him allegiance, nor respect to his work. His work, though incomprehensibly encompassing man, does not offer the stars by which he can set his course, and neither does his proclaimed wish and will. Since not the true God can be the creator of that to which selfhood feels so utterly a stranger, nature merely manifests its lowly demiurge: as a power deep beneath the Supreme God, upon which even man can look down from the height of his god-kindred spirit, this perversion of the Divine has retained of it only the power to act, but to act blindly, without knowledge and benevolence. Thus did the demiurge create the world out of ignorance and passion.

The world, then, is the product, and even the embodiment, of the negative of *knowledge*. What it reveals is unenlightened and therefore malignant force, proceeding from the spirit of self-assertive power, from the will to rule and coerce. The mindlessness of this will is the spirit of the world, which bears no relation to understanding and love. The laws of the universe are the laws of this rule, and not of divine wisdom. *Power* thus becomes the chief aspect of the cosmos, and its inner essence is ignorance (agnosia). To this, the positive complement is that the essence of man is knowledge—knowledge of self and of God: this determines his situation as that of the potentially knowing in the midst of the unknowing, of light in the midst of darkness, and this relation is at the bottom of his being alien, without companionship in the dark vastness of the universe.

That universe has none of the venerability of the Greek *cosmos*. Contemptuous epithets are applied to it: "these miserable elements" (*paupertina haec elementa*), "this puny cell of the creator" (*haec cellula creatoris*).[7] Yet it is still *cosmos,* an order—but order with a vengeance, alien to man's aspirations. Its recognition is compounded of fear and disrespect, of trembling and defiance. The blemish of nature lies not in any deficiency of order, but in the all too pervading completeness of it. Far from being chaos, the creation of the demiurge, unenlightened as it is, is still a system of law. But cosmic law, once worshiped as the expression of a reason with which man's reason can communicate in the act of cognition, is now seen only in its aspect of compulsion which thwarts man's freedom. The cosmic *logos* of the Stoics, which was identified with providence, is replaced by *heimarmene,* oppressive cosmic fate.

This *fatum* is dispensed by the planets, or the stars in general, the personified exponents of the rigid and hostile law of the universe. The change in the emotional content of the term *cosmos* is nowhere better symbolized than in this depreciation of the formerly most divine part of the visible world, the celestial spheres. The starry sky—to the Greeks since Pythagoras the purest embodiment of reason in the sensible universe, and the guarantor of its harmony—now stared man in the face with the fixed glare of alien power and necessity. No longer his kindred, yet powerful as before, the stars have become tyrants—feared but at the same time despised, because they are lower than man. "They (says Plotinus indignantly of the Gnostics), who deem even the basest of men worthy to be called brothers by them, insanely deny this title to the sun, the stars in the heavens, nay, to the world-soul, our sister, itself!" (*Enn.* II. 9. 18). Who is more "modern," we may ask—Plotinus or the Gnostics? "They ought to desist (he says elsewhere) from their horror-tales

---

[7] Marcion: Tertullian, *Contra Marcionem,* I. 14.

about the cosmic spheres . . . If man is superior to the other animate beings, how much more so are the spheres, which not for tyranny are in the All, but to confer upon it order and law" (*ibid*. 13). We have heard how the Gnostics felt about this law. Of providence it has nothing, and to man's freedom it is inimical. Under this pitiless sky, which no longer inspires worshipful confidence, man becomes conscious of his utter forlornness. Encompassed by it, subject to its power, yet superior to it by the nobility of his soul, he knows himself not so much a part of, but unaccountably placed in and exposed to, the enveloping system.

And, like Pascal, he is frightened. His solitary otherness, discovering itself in this forlornness, erupts in the feeling of dread. Dread as the soul's response to its being-in-the-world is a recurrent theme in gnostic literature. It is the self's reaction to the discovery of its situation, actually itself an element in that discovery: it marks the awakening of the inner self from the slumber or intoxication of the world. For the power of the star spirits, or of the cosmos in general, is not merely the external one of physical compulsion, but even more the internal one of alienation or self-estrangement. Becoming aware of itself, the self also discovers that it is not really its own, but is rather the involuntary executor of cosmic designs. Knowledge, *gnosis,* may liberate man from this servitude; but since the *cosmos* is contrary to life and to spirit, the saving knowledge cannot aim at integration into the cosmic whole and at compliance with its laws, as did Stoic wisdom, which sought freedom in the knowing consent to the meaningful necessity of the whole. For the Gnostics, on the contrary, man's alienation from the world is to be deepened and brought to a head, for the extrication of the inner self which only thus can gain itself. The world (not the alienation from it) must be overcome; and a world degraded to a power system can only be overcome through power. The overpowering here in question is, of course, anything but technological mastery. The power of the world is overcome, on the one hand, by the power of the Savior who breaks into its closed system from without, and, on the other hand, through the power of the "knowledge" brought by him, which as a magical weapon defeats the force of the planets and opens to the soul a path through their impeding orders. Different as this is from modern man's power relation to world-causality, an ontological similarity lies in the formal fact that the countering of power with power is the sole relation to the totality of nature left for man in both cases.

Before going any further, let us stop to ask what has here happened to the old idea of the *cosmos* as a divinely ordered whole. Certainly nothing remotely comparable to modern physical science was involved in this catastrophic devaluation or spiritual denudation of the universe. We need only observe that this universe became thoroughly demonized in the gnostic period. Yet this, together with the transcendence of the acosmic self, resulted in curious analogies to some phenomena which existentialism exhibits in the vastly different modern setting. If not science and technology, what caused, for the human groups involved, the collapse of the cosmos piety of classical civilization, on which so much of its ethics was built?

The answer is certainly complex, but at least one angle of it may be briefly indicated. What we have before us is the repudiation of the classical doctrine of "whole and parts," and some of the reasons for this repudiation must be sought in the social and political sphere. The doctrine of classical ontology according to which the whole is prior to the parts, is better than the parts, and is that for the sake of which the parts are, and wherein they find the meaning of their existence—this time-honored axiom had lost the social basis of its validity. The living example of such a whole had been the classical *polis*. . . . [For the remainder of this section of the original essay, the reader is referred to pp. 248-249 of the present volume, which almost verbatim duplicates it. I resume the thread with the last sentence on p. 249.] . . . The new atomized masses of the empire, who had never shared in that noble tradition, might react differently to a situation in which they found themselves passively involved: a situation in which the part was insignificant to the whole, and the whole alien to the parts. The aspiration of the gnostic individual was not to "act a part" in this whole, but—in existentialist parlance—to "exist authentically." The law of empire, under which he found himself, was a dispensation of external, inaccessible force; and for him the law of the universe, cosmic destiny, of which the world state was the terrestrial executor, assumed the same character. The very concept of law was affected thereby in all its aspects—as natural law, political law, and moral law.

This brings us back to our comparison.

The subversion of the idea of law, of *nomos,* leads to ethical consequences in which the nihilistic implication of the gnostic acosmism, and at the same time the analogy to certain modern reasonings, become even more obvious than in the cosmological aspect. I am thinking of gnostic antinomianism. It is to be conceded at the outset that the denial of every objective norm of conduct is argued on vastly different theoretical levels in Gnosis and Existentialism, and that antinomistic Gnosis appears crude and naive in comparison with the conceptual subtlety and historical reflection of its modern counterpart. What was being liquidated, in the one case, was the moral heritage of a millennium of ancient civilization; added to this, in the other, are two thousand years of Occidental Christian metaphysics as background to the idea of a moral law.

Nietzsche indicated the root of the nihilistic situation in the phrase "God is dead," meaning primarily the Christian God. The Gnostics, if asked to summarize similarly the metaphysical basis of their own nihilism, could have said only "the God of the cosmos is dead"—is dead, that is, as a god, has ceased to be divine for us and therefore to afford the lodestar for our lives. Admittedly the catastrophe in this case is less comprehensive and thus less irremediable, but the vacuum that was left, even if not so bottomless, was felt no less keenly. To Nietzsche the meaning of nihilism is that "the highest values become devaluated" (or "invalidated"), and the cause of this devaluation is "the *insight* that we have not the slightest justification for positing a beyond, or an 'in itself' of things, which is 'divine,' which is morality in person." [8] This statement taken with that about the death of God, bears out Heidegger's contention that "the names God and Christian God are in Nietzsche's thought used to denote the transcendental (supra-sensible) world in general. God is the name for the realm of ideas and ideals" (*Holzwege,* p. 199). Since it is from this realm alone that any sanction for values can derive, its vanishing, that is, the "death of God," means not only the actual devaluation of highest values, but the loss of the

[8] *Wille zur Macht* § § 2; 3.

very possibility of obligatory values as such. To quote once more Heidegger's interpretation of Nietzsche, "The phrase 'God is dead' means that the supra-sensible world is without effective force." (*Ibid.* p. 200.)

In a modified, rather paradoxical way this statement applies also to the gnostic position. It is true, of course, that its extreme dualism is of itself the very opposite of an abandonment of transcendence. The transmundane God represents it in the most radical form. In him the absolute beyond beckons across the enclosing cosmic shells. But this transcendence, unlike the "intelligible world" of Platonism or the world lord of Judaism, does not stand in any positive relation to the sensible world. It is not the essence or the cause of it, but its negation and cancellation. The gnostic God, as distinct from the demiurge, is the totally different, the other, the unknown. Like his inner-human counterpart, the acosmic self or *pneuma*, whose hidden nature also reveals itself only in the negative experience of otherness, of non-identification and of protested indefinable freedom, this God has more of the *nihil* than the *ens* in his concept. A transcendence withdrawn from any normative relation to the world is equal to a transcendence which has lost its effective force. In other words, for all purposes of man's relation to the reality that surrounds him this hidden God is a nihilistic conception: no *nomos* emanates from him, no law for nature and thus none for human action as a part of the natural order.

On this basis the antinomistic argument of the Gnostics is as simple as, for instance, that of Sartre. Since the transcendent is silent, Sartre argues, since "there is no sign in the world," man, the "abandoned" and left-to-himself, reclaims his freedom, or rather, cannot help taking it upon himself: he "is" that freedom, man being "nothing but his own project," and "all is permitted to him." [9] That this freedom is of a desperate kind, and, as a compassless task, inspires dread rather than exultation, is a different matter.

Sometimes in gnostic reasoning the antinomian argument appears in the guise of conventional subjectivism: . . . [for the sequence, the reader again should turn to its duplication in the book, viz., the two paragraphs on pp. 272-273, beginning with "In

[9] J. P. Sartre, *L'existentialisme est un humanisme*, pp. 33 f.

this connection . . ." and ending with ". . . thwarting their design."] . . .

As to the assertion of the authentic freedom of the self, it is to be noted that this freedom is a matter not of the "soul" (*psyche*), which is as adequately determined by the moral law as the body is by the physical law, but wholly a matter of the "spirit" (*pneuma*), the indefinable spiritual core of existence, the foreign spark. The soul is part of the natural order, created by the demiurge to envelop the foreign spirit, and in the normative law the creator exercises control over what is legitimately his own. Psychical man, definable in his natural essence, for instance as rational animal, is still natural man, and this "nature" can no more determine the pneumatic self than in the existentialist view any determinative essence is permitted to prejudice the freely self-projecting existence.

Here it is pertinent to compare an argument of Heidegger's. In his *Letter on Humanism,* Heidegger argues, against the classical definition of Man as "the rational animal," that this definition places man within animality, specified only by a *differentia* which falls within the genus "animal" as a particular quality. This, Heidegger contends, is placing man too low.[10] I will not press the point whether there is not a verbal sophism involved in thus arguing from the term "animal" as used in the classical definition.[11] What is important for us is the rejection of any definable "nature" of man which would subject his sovereign existence to a predetermined essence and thus make him part of an objective order of essences in the totality of nature. In this conception of a trans-essential, freely "self-projecting"

[10] Heidegger, Ueber den Humanismus. Frankfurt 1949, p. 13.

[11] "Animal" in the Greek sense means not "beast," but any "animated being," including demons, gods, the ensouled stars—even the ensouled universe as a whole (cf. Plato, Timaeus 30 C): no "lowering" of man is implied in placing him within this scale, and the bogy of "animality" in its modern connotations is slipped in surreptitiously. In reality, the lowering to Heidegger consists in placing "man" in *any* scale, that is, in a context of *nature* as such. The Christian devaluation of "animal" to "beast," which indeed makes the term usable only in contrast to "man," merely reflects the larger break with the classical position—that break by which Man, as the unique possessor of an immortal soul, comes to stand outside "nature" entirely. The existentialist argument takes off from this new basis: the play on the semantic ambiguity of "animal," while scoring an easy point, conceals this shift of basis of which that ambiguity is a function, and fails to meet the classical position with which it ostensibly argues.

existence I see something comparable to the gnostic concept of the trans-psychical negativity of the *pneuma.* That which has no nature has no norm. Only that which belongs to an order of natures—be it an order of creation, or of intelligible forms—can have a nature. Only where there is a whole is there a law. In the deprecating view of the Gnostics this holds for the *psyche,* which belongs to the cosmic whole. Psychical man can do no better than abide by a code of law and strive to be just, that is, properly "adjusted" to the established order, and thus play his allotted part in the cosmic scheme. But the *pneumaticos,* "spiritual" man, who does not belong to any objective scheme, is above the law, beyond good and evil, and a law unto himself in the power of his "knowledge."

But what is this knowledge about, this cognition which is not of the soul but of the spirit, and in which the spiritual self finds its salvation from cosmic servitude? A famous formula of the Valentinian school thus epitomizes the content of *gnosis:* "What makes us free is the knowledge who we were, what we have become; where we were, wherein we have been thrown; whereto we speed, wherefrom we are redeemed; what is birth and what rebirth." [12] A real exegesis of this programmatic formula would have to unfold the complete gnostic myth. Here I wish to make only a few formal observations.

First we note the dualistic grouping of the terms in antithetical pairs, and the eschatological tension between them, with its irreversible direction from past to future. We further observe that the terms throughout are concepts not of being but of happening, of movement. The knowledge is of a history, in which it is itself a critical event. Among these terms of motion, the one of having "been thrown" into something strikes our attention, because we have been made familiar with it in existentialist literature. We are reminded of Pascal's "Cast into the infinite immensity of spaces," of Heidegger's *Geworfenheit,* "having been thrown," which to him is a fundamental character of the *Dasein,* of the self-experience of existence. The term, as far as I can see, is originally gnostic. In Mandaean literature it is a standing phrase: life has been thrown into the world, light into darkness, the soul into the body. It ex-

[12] Clemens Alex., *Exc. ex Theod.,* 78. 2.

presses the original violence done to me in making me be where I am and what I am, the passivity of my choiceless emergence into an existing world which I did not make and whose law is not mine. But the image of the throw also imparts a dynamic character to the whole of the existence thus initiated. In our formula this is taken up by the image of speeding toward some end. Ejected into the world, life is a kind of trajectory projecting itself forward into the future.

This brings us to the final observation I wish to make apropos of the Valentinian formula: that in its temporal terms it makes no provision for a *present* on whose content knowledge may dwell and, in beholding, stay the forward thrust. There is past and future, where we come from and where we speed to, and the present is only the moment of *gnosis* itself, the peripety from the one to the other in a supreme crisis of the eschatological *now*. There is this to remark, however, in distinction to all modern parallels: in the gnostic formula it is understood that, though thrown into temporality, we had an origin in eternity, and so also have an aim in eternity. This places the innercosmic nihilism of the Gnosis against a metaphysical background which is entirely absent from its modern counterpart.

To turn once more to the modern counterpart, let us ponder an observation which must strike the close student of Heidegger's *Sein und Zeit,* that most profound and still most important manifesto of existentialist philosophy. Heidegger there develops a "fundamental ontology" according to the modes in which the self "exists," that is, constitutes its own being in the act of existing, and with it originates, as the objective correlates thereof, the several meanings of Being in general. These modes are explicated in a number of fundamental categories which Heidegger prefers to call "existentials." Unlike the objective "categories" of Kant, they articulate primarily structures not of reality but of realization, that is, not cognitive structures of a world of objects given, but functional structures of the active movement of inner time by which a "world" is entertained and the self originated as a continuous event. The "existentials" have, therefore, each and all, a profoundly temporal meaning. They are categories of internal or mental time, the true dimension of existence, and they articulate that dimension in its tenses. This being the case, they must exhibit, and distribute between them, the three horizons of time—past, present, and future.

Now if we try to arrange these "existentials," Heidegger's categories of existence, under those three heads, as it is possible to do, we make a striking discovery—at any rate one that struck me very much when, at the time the book appeared, I tried to draw up a diagram, in the classical manner of a "table of categories." It is the discovery that the column under the head of "present" remains practically empty—at least insofar as modes of "genuine" or "authentic" existence are concerned. I hasten to add that this is an extremely abridged statement. Actually a great deal is said about the existential "present," but not as an independent dimension in its own right. For the existentially "genuine" present is the present of the "situation," which is wholly defined in terms of the self's *relation* to its "future" and "past." It flashes up, as it were, in the light of decision, when the projected "future" reacts upon the given "past" (*Geworfenheit*) and in this meeting constitutes what Heidegger calls the "moment" (*Augenblick*): moment, not duration, is the temporal mode of *this* "present"—a creature of the other two horizons of time, a function of their ceaseless dynamics, and no independent dimension to dwell in. Detached, however, from this context of inner movement, by itself, mere "present" denotes precisely the renouncement of genuine future-past relation in the "abandonment" or "surrender" to talk, curiosity, and the anonymity of "everyman" (*Verfallenheit*): a failure of the tension of true existence, a kind of slackness of being. Indeed, *Verfallenheit,* a negative term which also includes the meaning of degeneration and decline, is *the* "existential" proper to "present" as such, showing it to be a derivative and "deficient" mode of existence.

Thus our original statement stands that all the relevant categories of existence, those having to do with the possible authenticity of selfhood, fall in correlate pairs under the heads of either past or future: "facticity," necessity, having become, having been thrown, guilt, are existential modes of the past; "existence," being ahead of one's present, anticipation of death, care, and resolve, are existential modes of the future. No present remains for genuine existence to repose in. Leaping off, as it were, from its past, existence projects itself into its future; faces its ultimate limit, death; returns from this eschatological glimpse of nothingness to its sheer factness, the unalterable datum of its already having become this, there and then; and carries this forward with its death-begotten resolve, into which the past has now been gathered up. I repeat, there is no present to dwell in, only the crisis between past and future, the pointed moment between, balanced on the razor's edge of decision which thrusts ahead.

This breathless dynamism held a tremendous appeal for the contemporary mind, and my generation in the German twenties and early thirties succumbed to it wholesale. But there is a puzzle in this evanescence of the present as the holder of genuine content, in its reduction to the inhospitable zero point of mere formal resolution. What metaphysical situation stands behind it?

Here an additional observation is relevant. There is, after all, besides the existential "present" of the moment, the presence of things. Does not the co-presence with them afford a "present" of a different kind? But we are told by Heidegger that things are primarily *zuhanden,* that is, usable (of which even "useless" is a mode), and therefore related to the "project" of existence and its "care" (Sorge), therefore included in the future-past dynamics. Yet they can also become neutralized to being merely *vorhanden* ("standing before me"), that is, indifferent objects, and the mode of *Vorhandenheit* is an objective counterpart to what on the existential side is *Verfallenheit,* false present. *Vorhanden* is what is merely and indifferently "extant," the "there" of bare nature, there to be looked at outside the relevance of the existential situation and of practical "concern." It is being, as it were, stripped and alienated to the mode of mute thinghood. This is the status left to "nature" for the relation of theory—a deficient mode of being—and the relation in which it is so objectified is a deficient mode of existence, its defection from the futurity of care into the spurious present of mere onlooking curiosity.[13]

This existentialist depreciation of the concept of nature obviously reflects its spiritual denudation at the hands of physical science, and it has something in common with the gnostic contempt for nature. No philosophy has ever been less concerned about nature than Existentialism, for which it has no dignity left:

[13] I am speaking here throughout of *Sein und Zeit,* not of the later Heidegger, who is certainly no "Existentialist."

this unconcern is not to be confounded with Socrates' refraining from physical inquiry as being above man's understanding.

To look at what is there, at nature as it is in itself, at Being, the ancients called by the name of contemplation, *theoria*. But the point here is that, if contemplation is left with only the irrelevantly extant, then it loses the noble status it once had—as does the repose in the present to which it holds the beholder by the presence of its objects. *Theoria* had that dignity because of its Platonic implications—because it beheld eternal objects in the forms of things, a transcendence of immutable being shining through the transparency of becoming. Immutable being is everlasting present, in which contemplation can share in the brief durations of the temporal present.

Thus it is eternity, not time, that grants a present and gives it a status of its own in the flux of time; and it is the loss of eternity which accounts for the loss of a genuine present. Such a loss of eternity is the disappearance of the world of ideas and ideals in which Heidegger sees the true meaning of Nietzsche's "God is dead": in other words, the absolute victory of nominalism over realism. Therefore the same cause which is at the root of nihilism is also at the root of the radical temporality of Heidegger's scheme of existence, in which the present is nothing but the moment of crisis between past and future. If values are not beheld in vision as being (like the Good and the Beautiful of Plato), but are posited by the will as projects, then indeed existence is committed to constant futurity, with death as the goal; and a merely formal resolution to be, without a *nomos* for that resolution, becomes a project from nothingness into nothingness. In the words of Nietzsche quoted before, "Who once has lost what thou hast lost stands nowhere still."

Once more our investigation leads back to the dualism between man and *physis* as the metaphysical background of the nihilistic situation. There is no overlooking one cardinal difference between the gnostic and the existentialist dualism: Gnostic man is thrown into an antagonistic, anti-divine, and therefore anti-human nature, modern man into an indifferent one. Only the latter case represents the absolute vacuum, the really bottomless pit. In the gnostic conception the hostile, the demonic, is still anthropomorphic, familiar even in its foreignness, and the contrast itself gives direction to existence—a negative direction, to be sure, but one that has behind it the sanction of the negative transcendence to which the positivity of the world is the qualitative counterpart. Not even this antagonistic quality is granted to the indifferent nature of modern science, and from that nature no direction at all can be elicited.

This makes modern nihilism infinitely more radical and more desperate than gnostic nihilism ever could be for all its panic terror of the world and its defiant contempt of its laws. That nature does not care, one way or the other, is the true abyss. That only man cares, in his finitude facing nothing but death, alone with his contingency and the objective meaninglessness of his projecting meanings, is a truly unprecedented situation.

But this very difference, which reveals the greater depth of modern nihilism, also challenges its self-consistency. Gnostic dualism, fantastic as it was, was at least self-consistent. The idea of a demonic nature against which the self is pitted, makes sense. But what about an indifferent nature which nevertheless contains in its midst that to which its own being does make a difference? The phrase of having been flung into indifferent nature is a remnant from a dualistic metaphysics, to whose use the non-metaphysical standpoint has no right. What is the throw without the thrower, and without a beyond whence it started? Rather should the existentialist say that life—conscious, caring, knowing self—has been "tossed up" *by* nature. If blindly, then the seeing is a product of the blind, the caring a product of the uncaring, a teleological nature begotten unteleologically.

Does not this paradox cast doubt on the very concept of an indifferent nature, that abstraction of physical science? So radically has anthropomorphism been banned from the concept of nature that even man must cease to be conceived anthropomorphically if he is just an accident of that nature. As the product of the indifferent, his being, too, must be indifferent. Then the facing of his mortality would simply warrant the reaction "Let us eat and drink for tomorrow we die." There is no point in caring for what has no sanction behind it in any creative intention. But if the deeper insight of Heidegger is right—that, facing our finitude, we find that we care, not only whether we exist but how we exist—then the mere fact of there being such a supreme care, anywhere within the world, must also qualify the totality which harbors that fact, and even more so if "it" alone was the productive cause of that fact, by letting its subject physically arise in its midst.

The disruption between man and total reality is at the bottom of nihilism. The illogicality of the rupture, that is, of a dualism without metaphysics, makes its fact no less real, nor its seeming alternative any more acceptable: the stare at isolated selfhood, to which it condemns man, may wish to exchange itself for a monistic naturalism which, along with the rupture, would abolish also the idea of man as man. Between that Scylla and this her twin Charybdis, the modern mind hovers. Whether a third road is open to it—one by which the dualistic rift can be avoided and yet enough of the dualistic insight saved to uphold the humanity of man—philosophy must find out.

CORRECTIONS AND ADDITIONS

To p. 69, note 23, and p. 219: the Turfan-text rendered after C. Salemann's translation should have been rendered after the more recent and improved one by W. Henning. The complete passage then reads:

And from the impurity of the he-demons and from the filth of the she-demons she [*Az*—"the evil mother of all demons"] formed this body, and she herself entered into it. Then from the five Light-elements, Ormuzd's armor, she formed [?] the good Soul and fettered it in the body. She made it as if blind and deaf, unconscious and confused, so that at first it might not know its origin and kinship.

> (W. Henning, "Geburt und Entstehung des manichäischen Urmenschen," *Nachricht. Gött. Ges. Wiss.*, Phil.-hist. Kl. 1932, Göttingen, 1933, 217 ff.)

To p. 199, "Apocryphon of John": the recent edition of this text referred to is in W. Till, *Die gnostischen Schriften des koptischen Papyrus Berolinensis 8502* (Texte und Untersuchungen 60), Berlin, 1955.

Selected Bibliography

With the exception of some articles of particular importance, only books have been included in this bibliography.

I. Background

Angus, S. *The Mystery Religions and Christianity*. New York, 1925.

———. *The Religious Quests of the Graeco-Roman World*. New York, 1929.

Barker, Sir E. (ed. and tr.). *From Alexander to Constantine*. Oxford, 1956.

Bevan, E. R. *Hellenism and Christianity*. London, 1921.

———. *Later Greek Religion*. London, 1927.

———. *Stoics and Sceptics*. Oxford, 1913.

Bidez, J., and Cumont, F. *Les mages hellenisés*. 2 vols. Paris, 1938.

Boll, F. *Sternglaube und Sterndeutung*. 4th edition. Leipzig, 1931.

Bousset, W. *Die Religion des Judentums im späthellenistischen Zeitalter*. 3rd edition. Tübingen, 1926.

Bréhier, E. *La philosophie de Plotin*. Paris, 1928.

Bultmann, R. *Primitive Christianity in its Contemporary Setting*. London, New York, 1956.

———. *Theology of the New Testament*. 2 vols. New York, 1951-55.

Caird, E. *The Evolution of Theology in the Greek Philosophers*. 2 vols. Glasgow, 1904.

Cicero. *De Natura Deorum*. Translated by H. M. Poteat. Chicago, 1950.

Clark, G. H. (ed.). *Selections from Hellenistic Philosophy*. New York, 1940.

Cumont, F. *After Life in Roman Paganism*. New Haven, 1922.

———. *Astrology and Religion among the Greeks and Romans*. New York, 1912.

———. *Lux Perpetua*. Paris, 1949.

———. *The Mysteries of Mithras*. Chicago, London, 1903.

———. *The Oriental Religions in Roman Paganism*. Chicago, 1911.

Deissmann, A. *Light from the Ancient East*. Revised edition. London, 1922.

Dieterich, A. *Eine Mithrasliturgie*. Leipzig, 1903.

Dodd, C. H. *The Bible and the Greeks*. London, 1935.

Duchesne-Guillemin, J. *Zoroastre*. Paris, 1948.

———. *The Western Response to Zoroaster*. Oxford, 1958.

Festugière, H. J. and Fabre, P. *Le monde gréco-romain au temps de Notre-Seigneur*. 2 vols. Paris, 1935.

Festugière, H. J. *Personal Religion among the Greeks*. Berkeley, 1954.

Gaster, T. H. (tr.). *The Dead Sea Scriptures*. New York, 1956.

Geffcken, J. *Der Ausgang des griechisch-römischen Heidentums*. Heidelberg, 1929.

Grant, F. C. *Hellenistic Religions: The Age of Syncretism*. New York, 1953 (Sources).

Grant, R. M. *Second Century Christianity: A Collection of Fragments*. London, 1946.

Gressmann, H. *Die hellenistische Gestirnreligion*. Leipzig, 1925.

———. *Die orientalischen Religionen im hellenistisch-römischen Zeitalter*. Berlin, 1930.

Gunkel, H. *Zum religionsgeschichtlichen Verständnis des Neuen Testaments.* Göttingen, 1903.

Guthrie, W. K. C. *Orpheus and Greek Religion.* 2nd edition. London, 1952.

Harnack, A. *The Mission and Expansion of Christianity in the First Three Centuries.* 2 vols. New York, 1908.

Hatch, E. *The Influence of Greek Ideas on Christianity* (Hibbert Lectures, 1888). New edition. New York, 1957.

Hepding, H. *Attis, seine Mythen und sein Kult.* Giessen, 1903.

Inge, W. R. *The Philosophy of Plotinus.* 2 vols. 3rd edition. London, 1929.

Jaeger, W. *Paideia: The Ideals of Greek Culture.* 3 vols. Oxford, 1939-45.

Jonas, H. *Augustin und das paulinische Freiheitsproblem.* Göttingen, 1930.

Kaerst, J. *Geschichte des Hellenismus.* 2 vols. 2nd edition. 1917-26.

Kern, O. *Die Religion der Griechen.* 3 vols. Berlin, 1926-38.

Labriolle, P. de. *La réaction païenne: Étude sur la polémique anti-chrétienne du 1er au 6e siècles.* Paris, 1934.

Laqueur, R. *Hellenismus.* Giessen, 1925.

Lietzmann, H. *The Beginnings of the Christian Church.* New York, 1937.

————. *History of the Early Church.* 4 vols. New York, 1938.

Meyer, E. *Ursprung und Anfänge des Christentums.* 3 vols. Stuttgart, 1923-25.

Moore, G. F. *Judaism in the First Centuries of the Christian Era.* 3 vols. Cambridge, 1927-30.

More, P. E. *Hellenistic Philosophies.* Princeton, 1923.

Murray, G. *Five Stages of Greek Religion.* Oxford, 1925; New York, 1955.

Nilsson, M. P. *History of Greek Religion.* Revised edition. Oxford, 1949.

Nock, A. D. *Conversion: the Old and the New in Religion from Alexander the Great to Augustine of Hippo.* Oxford, 1933.

———— (ed. and tr.). *Sallustius: Concerning the Gods and the Universe.* Cambridge, England, 1926.

Oates, W. J. (ed.). *The Stoic and Epicurean Philosophers.* New York, 1940.

Pohlenz, M. *Die Stoa.* 2 vols. Göttingen, 1948.

Reinhardt, K. *Kosmos und Sympathie.* Munich, 1926.

Reitzenstein, R. *Die hellenistischen Mysterienreligionen.* 3rd edition. Leipzig, 1927.

Rohde, E. *Psyche: Seelenkult und Unsterblichkeitsglaube der Griechen.* 8th edition. Tübingen, 1925; English translation, London, 1925.

Rostovtzeff, M. I. *Social and Economic History of the Hellenistic World.* 3 vols. Oxford, 1941.

————. *Social and Economic History of the Roman Empire.* 2 vols. New edition. Oxford, 1957.

Schoeps, H. J. *Theologie und Geschichte des Judenchristentums.* Tübingen, 1949.

Schürer, E. *History of the Jewish People in the Time of Jesus.* 5 vols. Edinburgh, 1885-91; 3 vols. New York, 1892.

Spengler, O. *The Decline of the West.* Vol. II. New York, 1928.

Tarn, W. W. *Hellenistic Civilization.* 3rd edition. London, 1952.

Wendland, P. *Die hellenistisch-römische Kultur in ihren Beziehungen zu Judentum und Christentum.* 2nd edition. Tübingen, 1912.

Whittaker, T. *The Neoplatonists.* 2nd edition. Cambridge, England, 1918.

II. Gnosticism: General

A. Sources

Buonaiuti, E. *Frammenti gnostici.* Rome, 1923.

————. *Gnostic Fragments.* English translation. London, 1924.

Charles, R. H. *The Apocrypha and Pseudepigrapha of the Old Testament.* Oxford, 1913.

Clement of Alexandria. *Stromata; Excerpta ex Theodoto.* Edited by O. Stählin (Die griech. christl. Schriftsteller der ersten drei Jahrhunderte, 15, 17). Leipzig, 1906-09.

——. *The Excerpta ex Theodoto* . . . . Edited and translated by R. P. Casey. London, 1934.

——. *Extraits de Théodote.* Edited and translated by F. Sagnard. Paris, 1948.

Ephiphanius of Salamis. *Panarion Haeresium.* Edited by K. Holl (Griech. christl. Schriftsteller, 25, 31, 37). Leipzig, 1915-31.

Grant, R. M. *Gnosticism. A Sourcebook of Heretical Writings.* New York, 1961.

Hennecke, E. (ed.). *Neutestamentliche Apokryphen.* 2nd edition. Tübingen, 1924.

Hippolytus of Rome. *Refutatio Omnium Haeresium* [=*Philosophumena*]. Edited by P. Wendland (Griech. christl. Schriftsteller, 26). Berlin, 1916.

Irenaeus of Lyon. *Adversus Haereses.* Edited by W. W. Harvey. 2 vols. Cambridge, England, 1857.

James, M. R. (tr.). *The Apocryphal New Testament.* Oxford, 1924.

Lipsius, R. A. and Bonnet, M. (ed.). *Acta Apostolorum Apocrypha.* Leipzig, 1891 ff.

Malinine, M., Puech, H. C., Quispel, G. (ed. and tr.). *Evangelium Veritatis.* Zürich, 1956.

Origenes. *Contra Celsum.* Edited by P. Koetschau (Griech. christl. Schriftsteller, 2-3). Leipzig, 1899.

——. *Id.* Edited and translated by H. Chadwick. Cambridge, England, 1953.

Puech, H. C. and Quispel, G. "Les écrits gnostiques du Codex Jung," *Vigiliae Christianae,* 8 (1954), 1-54.

——. "Le quatrième écrit du Codex Jung," *ibid.,* 9 (1955), 65-102.

Schmidt, C. *Koptisch-gnostische Schriften* (Griech. christl. Schriftsteller, 13). Leipzig, 1905.

——. *Pistis Sophia.* Revised edition (Coptica II). Leipzig, 1925.

Tertullian of Carthage. *De Praescriptione Haereticorum; Adversus Valentinianos; Adversus Marcionem.* Edited by E. Kroymann (Corpus script. eccles. lat., 47). Vienna, 1906.

——. *De Anima.* Edited and translated by J. H. Waszink. Amsterdam, 1947.

Till, W. (ed. and tr.). *Die gnostischen Schriften des koptischen Papyrus Berolinensis 8502* (Texte und Untersuchungen, 60). Berlin, 1955.

Völker, W. *Quellen zur Geschichte der christlichen Gnosis.* Tübingen, 1932.

B. Studies

Alfaric, P. *Christianisme et gnosticisme.* Paris, 1924.

Anrich, G. *Das antike Mysterienwesen in seinem Einfluss auf das Christentum.* Göttingen, 1894.

Anz, W. *Zur Frage nach dem Ursprung des Gnostizismus* (Texte und Untersuchungen, 15, 4). Leipzig, 1897.

Bauer, W. *Rechtgläubigkeit und Ketzerei im ältesten Christentum.* Tübingen, 1934.

Baur, F. C. *Die christliche Gnosis.* Tübingen, 1835.

Becker, H. *Die Reden des Johannesevangeliums und der Stil der gnostischen Offenbarungsrede.* Göttingen, 1956.

Bousset, W. *Hauptprobleme der Gnosis.* Göttingen, 1907.

——. "Gnosis," in Pauly-Wissowa, *Real-Encycl. d. klass. Altertumswiss.* VII (1912), 1503.

Bultmann, R. *Das Johannesevangelium.* Göttingen, 1941.

——. *Gnosis* (*Bible Keywords from G. Kittel's Theolog. Wörterbuch zum Neuen Testament V*). London, 1952.

Buonaiuti, E. *Lo Gnosticismo; storia di antiche lotte religiose.* Rome, 1907.

Burkitt, F. C. *Church and Gnosis.* Cambridge, England, 1932.

Cross, F. L. (ed.). *The Jung Codex . . . Three Studies* (by H. C. Puech, G. Quispel, W. C. Van Unnik). London, New York, 1955.

Dodd, C. H. *The Interpretation of the Fourth Gospel.* Cambridge, England, 1953.

Döllinger, I. von. *Geschichte der gnostisch-manichäischen Sekten im früheren Mittelalter.* Munich, 1890.

Dupont, D. J. *Gnosis. La connaissance religieuse dans les Épitres de Saint Paul.* Louvain, Paris, 1949.

Faye, E. de. *Gnostiques et gnosticisme.* 2nd edition. Paris, 1925.

Foerster, W. "Das Wesen der Gnosis," *Die Welt als Geschichte* (1955), 100-114.

Friedländer, M. *Der vorchristliche jüdische Gnosticismus.* Göttingen, 1898.

Graetz, H. *Gnosticismus und Judenthum.* Krotoschin, 1846.

Harnack, A. *Lehrbuch der Dogmengeschichte.* Vol. I. 4th edition. Tübingen, 1909; English translation of 1st edition, Boston, 1895-1903.

————. *Marcion. Das Evangelium vom fremden Gott.* 2nd edition. Leipzig, 1924.

Hilgenfeld, A. *Die Ketzergeschichte des Urchristentums.* Leipzig, 1884.

Jonas, H. *Gnosis und spätantiker Geist.* 2 vols.: I, Göttingen, 1934, 1954; II, 1, Göttingen, 1954.

———— "Gnosticism and Modern Nihilism," *Social Research,* 19 (1952), 430-52.

King, C. W. *The Gnostics and Their Remains.* 2nd edition. London, 1887.

Kraeling, C. H. *Anthropos and Son of Man: a Study in the Religious Syncretism of the Hellenistic Orient.* New York, 1927.

Leisegang, H, *Die Gnosis.* 4th edition. Stuttgart, 1955.

Liboron, H. *Die karpokratianische Gnosis.* Leipzig, 1938.

Maurer, C. *Ignatius von Antioch und das Johannesevangelium.* Zürich, 1949.

Nilsson, M. P. *Geschichte der griechischen Religion II.* Munich, 1950.

Norden, E. *Agnostos Theos.* Leipzig, 1913.

Odeberg, H. *The Third Enoch or the Hebrew Book of Enoch.* Cambridge, England, 1928.

————. *The Fourth Gospel.* Uppsala, 1929.

Pétrement, S. *Le dualisme chez Platon, les gnostiques et les manichéens.* Paris, 1947.

Quispel, G. *Gnosis als Weltreligion.* Zürich, 1951.

Reitzenstein, R. *Die Göttin Psyche in der hellenistischen und frühchristlichen Literatur* (Sitz. Ber. Ak. Wiss. Heidelberg, 1917, 10). Heidelberg, 1917.

Rylands, L. G. *The Beginnings of Gnostic Christianity.* London, 1940.

Schlier, H. *Religionsgeschichtliche Untersuchungen zu den Ignatiusbriefen.* Giessen, 1929.

Schmidt, C. *Plotin's Stellung zum Gnostizismus und kirchlichen Christentum* (Texte u. Untersuch., N. F., 5, 4). Leipzig, 1901.

Schoeps, H. J. *Aus frühchristlicher Zeit.* Tübingen, 1950.

————. *Urgemeinde, Judenchristentum, Gnosis.* Tübingen, 1956.

Scholem, G. *Major Trends in Jewish Mysticism.* New York, 1946.

Söderberg, H. *La religion des Cathares.* Uppsala, 1949.

Völker, W. *Der wahre Gnostiker nach Clemens Alexandrinus.* Berlin, 1952.

III. Mandaeans (Ch. 3)

A. Sources

Drower, E. S. (ed. and tr.). *Diwan Abatur, or Progress through the Purgatories.* Bibl. apost. vaticana, 1950.

———— (ed. and tr.). *The Book of the Zodiac.* London, 1949.

Lidzbarski, M. (tr.). *Ginza. Der Schatz oder das Grosse Buch der Mandäer.* Göttingen, 1925.

———— (ed. and tr.). *Das Johannesbuch der Mandäer.* Giessen, 1915.

———— (tr.). *Mandäische Liturgien.* Berlin, 1920.

————. "Uthra und Malakha," *Orientalische Studien Theodor Nöldeke . . . gewidmet.* Giessen, 1906.

Mead, G. R. S. (tr.). *The Gnostic John the Baptizer. Selections from the Mandaean John-book.* London, 1924.

Pognon, H. (ed. and tr.). *Inscriptions mandaites des coupes de Khouabir.* Paris, 1898-99.

B. Studies

Baumgartner, W. "Zur Mandäerfrage," *Hebrew Union College Annual,* 23 (1950-51), 41-71.

Bultmann, R. "Die Bedeutung der neuerschlossenen mandäischen und manichäischen Quellen für das Verständnis des Johannesevangeliums," *ZNW,* 24 (1925), 100-146.

Brandt, W. *Die Mandäer, ihre Religion und ihre Geschichte.* Amsterdam, 1915.

————. *Elchasai.* Leipzig, 1912.

Chwolson, D. A. *Die Ssabier und der Ssabismus.* 2 vols. St. Peterburg, 1856.

Drower, E. S. *The Mandaeans of Iraq and Iran: Their Cults, Customs, Legends,' and Folklore.* Oxford, 1937.

Kraeling, C. H. "A Mandaic Bibliography," *Journal of the American Oriental Society,* 46 (1926), 49-55.

Loisy, A. F. *Le mandéisme et les origines chrétiennes.* Paris, 1934.

Odeberg, H. *Die mandäische Religionsanschauung.* Uppsala, 1930.

Pallis, S. A. *Mandaean Studies.* London, 1926.

————. *Essay on Mandaean Bibliography, 1560-1930.* London, 1933.

Reitzenstein, R. *Das mandäische Buch des Herrn der Grösse und die Evangelienüberlieferung.* Heidelberg, 1919.

Säve-Söderbergh, T. *Studies in the Coptic-Manichaean Psalm-book, Prosody*

and Mandaean Parallels. Uppsala, 1949.

Stahl, R. *Les Mandéens et les origines chrétiennes.* Paris, 1930.

Thomas, J. *Le mouvement baptiste en Palestine et Syrie.* Gembloux, 1935.

Tondelli, L. *Il Mandeismo e le origine cristiane.* Rome, 1928.

Widengren, G.: see section VIII (B) of this bibliography.

IV. Simon Magus (Ch. 4)

A. Sources

Irenaeus; Hippolytus; Epiphanius; Tertullian (*De Anima*): see section II (A) of this bibliography.

"Clement of Rome": the [pseudo-] Clementine Homilies and Recognitions, ed. P. de Lagarde, *Clementina,* Leipzig, 1865; also Migne, PP.Gr. 1; 2.

Justin the Martyr. *Apology,* I. Edited by G. Krüger, *Die Apologien Justins des Märtyrers.* 4th edition. Tübingen, 1915.

B. Studies

Butler, E. M. *The Myth of the Magus.* Cambridge, England, 1948.

————. *The Fortunes of Faust.* Cambridge, England, 1952.

Cerfaux, L. "La gnose simonienne," *Recherches de science religieuse,* 15 (1925), 489 ff.; *ibid.,* 16 (1926), 5 ff.; 265 ff.; 481 ff.

————. "Simon le magicien à Samarie," *ibid.,* 27 (1937), 615 ff.

Cullmann, O. *Le problème littéraire et historique du roman pseudo-Clémentin.* Paris, 1930.

Quispel, G. *Gnosis als Weltreligion.* Zürich, 1951, 45-70.

————. "Simoh en Helena," *Nederlands Theol. Tijdenschrift,* 5 (1951), 339 ff.

Vincent, L. H. "Le cult d'Hélène à Samarie," *Revue biblique,* 45 (1936), 221 ff.

V. The "Hymn of the Pearl"; the Odes of Solomon (Ch. 5)

A. Sources

Hymn of the Pearl:

Bevan, A. A. (ed. and tr.). *The Hymn of the Soul* (Texts and Studies 5, 3). Cambridge, England, 1897. Syriac text and English translation.

Preuschen, E. (ed. and tr.). *Zwei gnostische Hymnen*. Giessen, 1904. Syriac text and German translation.

Lipsius, A. and Bonnet, M. *Acta Apostolorum Apocrypha*. Vol. II, 2. Leipzig, 1903, 218 ff. Greek text.

Odes of Solomon:

Bauer, W. (ed. and tr.). *Die Oden Salomos* (Kleine Texte . . . ed. H. Lietzmann, 64). Berlin, 1933.

Harris, J. R. and Mingana, A. (ed. and tr.). *The Odes and Psalms of Solomon*. 2 vols. Manchester, 1916-1920.

Labourt, J. and Batiffol, P. (ed. and tr.). *Les odes de Salomon*. Paris, 1911.

B. Studies

Hymn of the Pearl:

Bornkamm, G. *Mythos und Legende in den apokryphen Thomasakten*. Göttingen, 1933.

Haase, F. *Untersuchungen zur bardesanischen Gnosis* (Texte u. Unters. 34, 4). Leipzig, 1910.

Reitzenstein, R. *Hellenistische Wundererzählungen*. Leipzig, 1906.

―――. *Das iranische Erlösungsmysterium*. Bonn, 1921.

Schaeder, H. H. "Bardesanes von Edessa," *Zeitschr. f. Kirchengeschichte,* 51 (1932), 21 ff.

Widengren, G. "Der iranische Hintergrund der Gnosis," *Zeitschr. f. Religions- und Geistesgeschichte,* 4 (19-52), 97 ff.

Odes of Solomon:

Frankenberg, W. *Zum Verständnis der Oden Salomos*. Giessen, 1911.

Harnack, A. *Ein jüdisch-christliches*

Psalmbuch aus dem 1. Jahrhundert (Texte u. Unters. 35, 4). Leipzig, 1910.

Kittel, G. *Die Oden Salomos*. Leipzig, 1914.

Newbold, R. "Bardaisan and the Odes of Solomon," *Journal of Bibl. Literature,* 30 (1911), 161 ff.

VI. Hermes Trismegistus (Ch. 7)

A. Sources

Nock, A. D. (ed.) and Festugière, A. J. (tr.). *Hermès Trismégiste*. Vols. I-IV. Paris, 1945-54. (Vol. I: *Corpus Hermeticum*).

Scott, W. and Ferguson, A. S. (ed. and tr.). *Hermetica*. Vols. I-IV. Oxford, 1924-36.

B. Studies

Festugière, A. J. *La révélation d'Hermès Trismégiste*. Vols. I-IV. Paris, 1944-54.

―――. *L'Hermétisme*. Lund, 1948.

Gundel, H. "Poimandres," in Pauly Wissowa, *Real-Encyclopädie . . . ,* 21, 1193 ff.

Heinrici. *Die Hermesmystik und das Neue Testament*. Leipzig, 1918.

Kroll, J. *Die Lehren des Hermes Trismegistos*. Münster, 1914.

Moorsel, G. van. *The Mysteries of Hermes Trismegistos*. Utrecht, 1955.

Nilsson, M. P. *Geschichte der griechischen Religion*. Vol. II. Munich, 1950, 556 ff.

Quispel, G. "Der gnostische Anthropos und die jüdische Tradition," *Eranos-Jahrbücher,* 22 (1954), 195 ff.

Reitzenstein, R. *Poimandres. Studien zur griechisch-ägyptischen und frühchristlichen Literatur*. Leipzig, 1904.

VII. The Valentinians (Ch. 8)

A. Sources

Clement of Alexandria (*Strom., Exc. ex Theod.*); Irenaeus; Hippolytus; Tertullian (*Adv. Valentinianos*); Epiphanius; *Evangelium Veritatis:* see section II (A) of this bibliography.

Origenes. *Commentary on St. John's Gospel.* Edited by E. Preuschen (Griech. christl. Schriftsteller 10). Leipzig, 1903: contains the fragments of Heracleon; see their collection in W. Völker, *Quellen zur Geschichte der christlichen Gnosis,* Tübingen, 1932, 63-86.

Quispel, G. (ed.). *Ptolémée: Lettre à Flora.* Paris, 1949.

B. Studies

Baur, F. C. *Die christliche Gnosis.* Tübingen, 1835, 124-170.

Festugière, A. J. "Notes sur les Extraits de Théodote," *Vigiliae Christianae,* 3 (1949), 193 ff.

Foerster, W. *Von Valentin zu Herakleon.* Giessen, 1928.

Markus, R. A. "Pleroma and Fulfillment," *Vigiliae Christianae,* 8 (1954), 193 ff.

Quispel, G. "The Original Doctrine of Valentine," *ibid.,* 1 (1947), 43 ff.

Sagnard, F. M. *La gnose valentinienne et le témoignage de saint-Irenée.* Paris, 1947.

VIII. Manichaeism (Ch. 9)

A. Sources

Adam, A. *Texte zum Manichäismus* (Kleine Texte . . . [H. Lietzmann] ed. K. Aland, 175). Berlin, 1954.

Al-Biruni. *Chronology of Ancient Nations.* Edited and translated by C. E. Sachau. London, 1879.

Alexander of Lycopolis. *Contra Manichaei Opiniones Disputatio.* Edited by A. Brinkmann (Bibl. Teubner.). Leipzig, 1895.

Allberry, C. R. C. (ed. and tr.). *A Manichaean Psalm-book.* Stuttgart, 1938.

Andreas, F. C. and Henning, W. *Mitteliranische Manichaica aus Chinesisch-Turkestan.* I; II (Sitz. Ber. Ak. Wiss. Berlin, 1932; 1933).

Augustine: anti-Manichaean writings collected in *Corp. Script. Eccl. Lat.,* vol. 25, rec. J. Zycha, Vienna 1891-92.

———. *De Natura Boni.* Translated by A. A. Moon. Washington, 1955.

Bang, W. "Manichäische Laien-Beichtspiegel," *Muséon,* 36 (1922), 137 ff.

———. "Manichäische Hymnen," *ibid.,* 38 (1925), 1 ff.

———. "Die Mailänder Abschwörungsformel," *ibid.,* 53 ff.

Boyce, M. *The Manichaean Hymn-cycles in Parthian.* Oxford, 1954.

Chavannes, E. and Pelliot, P. *Un traité manichéen retrouvé en Chine* (Extrait du Journal Asiatique, Nov.-Dec. 1911). Paris, 1912.

En-Nadim. *Fihrist al-Ulum.* Arabic text and German translation in G. Flügel, *Mani.* Leipzig, 1862.

Ephraem Syrus. *S. Ephraim's prose refutations of Mani, Marcion, and Bardaisan.* Edited and translated by C. W. Mitchell. Vols. I, II. London, 1912, 1921.

Epiphanius of Salamis. *Panarion Haeresium,* 66. Edited by K. Holl.

Hegemonius. *Acta Archelai.* Edited by C. H. Beeson (Griech. christl. Schriftsteller 16). Leipzig, 1906.

Henning, W. (ed. and tr.). "Ein manichäischer kosmogonischer Hymnus," *Nachricht. Gött. Ges. Wiss.* (Philhist. Kl. 1932). Göttingen, 1933, 214 ff.

———. (ed. and tr.). "Geburt und Entsendung des manichäischen Urmenschen," *ibid.* (1933). Göttingen, 1934, 1 ff.

———. (tr.). *Ein manichäisches Bet- und Beichtbuch.* Berlin, 1937.

———. *Sogdica.* London, 1940.

Jackson, A. V. W. *Researches in Manichaeism, with Special Reference to the Turfan Fragments.* New York, 1932.

Le Coq, A. von. *Chuastuanift, ein Sün-*

denbekenntnis der manichäischen Auditores (Abh. Akad. Wiss. Berlin, 1910).

———. *Türkische Manichaica aus Chotscho.* I-III (Abh. Akad. Wiss. Berlin, 1911-22).

Müller, F. W. K. *Handschriftenreste in Estrangelo-Schrift aus Turfan.* I (Sitz. Ber. Akad. Wiss. Berlin, 1904). II (Abh. Akad. Wiss. Berlin, 1912).

Polotsky, H. J. and Böhlig, A. (ed. and tr.). *Kephalaia.* Stuttgart, 1940.

Polotsky, H. J. (ed. and tr.). *Manichäische Homilien.* Stuttgart, 1934.

Radloff, W. (ed. and tr.). *Chuastuanit, das Bussgebet der Manichäer.* St. Petersburg, 1909.

Serapion of Thmuis. *Against the Manichees.* Edited by R. B. Casey (Harvard Theol. Studies 15). Cambridge, 1931.

Severus of Antioch. *123rd Homily.* Syriac text with French translation in F. Cumont, M. A. Kugener, *Recherches sur le Manichéisme,* 89-150; German translation in A. Adam, *Texte zum Manichäismus,* 11-14.

Shahrastani. *Kitab ul Milal.* Translated by T. Haarbrücker. Halle, 1850-51.

Simplicius. *In Epicteti Enchiridion Commentarium (c. 27).* Edited by F. Dübner. Paris, 1840.

Theodore bar Konai, *Liber Scholiorum XI:* Syriac text in *Corp. Script. Christ. Or.* 66, edited by A. Scher, Paris, Leipzig, 1912; French translation of the cosmogony in F. Cumont, M. A. Kugener, *Recherches sur le Manichéisme;* English translation by A. Yohannan, in A. V. W. Jackson, *Researches in Manichaeism;* German translation in A. Adam, *Texte zum Manichäismus.*

Theodoret, *Haereticorum Fabularum Compendium* (I. 26). Migne PP.Gr. 83.

Titus of Bostra. *Adversus Manichaeos.* Edited by P. de Lagarde. 1859 (also Migne PP.Gr. 18).

Waldschmidt, E. and Lentz, W. *Die Stellung Jesu im Manichäismus* (Abh. Akad. Wiss. Berlin, 1926, 4).

———. *Manichäische Dogmatik aus chinesischen und iranischen Quellen* (Sitz. Ber. Akad. Wiss. Berlin, 1933, 13).

West, E. W. (tr.). *Pahlavi Texts.* 5 vols. Oxford, 1880-1897 (vol. 3: Sikand Gumanik Vigar).

B. Studies

Alfaric, P. *Les écritures manichéennes.* 2 vols. Paris, 1918-19.

Baur, F. C. *Das manichäische Religionssystem.* Tübingen, 1831 (reprinted, Göttingen, 1928).

Beausobre, G. *Histoire critique de Manichée et du manichéisme.* 2 vols. Amsterdam, 1734-39.

Bornkamm, G. *Mythos und Legende in den apokryphen Thomasakten. Beiträge zur Geschichte der Gnosis und zur Vorgeschichte des Manichäismus.* Göttingen, 1933.

Burkitt, F. C. *The religion of the Manichees.* Cambridge, England, 1925.

Cumont, F. *Recherches sur le Manichéisme.* Brussels, 1912.

Flügel, G. *Mani, seine Lehre und seine Schriften.* Leipzig, 1862.

Kessler, K. *Mani. Forschungen über die manichäische Religion.* Vol. I. Berlin, 1889.

Lentz, W. "Fünfzig Jahre Arbeit an den iranischen Handschriften der deutschen Turfan-Sammlung," *Zeitschrift d. Deutsch. Morgenländ. Gesellschaft,* 106 (N. F. 31), 1956, *3-*22.

Pétrement, S. *Le dualisme chez Platon, les gnostiques et les manichéens.* Paris, 1947.

Polotsky, H. J. "Manichäismus," in Pauly-Wissowa, *Real-Encyclopädie* . . . Suppl. VI. Stuttgart, 1935, 240-271.

Puech, H. C. *Le Manichéisme, son fondateur, sa doctrine* (Publications du Musée Guimet 66). Paris, 1949 [latest bibliography].

Reitzenstein, R. *Das iranische Erlö-sungsmysterium.* Bonn, 1921.

Roché, D. *Études manichéenes et cathares.* Arques, 1952.

Runciman, S. *The Medieval Manichee.* Cambridge, England, 1947.

Säve-Söderbergh, T: see section III (B) of this bibliography.

Salemann, C. *Manichäische Studien.* St. Petersburg, 1908.

Schaeder, H. H. "Urform und Fortbildungen des manichäischen Systems," (*Vorträge Bibl. Warburg* 4, 1924-25). Leipzig, 1927.

————. "Zur manichäischen Urmensch-lehre," in R. Reitzenstein and H. H. Schaeder, *Studien zum antiken Synkretismus.* (Studien Bibl. Warburg 7) Leipzig, 1926.

————. "Der Manichäismus nach neuen Funden und Forschungen," *Morgenland,* 28. Leipzig, 1936.

Schmidt, C. and Polotsky, H. J. *Ein Mani-Fund in Aegypten* (Sitz. Ber. Akad. Wiss. Berlin, 1933, 1).

Troje, L. *Die Dreizehn und die Zwölf im Traktat Pelliot.* Leipzig, 1925.

Wesendonk, O. G. von. *Urmensch und Seele in der iranischen Ueberlieferung.* 1924.

Wetter, G. P. *Phos. Eine Untersuchung über hellenistische Frömmigkeit, zugleich ein Beitrag zum Verständnis des Manichäismus.* Uppsala, 1915.

Widengren, G. *The Great Vohu Manah and the Apostle of God; Studies in*

Iranian and Manichaean Religion. Uppsala, 1945.

————. *Mesopotamian Elements in Manichaeism; Studies in Manichaean, Mandaean, and Syrian-Gnostic Religion.* Uppsala-Leipzig, 1946.

————. *The Ascension of the Apostle and the Heavenly Book.* Uppsala, 1950.

IX. Philo Judaeus (Ch. 11, 6)

Works, Greek and in English translation, in *Loeb Classical Library.*

Bréhier, E. *Les idées philosophiques et religieuses de Philon d'Alexandrie.* 2nd edition. Paris, 1925.

Goodenough, E. R. *By Light, Light; the Mystic Gospel of Hellenistic Judaism.* Oxford, 1935.

————. *An Introduction to Philo Judaeus.* New Haven, 1940.

Heinemann, I. *Philons griechische und jüdische Bildung.* Breslau, 1932.

Jonas, H. *Gnosis und spätantiker Geist* II, 1. Göttingen, 1954. 70-121.

Lewy, H. *Sobria Ebrietas; Untersuchungen zur Geschichte der antiken Mystik* (Beihefte zur *ZNW* 9). Giessen, 1929.

———— (tr.). *Philo Selections* (Philosophia Judaica). Oxford, 1946.

Wolfson, H. A. *Philo. Foundations of Religious Philosophy in Judaism, Christianity, and Islam.* 2 vols. Cambridge, Mass., 1948.

Selected Supplementary Bibliography

The literature has been growing fast in the decade since the first publication of this volume, especially under the stimulus of the new Coptic sources from Nag Hammadi. For fuller information on the progress of research and on bibliography (especially regarding the important part of the literature dispersed in scholarly journals, which is listed here in only a few exceptional cases), one should turn to the following progress reports for the whole field: S. Schulz, "Die Bedeutung neuer Gnosisfunde für die neutestamentliche Wissenschaft," *Theologische Rundschau* 26 (1960), 209-266, 301-334; K. Rudolph, "Gnosis und Gnostizismus, ein Forschungsbericht," *ibid.,* 34 (1969), 121-175, 181-231. Particular surveys of Mandaean studies and the Nag Hammadi complex are listed below at the heads of the respective subdivisions. This bibliography was assembled at the beginning of 1970.

General

Ambelain, R. *La notion gnostique du demiurge dans les Ecritures et les traditions judeo-chrétiennes.* Paris, 1959.

Bianchi, U. (ed.). *Le Origini dello Gnosticismo. Colloquio di Messina 13-18 Aprile 1966 (Studies in the History of Religions* XII). Leiden, 1967. [Papers and discussion in English, French, German, Italian.]

Böhlig, A. *Mysterion und Wahrheit. Gesammelte Beiträge zur spätantiken Religionsgeschichte.* Leiden, 1968.

Brox, N. *Offenbarung, Gnosis und gnostischer Mythos bei Irenäus von Lyon. (Salzburger Patrist. Studien* I). Salzburg and München, 1966.

Colpe, C., E. Haenchen, G. Kretschmar. Article "Gnosis" in *Religion in Geschichte und Gegenwart [RGG],* 3rd ed., vol. 2 (1958), cols. 1648-1661.

Colpe, C. *Die religionsgeschichtliche Schule: Darstellung und Kritik ihres Bildes vom gnostischen Erlösermythus.* Göttingen, 1961.

Eltester, W. (ed.). *Christentum und Gnosis. Aufsätze hrsg. von Walther Eltester. (BZNW* 37). Berlin, 1969.

Foerster, W. (ed.). *Die Gnosis.* vol. I [Greek and Latin texts], Zürich, 1969; vol. II [Coptic and Mandaic texts], ibid., forthcoming.

Frickel, J. *Die "Apophasis Megale" in Hippolyt's Refutatio (VI 9-18): Eine Paraphrase zur Apophasis Simons. (Orientalia Christiana Analecta* 182). Rome, 1968.

Grant, R. M. *Gnosticism and Early Christianity.* 2nd ed. New York, 1966.

van Groningen, G. *First Century Gnosticism: Its Origins and Motifs.* Leiden, 1967.

Haardt, R. *Die Gnosis. Wesen und Zeugnisse.* Salzburg, 1967. [General exposition and selected sources in German translation.]

————. Articles "Gnosis" and "Gnosticism" in *Sacramentum Mundi* II, 374-379; 379-381. New York, 1968.

Hilgenfeld, A. *Die Ketzergeschichte des Urchristentums.* Hildesheim, 1963. [Facsimile reprint of the edition of Leipzig, 1884.]

Jervell, J. *Imago Dei: Gen. 1, 26 f. im Spätjudentum, in der Gnosis und in den paulinischen Briefen.* Göttingen, 1960.

Jonas, H. *Gnosis und spätantiker Geist* I, 377-476: *Ergänzungsheft zur 1. und 2. Auflage* [Supplement to 1st and 2nd eds. of vol. I]. Göttingen, 1964.

———. Article "Gnosticism" in *Encyclopedia of Philosophy,* vol. 3, 336-342. New York, 1967.

Klein, F. N. *Die Lichtterminologie bei Philon von Alexandrien und in den hermetischen Schriften.* Leiden, 1962.

Langerbeck, H. *Aufsätze zur Gnosis. Aus dem Nachlass hrsg. von H. Dörries (Abh. d. Akad. d. Wiss. in Göttingen, Phil.-hist. Kl. 3. F. 69).* Göttingen, 1967.

MacRae, G. W. Articles "Gnosis, Christian" and "Gnosticism" in *New Catholic Encyclopedia* VII, 522-523; 523-528. New York, 1967.

Merkelbach, R. *Roman und Mysterium in der Antike.* München, 1962.

Orbe, A. *Estudios valentinianos (Analecta gregoriana).* Rome: Univ. Gregor., I (1958); II (1955); III (1961); IV (1966); V (1956).

Puech, H.-Ch. "Gnostic Gospels and Related Documents" in Hennecke and Schneemelcher (eds.), *New Testament Apocrypha,* vol. I, 231-362. London and Philadelphia, 1963.

Quispel, G. *Makarius, das Thomasevangelium und das Lied von der Perle.* Leiden, 1967 *(Suppl. to Novum Testamentum* XV). [Cf. H. Jonas, "Response to G. Quispel on 'Gnosticism and the New Testament,'" in J. P.

Hyatt (ed.), *The Bible in Modern Scholarship.* Nashville and New York, 1965, 279-293.]

Salles-Dabadie, J. M. A. *Recherches sur Simon le Mage; I: L'"Apophasis megalè." Cahiers de la Revue Biblique* 10. Paris, 1969.

Schenke, H.-M. *Der Gott "Mensch" in der Gnosis.* Göttingen, 1962.

———. "Die Gnosis," in J. Leipoldt and W. Grundmann (eds.), *Die Umwelt des Urchristentums,* vol. II. Berlin, 1967, 350-418.

Schmidt, C., and W. Till. *Koptisch-gnostische Schriften* I. *(Die Griech.-Christl. Schriftsteller,* etc., 13) Akademie-Verlag, Berlin, 1959.

Schmithals, W. *Die Gnosis in Korinth.* 2nd ed. Göttingen, 1965.

Scholem, G. *Jewish Gnosticism.* 2nd ed. New York, 1965.

Wilson, R. McL. *The Gnostic Problem. A Study of the Relations between Hellenistic Judaism and the Gnostic Heresy.* London, 1958 (reissued 1964).

———. *Gnosis and the New Testament.* Philadelphia, 1968.

———. Articles "Simon Magus" and "Valentinus. Valentinianism" in *Encyclopedia of Philosophy* 7:444-45, and 8:226-27. New York, 1967.

Wlosok, A. *Laktanz und die philosophische Gnosis (Abhandl. d. Heidelberger Akad. d. Wiss., Phil.-hist. Kl.,* 1960, 2). Heidelberg, 1960.

Zandee, J. "Gnostic Ideas on the Fall and Salvation," *Numen* 11 (1964), 13-74.

Mandaeans

The most complete bibliography up to 1960 is found in K. Rudolph's *Die Mandäer* I and II (see below). Later surveys of research and literature may be found in R. Macuch, "Der gegenwärtige Stand der Mandäerforschung und ihre Aufgaben," *Orientalistische Literaturzeitung* 63 (1968), cols. 5-14; and K. Rudolph, "Problems of a History of the Development of the Mandaean Religion," *History of Religions* 8 (1969), 210-235.

Colpe, C. Article "Mandäer" in *RGG,* 3rd. ed., vol. 4 (1960), cols. 709-12.

Drower, E. S. *The Canonical Prayerbook of the Mandaeans.* Leiden, 1959.

———. *The Secret Adam. A Study of Nasoraean Gnosis.* Oxford, 1960.

———. (ed., tr.). *The Thousand and Twelve Questions. A Mandaean Text (Dt. Aḳad. d. Wiss., Institut f. Orientforschung,* Nr. 32). Berlin, 1960.

———. (ed., tr.). *The Coronation of the Great Šišlam.* Leiden, 1962.

———. (ed., tr.). *A Pair of Naṣoraean Commentaries.* Ibid., 1963.

———. and R. Macuch. *A Mandaean Dictionary.* Ibid., 1963.

Lidzbarski, M. (tr.). *Mandäische Liturgien.* Berlin and Hildesheim, 1962. [Facsimile reprint.]

Macuch, R. *Handbook of Classical and Modern Mandaic.* Berlin, 1965.

Rudolph, K. *Die Mandäer. I. Prolegomena: Das Mandäerproblem.* Göttingen, 1960; *II. Der Kult.* Ibid., 1961.

———. *Theogonie, Kosmogonie und Anthropogonie in den mandäischen Schriften.* Göttingen, 1965.

Widengren, G. Article "Die Mandäer" in *Handbuch der Orientalistik,* vol. 8,2 (1961), 83-101.

Yamauchi, E. *Mandaic Incantation Texts.* New Haven, 1967.

Manichaeans

Adam, A. *Die Psalmen des Thomas und das Perlenlied als Zeugnisse der vorchristl. Gnosis* (BZNW 24). Berlin, 1959.

———. Article "Manichäismus" in *Handbuch der Orientalistik,* vol. 8,2 (1961), 102-119.

Böhlig, A. *Probleme des manichäischen Lehrvortrags.* München, 1953.

———. "Der Manichäismus im Lichte der neueren Gnosisforschung," in K. Wessel (ed.), *Christentum am Nil.* Recklinghausen, 1964, 114-123.

Boyce, M. *Catalogue of the Iranian Manuscripts in Manichaean Script in the German Turfan Collection.* Leiden, 1960.

Colpe, C. Article "Manichäismus" in *RGG,* 3rd ed., vol. 4 (1960), cols. 714-22.

Klíma, O. *Manis Zeit und Leben.* Prague, 1962.

Manselli, R. "Modern Studies on Manichaeism," *East and West* 10 (1959), 77-86.

de Menasce, P. J. (ed., tr., com.). *Škand-Gumānīk Vičār. La Solution décisive des doutes (Collectanea Friburgensia,* N.S. 30). Fribourg, 1945.

Reis, J. "Introduction aux études manichéennes," I, *Ephemerides Theol. Lovaniensis* 33 (1957), 453-82; II, *ibid,* 35 (1959), 362-409.

Rudolph, K. "Gnosis und Manichäismus nach den koptischen Quellen," *Koptologische Studien in der DDR* (Sonderheft, *Wiss. Ztschr. der Martin-Luther-Univ. Halle-Wittenberg,* 1965), 155-190.

Widengren, G. *Mani and Manichaeism.* London, 1965; New York, 1966.

Wilson, R. McL. Article "Mani. Manicheism" in *Encyclopedia of Philosophy,* vol. 5, 149-50, New York, 1967.

Nag Hammadi

In this area, the growth of literature is most marked, although the work of editing and translating the new texts is still far from complete. The following interim reports on research and literature may be consulted for information beyond the selection offered here, which is mostly confined to books: S. Giversen, "Nag Hammadi Bibliography 1948-1963," *Studia Theologica* 17 (1963), 139-187; R. Haardt, "Zwanzig Jahre der Erforschung der koptisch-gnostischen Schriften von Nag Hammadi," *Theologie und Philosophie* 42 (1967), 390-401; E. Haenchen, "Literatur zum Thomasevangelium," *Theologische Rundschau,* N.F. 27 (1961/62), 147-178, 306-338; id., "Literatur zum Codex Jung," *ibid.,* 30 (1964), 39-82; J. M. Robinson, "The Coptic

Gnostic Library Today," *New Testament Studies* 14 (1967/68), 356-401 [bibliography p. 383ff.]: updated in *NTS* 16 (1969/70), 185-90 (also, *Novum Testamentum*, Spring 1970); H.-M. Schenke, "Die Arbeit am Philippus-Evangelium," *Theol. Literaturzeitung* 90 (1965), cols. 321-332; id., "Zum gegenwärtigen Stand der Erforschung der Nag Hammadi-Handschriften," *Koptologische Studien in der DDR.* (Sonderheft, *Wiss. Ztschr. der Martin-Luther-Univ. Halle-Wittenberg,* 1965), 124-135. D. M. Scholer, *Nag Hammadi Bibliography 1948-1969 (Nag Hammadi Monograph Series,* vol. I), Leiden, forthcoming. The bibliography which follows lists primary and secondary literature together.

Arai, S. *Die Christologie des Evangelium Veritatis.* Leiden, 1964.

Böhlig, A., and P. Labib (ed., tr., com.). *Die koptisch-gnostische Schrift ohne Titel aus Codex II von Nag Hammadi* (Dt. Akad. d. Wiss., Institut für Orientforschung 58). Berlin, 1962.

———— (ed., tr.). *Koptische-gnostische Apokalypsen aus Codex V von Nag Hammadi* (Sonderband, *Wissensch. Zeitschr. der Martin-Luther-Univ. Halle-Wittenberg* 1963). Halle-Wittenberg, 1963.

Bullard, R. A. (ed., tr., com.). *The Hypostasis of the Archons (Patrist. Texte und Studien).* Berlin, forthcoming.

Doresse, J. *The Secret Books of the Egyptian Gnostics.* New York, 1960. [See my review in *The Journal of Religion* 42 (1962), 262-273.]

————. " 'Le Livre sacré du grand esprit invisible' ou 'L'Évangile des Égyptiens,' " *Journal Asiatique* 254 (1966). 317-435.

Gaffron, H.-G. *Studien zum koptischen Philippusevangelium.* Inaugural-Dissert., Evang.-Theol. Fakultät, Rhein. Friedrich-Wilhelm Univ., Bonn, 1969.

Gärtner, B. *The Theology of the Gospel according to Thomas.* New York, 1961.

Giversen, S. (ed., tr., com.). *Apocryphon Johannis (Acta Theologica Danica 5).* Copenhagen, 1963. [Translation and Commentary in English.]

Grant, R. M. (collab. with D. N. Freedman). *The Secret Sayings of Jesus.* With an English translation of the Gospel of Thomas by W. R. Schoedel.

Garden City, New York, 1960.

Grobel, K. *The Gospel of Truth* (Translation and Commentary). New York and Nashville, 1960.

Guillaumont, A., H.-Ch. Puech, G. Quispel, W. Till, Y. 'Abd al Masīh (ed., tr.). *The Gospel according to Thomas.* Leiden and New York, 1959.

Haenchen, E. *Die Botschaft des Thomas-Evangeliums* (Theologische Bibliothek Töpelmann 6). Berlin, 1961.

Helmbold, A. *The Nag Hammadi Gnostic Texts and the Bible.* Grand Rapids, 1967.

Kasser, R. *L'Évangile selon Thomas.* Neuchatel, 1961.

Krause, M., and P. Labib (ed., tr.). *Die drei Versionen des Apokryphon des Johannes im Koptischen Museum zu Alt-Kairo (Abhandl. d. Dt. Archäol. Instituts Kairo, Kopt. Reihe,* 1). Wiesbaden, 1962.

————. (ed., tr.). *Gnostische und hermetische Schriften aus Codex II und VI (ibid.,* 2). Ibid., forthcoming.

Labib, P. (ed.). *Coptic Gnostic Papyri in the Coptic Museum at Old Cairo.* Vol. I. Cairo, 1956 (photogr.).

Leipoldt, J., and H.-M. Schenke. *Koptisch-gnostische Schriften aus den Papyrus-Codices von Nag Hamadi (Theol. Forschung* 20). Hamburg, 1960.

Leipoldt, J. *Das Evangelium nach Thomas (TU* 101). Berlin, 1967.

Malinine, M., H.-Ch. Puech, G. Quispel, W. Till (ed., tr.). *Evangelium Veritatis (Supplementum).* Zürich and Stuttgart, 1961.

————. *De Resurrectione Epistula ad*

Rheginum. Ibid., 1963.

―――― and R. Kasser (ed., tr.). *Epistula Jacobi Apocrypha.* Ibid., 1968.

Ménard, J. E. L'Évangile de Vérité. *Rétroversion grecque et Commentaire.* Paris, 1962.

――――. *L'Évangile selon Philippe* (Publ. de la Faculté de Théol. de l'Univ. de Montréal 35). Paris, 1964.

――――. *L'Évangile selon Philippe. Introd., Texte, Trad., Comm.* (Thèse pour le Doctorat en Théologie, Univ. de Strasbourg, 1967).

Peel, M. L. *The Epistle to Rheginos; A Valentinian Letter on the Resurrection: Introduction, Translation, Analysis and Exposition.* London and Philadelphia, 1969.

Schenke, H.-M. *Die Herkunft des sogenannten Evangelium Veritatis.* Göttingen, 1959.

――――. "Nag Hammadi Studien" I. II. III. *Ztschr. f. Religions und Geistesgeschichte* 14 (1962), 57-63, 263-278, 352-361.

Schrage, W. *Das Verhältnis des Thomas-Evangeliums zur synoptischen Tradition,* etc. (*BZNW* 29). Berlin, 1964.

Summers, R. *The Secret Sayings of the Living Jesus: Studies in the Coptic Gospel According to Thomas.* Waco, Texas, 1968.

Till, W. C. (ed., tr.). *Das Evangelium nach Philippos* (*Patrist. Texte und Studien* 2). Berlin, 1963.

Turner, H. E. W., and H. Montefiore. *Thomas and the Evangelists.* London, 1962.

van Unnik, W. C., et al. *Evangelien aus dem Nilsand.* Frankfurt a. M., 1960. (Partial translation in English: *Newly Discovered Gnostic Writings, Studies in Biblical Theology* 30. London, 1960.)

Wilson, R. McL. *Studies in the Gospel of Thomas.* London, 1960.

―――― (tr., com.). *The Gospel of Philip.* New York, 1962.

Zandee, J. *The Terminology of Plotinus and of Some Gnostic Writings, Mainly the Fourth Treatise of the Jung Codex.* Istanbul, 1961.

Index to Proper Names

Abathur: 155n10, 164n16

Abel: 95, 140n11, 205

Abiram: 95

Abraham: 95, 280n12

Abram: 281n13

Achamoth: 186. *See also* Sophia

Adam: 64, 69, 72, 73 f., 76, 81, 83 ff.,
86-89, 92 ff., 117, 154 f., 203 ff., 209,
226-231

Adonaios (*also* Adoni): 43, 133n4, 201

Ahriman: 69n23, 142, 217, 219, 224,
225

Ahura Mazda: 217. *See also* Ormuzd

Al-Biruni: 230n36

Alexander the Great: 3-7, 10-14, 18, 20,
211

Alexander of Lycopolis: 38, 210, 220n23,
231, 234

Amenhotep IV: 256

Anosh (*also* Enosh): 65 f., 80, 97

Ardashir I: 208

Aristotle: 6, 8, 211, 251, 255, 258n12,
259n14

Arnobius: 157

Artaxerxes: 5

Artemis: 109n9

Augustine, St.: 38, 61, 73, 210, 226n32,
233

Authades: 68

Bahram I: 208

Barbelo: 135n5, 200

Bardesanes: 9, 160

Bartholomae: 123

Basileus: 9. *See also* Malchus

Basilides: 42, 43, 109n10, 133, 135n5,
159, 162, 214n10, 283, 288

B'haq-Ziva: 135, 155n10

Buddha: 208, 230

Caesar: 20

Cain: 95, 140n11, 205

Carpocrates: 274

Celsus: 103, 104n2, 168

Cerdon: 136

Cerinthus: 136

Christ, Jesus: 20, 32, 39, 53, 67, 78,
78n29, 86, 93 ff., 103, 108, 109, 132 f.,
136-146 *passim*, 181n9, 183-199 *passim*, 207n2, 208, 228-231, 282

Chroshtag: 82n31

Chrysippus: 245

Cicero: 243 ff., 247n7, 250, 255, 260

Clement of Alexandria: 37, 159

Clement of Rome: 104

Cornford, F. M.: 159n13

Daniel: 13

Dathan: 95

Droysen, G.: 12, 18

Edem: 136n6, 223n27

Eloaios: 201. *See also* Elohim

Elohim (*also* Eloim): 43, 133n4, 136n6,
191n25, 205, 223n27

El-shaddai (Esaldaios): 43, 133n4

En-Nadim: 210, 216, 217n18, 218n20,
222n24, 233, 233n40, 234, 236

Ennoia (*also* Epinoia): 106-110 *passim*,
130, 204. *See also* Helen, Helena

Enoch: 95

Ephraem: 9, 211, 234

Epicurus: 266

Epimetheus: 96

Epiphanius: 37, 38, 104, 108, 135n5,
168, 169, 178, 180n8, 234

Esau: 95

Eustathius: 109n9

Eve: 59, 64, 84n34, 87, 93, 204 f., 226-
231

Festugière, A. J.: 151n8, 172n20

356